The First

American Frontier

The First American Frontier

Advisory Editor: Dale Van Every

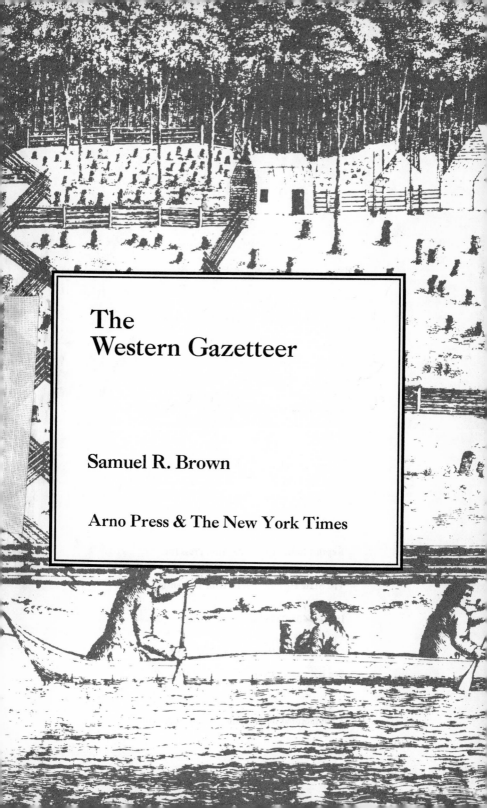

The
Western Gazetteer

Samuel R. Brown

Arno Press & The New York Times

134529

Reprint Edition 1971 by Arno Press Inc.

Reprinted from a copy in
The State Historical Society of Wisconsin Library

LC #   79-146380
ISBN 0-405-02831-8

The First American Frontier
ISBN for complete set: 0-405-02820-2

See last pages of this volume for titles.

Manufactured in the United States of America

THE
WESTERN GAZETTEER;
OR
EMIGRANT'S DIRECTORY,

CONTAINING

A GEOGRAPHICAL DESCRIPTION

OF THE

WESTERN STATES AND TERRITORIES, VIZ.

THE STATES OF

KENTUCKY, INDIANA, LOUISIANA, OHIO, TENESSEE AND MISSISSIPPI:

AND THE TERRITORIES OF

ILLINOIS, MISSOURI, ALABAMA, MICHIGAN, AND NORTH-WESTERN.

WITH

AN APPENDIX,

CONTAINING SKETCHES OF SOME OF THE WESTERN COUNTIES OF NEW-YORK, PENNSYLVANIA AND VIRGINIA; A DESCRIPTION OF THE GREAT NORTHERN LAKES; INDIAN ANNUITIES AND, DIRECTIONS TO EMIGRANTS.

BY SAMUEL R. BROWN.

AUBURN, N. Y.
PRINTED BY H. C. SOUTHWICK.

INDEX.

PREFATORY.

In the following sketches of Western America, the several states and territories described, are arranged alphabetically; but for the reader's convenience, and for the purpose of preserving continuity to the description of any particular state or territory, when commenced, the disposition of the articles is geographical. The immense extent of country embraced in the plan of the work, has in many instances prevented minuteness of description, even where personal knowledge was most perfect. The field was rich, ample—unbounded; but the circumscribed limits of a single volume, permitted only a glance at the infinity of interesting objects, which presented themselves at every step; for instance, more than *one hundred* great rivers of the west, the greater part of which I have disposed of in a single paragraph, or by merely *naming* them, would afford ample materials, for a volume of much interest.

In preparing this work for the press, it has been the writer's principal aim, to make it a useful, correct and faithful guide to enterprising farmers, and mechanics, of the Atlantic states, who may wish to establish themselves in any of the *transmontane* territories.

Business and curiosity has made the writer acquainted with a large proportion of the Western Country, and many parts never before particularly described. Where personal knowledge was wanting, he has availed himself of the correspondence of many of the most intelligent gentlemen resident in the west.

The chief objects embraced are, Boundaries, Latitude and Aspect of the Country, Soil, Climate, Diseases, Vegetable, Mineral and Animal Productions, Rivers, Lakes, Swamps, Prairies, Portages, Roads, Counties, Settlements, and Villages; Population, Character and Customs of the Inhabitants, Indians, Antiquities, Military Posts, Situation and Price of Lands, Price Current, Trade, Extent of Navigable Waters, Expences of Travelling, Directions to Emigrants, &c. &c.

The vast region of which I have attempted to sketch the most prominent features, is bounded north by the great Lakes, Erie, Huron, and Superior, and the chain of waters between the Grand Portage and the Lake of the Woods, west by the

Rocky Mountains; south by the Gulf of Mexico, and east by the Alleghany Mountains—comprising almost *one thousand millions* of acres; watered by several hundred rivers: and containing an extent of upwards 50,000 miles of internal ship and boat navigation. The "Western Country," has, therefore, the outlines of an immense empire. The mind wants new powers of comprehension to form an adequate conception of its extent. It has 2000 miles of *Lake*, 1000 of *Gulf*, and 100,000 of *River* coast; in short the whole country is one continued net-work of rivers, interlocking with each other, and intersecting the country in every direction. By incurring an expence of less than 50,000 dollars, it is believed by good judges, that a sloop navigation might be opened between Buffalo and the Fond du Lac, a distance of nearly 1800 miles, the only interruption at present being the rapids of St. Marie, between lakes Huron and Superior. The Ohio by one of its branches, (French creek) approaches with a boatable navigation to within *seven* miles of lake Erie; by the Connewango, to within *nine*; by the Muskingum, to the very source of the Cayahoga. The Scioto interweaves its branches with the Sandusky, between which there is a practicable portage of eight miles. The Wabash mingles its waters occasionally with those of the Miami-of-the-lakes; so do those of the *Illinois*, with those of *Lake Michigan*, between which, *Nature* has herself scooped out a *canal*. Well might *Lefebvre Desnouettes*, exclaim, on beholding boats arrive at St. Louis, from lake Michigan, without meeting with a portage; "*What a wonderful river, communicating with the sea by its mouth and its source!*"

ALABAMA TERRITORY,

Is situated between 30 and 35 degrees of north latitude. Its boundaries as established by law on the 3d of March, 18i7, are as follows : Beginning at the point where the line of the thirty-first degree of north latitude intersects the Perdido river, thence east to the western boundary line of the state of Georgia,thence along said line to the southern boundary line to the state of Tennessee, thence west along said boundary line to the Tennessee river, thence up the same to the mouth of Bear creek, thence by a direct line to the north west corner of Washington county, thence due south to the Gulf of Mexico, thence eastwardly, including all the islands within six leagues of the shore, to the Perdido river, and thence up the same to the beginning." It has the new state (formed from the western part of the Mississippi territory)on the west; Tennessee north; Georgia and the remnant of West Florida east, and the gulf of Mexico and West Florida south. These boundaries comprise about one half of the late Mississippi territory, which contained about 93,480 square miles, or 59,827,200 acres.

RIVERS.

The main rivers of this territory run south and fall into the gulf of Mexico. The Alabama is the most considerable.

It takes its rise in the Cherokee nation, near the boundary line between the states of Georgia and Tennessee, and not far from the 35th degree of north latitude, and proceeding in a southwestwardlydirection,unites with the Tombigbee,nine miles above the 31st degree of north latitude,and forms with it, the river Mobile. The junction of the two rivers is about forty-five miles from the head of Mobile bay, and the river is navigable thus far, and indeed several miles further, for any vessel which can come up the bay. From the junction to Fort Claiborne [says Judge Toulmin] the distance is about sixty miles, and the river is navigable thus far, at the lowest time for any vessel which will not draw more than six feet of water. The distance from thence to the mouth of the Cahawba, on the western side of the Alabama, is estimated at one hundred and fifty miles, and the river affords to this place four or five feet depth of water. From the mouth of the Cahawba to the forks of the Coose and Tallapoose, it is said to be 160 miles, though some do not estimate the distance so great, and the navigation is still good except at two ripples, in which however there is a plenty of water, and they pass over them with boats. In this part of the river it is three feet deep in the shallowest places.

The river here loses its name : the eastern branch being called the Tallapoose, which, except near the mouth, runs through the territory still belonging to the Creeks, whilst the western branch of the Alabama is called the Coose. The Tallapoose is boatable to the great falls, thirty or forty miles above the fork. About eight miles by water, tho' not three in a straight line, above the junction of the Coose and Tallapoose, the two rivers approach very near to each other; and it is in this point of land that Fort Jackson stands.

From thence to the falls of Coose, the distance is seven or eight miles, and here the navigation of the Coose may, in the present state of things, be considered as terminating. There is a continuation of rocky shoals to Fort Williams, a distance of 50 miles ; a circumstance the more to be regretted, as the navigation is not materially obstructed above, and can be pursued up the Coose to one of its head streams called the Connesangah, which is about forty-six feet wide, and from the boatable part of which to the boatable part of the Amoy it is but eight or ten miles over a firm level country. The Amoy is about sixty feet wide, and is a branch of the Hiwassee, which discharges itself into the Tennessee about eight miles below Knoxville. The distance from Fort Williams to Fort Strother, at the Ten-Islands, where the Cherokee line strikes the Coosa river, is nearly sixty miles by land, but considerably more by water. From thence to the portage, or highest point of navigation on the Connesaugah, it is probably 120 or 130 miles by land.

As to the great falls between Fort Williams and Fort Jackson; it is the opinion of some that they might be rendered navigable, with no very great difficulty. There is water enough; but the shoals are very numerous. Indeed, boats loaded with provisions for the troops, did descend the river, and pass them during the late Creek war; but the hazard was very considerable, and some of them were destroyed.

As to the time it takes to navigate the Alabama, it may be stated, that to go from Mobile to Fort Jackson, a distance of about 420 miles, it will take from a month to six weeks, according to the state of the river. A barge with five hands, and carrying 125 barrels, has gone from Mobile to Fort Jackson in 30 days : but it was reckoned a remarkable good trip. The business however is new, and experience will probably lead to expedition.

The Coosa, under the names of Connesangah, Estenaury, Hightour, &c. runs probably about 150 miles, estimating the distance by land, through the Cherokee territory, in the north-western corner of the state of Georgia.

The country between the Mobile and the Catahouchy, is about 180 miles wide, and watered by the *Perdido* river, which forms the boundary between the Alabama territory and the remnant of West Florida ; it runs parallel to the Mobile, and falls into Perdido bay. The streams are the Conecah and Escambia, whose waters unite and flow into Pensacola bay ; the Conecah is navigable upwards of 160 miles, and is lined by forests of valuable timber. Beyond the Escambia is Yellowwater river, which falls into the bay of Pen-

B

sacola. Choctaw and Pea rivers still further east, fall into the bay of St. Roses. These streams are all navigable from 50 to 100 miles; the country which they drain is mostly of a sandy soil, and pine timber.

The Catahouchy is a noble river, affording a navigation of 400 miles; heads in the S. E. corner of Georgia, pursues a S. W. course 390 miles until it strikes the boundary line between Georgia and the Alabama territory, when itself becomes the division line to the limits of West Florida, a distance of 120 miles.

SURFACE, SOIL, TIMBER.

The northern parts of this territory are broken; near the Tennessee line, towards the S. E. corner, it may be said to be mountainous. The middle is hilly, with here and there tracts of level prairie land. Along the Florida line is a strip of country 50 or 60 miles wide, covered with the short and long leaved pine, cypress and loblolly, so closely resembling the country between Pearl river and the Mobile, as to render a description of the one applicable to the other. Such are its general aspects. The soil between the Mobile and the Catahouchy, bordering West Florida is better than that on the east side of Flint river; between the Conecah and the Catahouchy, the land is broken and waving; the ridge dividing their waters has high flats of light sandy land, well set with willow leafed hickory, and iron ore in places; all the streams have cane on their margins, and are frequently ornamented with the sour orange tree; the country healthy, and affording a fine range for cattle, hogs and horses. The pine flats have the wire grass and saw palmetto: the soil of the waving land, stiff and red loam, with stone on the ridges; the pine land pretty good for corn. Between the Mobile and the Perdido, the soil is thin, timber pine, loblolly bay, cypress. The head waters of Escambia and Conecah embrace large quantities of fine cotton and sugar lands, and orange groves.

Along the Tensaw pine and cypress forests, of a heavy growth; canebrakes along the river; and sometimes cypress swamps. The Alabama is margined with cane swamps; these at intervals with pine flats of good soil, suitable for sugar, cotton and corn. The swamps at the confluence with the Tombigbee, and for some distance below are subject to periodical inundations, for which reason the inhabitants never fence their improvements. Above they are very wide, intersected with slashes and crooked drains, and much infested with musquetoes. The land bordering on the swamps is a poor stiff clay, for one mile back; the growth pine and underbrush; back of this, broken pine barren; cypress ponds and canebrakes on the branches. Fifty miles from the union of the Alabama with Tombigbee, the high broken lands commence, extending for 60 miles upwards; timber, oak, hickory, poplar, and very large cedars.

The best part of the territory is to be found between the Alabama and Tombigbee; the Black Warrior, and Bear creek, have some fine bottoms; and those of the Tallapoosa from Tookabatchee to its confluence with the Coosa, about thirty miles, are excellent; the broken land terminates on its right bank, the good land spreads out on the left. Proceeding towards the dividing ridge between the Alabama waters and those of the Conecah, we pass over an extensive tract of rich land, the timber large, and cane abundant, liberally watered by creeks; this tract is thirty miles long including the plains, and twenty wide. The plains are waving, hill and dale, and appear divided into fields, interspersed or bounded with clumps of woodland; soil lead colored or dark clay, very rich and covered with weeds and tall grass. Below the plains, soil stiff, very red in places, and gravelly; surface broken for thirty miles, then pine barren. At the sources of Limestone creek, there is an excellent body of land called the " Dog wood;" the growth oak, chesnut, poplar, pine, and dogwood. This vein of land, is 20 miles in length, and 8 broad; the dogwood is very thick set, and tall the whole finely watered.

Sixty miles above the confluence of Coosa and Tallapoosa, there is a high waving country, settled by the Creek Indians, who live generally on rich flats of oak, hickory, poplar, walnut and mulberry—the springs are fine ; cane on the creeks, and reed on branches ; the surrounding crountry broken and gravelly. Most kinds of game are scarce throughout the terri, tory. Stone coal abounds on the Cahaba, Black Warrior, &c. The late Col. Hawkins long resident in the Creek nation, pourtrays the surface and soil of this country in these words :

The country lying between Coosa, Tallapoosa, and Chatahouchee, above their falls, is broken—the soil stiff, with coarse gravel, and in some places stone. The trees post oak, white and black oak, pine, hickory and chesnut—all of them small—the whole well watered, and the rivers and creeks have rocky beds, clad in many places with moss, greatly relished by cattle, horses and deer, and are margined with cane and reeds, and narrow strips or coves of rich flats. On the Coosa, sixty miles above its junction with Tallapoosa, there is limestone, and it is to be found in several places from thence to E-tow-woh and its western branches.

The country above the falls of Ocmulgee and Flint rivers is low and broken, as that of the other rivers. These have their sources above each other, on the left side of Chatahouchee, in open flat land, the soil stiff, the trees post and black oak, and small.

The land is generally rich, well watered, and lies well, as a waving country, for cultivation ; the growth of timber, oak, hickory, and the short leaf pine, pea vine on the hill sides and in the bottoms, and a late (or autumnal) broad leaf grass on the richest land—the whole a very desirable country. Below the falls of these two rivers the land is broken or waving, the streams are some of them margined with oak woods, and all of them with cane or reed. The uplands of Ocmulgee are pine forest ; the swamp wide and rich ; the whole fine for stock. On its right bank, below the old Uchee path, there is some light pine barren, with some light Palmeto grass.

Flint river has also below its falls some rich swamp for not more than 20 miles ; its left bank is then poor, with pine flats and ponds, down within fifteen miles of its confluence with Chatahouchee. These fifteen miles are waving, with some good oak land in small veins. On its right bank there are several large creeks which rise out of the ridge dividing the waters of Flint and Chatahouchee. Some of them margined with oak woods and cane, and all the branches for seventy miles below the falls have reeds ; from thence down there are bay-galls, dwarf evergreens, and cypress ponds, with some live oak. Between these rivers there is good post and black oak land, strewed over with iron ore, and the ridge dividing their waters has a vein extending itself in the direction of the ridge. Within twenty-five miles of the confluence of the rivers the live oak is to be seen near all the ponds ; here are limestone sinks ; the land is good in veins, in the flats and on the margins of the rivers. The trees of every description small—the range a fine one for cattle.

The extensive body of land between Flint river and O-ke-fau-no-cau, Altamaha and the eastern boundary of the Creek claims, is pine land, with cypress ponds and bay-galls. The small streams are margined with dwarf evergreens ; the uplands have yellow pine, with dwarf, saw palmeto and wire grass ; the bluffs on St. Illas are some part of them sandy pine barren ; the remainder a compact, stiff, yellowish sand or clay, with large swamps ; the growth loblolly bay, gum and small evergreens ; the whole of those swamps are bogs. In the rainy season, which commences after midsummer, the ponds fill, and then the country is, a greater part of it, covered with water ; and in the dry season it is difficult to obtain water in any direction for many miles.

The bees abound in the Okefaunocau and other swamps eastward of Flint river ; the whortleberry is to be found in swamps and on the poorest land bordering on the cypress ponds, when the woods are not burnt for a year or more ; the latter are on dwarf bushes, grow large, and in great abundance.

The dwarf saw-palmetto, when the woods are not burnt, in like manner, bears a cluster of berries on a single stone, which are eaten by bear, deer, turkeys and Indians. The berries half an inch in diameter, covered with a black skin, and have a hard seed : they are agreeable to the taste, sweet accompanied with bitter, and when fully ripe they burst, and the bees extract much honey from them. The China briar is in the flat, rich, sandy margin of streams. The Indians dig the roots, pound them in a mortar, and suspend them in coarse cloth, pour water on them, and wash them : the sediment which passes through with the water is left to subside ; the water is then poured off, and the sediment is baked into cakes, or made into gruel sweetened with honey. This briar is called Coonte, and the bread of it Coontetucal ga, and is an important article of food among the hunters. In the old beaver ponds, and in thick boggy places, they have the bog potatoe, a small root used as food in years of scarcity.

The *Okefaunocau* is the source of St. Marys and Little St. Johns, called by the Indians Sau-wau-he. It is sometimes pronounced Ecunfinocau, from Ecunau earth, and finocau quivering; the first is the most common among the Creeks—it is from Ocka, a Choctaw word for fire and water ; Ocau, quivering. This is a very extensive swamp, and much of it a bog; so much so, that a little motion will make the mud and water quiver to a great distance ; hencethe name is given

Ho-eth-le-poie Tus-tun-ug-go Thlucco, an Indian who resided in it many years, says, " that Little St. Johns may be ascended far into the swamp, but that it is not practicable to go far up the St. Marys, as it loses itself in the swamp ; that there is one ridge on the west side of St. Johns, and three on the east ; the growth pine, live and white oak—the soil good ; the lakes abound in fish and alligators ; on the ridges, and in the swamps, there were a great many bear, deer, and and tigers—he lived on the ridge west of St. Johns, and was, with his family, very healthy ; beasts of prey destroyed most of his cattle and horses : he could walk round the swamp in five days."

INDIAN CESSION.

The Indian claims are now extinguished to about three fourths of the territory. By Jackson's treaty, the Coose river was made the boundary line between the lands of the United States and Creeks, from the Ten Islands on the Coosa river, to Wetumke, or the great Falls near Fort Jackson. From Wetumke, the line runs across eastwardly about 18 miles, then southwardly across the Tallapoose to the mouth of Ofuskee, and up the Ofuskee ten miles, and thence S. 49. 16. E. 67 miles to the mouth of Sumuchichoba, on the Chattahouchee, 46 miles above the 31st degree of north latitude, or the boundary line between the Alabama territory and West Florida, and from the mouth of Sumuchichoba, due east through the state of Georgia to the Altamaha, two miles east of Goose creek. The whole of the Creek country, west and south of the Alabama and the line above mentioned, was ceded to the United States by the treaty with general Jackson. That part of the cession which falls within the Alabama territory, amounts probably to about 17,000 square miles.

SETTLEMENTS, POPULATION.

The settlements extend here from Mobile point to Fort Jackson on the Coosa. On the Alabama the country is pretty well settled near the river, 25 miles above Fort Jackson. There are also settlements on the Conecah, Cahaba, and Black Warrior. The country is very thinly settled below St. Stephens. But it is now rapidly settling between the Alabama and Tombigbee.

There are several new towns laid off; the village of Blakely is situated at the mouth of Tensaw, on the east side of the Mobile bay. Its site is high, commanding and pleasant. Its fountains of fresh spring water, are pure, cool, numerous and copious. A good road can be found along the dividing ridge

separating the branches of Conecah and Escambia from those
of the Alabama; and the distance from Mobile to Fort Claiborne, by this route is 30 miles shorter, than by that of St.
Stevens. The main road from Georgia to New-Orleans will
probably strike Mobile bay at this point. The borders of the
Conecah are fast settling, especially by the poorer class of
people, and stock owners; it being better calculated for men
of small capital than the Alabama The rapidity of the settlement of Madison county is probably without a parallel
in the history of the union. The census of 1816 gave the
following result:

Counties.	Whites.	Slaves	Total
Wayne,	1,566	517	2,083
Baldwin,	411	752	1,163
Clarke,	2,763	1,333	4,196
Greene,	992	729	1,721
Monroe,	3,593	1,603	5,296
Jackson,	714	255	969
Washington,	1,888	671	2,559
Madison,	10,000	4,200	14,200
Mobile,	867	433	1,300
Total,	22,794	10,493	33,287

This population is scattered, in lines, over an immense
extent of territory. It is rapidly augmenting by emigrants
from Georgia, the Carolinas, and from Kentucky and Tennessee. A writer well acquainted with the country, predicts
that *five years will not elapse* before the population of this
territory will exceed 60,000 free white inhabitants, the number which gives a right to admission into the union, as an independent state.

The Creeks or Muscogees, are the only Indians inhabiting
the territory, and reside chiefly on the waters of Alabama and
Catahouchy, in about thirty towns; they are brave, raise stock,
and cultivate the soil, and although greatly reduced by war
and famine, in 1813-14, their number at this moment exceeds
20,000 souls.

ILLINOIS TERRITORY.

THE boundaries of the Illinois territory are defined by law :—the Ohio washes its southern border, extending from the mouth of the Wabash to its junction with the Mississippi, a distance of 160 miles ; the Mississippi constitutes the western boundary from the mouth of the Ohio to the Rocky Hills, in north latitute 41 50, a distance, measuring the meanderings of that river, of more than 600 miles ; a line due east from the Rocky Hills (not yet run) divides it from the North Western Territory; the Wabash separates it from Indiana, from its mouth to within 16 miles of Fort Harrison, where the division line leaves the river, running north until it intersects the northern boundary line in N. lat. 41 50. The length of the territory in a direct line from north to south is 347 miles—its mean breadth 206. Its southern extremity is in 36 57 N. lat. It contains 52,000 square miles, or 33,280,000 acres.

The form of this extensive country is that of an imperfect triangle—its base being the northern boundary of the territory, or the parallel of the southern extremity of lake Michigan; and the Mississippi its hypothenuse.

The present population is estimated at 20,000 souls ; all whites. It increases, it is supposed, in the ratio of thirty per cent. annually, which is accellerating. Slavery is not admitted. The inhabitants principally reside on the Wabash below Vincennes, on the Mississippi, Ohio and Kaskaskia.

No state or territory in North America can boast of superior facilities of internal navigation. Nearly 1000 miles,

or, in other words, two-thirds of its frontier is washed by
the Wabash, Ohio, and Mississippi. The placid Illinois traverses this territory in a southwestern direction, nearly 400
miles. This noble river is formed by the junction of the
rivers Theakaki and Plein in N. lat. 41 48. Unlike the other
great rivers of the western country, its current is mild and
unbroken by rapids, meandering *at leisure* through one of the
finest countries in the world. It enters the Mississippi about
200 miles above its confluence with the Ohio and 18 above the
mouth of the Misouri, in 38 42 N. lat. Is upwards of 400
yards wide at its mouth, bearing from the Mississippi N. 75
deg. west. The tributaries of this river entering from the
north or right bank, are, 1. The Mine, 70 miles long, falls into the *Illinois* about 75 miles from its mouth. 2. The Sagamond, a crooked river, enters the Illinois 130 miles from
the Mississippi. It is 100 yards wide at its entrance, and
navigable 150 miles for small craft—general course south east.
3. Demi Quain, enters 28 miles above the mouth of the Sagamond ; its course nearly south east, and is said to be navigable 120 miles. On the northern bank of this river is an
extensive morass called Demi Quain Swamp. 4. Seseme
Quain is the next river entering from the north west, 30
miles above the mouth of Demi Quain ; 60 yards wide and
boatable 60 miles. The land on its banks is represented to
be of superior excellence. 5. La Marche, a little river from the
north—navigable but a short distance. 6. Fox river comes
in nearly equi-distant between the *Illinois* lake and the junction of the Plein and Theakaki rivers, is 130 yards wide—
heads near the sources of Rocky river (of the Mississippi,) and
pursues a north eastern course for the first 50 miles, as though
making an effort to get into lake Michigan, approaches to
within *two miles* of Plein river ; it then takes a southern direction and is navigable 130 miles. 7. Plein, or *Kickapoo*
river, interlocks in a singular manner, with the Chicago, running into lake Michigan ; sixty miles from its head it expands
and forms lake Depage, five miles below which it joins the

Theakaki from the north east. These streams united, are to the Illinois what the Allegany and Monongahela, are to the Ohio—they water parts of Indiana and the N. W. Territory.

The rivers of the left branch of the Illinois fall in in the following order : 1. The Macopin, a small river, 25 yards wide, 20 miles from the Mississippi; boatable 9 miles to the hills. 2. The Little Michillimackinac, 200 miles from the Mississippi; navigable 90 miles; comes from the S. E. It interweaves its branches with the *Kaskaskia*—has several considerable forks. 3. Crow Meadow river; heads in the Knobs, near the head waters of the Vermillion (of the Wabash)—its course is N. W.—is but 20 yards wide at its mouth, and navigable about 15 miles. 4. Vermillion river, from the S. E.—30 yards wide ; rocky and unnavigable, falls into the Illinois 160 miles from the Mississippi, near the S. E. end of the Little Rocks. 5. Rainy Island river, from the S. E. narrow and navigable but a few miles.

"The banks of the Illinois are generally high. The bed of the river being a white marble, or clay, or sand, the waters are remarkably clear. It abounds with beautiful islands, one of which is ten miles long; and adjoining or near to it, are many coal mines, salt ponds, and small lakes. It passes through one lake, two hundred and ten miles from its mouth, which is twenty miles in length, and three or four miles in breadth, called Illinois lake."*

The Kaskaskia is the next river in magnitude. It heads in the extensive prairies south of lake Michigan—its course is nearly north. It enters the Mississippi 100 miles above the mouth of the Ohio, and 84 below the Illinois, and is navigable 130 miles. Its tributaries from the west and north-west are Water-Cress and Lalande creeks—those entering from the east are Blind River, Bighill creek, Beaver, Yellow creek, and Copper mine creek.

---

* A late Officer of the U. S. Army.

A respectable correspondent, residing on the Kaskaskia, gives the following interesting sketch, under date of January 20, 1817:

"The Kaskaskia river waters the finest country I have ever seen—it is neither flat nor mountainous, but maintains a happy undulating medium between the extremes—it is suited to the growth of Indian corn, wheat, rye, oats, barley, hemp, tobacco, &c. &c. The climate is too cold for cotton, as a staple, or for sugar. On the streams of this river there are already built, and now building a great number of mills—it is navigable at least 150 miles on a straight line—it is generally conceded that the permanent seat of government for the state, will be fixed on this river, near a direct line from the mouth of Missouri to Vincennes, in the state of Indiana. The inhabitants residing on this river and its waters, may not be as polished as some; but I will say, without fear of contradiction, that no people have a more abundant stock of hospitality, morality, and religion. On the bank of this river, a few miles above its mouth, is situated the town of Kaskaskia, the present seat of government. Here is a fine harbor for boats.

"The great American bottom of the Mississippi begins at the mouth of the Kaskaskia river, extending nearly to the mouth of the Illinois river, supposed to contain six hundred square miles. No land can be more fertile—Some of it has been in cultivation one hundred and twenty years, and still no deterioration has yet manifested itself—it is unquestionably the Delta of America. Great numbers of cattle are bought in that country for the Philadelphia and Baltimore markets—it is undoubtedly a very fine stock country."

Au Vase river empties into the Mississippi 55 miles above the mouth of the Ohio; it is boatable 60 miles, through a fine prairie country. It drains a district 70 by 25 miles. The little river *Marie* waters a district between the Au Vase and and Kaskaskia. Wood river is the principal stream between the mouths of the Kaskaskia and Illinois.

Rocky river waters the north-west corner of the territory. It heads in the hills west of the south end of lake Michigan, and is 300 yards wide at its entrance into the Mississippi—it bears from the Mississippi almost due east—about three miles up this river is an old Indian town, belonging to the Sac nation. Sand Bay river discharges itself into the Mississippi between the mouths of Rocky and Illinois rivers.

The streams falling into the Ohio, from this territory, below the mouth of the Wabash, are few and inconsiderable in size. The Saline is the first—it empties its waters 26 miles below the mouth of the Wabash. It is 150 yards wide at its mouth —navigable for keels and batteaux for 30 miles. The famous U. S. Salt-Works, are upon this stream, 20 miles up by the windings of the river, but not more than ten in a direct line. Sandy creek between this and fort Massac; and Cash river, 15 miles below Wilkinsonville, are the only ones deserving mention, though there are others sufficiently large to afford mill seats.

In addition to the rivers and rivulets already described, the eastern part of the territory is watered by several respectable rivers running into the Wabash. 1. Little Wabash river, from the north-west—60 yards wide. 2. Fox river, which interlocks with eastern branches of the Kaskaskia—enters the Wabash about 50 miles below Vincennes. 3. The Embarras, or river of Embarasment, enters the Wabash a little below Vincennes—course south-east. 4. Mascontin, from the north-west, 50 yards wide. 5. St. Germain, from the west; a mere rivulet. 6. Tortue, from the west, a crooked, long river. The three last mentioned rivers enter the Wabash, in the order named, between Vincennes and fort Harrison. 7. Brouette. 8. Duchat. 9. Erabliere. 10. Rejoicing. These rivers all head in the Illinois territory, and enter the Wabash, between fort Harrison and Tippecanoe. The last is 100 yards wide at its mouth.

There are many small lakes in this territory. Several of the rivers have their sources in them. They abound with wild fowl and fish.   On the left bank of the Illinois, 40 miles from its mouth, are a chain of small lakes communicating by narrow channels, with each other; one of them discharges into the Illinios.   The prairies bordering these lakes constitute the Peorias' wintering ground.   Illinois and Depage lakes are merely expansions of the Illinois and Plein rivers.   Demiquain lake is situated on the right bank of the Illinois, above the mouth of the river of the same name—it is of a circular form; six miles across; and empties its waters into the Illinois.   There are also several small lakes in the American Bottom, such as Marrodizua, five miles long, twenty two miles below the mouth of Wood river—Bond lake 3 miles further down; their outlets discharge into the Mississippi.   On their margins are delightful plantations.

FACE OF THE COUNTRY.

There are six distinct kinds of land in Illinois.   1. Bottoms, bearing honey locust, pecan, black walnut, beach, sugar maple, buckeye, pawpaw, &c.   This land is of the first quality, and may be said to be *ripe* alluvion, and is found in greater or less quantities, on all the rivers before enumerated.   It is called the first bottom.   It is almost invariably covered with a pretty heavy growth of the foregoing trees, grape vines, &c. and in autumn the air of these bottoms is agreeably impregnated with an aromatic smell, caused no doubt by the fruit and leaves of the black walnut.   This land is inexhaustible in fecundity; as is proved by its present fertility, where it has been annually cultivated without manure, for more than a century.   It varies in width from 50 rods to two miles and upwards.   2. The newly formed or *unripe* alluvion;   this kind of land is always found at the mouths and confluences of rivers; it produces sycamore, cotton wood, water maple, water ash, elm willow oak, willow, &c. and is covered in autumn, with a luxuriant growth of weeds.   These bottoms are subject to inundations, the banks being several feet below high water mark.

There are many thousand acres of this land at the mouth of the Wabash, and at the confluence of the Mississippi. Woe be to the settler, who locates himself upon this deleterious soil. 3. Dry prairie, bordering all the rivers, lies immediately in the rear of the bottoms; from 30 to 100 feet higher; and from one to ten miles wide, a dry rich soil, and most happily adapted to the purposes of cultivation, as it bears drought and rain with equal success. These prairies are destitute of trees, unless where they are crossed by streams and occasional islands of wood land. The prairies of the Illinois river are the most extensive of any east of the Mississippi, and have alone been estimated at 1,200,000 acres. This soil is some places black, in others of the colour of iron rust interspersed with a light white sand. In point of productiveness, it is not inferior to the first rate river bottoms, and in some respects superior. 4. Wet prairie, which are found remote from streams, or at their sources, the soil is generally cold and barren, abounding with swamps, ponds, and covered with a tall coarse grass. 5. Timbered land, moderately hilly, well watered, and of a rich soil. 6. Hills, of a sterile soil and destitute of timber, or covered with stinted oaks and pines.

Between the mouths of the Wabash and the Ohio, the right bank of the Ohio, in many places presents the rugged appearance of bold projecting rocks. The banks of the Kaskaskia and Illinois in some places present a sublime and picturesque scenery. Several of their tributary streams have excavated for themselves deep and frightful gulfs, particularly, those of the first named river, the banks of which near the junction of Big hill creek, present a perpendicular front of 140 feet high, of solid limestone. The north western part of the territory is a hilly, broken country, in which most of the rivers emptying into the Wabash from the north, have their heads. A great part of the territory is open prairie, some of which are of such vast extent that the sun apparently rises and sets within their widely extended borders.

"The large tract of country through which the Illinois river and its branches meander, is said not to be exceeded in beauty, levelness, richness, and fertility of soil, by any tract of land, of equal extent, in the United States. From the Illinois to the Wabash, excepting some little distance from the rivers, is almost one continued prairie, or natural meadow, intermixed with groves, or copses of wood, and some swamps and small lakes. These beautiful, and to the eye of the beholder, unlimited fields, are covered with a luxuriant growth of grass, and other vegetable productions."

Travellers describe the scenery skirting the Illinois as beautiful beyond description. There is a constant succession of prairies, stretching in many places, from the river farther than the eye can reach, and elegant groves of wood land. The trees are represented as peculiarly handsome; having their branches overspread with rich covering of the vine. Neverthsless, it is the empire of solitude, for the cheering voice of civilized men is seldom heard on this delightful stream.

According to the late General Pike, the east shore of the Mississippi, from the mouth of the Missouri to that of the Illinois (20 miles) is bordered by hills from 80 to 100 feet high; above, they are of gentle ascent, alternately presenting beautiful cedar clifts and distant ridges. The bottoms afford many eligible situations for settlements. Above and below the mouth of Rocky river are beautiful prairies.

TREES, PLANTS, MINERALS.

The oak family may be said to be the prevailing forest tree of Illinois. There are four species of white oak; two of chesnut oak, mountain and Illinois; three of willow oak, upland, swamp, and *shingle*, so called from its being an excellent material for shingles, and which is used for that purpose by the inhabitants. It is found on all the rivers of the territory. Its height is from 40 to 50 feet—grey bark, straight branches, large, sessile, dark green leaves, a little downy underneath; spnerical acorns. Black jack, black oak,

swamp oak, scarlet oak, so called from its scarlet colored
leaves in autumn; grows to the height of 80 feet, useful for
rails. The honey locust is found in all the swails, bottoms,
and rich hills of the west, from the lakes to the latitude of
Natchez. It invariably rejects a poor soil; grows to the
height of 40 or 60 feet, dividing into many branches, which
together with the trunk, are armed with long, sharp, pithy
spines of the size of goose quills, from five to ten inches in
length, and frequently so thick as to prevent the ascent of a
squirrel. The branches are garnished with winged leaves,
composed of ten or more pair of small lobes, sitting close to
the midrib, of a lucid green colour. The flowers come out
from the sides of the young branches, in form of katkins, of
an herbaceous colour, and are succeeded by crooked, com-
pressed pods, from nine or ten to sixteen or eighteen inches
in length, and about an inch and a half or two inches in
breadth, of which near one half is filled with a sweet pulp,
the other containing many seeds in separate cells. The pods,
from the sweetness of their pulp, are used to brew in beer,
and afford for hogs and many other animals a nutritious and
abundant food. I have myself been in situations, when I was
obliged to resort to them as a substitute for something better,
and always found them to allay hunger, and renew almost exhausted strength. The black walnut is found on the bottoms
and rich hills—it often rises to the height of 70 feet ; large
trunk, dark, furrowed bark ; winged leaves, which emit an
aromatic flavor when bruised; fruit round and nearly as large
as a peach. The wood is light and durable. Butternut is a
companion of the black walnut. Besides all the species of
hickory found in the northern states, the pecan or Illinois nut
grows plentifully in the rich swails and bottoms ; the nuts are
small and thin shelled. The banks of the Illinois are the favorite soil of the mulberry, and of the plum. Sugar maple,
blue and white oak, black locust, elm, basswood, beach, buckeye, hackberry, coffee-nut tree, and sycamore, are found in
their congenial soils, throughout the territory. White pine

B

is found on the head branches of the Illinois. Spice wood,
sassafras, black and white haws, crab apple, wild cherry, cucumber, and pawpaw, are common to the best soils. The last
yields a fruit of the size of a cucumber, of a yellow colour—
in taste resembling the pine apple. They grow in clusters
of three, four, and five, in the crotches of a soft straight and
beautiful shrub from 10 to 25 feet high—it is rarely found on
the hills however rich their soil. The forests and banks of the
streams abound with grape vines, of which there are several
species; some valuable. The herbage of the woods varies
little from that of Kentucky, Ohio, and Indiana.

Copper and lead are found in several parts of the territory.
I am not informed as to the existence of iron ore. Travellers
speak of an *allum hill* a considerable distance up Mine river,
and of another hill, producing the fleche or arrow stone. The
French while in possession of the country, procured mill-
stones above the Illinois lake. Coal is found upon the banks
of the Au Vase or Muddy river, and Illinois 50 miles above
Peoria lake; the latter mine extends for half a mile along
the right bank of the river. A little below the coal mines
are two salt ponds one hundred yards in circumference, and
several feet in depth; the water is stagnant, and of a yellowish
colour. The French inhabitants and Indians make good salt
from them. Between two and three hundred thousand bushels of salt are annually made at the U. S. Saline, 26 miles below the mouth of the Wabash. These works supply the
settlements of Indiana and Illinois. The salt is sold at the
works at from fifty to seventy-five cents a bushel. Government have leased the works to Messrs. Wilkins and Morrison,
of Lexington. Beds of white clay are found on the rivers
Illinois and Tortue. The prevailing stone is lime.

VILLAGES, ROADS, AND SETTLEMENTS.

There are several old French villages on both banks of the
Illinois, which are antique in appearance, inhabited by a people inured to the habits of savage life.

Cahokia—Is situated on a small stream, about one mile east of the Mississippi, nearly opposite to St. Louis. It contains about 160 houses, mostly French, who were its founders. "This town, although apparently of considerable elevation, is still a damp and disagreeable situation, owing to its being too level to permit the rains to run off very easily." It formerly enjoyed a considerable share of the fur trade. At present the inhabitants confine their attention chiefly to agriculture, but not with much spirit. There is a post-office and a chapel for the Roman Catholic worship; and is the seat of justice for St. Clair county.

St. Philippe—In the American bottom, 45 miles below Cahokia, a pleasant old French village.

Prairie du Rochers—Twenty miles below St. Phillippe, contains from sixty to seventy French families; the streets are narrow—there is a catholic chapel. The country below and above is a continued prairie of the richest soil.

Kaskaskia—Situated on the right shore of the river of the same name, eleven miles from its mouth, and six from the Mississippi, in a direct line. It is at present the seat of the territorial government and chief town of Randolph county—contains 160 houses, scattered over an extensive plain ; some of them are of stone. Almost every house has a spacious picketed garden in its rear. The houses have a clumsy appearance ; it is 150 miles south-west of Vincennes, and 900 from the city of Washington. The inhabitants are more than half French ; they raise large stocks of horned cattle, horses, swine, poultry, &c. There is a post office, a land office for the sale of the public lands, and a printing office, from which is issued a weekly newspaper entitled the *"Illinois Herald."* This place was settled upwards of 100 years ago, by the French of Lower Canada. The surrounding lands are in a good state of cultivation.

The villages on the Ohio, below the Wabash are,

Shawannetown, above the mouth of the Saline, containing 30 or 40 log buildings ; the inhabitants live by the profits of the salt trade. The growth of the town has been greatly re-. tarded in consequence of the United States having reserved to themselves the property of the scite of this place, the salt licks, as well as the intermediate tract between this and Saline river, 9 miles distant. It is a place of great resort for boats, and in time will no doubt become a place of consequence, as the lands in its vicinity are of a good quality. Here formerly stood an Indian village of the Shawanroe nation.

Wilkinsonville—About half way between fort Massac and the mouth of the Ohio, stands upon a beautiful savanna of 100 acres, 60 cr 70 feet above the river. It is a place of little or no trade at present, and has sensibly declined since it lost the governmental patronage of a garrison. It has a fine eddy for boats.

There are several other small villages, such as Belle Fontaine, L'Aigle, Edwardsville, &c. A new village is about to be laid out at the mouth of Cash. There are two roads leading through the Ohio to Kaskaskia. The first leaves the Ohio at Robin's ferry, 17 miles below the Saline ; distance to Kaskaskia, 135 miles. The other leaves the river at Lusk's ferry, 15 miles above the mouth of Cumberland. This is the shortest route by 15 or 20 miles. A post route passes from Vincennes to Kaskaskia, about 150 miles long—travellers are obliged to camp out two or three nights. Government have leased out a number of lots upon these roads ; and receive the rents in repairs of a given distance of road. There is a tolerable road between the mouth of Au Vase and Wood river, passing through Kaskaskia, Prairie du Rochers, St. Philippe, and Cahokia. Most of the settlements are connected by practicable roads, at least for packers and travellers on horseback. The bulk of the population is settled upon the Mississippi, Kaskaskia and its branches. There are a few detached settlements on the Wabash, and some of the streams entering the west bank; and detached ones on the Ohio. Those on the Illinois are small, insulated, and sometimes 50 miles apart. The American and Turky hill settlements, between the Illinois and Wood rivers, are flourishing; the inhabitants are mostly from Kentucky and the southern states.

NATURAL CURIOSITIES, ANTIQUITIES.

The "Cave in Rock," nineteen miles below Saline, has been often visited and described by travellers. The entrance into this cave is of a semi-circular form, twenty feet above the ordinary level of the river, in a perpendicular rock, thirty feet high. A few yards from the mouth you enter a spacious room, sixty paces in length, and nearly as wide. Near the centre of the roof is an aperture resembling the funnel of a chimney, which, according to Ash, the British traveller, leads to an upper room, "not unlike a Gothic Cathedral." At one end of this vault, our traveller found an opening, which served as a descent to another vault, of very great depth, as he judged, since "a stone cast in, whose reverbration was not returned for the space of several seconds." Our adventurer, who is always full of the marvellous, found the remains of several human skeletons, in this "drear abode;" while searching for others, he got bewildered, and was unable to find the place of his descent. He fired his pistol, as a signal of distress—its effect was "terrific"—its report "tremendous." "No thunder could exceed the explosion, no echo return so strong a voice!"* Mason's gang of robbers made this cave their principal rendezvous, in 1   7, where they frequently plundered or murdered the crews of boats descending the Ohio.

The Battery Rocks, so called from their resemblance to a range of forts and batteries, are noticed by travellers, as a natural curiosity. They are nothing more than the perpendicular bank of the river, seven miles above the Cave in Rock. The *Devil's Oven* is situated upon an elevated rocky point,

---

* See Ash's Travels, page 234.

projecting into the Mississippi, fifteen miles below the mouth of Au Vase. It has a close resemblance to an oven. On the large prairies are frequently found *sink-holes*, some of which are 150 feet across, circular at the top, gradually narrowing to the bottom, and frequently so steep as to make the descent difficult. At the bottom, the traveller finds a handsome sub-terranean brook, in which he can conveniently allay his thirst. These sinks have, doubtless, been formed by the waters' un-dermining the earth, the weight of which produces successive excavations.

Ancient fortifications and mounds, similar to those found in Kentucky, Ohio, and Indiana, are also met with in Illinois. Four miles above the Prairie du Rochers, are the ruins of fort Chartres, built by the French, at the expence of one hundred thousand dollars. At the period of its construction, it was one quarter of a mile from the river, but at present is nearly undermined by the Mississippi. Fort Massac, 45 miles above the mouth of the Ohio, built by the French about the middle of the last century, and occupied by the Americans for many years after the close of the revolutionary war; is at present dismantled.

ANIMALS, BIRDS, FISH, SERPENTS.

The buffaloe, which formerly roamed at will, and in vast numbers, through the immense prairies of Illinois, have lately disappeared, preferring the more distant plains of the Mis-souri. Deer, elk, bear, wolves, foxes, oposum, and raccoon, remain in considerable numbers. The inhabitants of a fine breed of horses from the Spanish stock. Their cattle have a lively and sleek appearance. Hogs are easily raised.

Wild turkies abound in the hilly districts. Quails are plenty—pheasants, scarce. Geese and ducks frequent the ponds, lakes, and rivers; particularly the head branches of the Illinois, and small lakes towards lake Michigan, whither they are attracted in prodigious numbers, in quest of the wild rice, which furnishes an abundant and favorite aliment. Buzzards, pigeons, black birds, paroquets, and several species of hawks, abound in the same numbers, as in other parts of the western country.

Most kinds of fish which are found in the Missssippi and the great northern lakes, frequent the rivers of this territory. Sturgeon are found in Peoria or Illinois lake.

The only venomous serpents, are the common and *prairie* rattlesnakes, and copper-heads.

INDIANS.

The Sacs or Saukies, inhabit the country bordering on Sand Bay and Rocky Rivers—they have three villages. A part of this tribe reside on the west side of the Mississippi. Pike gives the total number of souls at 2850. Four miles below Sand Bay, the U. S. had an agricultural establishment, under the direction of a Mr. Ewing. It did not succeed, because these Indians hold labor in the greatest contempt. The Kaskaskias, Cohokias and Peorias, are remnants of formidable tribes. They have been nearly annihilated in their wars with the Saukies and Foxes, originally provoked by the assassination of the Saukie chief Pontiac. They are reduced to 250 warriors—reside principally between the Kaskaskia and Illinois. The Delawares and Shawanese have a summer residence four miles below Au Vase river. The Piankashaws and Mascontins mostly inhabit the Mascontin, Tortue and Rejoicing branches of the Wabash; their total number of souls about 600.

AGRICULTURE, PRODUCTS.

Corn is at present the staple—no country produces finer. The traveller often meets with cornfields containing from 100 to 1000 acres, these are cultivated *in common* by the people of a whole village, or a settlement. By this method the inhab-

itants obviate the expense of *division* fences, where it would
be necessary to haul timber several miles to the centre of a
vast prairie. Cotton is raised for domestic use. There is no
doubt, that ultimately, considerable quantities will be produced for exportation. Tobacco grows to great perfection.
Wheat does well, when properly managed, except on the bottoms where the soil is too rich. Flax, hemp, oats, rish and
sweet potatoes do as well as in Kentucky. Notwithstanding
the abundance of wild grapes to be found in the forests, it is
very doubtful, I think, whether the French inhabitants ever
made 80 hogsheads of good wine, in any single year. The
successful experiment at Vevay, in Indiana, warrants the belief that vineyards, at no remote period, will embellish the
hills of the southern half of this territory.

MANUFACTURES.

These are all of the domestic kind. In 1810, according to
the Marshall's returns, there were,

Spinning-Wheels,	630
Looms,	460
Cloth produced, (yards)	90,039
Value, (dollars)	54,028
Tanneries,	9
Value of Leather dressed,	7,750
Distilleries,	19
Produced (gallons) 10,200	7,500
Flour, 6440 barrels—value,	32,200
Maple Sugar, 15,600 lbs.—value,	1,980

The population has nearly doubled since that period, and
the manufactures have advanced in a corresponding ratio.

MILITARY BOUNTY LANDS.

The lands in this territory appropriated to reward the valor
of our soldiers, during the late war, amount to 3,500,000

ãcres. This tract lies on the nortʊ bank of the Illinois, near its junction with thꞁ Mississippi. Ӏt has never been particularly described. Mr. Tiffin, commissioner of the general land office, declares it to be of the first quality. A gentleman, high in office in that territory, writes—"Ӏ have never been on the north side of the illinois river, but my information authorises me to say, that it is a very good country." Another correspondent writes—"This tract is of good quality, and desirable to settlers—it is inferior to none of the public lands of the United States." The U. S. are now engaged in surveying them. They are watered by several respectable streams, and are advantageously situated, either for the lake or Orleans trade, having the Mississippi west ; illinois south ; Mine river east, and lands belonging to the Sac and Fox Indians, north. The growth of vegetation is so luxuriant that the surveyors can make no progress in summer.

LANDS, TITLES, PRICES.

The public lands have rarely sold for more than $5 per acre, *at auction*. Those sold at Edwardsville in October, 1816, averaged $4. Private sales at the land office, are fixed by law, at $2 per acre. The old French locations command various prices from $1 to 50. Titles derived from the United States' government are always valid ; and those from individuals rarely false.

There are upwards of sixteen millions of acres belonging to the United States, obtained at different cessions from the Indians, and consequently a wide field open for purchase and selection.

The lands belonging to the aboriginal proprietors lie principally between the Wabash and the Illinois, north of the head of the Kaskaskia. They have large reservations north of the Illinois, upon Rocky river, Sagamond. &c. The United States have obtained a cession of six miles square at the east end of Peoria lake, north of the Illinois river.

FUTURE POPULATION.

The territorial population being at this moment 20,000 souls, and the ratio of increase 30 per cent. per annum, it will require *ten years* to give Illinois the necessary qualification for being admitted into the Union. It is capable of sustaining a denser population than New York, and contains nearly as many acres. Comparatively speaking, there are no waste lands. It would, therefore, allowing twenty souls to the square mile, conveniently sustain a population of 1,000,000. But on the ratio of 54 to a square mile, which was that of Connecticut, at the census of 1810, it would contain, in time, 2,600,000.

EXTENT OF NAVIGABLE WATERS.

Nature has been peculiarly bountiful to Illinois, for not only has she blessed this favored region with a temperate climate, and highly productive soil, but has prepared convenient channels of communication, for the transportation of products to market, and to facilitate settlement and internal intercourse. The Illinois, which hitherto has been little navigated, except by the North-West Company's boats, must in a few years become the theatre of an active commerce. American enterprize will force its way thither. The tide of navigation, like water, will overspread the fine vallies of Illinois, Mine and Demi-Quain. A trifling expence, comparitively to the importance of the undertaking, will unite the Illinois to the Chicago in *all* seasons of the year. Then the lead of of Missouri, and the cotton of Tennessee will find their way to Detroit and Buffalo. The following rough estimate, which does not exceed the actual distance, will enable uninformed readers to form a pretty correct idea of the extent of *frontier*

and *internal* navigation, for boats, which the future state of
Illinois will enjoy.

FRONTIER NAVIGATION.

Wabash, ...	240 miles.
Ohio, ...	164
Mississippi, ...	620

Total 1024

INTERNAL NAVIGATION.

Illinois, navigable	320 miles.
Tributaries from the N. W.	550
Ditto, from the S. E.	200
Kaskaskia, and branches, ...	300
Tributaries of the Wabash, ...	500
Minor rivers, such as Au Vase, Marie, Cash, &c.	200

Internal 2070
Frontier 1024

Total 3094

The distance by water, from the mouth of the Illinois to
New Orleans, is 1174 miles, and to Buffalo, through the lakes,
1400.

INDIANA,

IS bounded west by the Wabash river, from its mouth to 40 miles above Vincennes, and thence by a meridian line to the parallel of the south end of lake Michigan, (supposed to be in N. lat. 41, 50.) which divides it from Illinois territory. Its northern limit is the above parallel, which separates it from the Michigan territory. A meridian line running from the mouth of the Big Miami, until it intersects the aforesaid parallel of the south end of lake Michigan, divides it from the state of Ohio, on the east. The Ohio river forms its southern boundary. Length, from north to south, 284 miles ; breadth, from east to west, 155 miles—contains 39,000 square miles, or 24,960,000 acres. Its form would be that of a paralello-gram, were the course of the Ohio due west.

RIVERS, LAKES.

The Ohio washes the southern border of Indiana, from the mouth of the Big Miami, to that of the Wabash, a dis-tance, measuring its windings, of 472 miles—all the streams which intersect this extensive line of coast, are comparitively short; for the southern fork of White river, having its source within a few miles of the Ohio boundary line, runs nearly par-allel with Ohio, at the distance of from forty to sixty miles. The principal of these enter the Ohio in the order named :

Tanner's Creek—Two miles below Lawrenceburgh, thirty miles long ; thirty yards wide at its mouth—heads in the Flat woods to the south of Brookville .

Loughery's Creek—Fifty yards wide at its mouth, and forty miles long, is the next stream worthy of mention, below the Big Miami, from which it is distant eleven miles.

Indian Creek—Sometimes called Indian Kentucky, and by the Swiss *Venoge*, after a small river in the Pays de Vaud (Switzerland) constitutes the southern limit of the Swiss settlement, eight miles below the mouth of Kentucky river. It rises in the hills near the south fork of White River, 45 miles north east of Vevay.

Wyandot creek, heads in the range of hills extending in a transverse direction, from near the mouth of Blue river, to the *Muddy* fork of White river, and falls into the Ohio about equidistant from the falls and Blue river.

Big Blue River, heads still further north; but near the south fork of White river. After running fifty miles southwest, it inclines to the east of south, and enters the Ohio 32 miles below the mouth of Salt river, from the south. Its name indicates the colour of its water, which is of a clear blueish cast; but in quality pure and healthful.

Little Blue River empties into the Ohio 13 miles below the mouth of Big Blue River—it is about forty yards wide at its mouth—its course is from north east to south west. Ten miles below is Sinking creek, fifty yards wide at its mouth.

Anderson's river, sixty miles farther down, is the most considerable stream between Blue river and the Wabash. Below this, are Pegion and Beaver creeks. In addition to the preceding creeks and rivers, a large number of respectable creeks and runs also enter the Ohio, at different points between the Miami and the Wabash, so that that part of Indiana, lying between White river and the Ohio, may be pronounced *well watered*. It is the character of most of the foregoing streams, to possess a brisk current and pure water; the consequence is, an abundance of convenient mill seats, and a salubrious and healthful climate.

The *Wabash* waters the central and western parts of the state. The main branch of this fine river, heads two miles east of old fort St. Mary's, and intersects the portage road between Loramie creek and the river St. Mary's, in Darke county, Ohio. There are three other branches, all winding through a rich and extensive country. The first, called *Little river*, heads seven miles south of fort Wayne, and enters the Wabash, about eighty miles below the St. Mary's portage. The second is the Massasinway, which heads in Darke county, Ohio, about half way between forts Greenville and Recovery, and unites with the others, 5 miles below the mouth of Little river. The third is *Eel river*, which issues from several lakes and ponds, eighteen miles west of fort Wayne; it enters the Wabash, eight miles below the mouth of the Massissinway. From the entrance of Eel river, the general course of the Wabash is about ten degrees south of west, to the mouth of Rejoicing river, (85 miles) where it takes a southern direction, to the mouth of Rocky river (forty miles) —here it inclines to the west, to the mouth of the Miscontin, (thirty-six miles)—where it pursues a south eastern course, to Vincennes, (fifty miles)—from this town to the Ohio, its general course is south, (one hundred miles.) It is three hundred yards wide at its mouth, and enters the Ohio at right angles. Its length, from its mouth to its extreme source, exceeds five hundred miles. It is navigable for keel boats, about four hundred miles, to Ouitanon, where there are rapids. From this village small boats can go to within six miles of St. Mary's river; ten of fort Wayne; and eight of the St. Josephs of the Miami-of-the-lakes. Its current is generally gentle above Vincennes—below this town there are several rapids; but not of sufficient magnitude to prevent boats from ascending. The principal rapids are between Deche and White rivers, ten miles below Vincennes.

The tributary waters, which enter from the left bank of the Wabash, and which are called rivers, are:

1. The *Petoka*, from the north east, comes in twenty miles below Vincennes; it heads a few miles south east of the Muddy fork of White river, with which it runs parallel, at the distance of ten or twelve miles. It is about seventy-five miles in length, and meanders through extensive rich bottoms.

2. *White River* enters four miles above the Petoka, and sixteen below Vincennes. This is an important river, as it reaches nearly across the state in a diagonal direction, watering a vast body of rich land—thirty-five miles from its mouth there is a junction of the two principal forks—the north or Drift-wood Branch, interlocks with the north fork of *White-water*, and with the branches of Stillwater, a tributary of the Big Miami. The south or Muddy fork heads between the branches of the west fork of *Whitewater*. The country between the two main forks of Whiteriver is watered by the Teakettle branch, which unites with the north fork, twenty miles above the junction of the two principal forks.

3. *Deche river*, unites with the Wabash, about half way between Vincennes and the mouth of Whiteriver—it comes from the north east—is a crooked, short stream, but receives several creeks.

4. *Little river*, called by the French *Le Petite Reviere*, winds its devious course, from the north east, among wide spreading bottoms, and enters its estuary a little above Vincennes. Between this river and the Wabash lies an alluvion of several thousand acres, uniformly bottom, of exhaustless fertility.

5. The *St. Marie*, from north east, enters eighteen miles above Vincennes, and is about fifty miles long.

6. *Rocky river*, sixty miles further up, comes in from the east, and interweaves its branches with those of the Main fork of White river. It is one hundred yards wide at its mouth, and has several large forks.

7. *Petite*, or *Little* river, is the only *river* entering from the left, for seventy miles above Rocky river. It comes from the south east, and heads near the sources of Rocky river.

8. *Pomme* river comes in from the south east—forty miles higher up, and twenty miles below the mouth of Massissinway. It rises near the Ohio boundary, a little to the north of the head branches of Whitewater. Besides the rivers above enumerated, which water the left bank of the Wabash,

there are an immense number of creeks and runs, affording, in most places a sufficient supply of water. But there are pretty extensive districts between the *Little* and *Rocky* rivers, where water cannot be readily procured.

The right or north west bank of the Wabash, receives a greater number of rivers than the left. Crossing this noble stream, at the mouth of Pomme river, and descending upon its right shore, the first considerable water that obstructs our progress, is *Richard's creek*, from the north west—ten miles below. Ten miles farther enters *Rock river*, from the north west—its banks are high, and the country around it broken.

Eight miles farther down, is the *Tippacanoe*, rendered famous by the battle upon its banks, between the Americans and Indians, in Nov. 1811. This river heads about thirty miles to the West of fort Wayne. Several of its branches issue from lakes, swamps, and ponds, some of which have *double outlets*, running into the St. Josephs of the Miami-of-the-lakes. Upon this stream, and on the Wabash, above and below its junction, are Indian villages, and extensive fields. Two Indian roads leave these towns for the northern lakes— one ascends the right bank of the Wabash, to Ouitanan and fort Wayne; the other ascends the Tippacanoe, and crosses the head branches of the Illinois, to the St. Josephs of lake Michigan.

From the mouth of Tippacanoe, we successively pass Pine, and Redwood creeks; Rejoicing, or Vermillion Jaune, Little Vermillion, Erabliere, Duchat, and Brouette rivers, at the distance of from ten to fifteen miles from each other, and all coming from the west or north west; mostly small, and having their heads in the Illinois territory.

Whitewater, rises near the eastern boundary line, twelve miles west of fort Greenville, and nearly parallel with this line, at the distance of from six to ten miles, and watering in its progress, twenty-two townships, in Wayne, Franklin, and Dearborn counties. At Brookville, thirty miles from its entrance into the Miami, it receives the West fork, which Leads in the Flat woods, thirty miles west of that village, and interlocks with the branches of White river. This beautiful little river waters nearly one million of acres of fine land, and owes its name to the unusual transparency of its water. A fish or a pebble can be seen at the depth of twenty feet. It is sufficiently cool for drinking during summer. The inhabitants contend that bodies floating on its surface are less buoyant than those on any other river; and endeavored to dissuade me from bathing in it. I nevertheless, swam several times across the stream, where it was one hundred yards wide; and, although an experienced swimmer, was not a little fatigued by the exercise. But I ascribed the effect to the *coldness* rather than to any extraordinary *weakness* in the water.

One of the eastern branches of this river, heads six miles east of the state line, in the state of Ohio; and Greenville creek, a tributary of the Stillwater fork of the Big Miami, heads about the same distance within the state of Indiana.

The north eastern part of the state is watered by the St. Josephs of the Miami-of-the-lakes, and its tributaries—this river heads about sixty miles to the north west of fort Wayne, and forms a junction with the St. Mary's, just above the post. Panther's creek, from the south, is its largest fork. Its remote branches interlock with those of the rivers Raisin, Black, St. Josephs of lake Michigan, and Eel river.

That part of the state bordering on the Michigan territory, is liberally watered by the head branches of the river Raisin, (of lake Erie;) the numerous forks of Black river, (of lake Michigan;) and the St. Josephs of lake Michigan—the latter heads near, and interlocks with the branches of Eel river; and pursues a serpentine course, seventy miles, through the northern part of Indiana.

The rivers Chemin, Big and Little Kennomic, all of which fall into lake Michigan; the Theakaki, Kickapoo, and a part of the chief branch of the Illinois, all wind through the north western section of the state: and all, except the last, are entirely within its boundaries: the three first run from south to north; the latter south and south west. Besides, the country is chequered by numerous creeks. The Vermillion of the Illinois rises in Indiana, near the sources of Tippacanoe.

The northern half of the state is a country of lakes—38 of which, from two to ten miles in length, are delineated on the latest maps; but the actual number probably exceeds one hundred—many of these, however, are mere ponds, less than one mile in length. Some have *two distinct outlets;* one running into the northern lakes; the other into the Mississippi.

The phenomenon of waters with double outlets, is not uncommon. The great Ganges, the greater Burrumpooter, and the great river of Ava, all rise and issue from the same fountain—so do the Rhine and the Rhone ; the Suir, the Nore, and the Barrow, in Ireland, spring from the same well—and after traversing a vast range of country, in three opposite directions, re-unite and form one basin, in Waterford Harbor; there are two rivers in the Isthmus of Panama, whose head waters are not farther apart than the Ouisconsin and Fox river; one stretches into the southern ocean; the other into the Mexican sea.

The greater part of these lakes, are situated between the head waters of the two St. Josephs, Black river, Raisin, Tippacanoe, and Eel rivers.

ASPECT OF THE COUNTRY.

A range of hills, called the knobs, extends from the falls of the Ohio, to the Wabash, nearly in a south western direction, which, in many places, produces a broken and uneven surface. North of these hills, lie the Flat woods, seventy miles wide and reaching nearly to the Guitanan country. Bordering all the principal streams, except the Ohio, there are strips of bottom and prairie land; both together are from three to six miles in width. Between the Wabash and lake Michigan the country is mostly champaign, abounding alternately with wood lands, prairies, lakes, and swamps.

A range of hills run parallel with the Ohio, from the mouth of the Big Miami, to Blue river, alternately approaching to within a few rods, and receding to the distance of two miles; but broken at short intervals by numerous creeks. Immediately below Blue river, the hills disappear, and the horizon presents nothing to view but an immense tract of level land, covered with a heavy growth of timber.

That part of the state lying west of the Ohio boundary line, north of the head branches of White river, east and south of the Wabash, has been described by the conductors of expeditions against the Indians, as a "country containing much good land; but intersected at the distance of four or six miles, with long, narrow swamps, boggy and mirey, the soil of which is a stiff blue clay."

North of the Wabash, between Tippacanoe and Ouitanan, the banks of the streams are high, abrupt, and broken—and the land well timbered, except on the prairies.

Between the Plein and Theakaki, the country is flat, wet, and swampy, interspersed with prairies of an inferior quality of soil.

In going from the Ohio to the Wabash, say from Clark's ville or Madison to Vincennes, you ascend from two to three hundred feet before you find yourself at the top of the *last* bank of the Ohio. You have then before you a strip of country, twenty miles wide, tolerably level, except where gullied by the actions of streams. This brings you at the foot of the " *Knobs*," which are at least 500 feet higher than the land in your rear; after this you pass no very tedious hills, until you find yourself within three miles of Vincennes. In travelling from this place to the Ohio, you are not sensible of *ascending* to the height at which you find yourself, on the summit of the " *Knobs*," from which you have a boundless prospect to the east. You can distinctly trace, with the eye, at the distance of twenty miles, the deep, serpentine vale of the Ohio, and the positions of New-Lexington, Corydon, and Louisville, in Kentucky.

PRAIRIES.

There are two kinds of these meadows—the *river* and *upland* prairies: the first are found upon the margins of rivers, and are *bottoms* destitute of timber; most of these exhibit vestiges of former cultivation. The last are plains, from thirty to one hundred feet higher than the alluvial bottoms; and are far more numerous and extensive; but are indeterminate in size and figure—since some are not larger than a common field, while others expand beyond the reach of the eye, or the limits of the horizon. They are usually bounded by groves of lofty forest trees; and not unfrequently adorned with "islands," or copses of small trees, affording an agreeable shade for man and beast. In spring and summer they are covered with a luxuriant growth of grass, and fragrant flowers, from six to eight feet high, through which it is very fatiguing to force one's way with any degree of celerity. The soil of these plains is often as deep and as fertile as the best bottoms. The prairies bordering the Wabash, are particularly rich—wells have been sunk in them, where the vegetable soil was *twenty-two feet deep*, under which was a stratum of fine white sand, containing horizontal lines, plainly indicating to the geologist, the gradual subsidence of water. Yet the ordinary depth is from two to five feet.

The several expeditions against the Indians, during the late war, enabled many of our officers, to become extensively acquainted with the geography of the Indiana and Michigan territories.

An officer, who conducted several expeditions against the Indians, and who was at the Putawatomie villages, on the St. Joseph's of lake Michigan, writes to me as follows:

"The country [between fort Wayne and the St. Joseph's of lake Michigan,] in every direction, is beautiful, presenting a fine prospect. There are no hills to be seen; a champaign country, the greater part prairie, affording inexhaustible grazing, and presenting the most delightful natural meadows, and the grass cured would be almost equal to our hay; there are also, vast forests of valuable timber, and the soil exceedingly rich. The rivers have their sources in swamps, and sometimes from delightful inland lakes. It is not unfrequent to see two opposite streams supplied by the same water or lake, one running into the waters of the Mississippi, and the other into the northern lakes. Neither China nor Holland ever had such natural advantages for inland water communications."

Another officer, who had opportunities of seeing and exploring the country between the Wabash and lake Michigan, describes it as a country, "admirably calculated for the convenience of inland navigation. The sources of the rivers are invariably in swamps or lakes, and the country around them perfectly level. A trifling expence would open a navigable communication between Eel river, and a branch of the Little St. Joseph's; the two St. Joseph's; the Raisin of lake Erie, and the Lenoir (Black river) of lake Michigan. Small lakes are discovered in every part of this extensive and romantic country. We found them covered with ducks, and other water fowls. For the diversion of fishing, we had no leisure ; consequently, I am not able to inform you whether they abound with fish, but presume they do, as many of their outlets empty into the tributaries of the great lakes.

"The country around the head branches of Eel river, Panther's creek, and St. Joseph's, (of the Miami) is generally low and swampy ; and too wet for cultivation. But even in that quarter, there are many beautiful situations. The timber is oak, hickory, black walnut, beach, sugar maple, elm, and honey locust. The wood lands line the water courses; but branch out frequently into the prairies.

"The immense prairies on the south bank of the St. Josephs, (of lake Michigan) afforded us many rich, beautiful, and picturesque views. They are from one to ten miles wide; and of unequal lengths. They are as level as lakes; and in point of fertility, not inferior to the lands around Lexington,

Ken. or the best bottoms of the Ohio. We crossed two, whose southern limits were not descernable to the naked eye; they were doubtless capacious enough to form two or three townships each; and perfectly dry, being at least one hundred feet above the river bottoms. These natural meadows are covered with a tall grass; and are separated by strips of woods, containing oak, maple, locust, lyn, poplar, plum, ash, and crab-apple. In these wood lands, we generally meet with creeks, runs, or springs; but *never* in the open prairies, unless in wet and rainy seasons, when the waters form temporary sluggish brooks, wherever there is sufficient descent for the purpose.

"The St. Josephs [of lake Michigan] is a charming river, and navigable to within a short distance of the river of the same name. Its current is brisk, and at the upper villages, one hundred yards wide. The Indians have cleared large fields upon its banks: several Canadian French families reside with them. Their manners and habits of life are semi-savage.

"All the rivers in the interior of Indiana and Michigan, have spacious bottoms, and they uniformly wander from the line of their courses, so that in making fifty miles progress, in a direct line, they water one hundred miles of territory by their sinuosities. By these frequent bends, the length of *river coast,* and the quantity of bottom land is nearly doubled, which amply compensates for extra toil and expence of navigation."

Mr. D. Buck, of Auburn, (N. Y.) who assisted in the survey of twenty-two townships, six miles square each, writes to his correspondent as follows :

I have seen a great deal of excellent land; the prairies on the Wabash in the vicinity of fort Harrison, exceed every thing for richness of soil and beauty of situation, I ever beheld. The prairies are from one to five miles wide, bordering on the river, and from one to twelve in length; the streams which run into the Wabash, divide one prairie from another ; on these streams are strips of woods from half a mile to a mile wide, the timber of which is excellent; the soil of the prairies is a black vegetable mould, intermixed with fine sand, and sometimes gravel. In choosing a situation for a farm, it is important so to locate a tract, as to have half prairie and half wood land ; by which means you will have a plantation cleared to your hand.

The new purchase contains one hundred and twenty townships, or 2,765,040 acres. The lands sell very high in the neighborhood of fort Harrison, for it is the most delightful situation for a town on the Wabash—the soil is the richest of any in the state. This will undoubtedly become the seat of a new county, and that at no remote period. The fort is garrisoned by one hundred and fifty riflemen, of the regular army, under the command of Major Morgan. There are six families living in log cabins, near the fort, who improve congress lands. They have been here five years. Wherever they have cultivated the ground, it produces abundantly. Besides these, there are several Indian traders—Great numbers of Indians resort hither to sell their peltries. The tribes who frequent this place and reside on the Wabash, are the Kickapoos Miamis, Putawatomies, Shawanoese, Weaws, and Delawares. They encamp in the woods convenient to water, where they build wigwams. We came across a great many while surveying in the wilderness—they appeared friendly, and offered us honey and venison. Our business has principally been near the Indian boundary line, sixty miles from any white settlements. The woods abound with deer, bears, wolves, and wild turkies. About three-eighths of the land we surveyed is excellent for most kinds of produce; the remainder is good for grazing, but too hilly, flat, or wet, for grain.

The lands on White river are well watered with springs and brooks. You can hardly find a quarter section without water; the country in this quarter is, in many places, hilly and broken, and in some parts stony. Limestone is most predominant ; but there are quarries of free stone. Although the country is well watered, good mill seats are scarce. There can be a sufficiency of small mills for the accommodation of the inhabitants. Steam mills, without doubt, will be in operation as soon as the country is sufficiently settled for the purpose of flouring for exportation.

" There are some excellent tracts of land in Indiana and Illinois—corn is raised pretty easy ; and stock with little attention, and in some places with little or no fodder. This country is full of prairies ; some of which are excellent land. The timber around them consists principally oak, of which the inhabitants make most of their rails, and sometimes draw them three miles. These prairies are destitute of water; but it can be obtained by digging twenty or thirty feet. Wheat grows stout; but the grain is not so plump as it is in the state of New York."

" It is difficult building in Knox county, and always will be, on account of the scarcity of mill seats. Horse mills are common ; the miller takes one eighth part of the grain for toll; customers finding their own horses."

He further states, that the two branches of Whiteriver are navigable with boats in high water for the distance of 130 miles; that coal mines are numerous near the Wabash. Iron ore is found on Whiteriver. That wheat yields the inhabitants, who are neat farmers, 68 lbs. a bushel, and never gets winter-killed or smutty ; the only difficulty they experience in its culture is, that the land in many places is too rich until it has been improved. Apple trees bear every year. Peaches some years do exceedingly well; so do cherries, currents, and most kinds of fruit. Wheat is 75 cents a bushel ; flour $3 a hundred—delivered at Fort Harrison four; corn 25 cents a bushel—pork $4—beef $4; butter and cheese from 12 1-2 to 25 cents; honey 50 cents per gallon. Maple sugar 25 cents. European goods exorbitantly high.

Reptiles and venomous serpents are not numerous. A few rattle snakes and some copperheads comprise all that are dangerous.

G

The banks of the Wabash are in many places, subject to be overflowed in high water. When the Ohio is at full height its waters set back and inundate the bottoms of the Wabash to the distance of four or five miles.

Mr. Buck, who descended this river in March, 1816, says, "I came down the river at the highest stage of water; the banks were completely overflowed almost all the way. The prairies extending to the river appeared like small seas; and in many places, it was with difficulty that we could keep our boat from running into the woods. The distance from Fort Harrison to Vincennes by water, is 120 miles; by land only 65. Below the fort the river is very crooked to its mouth; above, as far as the Indian title is extinguished, it is quite strait in a north and south direction. The breadth of the river (at Vincennes) is from 40 to 70 rods. It overflows its banks every spring, except at a few places where there are handsome situations for towns. It inundates a considerable extent of country opposite Vincennes. The floods do not last long; nor are they dangerous, if people will use a little precaution in removing their stock and swine.

"The winters are mild, compared with those of the northern states. By all accounts, last winter was uncommonly severe for this country. There were three or four weeks of freezing weather, during which the snow was from six to nine inches deep. The Wabash was frozen over so that it was crossed in many places upon the ice with safety. I think that autumnal frosts are earlier here than in the western counties of New York; but the weather is very fine till Christmas; then changeable until about the middle of February, when winter breaks up, and spring soon commences. Peaches are in blossom by the first of March, and by the 10th of April, the forests are "clad in green." The flowering shrubs and trees are in full bloom some days before the leaves get their growth, which gives the woods a very beautiful appearance."

"Salt, at and above Vincennes is two dollars a bushel, though considerable quantities are made at the U. S. Saline

30 miles below the mouth of the Wabash, in the Illinois territory, where it is sold for one dollar a bushel. The chief supply comes from the salt works on the Great Kenhaway.— There have been salt wells sunk, (by boring) near the Ohio, to the depth of 500 feet, where the water is said to be very strong. There are likewise salt springs on the Indian lands, not far from the northern boundary of the new purchase."

POPULATION, COUNTIES, VILLAGES.

Population of Indiana in November, 1815.

Counties.	No. of inhabitants.
Wayne,	6,290
Franklin,	7,970
Dearborn,	4,426
Jefferson,	4,093
Washington,	6,606
Harrison,	6,769
Gibson,	5,330
Knox,	6,800
Switzerland,	3,500
Clark,	7,000
Posey,	3,000
Perry,	3,000
Warwick,	3,000
Total,	68,780

DEARBORN COUNTY,

Is bounded east by the state of Ohio, south by the Ohio river, west by Switzerland county, and north by Franklin county. It is well watered by Tanner's Hougelane's and Loughery's creeks, Whitewater and the head branches of Indian Kentucky. The south part of this county is broken ; the north end level, being in the Flat Woods. The Ohio

bottoms are low but fertile.   The timber in the middle and
northern parts is oak, hickory, poplar, and sugar maple.

Lawrenceburgh—Stands on the bank of the Ohio, two
miles below the mouth of the Big Miami.   It has not flourished for several years past, owing, principally to its being subject to inundation, when the Ohio is high.   A new town called Edinburgh, half a mile from the river, on a more elevated
situation promises to eclipse it.

Rising-Sun—Is delightfully situated on the second bank of
the Ohio, with a gradual descent to the river.   It contains
thirty or forty houses, and is half way between Vevay and
Lawrenceburgh.   It has a post office, and a floating mill an-
chored abreast of the town.   It has had a very rapid growth,
and will probably become a place of considerable trade.

FRANKLIN,

Has the state of Ohio on the east, Dearborn county south
and Indian lands west and north.   It is one of the best counties in the state, and was established about four years ago.—
It is principally watered by Whitewater and its branches,
upon which there is some of the best bottom lands in the
western country and has been the centre of an ancient population, as is proved by the great number of mounds and fortifications, to be seen on the bottoms and hills.   There are no
prairies in this county.   Both sides of Whitewater, from its
mouth, to Brookville, are tolerably well settled.   Here are
some of the finest farms to be met with in the western country.   A number of mills have been erected.   The upland is
pretty level, and the principal timber white oak, hickory and
black walnut.   The oak trees are remarkably tall and handsome ; and well suited either for rails, staves, or square timber.
The soil is free from stones, and easily cleared and ploughed ;
producing fine crops of wheat and corn.   In July last, I saw
several corn-fields, which in the preceding March, were in a
state of nature with the trees and brushwood all growing.

Yet the corn looked as flourishing as it did upon the bottoms. In the woods, on the bottoms of Whitewater, I discovered several *natural wells*, formed in a most singular manner. They were from ten to fifteen feet deep, substantially curbed, being nothing more nor less than parts of the upright trunks of the largest sycamores, which had been hollowed out by the hand of time. To explain: When these trees were in their infancy, their roots spread near the surface of the ground; but in the course of time, successive inundations and the annual decay of a luxuriant vegetation, have formed a stratum of the richest soil, from ten to fifteen feet deep, over the roots of these venerable trees. At length these vegetable Mathusalems die, and are prostrated by the winds of heaven, and where once stood a tree of giant growth, now yawns a well scooped out by nature's hand.

Genseng grows in the bottoms to a perfection and size, I never before witnessed; and so thick, where the hogs have not thinned it, that one could dig a bushel in a very short time. Upon the spurs of the hills, and the poorest soil, is found the wild columbo root, and is easily procured in any quantity. There are two villages in this county—Brookville and Harrison.

Brookville—Is pleasantly situated in the forks of Whitewater, thirty miles north of Lawrenceburgh and the Ohio river; twenty miles south of Salisbury—about forty-two north west of Cincinnati, and twenty-five from Hamilton, "It was laid out in the year 1811; but no improvements were made until the succeeding year, and then but partially; owing to the unsettled state of the frontiers, and its vicinity to the Indian boundary, being not more than fifteen miles. The late war completely checked the emigration to the country, and consequently the town ceased to improve. At the close of the war, there was not more than ten or twelve dwelling houses in the place; but since that period, its rapid accession of wealth and population has been unexampled in the western country.

" There are now in the town upwards of eighty buildings, exclusive of shops, stables, and out houses, the greater number of which were built during the last season. The buildings are generally frame, and a great part of them handsomely painted. There are within the precincts of the town, one grist mill and two saw mills, two fulling mills, three carding machines, one printing office,* one silversmith, two saddlers, two cabinet makers, one hatter, two taylors, four boot and shoemakers, two tanners and curriers, one chairmaker, one cooper, five taverns and seven stores. There are also a jail, a market house, and a handsome brick court house nearly finished.

" The ground on which the town stands, is composed of a rich and sandy loam, covering a thin stratum of clay, underneath which is a great body of gravel and pebbles—consequently the streets are but seldom muddy, and continue so but for a short time. The public square and a great part of the town stands on a beautiful level, that is elevated between seventy and eighty feet above the level of the river : and, in short, the situation of the town, the cleanlines of the streets, the purity of the waters, and the aspect of the country around, all combine to render it one of the most healthy and agreeable situations in the western country.

" There are, perhaps, few places that possess equal advantages, or that present a more flattering prospect of future wealth and importance than this. As a situation for manufactories, it is unequalled ; the two branches of Whitewater affording a continued succession of the best sites for the erection of water works, from their junction almost to their sources, and many valuable situations may be found below the town, on the main river.

———

* At this press is published a respectable and well conducted weekly Journal, entitled " THE PLAIN DEALER," edited by B. F. MORRIS, Esq. to whose pen and the politeness of N. D. GALLION, Post Master, I am indebted for the above interesting and correct account of Brookville, and which I have preferred to my own.

"The country watered by this stream is inferior to none. Along the river and all its tributary streams, are extensive and fertile bottoms, bounded by hills of various heights; and immediately from the top of these, commences a level and rich country, timbered with poplar, walnut, beech, sugar tree, oak, ash, hickory, elm, buckeye, &c. and a variety of shrubs and underbrush. The soil of this land is peculiarly adapted to the culture of small grain, and for grazing. The last harvest produced several crops of wheat, in the neighborhood of this place that weighed from sixty-five to sixty-eight pounds per bushel; and the best crops of grass I have ever seen, are produced without the aid of manure. Corn, oats, rye, flax, hemp, sweet and Irish potatoes, &c., &c. are produced in abundance.

"During the last season, 1816, many successful experiments were made in rearing tobacco, and the soil has been pronounced by good judges, to be as congenial to its growth, as the best lands in the state of Virginia, Kentucky, or the Carolinas. As an evidence of the fertility of the country, corn and oats are selling at twenty-five, rye at forty, and wheat a seventy-five cents per bushel, beef at three and a half, and pork at four cents per pound. The country is well supplied with good water, from a great number of springs, and water may also be obtained in almost any place by digging to a moderate depth.

"Another source from which this town must eventually derive great importance, is the ease and small experce with which the navigation of Whitewater, from the junction of the forks, can be so far improved as to carry out into the Ohio, all articles that may be raised for exportation.

"To the north and north west of this place, is an extensive and fertile country, that is fast growing into importance; and in wealth and population, will soon be inferior to but few districts on the waters of the Ohio; and, owing to the geographical situation of the country, all the intercourse of the inhabitants with the Ohio river, must be through this place."

I was at Brookville in July last, on business, and was highly pleased with the amenity of its situation, and the industry,
intelligence, and healthful appearance of the inhabitants.—
The road from thence to Harrison, was very fine.

Harrison.—This village is situated on the north-side of
Whitewater, eight miles from its mouth, eighteen north east
of Brookville, and in the centre of a large tract of some of the
best land in the state.   More than one half of the village
stands on the Ohio side of the state line.   There are about
thirty-five houses, mostly new.   A considerable number of
the inhabitants are from the state of New York.   Mr. Look-
er, from Saratoga county, Mr. Crane, from Schenectady, and
Mr. Allen, the post master, from New Jersey, own the surrounding lands.   They have all very fine and valuable farms,
worth from forty to sixty dollars an acre.   The settlement
was commenced about sixteen years ago.   The bottoms are
here from one to two miles wide; the soil remarkably deep
and rich, and the woods free from brushwood.   The trees are
of a moderate growth, but straight and thrifty.   The traces
of ancient population cover the earth in every direction.
On the bottoms are a great number of mounds, very unequal
in point of age and size.   The small ones are from two to four
feet above the surface, and the growth of timber upon them
small, not being over one hundred years old;   while the
others are from ten to thirty feet high, and frequently contain
trees of the largest diameters.   Besides, the bones found in
the small ones will bear removal, and exposure to the air,
while those in the large ones are rarely capable of sustaining
their own weight; and are often found in a decomposed or
powdered state.   There is a large mound in Mr. Allen's field,
about twenty feet high, sixty feet in diameter at the base,
which contains a greater proportion of bones, than any one
I ever before examined, as almost every shovel full of dirt
would contain several fragments of a human skeleton.   When
on Whitewater, I obtained the assistance of several of the
inhabitants, for the purpose of making a thorough examination

of the internal structure of these monuments of the ancient populousness of the country. We examined from fifteen to twenty. In some, whose height were from ten to fifteen feet, we could not find more than four or five skeletons. In *one*, not the least appearance of a human bone was to be found. Others were so full of bones, as to warrant the belief, that they originally contained at least one hundred dead bodies; children of different ages, and the full grown, appeared to have been piled together promiscuously. We found several scull, leg and thigh bones, which plainly indicated, that their possessors were men of gigantic stature. The scull of one skeleton was one fourth of an inch thick; and the teeth remarkably even, sound and handsome, all firmly planted. The fore teeth were very deep, and not so wide as those of the generality of white people. Indeed, there seemed a great degree of regularity in the form of the teeth, in all the mounds. In the progress of our researches, we obtained ample testimony, that these masses of earth were formed by a *savage people.* Yet, doubtless possessing a greater degree of civilization than the present race of Indians. We discovered a piece of glass weighing five ounces, resembling the bottom of a tumbler, but concave; several *stone axes,* with grooves near their heads to receive a withe, which unquestionably served as helves; arrows formed from flint, almost exactly similar to those in use among the present Indians; several pieces of earthen ware; some appeared to be parts of vessels holding six or eight gallons; others were obviously fragments of jugs jars, and cups; some were plain, while others were curiously ornamented with figures of birds and beasts, drawn while the clay or material of which they were made was soft and before the process of glazing was performed. The *glazier's art* appears to have been well understood by the potters who manufactured this aboriginal *crockery.* The smaller vessels were made of pounded or pulverized muscle shells, mixed with an earthen or flinty substance, and the large ones of clay and sand. There was no appearance of *iron:* one of the sculls was

H

found pierced by an arrow, which was still sticking in it, driv-
en about half way through before its force was spent. It was
about six inches long. The subjects of this mound were
doubtless killed in battle, and hastily buried. In digging to
the bottom of them we invariably came to a stratum of ashes,
from six inches to two feet thick, which rests on the original
earth. These ashes contain coals, fragments of brands, and
pieces of *calcined bones.* From the quantity of ashes and
bones, and the appearance of the earth underneath, it is evident that large fires must have been kept burning for several
days previous to commencing the mound, and that a considerable number of human victims must have been sacrificed,
by burning, on the spot! Prisoners of war were no doubt
selected for this horrid purpose. Perhaps the custom of the
age rendered it a signal honor, for the chieftains and most active warriors to be interred, by way of triumph, on the ashes
of their enemies, whom they had vanquished in war. If this
was not the case, the mystery can only be solved by suppos-
ing that the fanaticism of the priests and prophets excited
their besotted followers to voluntary self-devotion. The soil
of the mounds is always different from that of the immediately surrounding earth—being uniformly of a soft vegetable
mould or loam, and containing no stones or other hard sub-
stances, to "press upon the dead and disturb their repose."

Almost every building lot in Harrison village contains a
small mound; and some as many as three. On the neighboring hills, north east of the town, are a number of the remains
of stone houses. They were covered with soil, brush, and
full grown trees. We cleared away the earth, roots and rubbish from one of them, and found it to have been anciently occupied as a dwelling. It was about twelve feet square; the
walls had fallen nearly to the foundation. They appeared to
have been built of rough stones, like our stone walls. Not
the least trace of any iron tools having been employed to
smooth the face of them, could be perceived. At one end
of the building, we came to a regular hearth, containing ashes

and coals; before which we found the bones of eight persons
of different ages, from a small child to the heads of the family.
The positions of their skeletons clearly indicated, that their
deaths were sudden and simultaneous. They were probably
asleep, with their feet towards the fire, when destroyed by an
enemy, an earthquake, or pestilence.

WAYNE.

This county is bounded on the east by the state of Ohio, on
the south by the county of Franklin, on the west and north
by Indian lands. It is watered by the north fork of Whitewater, the head brooks of the north fork of Whiteriver,
sources of Rocky river, Massissinway, and main branch of
the Wabash. It is very extensive, of a level surface, well
timbered, contains fine lands, and has been settled ten years.
Its products are, Indian corn, wheat, rye, oats, and tobacco.

Salisbury—Lies thirty miles north of Brookville; contains
about thirty five houses, two stores and two taverns. It is at
present the seat of justice for Wayne county; but Centreville, a new village, being more central, threatens to become
its competitor for that privilege.

SWITZERLAND,

Is bounded west by Jefferson, south by the Ohio river,
north in part by Indian lands, and east by Dearborn county.
Its surface is, in some places, broken by the Ohio and Silver
creek hills, which, however, are of a pretty good soil. It is
watered by Venoge and Plum creeks, and several small runs;
some running into the Ohio, and others into Whiteriver.

New Switzerland—The settlement of New Switzerland
was commenced by a few emigrants, from the Pays de Vaud,
in the spring of 1805. It extends from about three quarters
of a mile above the mouth of Plum creek, down the river to
the mouth of Indian creek, now called Venoge; a distance of

about four miles and a half, fronting the river, and originally extended back far enough to cover 3,700 acres of land; about half of which was purchased under a law in favor of J. J. Dufour, and his associates, upon a credit of twelve years. Subsequent purchases have been made on the usual terms, excepting an extension of credit, in order to encourage the cultivation of the vine. There has been a gradual accession of numbers to this interesting colony. As early as 1810, they had eight acres of vineyard, from which they made 2,400 gallons of wine, which, in its crude state, was thought by good judges, to be superior to the claret of Bordeaux. A part of this wine was made out of the Madeira grape. They have now greatly augmented the quantity of their vineyard grounds, which, when bearing, present to the eye of the observer the most interesting agricultural prospect, perhaps, ever witnessed in the United States. The principal proprietors of the vineyards, are the Messrs. Dufours, Bettens, Morerod, Siebenthal. Mr. J. J. Dufour arrived from Switzerland in September last, with a large number of emigrants. The Swiss speak the French language in its purity ; and are a temperate, industrious and polished people, fond of music and dancing, and warmly attached to the United States. They are rapidly extending their vineyards; they also cultivate Indian corn, wheat, potatoes, hemp, flax, and other articles necessary to farmers—but in quantities barely sufficient for domestic use. Some of their women manufacture *straw hats.* They are made quite different from the common straw bonnets, by tying the straws together, instead of plaiting and sewing the plaits. They are sold in great numbers in the neighboring settlements, and in the Mississippi and Indiana territories.

Vevay—Half a mile above the upper vineyards, was laid out in 1813, but was a forest in 1814, till the first of February, when the first house was built. During the same year forty four others, four stores, and two taverns were erected, and the village selected as a suitable place for the seat of justice for Switzerland county. There are at present eighty-four dwelling houses, besides thirty four mechanics' shops, of different professions. The court house, jail, and school house are of brick. A brick market house and church are building. It has eight stores, three taverns, two lawyers, two physicians, and a printing office printing a weekly newspaper, called the *Indiana Register.* There is a library of 300 volumes; and a literary society in which are several persons of genius, science, and literature.

This delightful village is situated on the second bank of the Ohio, twenty-five feet above high water mark, and is nearly equidistant from Cincinnati, Lexington, and Louisville, or forty five miles from each. The view of the Ohio is extensive, being eight miles. The country in the rear is broken but fertile. The climate is mild, and the sweet potatoe is cultivated with success. Cotton would doubtless do well. There are several roads which diverge from the settlement. Three mails arrive weekly.

JEFFERSON,

Is bounded on the east by Switzerland county, on the south by the river Ohio, on the west by the county of Clark, on the north by Indian lands. It contains a great proportion of excellent land. It is watered by several small creeks running into the Ohio, and by the Mescatitak, a branch of the south fork of Whiteriver, which heads within five miles of the Ohio river.

New Lexington.—This flourishing town is famous for having produced the pretended monied institution, called "The Lexington Indiana Manufacturing Company," which has exploded. It is situated in a rich settlement, sixteen miles nearly west of Madison, and five miles east of the Knobs; and contains about forty houses, some of them handsome, brick and frame, and others built with hewn logs, in the true western style. There is a post-office, and printing establishment, in which is printed the "*Western Eagle.*" The sur-

134529

face of the surrounding country for several miles, is sufficiently *rolling* to give the water of the creeks and runs a brisk
motion. The stones towards the Ohio are calcareous: to the
west and north west, clayey slate. The soil is very productive. In the vicinity of this place, the enterprising General
M'Farland has, with astonishing perseverance, dug to the
depth of nearly five hundred feet, in quest of salt water.
His exertions have been crowned with success, inasmuch as
the water exceeds in strength any salt water in the western
country, and affords from three to four bushels of salt, to the
hundred gallons of water.

Madison.—This is the seat of justice for the county, and
is situated on the upper bank of the Ohio, thirty miles below
Vevay, contains sixty or seventy houses, mostly small and
new. The banking institution, called the "Farmers' and
Mechanics' Bank," is established here.

CLARK,

Is bounded east by Jefferson county, south by the Ohio
river, west by the counties of Harrison and Washington,
north by the county of Jackson and Indian lands. It is watered by several creeks running into the Ohio, such as Silver
creek, Cane run, &c. and several brooks falling into the Mescatitak branch of the south fork of Whiteriver. Its surface
is considerably broken in the central parts of the county.
Hickory and oak are the prevailing timber. It is thought
that this country contains many valuable minerals; some
have been discovered; copperas is found in the high banks of
Silver creek, about two miles from its mouth. A medicinal
spring, near Jeffersonville, has been much frequented—its waters are strongly impregnated with sulphur and iron. The
reed cane grows on the flats.

Charleston—The seat of justice for Clark county, is situated in the centre of a rich and thriving settlement, thirty-two
miles south of west from Madison, two miles from the Ohio

river, and fourteen from the falls.   This village, like many
others in the western country, has sprung up suddenly by
the magical influence of American enterprize, excited into action by a concurrence of favorable circumstances.

Jeffersonville—Stands on the bank of the Ohio, nearly opposite Louisville, and a little above the falls.   It contains
about one hundred and thirty houses, brick, frame and hewn
logs.   The bank of the river is high, which affords a fine view
of Louisville, the falls, and the opposite hills.   Just below
the town is a fine eddy for boats.   A post-office, and a land-
office, for the sale of the United States' lands, are established,
and it promises to become a place of wealth, elegance and extensive business.   The most eligible boat channel is on the Indiana side of the Ohio.

Clarksville—Lies at the lower end of the falls; and, although commenced as early as 1783, does not contain above
forty houses, most of them old and decayed.   It has a safe
capacious harbor for boats.

New Albany—A short distance below Clarksville, has been
puffed throughout the Union; but has not yet realized the
anticipations of the proprietors.

HARRISON,

Is bounded east by Clark county, south by the Ohio, west
by the new county of Perry, and north by Washington.   Its
principal stream is Blue river, which is navigable for boats
about forty miles.   Gen. Harrison owns a large tract of land
upon this river, and has erected a grist and saw mill, about
eight miles from its mouth, on a durable spring brook, running
into it.   On both banks of this river are large quantities of
oak and locust timber.   Gen. H. had it in contemplation,
shortly before the commencement of the late war, to establish
a ship yard at its mouth, where there is a convenient situation
for building and launching vessels.

Corydon—The seat of justice for Harrison county, is situated twenty-five miles nearly west from Jeffersonville, and ten miles from the Ohio river. It was commenced in 1809, and is the seat of government for the state. The selection of this place by the legislature, as the seat of government for the period of eight years, has excited great dissatisfaction in other parts of the state. It has rapidly encreased since the meeting of the state convention, in July, 1816. The *Indiana Gazette* is printed in this village.

WASHINGTON

County is bounded on the east by Clark county, on the south by the county of Harrison, on the west by the county of Orange, and on the north by the county of Jackson. It is watered by the south fork of Whiteriver—is moderately hilly, and was established in 1814.

Salem—Is the only village deserving notice; and is situated thirty-four miles north of Corydon, and twenty-five nearly west from Jeffersonville, on the Vincennes road.

JACKSON

Lies west of Clark and Jefferson counties, north of Washington, east of Orange, and south of the Indian country. It is watered by Whiteriver and its tributary creeks, and was set off in 1815. *Brownstown* is the seat of justice; and is situated twenty-five miles east of north from Salem.

ORANGE

County is bounded by the counties of Washington and Jackson on the east; by Harrison and Perry on the south; by the county of Knox on the west; and by Indian lands on the north. It has a rich soil, and is well watered by Whiteriver and Petoka. A gentleman, who surveyed several townships in the county, declares it to be equal in point of fertility

of soil, and excellence of water, to any county in the state.
" The surface is agreeably undulating. The timber on the
hills consist of black walnut, oak, hickory, ash, sugar maple;
on the low grounds, basswood, pawpaw, honey locust, buckeye
and spicewood; besides, grape vines, and a variety of shrubs.
We occasionally met with rattlesnakes and copperheads on
the uplands, but never in the bottoms. The most common
game are deer and bear. There is a coal-mine a little below
the forks of Whiteriver; besides, we met with frequent signs
of minerals; and the needle often refused to settle. The
bottoms of Whiteriver are nearly as wide as those of the Wabash, and contain evidence of having been formerly inhabited
by Indians, as the remains of their cabins and corn-hills are
yet visible. The new village of Paoli is the county seat. It
is forty miles nearly east of Vincennes; and thirty north of
west from Salem."

KNOX.

This county is bounded by Orange on the east; by the
county of Gibson on the south; by the Wabash river on the
west; and by Indian lands on the north. This is the oldest
and most populous county in the state. It is watered by the
Deche, Whiteriver, Wabash, Littleriver, St. Marie, Bus-
seron, Raccoon and Ambush creeks. It has upwards of
200,000 acres of the best prairie and bottom land, and is
rapidly encreasing in inhabitants and improvements.

Vincennes,—The seat of justice for Knox county, stands
on the east bank of the Wabash, one hundred miles from its
junction with the Ohio, in a direct line, but nearly two hundred by the courses of the river; and one hundred and twenty west of the falls of Ohio. It contains about one hundred
houses, most of which are small and scattering; some have a
neat and handsome aspect, while others are built in an un-
couth manner, having a frame skeleton filled up with mud
and stick walls, similar to some of the old German houses on

I

the Hudson and Mohawk rivers.   The best buildings are a
brick tavern, jail, and academy.   The latter, which is an honor
to the state, stands in the public square, and is under the direction of the Rev. Mr. Scott, a presbyterian minister, a gentleman of letters ; yet, hitherto, his pupils have not been numerous.   He teaches the ancient languages, mathematics, &c.
The meeting house, a plain building, stands on the prairie, one
mile from the town.   The plan of the town is handsomely
designed ; the streets are wide and cross each other at right
angles.   Almost every house has a garden in its rear, with
high, substantial picket fences to prevent the thefts of the Indians.   General Harrison is one of the principal proprietors
of the soil.   The common field near the town contains nearly 5000 acres, of excellent prairie soil, which has been cultivated for more than half a century, and yet retains its pris-
tine fertility.   The United States have a land office for the
disposal of the public lands ; and formerly kept a small garrison, in a little stockade near the bank of the river, for the protection of the inhabitants.   The Governor of the territory
resided, and the territorial legislature convened here.   The
place has possessed many political advantages.   "The bank
of Vincennes" enjoys a good character, and its paper has already attained an extensive circulation.   It has recently become a state bank.   There is also a printing office, which issues a paper, called the "Western Sun," edited by Mr. E.
Stout.   This village was settled nearly one hundred years
ago, by the French, who mostly came from Lower Canada.
Buried in the centre of an immense wilderness, unprotected,
and without intercourse with the civilized world, these colo-
nists gradually approximated to the savage state.   Many of
the males intermarried with the Indians, whose amity was
by these ties secured and strengthened, and their numbers
amounted to three hundred persons.

" During the revolutionary war, their remote situation exempted them from all its evils, till, in 1782, they were visited
by a detachment from Kentucky, who plundered and insulted

them, and killed or drove off the cattle which formed their chief wealth.

" The peace of 1783, gave them to the United States, under whose benign government they began to breathe again; but unluckily an Indian war commenced in 1788, and siding with the whites, as duty and discretion enjoined, they were annoyed by the savages, whose animosity was embittered by the remembrance of their ancient friendship and alliance. Their cattle were killed, their village closely beset, and, for several years, they could not carry the plough or hoe a musket shot from their huts.

" Military service was added to their other hardships ; but, in 1792, the compassion of the federal government gave four hundred acres of land to every one who paid the capitation, and one hundred more to every one who served in the militia. This domain, so ample to a diligent husbandman, was of little value to the hunting Frenchmen, who soon bartered away their invaluable ground for about 30 cents an acre, which was paid to them in goods, on which an exorbitant profit was charged. This land was of the best quality; it sold, as early as 1796, at two dollars an acre, and I may venture to say is now worth at least ten.   Thus, for the most part, reduced again to their gardens, or the little homestead which was indispensable to their subsistence, they had nothing to live on but their fruit, potatoes, maize, and now an then a little game; and, on this fare, no wonder they became as lean as Arabs.

" Their ignorance, indeed, was profound. Nobody ever opened a school among them, till it was done by the abbe R. a polite, well educated, and liberal minded missionary, banished hither by the French revolution.   Out of nine of the French, scarcely six could read or write, whereas nine-tenths of the Americans, or emigrants from the east, could do both. Their dialect is by no means, as I had been previously assured, a vulgar or provincial BROGUE, but pretty good French, intermixed with many military terms and phrases, all the settlements having been originally made by soldiers. The primitive stock of Canada was the regiment of Carignon."*

The country around Vincennes in every direction, being well adapted to settlements and cultivation, what is there to prevent this place from equalling, in a very few years, in numbers, wealth, and refinement, the fine towns of Lexington, Louisville and Cincinnati? Building lots in Vincennes sell at from fifty to one thousand dollars a lot. There are two roads leading to the Ohio; one to fort Harrison; one to Princeton; and one to Kaskaskia.

A new village has been laid out at *Terre Haute*, three miles below fort Harrison. This situation, for beauty of prospect, is exceeded by none in the state.

PRICES AND SALES OF PUBLIC LANDS.

Congress lands, after the auction sales are closed, sell invariably for $2 an acre. For a quarter section, $80 are to be paid down—the same sum in two years; and the remainder in annual payments, without interest, if punctually made. Those who pay in advance, are entitled to a discount of eight per cent.

Harrison's Purchase, containing upwards of 3,000,000 acres, lying between Whiteriver, the Wabash, and Rocky river, was opened for sale at auction, at Jeffersonville, in Sept. last, and altho' the Canadian volunteers had previously selected their donation lots, numerous tracts were sold at from $4 to $30 an acre. A fractional section on the Wabash, below fort Harrison, sold for $32 18, and several others from $20 to $30. Speculators from all quarters attended the sales.

The Canadian volunteers deserved the munificence of the United States, for they freely shed their blood under our banners, upon the Niagara frontier, under the intrepid Wil-

_____

* See Volney's View of the Soil and Climate of the United States, pages 334 and 335.

ocks, Delapierre, and Markle. But unfortunately the cup of generosity was upset before it reached their mouths. We gave them the choice of the best lands in the United States, merely to enrich the Mammon of speculation. Most of these brave men have blindly or necessitously parted with their lands for a song.

ANTIQUITIES.

On the hills, two miles east of the town, are three large mounds; and others are frequently met with on the prairies and upland, from Whiteriver to the head of the Wabash. They are in every respect similar to those in Franklin county, already described.

The French have a tradition, that an exterminating battle was fought in the beginning of the last century, on the ground where fort Harrison now stands, between the Indians living on the Mississippi, and those of the Wabash. The bone of contention was the lands lying between those rivers, which both parties claimed. There were about 1000 warriors on each side. The condition of the fight was, that the victors should possess the lands in dispute. The grandeur of the prize was peculiarly calculated to inflame the ardor of savage minds. The contest commenced about sunrise. Both parties fought desperately. The Wabash warriors came off conquerors, having *seven* men left alive at sunset, and their adversaries but *five*. The mounds are still to be seen where it is said the slain were buried.

GIBSON.

This county is bounded by the counties of Warwick and Orange on the east, the county of Posey on the south, the Wabash river on the west, and the county of Knox on the north. It is watered by several creeks and runs, falling into the Petoka and Wabash. About one half of this county has a fertile and highly favorable soil; and the greater part of the other half would be pronounced good, in any of the Atlantic states.

Princeton—Is the county seat; it lies thirty-five miles nearly south of Vincennes. It has a post-office; and has had a rapid growth, considering the newness of the surrounding settlements.

Harmony.—This village is situated on the Wabash, half a day's ride below Princeton, and is settled by the *Harmonists*, from Butler county, Pennsylvania. They are under the direction of the Rev. George Rapp; and hold their property in community. They have a very extensive establishment for the manufacturing of wool. Their *Merino* cloth is not surpassed by any in America. They also cultivate the vine; and are distinguished for their temperance, industry and skill in many of the mechanical professions.

POSEY,

Is situated south of Gibson, bounded on the east by the county of Warwick, on the south and west by the Ohio and Wabash rivers. It contains rich and extensive prairies; but the banks of the Wabash are in many places subject to inundation, both from its own floods, and those of the Ohio, which sets up the Wabash several miles.

WARWICK.

This county is situated east of the county of Posey, bounded on the east by the county of Perry, on the south by the Ohio river, on the west by the county of Posey, and on the north by the counties of Orange and Knox. It is a level and rich county, watered by several large creeks running into the Ohio, such as Beaver, Pigeon, &c. It is nevertheless but indifferently watered, owing to the early drying up of the streams. The prairies are numerous, but mostly inferior, in point of soil, to those bordering the Wabash.   The prevailing timber being oak, the range for hogs is excellent.

PERRY,

Is bounded east by Harrison, north by Orange and Washington, west by Warwick, and south by the Ohio river.   It is watered by the little river Anderson, and by creeks and runs falling into the Ohio.   It was established in 1615.

INDIANS.

These consist of Mascontins, Piankashaws, Kickapoos, Delawares, Miamis, Shawanoese, Weeaws, Ouitanans, Eelrivers, Hurons, and Pottawattamies.

The *Mascontins* and *Piankashaws* reside on the rivers falling into the right bank of the Wabash, between Vincennes and Tippacanœ.   Their numbers are given at 1000 souls. Hutchins affirms that they, together with the Kickapoos, could raise 1000 *warriors.*

The *Kickapoos* reside on the west side of the Wabash, above Tippacanœ, and on the head waters of the Illinois. They have several large villages, and can raise 400 warriors.

The *Delawares* reside on the head waters of Whiteriver, in a village surrounded by large open prairies.   I have no data for stating their numbers with accuracy; they are not numerous.

The *Miamis* inhabit the upper Wabash, Massissinway, Miami-of-the-lakes, and Little St. Josephs—mostly within one or two day's travel of fort Wayne.   General Harrison burnt four of their towns at the forks of the Wabash, in September, 1813.   They are the proprietors of excellent lands, and cultivate large quantities of Indian corn.   They are reduced to about 1100 souls.

The *Shawanœse* live on and near the banks of Tippacanœ, Ponce Passu creek, and the Wabash river.   They were for-

merly a very formidable and warlike tribe; but have been reduced by their frequent wars, to about 400 warriors. They
have fine lands, and raise an abundance of corn. Their country was invaded by General Wilkinson, in 1791, who destroyed their principal town, near the mouth of Tippacanœ,
called *Kathtippecamunk.* " It contained one hundred and
twenty houses, eighty of which were shingle roofed. The
best houses belonged to the French traders. The gardens
and improvements around were delightful. There was a tavern, with cellars, bar, public and private rooms; and the
whole marked no small degree of order and civilization." Not
far from the ruins of this town stands the celebrated Prophet's
town, destroyed by General Harrison, in Nov. 1811, but
since rebuilt. Above Tippacanœ is the old French post of
Ouitanan, situated on the north side of the Wabash, in the
centre of the Indian country. This place is as old as Vincennes. Several half civilized French inhabitants reside here
as well as at L'Anguille, on Eelriver. They raise corn, and
trade with the Indians.

The *Hurons* reside in a small village, ten or fifteen miles
south east of Ouitanan. There are only ten or twelve families of them. The *Eelrivers* and *Weeaws* are bands of the
Miamis; and reside on the Wabash and Eelriver. They
can collect about 100 warriors.

A part of the *Winnebagoes* occupy a village on Ponce
Passu creek, seven miles east of the Prophet's town, which
contains from forty-five to fifty houses, several of which are
fifty feet long; others reside on the branches of Plein and Fox
rivers, and frequent Chicago.

The *Pottawatlamies* are the most numerous tribe in the
state. They reside on the Elkhart branch of the St. Josephs, where they have five villages, one of which is situated
in an immense prairie, sixty miles west of fort Wayne. The
course of this branch is north west. The balance of this
tribe live on the St. Josephs, Chicago, Kennomic, and Theakaki rivers.

The best proof of the excellence of the land on the Upper Wabash, is the circumstance of its being the scene of a numerous Indian population. These sagacious children of nature are good judges of land. Indeed, they are rarely, if ever, found on a barren soil.

EXTENT OF NAVIGABLE WATERS.

	Miles.
The Ohio river washes the southern boundary of Indiana, for the distance of	472
Wabash, navigable	470
Whiteriver, and its forks,	160
Petoka,	30
Blueriver,	40
Whitewater,	40
Rocky River,	45
Panne,	30
Massissinway	45
Eel, and Little rivers,	60
Western Tributaries of the Wabash,	330
St. Josephs of Miami and Panther's Creek,	75
Elkhart and part of St. Josephs of L. Mich.	100
Great and Little Kennomic,	120
Chemin River,	40
Chicago and Kickapoo,	80
Theakaki, and parts of Fox, Plein, and Illinois,	300
Southern coast of Lake Michigan,	50
Total	2487

The foregoing estimate does not embrace streams boatable less than thirty miles; besides, several of those named are navigable for canoes and small boats many miles further than the given distances annexed.

The distance from Chicago, to New Orleans, by water, is 1680 miles—to Buffalo, about 800. The surplus products of three fourths of the state will find their way to the New Orleans market.

K

VIEW OF PORTAGES.

All the streams in the northern parts of the state, which empty into the Wabash and Illinois, have their branches interwoven with many of the rivers running into lakes Erie and Michigan. Indeed, as before observed, they not unfrequently issue from the same marsh, prairie, pond, or lake. There are upwards of twenty portages near the Michigan frontier, only two of which have hitherto been used by the whites. The first of these is between the St. Marys and the Littleriver branch of the Wabash, and is nine miles long. The road which is good in dry seasons, leaves the St. Marys near Fort Wayne, where teams are kept for the transportation of boats and merchandize. It was by this route that the French, while in possession of Canada, passed from the lakes to their posts on the Wabash. From the levelness of the intervening country, a canal could be easily opened, uniting the two streams. The second is the short portage between the Chicago and the Kickapoo branch of the Illinois, rendered important by the inundations, which at certain seasons cover the intermediate prairie, from which the two opposite streams flow. By this means nature has herself opened a navigable communication between the Great Lakes and the Mississippi; and it is a fact, however difficult it may be of belief to many, that boats not unfrequently pass from Lake Michigan into the Illinois, and in some instances without being subjected to the necessity of having their lading taken out. I have never been on this portage, and therefore cannot speak from personal knowledge, yet the fact has reached me through so many authentic channels, that I have no doubt of its truth. Gen. P. B. Porter, whose geographical knowledge of the countries bordering the lakes, is excelled by that of no gentleman in the western country, has given his corroborative testimony in his speech on internal navigation, delivered on the floor of congress in 1810. Lieutenant Hamilton of the United States' army, a meritorious officer, whose services have not been adequately requited, informed a friend of mine living at Detroit, that he had passed with a laden boat, and met with no obstructions on the portage, except from the grass, through which, however, the men easily forced the boat. But, in order to multiply proof and remove every doubt, I consulted the Hon. N. POPE, the Territorial Delegate in congress from Illinois, who in answer to my enquiries stated, that " at high water boats pass out of Lake Michigan into the Illinois river, and so *vice versa,* without landing. A canal uniting them is deemed practicable at a small expense," &c. When on the upper lakes, I frequently met with voyageurs who had assisted in navigating boats across this portage.

This morass is not the only one possessing two distinct outlets, I have myself witnessed this phenomenon in several instances ; but never where there was water sufficient to float a laden boat. Let us hear what the justly celebrated Volney, says on this interesting subject.

" During the vernal floods, the north branch of the Great Miami mixes its waters with the southern branch of the *Miami of the Lake.* The carrying place, or *portage,* of a league, which separates their heads, disappears beneath the flood, and we can pass in canoes from the Ohio to Lake Erie, as I myself witnessed in 1796.

" At Loremier's Fort, or store, an eastern branch of the Wabash serves as a simple canal to connect the two Miamis ; and the same Wabash, by a northern branch, communicates, above Fort Wayne, in the time of inundation, with the Miami of Lake Erie.

" In the winter of 1792-3, two boats *(perogues)* were detached from Detroit, by a mercantile house, from whom I received the information, which passed, without interruption, from the Huron river,* which enters Lake Erie, into *Grand River,* which falls into Lake Michigan, by means of the rise at the heads of the two streams.

---

* The river Huron mentioned by Volney, enters Lake Erie six miles below Malden. There are two other rivers of this name ; one falls into Lake Erie twelve miles below Sandusky bay, and the other into Lake St Clair.

" The Muskingum, which flows into the Ohio, communicates, at its sources, through some small lakes, with the Cayahoga, belonging to Lake Erie."

There is a portage of four miles between the St. Joseph's of Lake Michigan, and the Theakaki; of two miles between the Theakaki and the Great Kennomic; of half a mile between the Great and Little Kennomic; of four miles between the Chemin and Little Kennomic; and of three miles between the west fork of Chicago and Plein; besides numerous ones between the head branches of the two St. Josephs; Black, Raisin and Eel rivers, which vary in length according to the dryness or moisture of the season. There is a short portage between the St. Marys and the main branch of the Wabash, over which, in times of inundation the Indians pass with their light perogues.

In the great peninsula in Upper Canada, formed by the Lakes Ontario, Erie, Huron, Simcoe, &c. there are immense swamps from which the waters flow off almost imperceptibly in opposite directions. Through these swamps canoes can pass from the Chippewa creek into the Grand river, and from Lake Simcoe to Nautausawaga, running into Lake Huron.

MISCELLANEOUS.

Chicago is a small river, which forks sixteen miles from the lake, into the east and west branches. Sloops of forty tons burthen can enter its harbor. Six miles from the lake its current becomes brisk, and continues so as far as the portage. Fort Dearborn, famous for the murder of its garrison in September 1815, by the Pottawattamies, stood upon its left bank near the lake shore. The Indians have relinquished to the United States a tract of land six miles square, at the mouth of this river. The fort has been lately re-occupied.

The Great Kennomic.—This river rises twenty or thirty miles S. of lake Michigan, and running a N. W. course approaches within two or three miles of that lake. Thence winding to the S. W. and north, it forms a curviture nearly similar to the end of the lake, and parallel with it, keeping at the distance of 8 or 9 miles. It thence turns suddenly to the S. E. E. and N. E. in a contrary but parrellel direction to its former course, and empties into the lake 30 miles east of Chicago. It expands behind the sand hills near its mouth, and forms a spacious bay. It affords to the Indians an inexhaustible supply of fish, and an ample range for fowling and trapping. Its banks are low, and its current gentle.

Population.—I have recently received several letters from gentlemen residing in Indiana, which concur in stating that the population has doubled since May 1815. In other words, it now amounts to 128,000 souls, a rapidity of increase altogether unprecedented.

Price of Improved Lands.—Farms containing a log house and fifteen or twenty acres, sell as high as eight or ten dollars; in some instances the necessities or rambling dispositions of the inhabitants induce them to dispose of their plantations at a trifling advance upon the original price.

Falls of the Ohio.—An improvement of the navigation of the falls is about to be attempted by a canal round the rapids. The legislature have incorporated a company with a capital of $1,000,000. When this enterprize is accomplished, ship building will probably re-commence with vigor. It was the difficulties encountered in getting vessels over these rapids, which chiefly contributed to discourage this important business above the falls.

The Wabash.—The rapids at Ouitanan are impassable for boats; but the navigation is so good between Vincennes and this place, that Gen. Hopkins in his expedition to Tippecanoe in 1813, conveyed his baggage and stores in large keels, of thirty tons burthen. General Harrison in his expedition against the Prophet, was accompanied in his march through the wilderness by a caravan of *waggons !* They were enabled to proceed with tolerable speed by keeping in the prairies to the west of the woodlands bordering the Wabash.

Washington County.—In addition to the streams mentioned in page 66, is watered by Blueriver, which rises in the eastern part of the county, and pursuing a S. E. course, passes through Harrison county twelve miles south-west of Corydon.

Climate.—From the latitude of Ouitanan, (40 20) to the borders of the Ohio, the climate of Indiana may be pronounced mild.   North of the head branches of the Wabash, the north and north-west winds are formidable enemies to human comfort, and the winters severe and rigorous; though snow is rarely known to fall so deep as it does in the northern counties of New-York.   The southern shore of Lake Michigan, and the vast prairies in the direction of the Wabash have little to protect them from the rage of the brumal winds.

The Reed Cane.—This plant grows south of the ridge of hills extending from the falls of the Ohio to those of the Wabash above the mouth of Whiteriver.   It is sometimes found as far north as the mouth of the Big Miami.   Cotton, the vines of Spain, the silk worm, and the sweet potatoe will flourish wherever the reed cane grows, except, the first, which does not grow to perfection beyond 31 degrees of north latitude.   Rice and Indigo, I think would do well between Blueriver and the Wabash, though I have never seen either cultivated, or heard that the inhabitants have yet made the trial.   I have seen these plants growing luxuriantly in Overton county, Tennessee, which is a high broken country, near the Kentucky boundary line, in latitude 36 35.   The mouth of the Wabash is in 37 50.

The state will doubtless produce cotton sufficient for its own consumption.   It is already raised in considerable quantities at Vincennes, Princeton, Harmony, and in the settlements below the mouth of Anderson.   The Wabash will at no very remote period, serve as a canal to supply with cotton, a part of the market on the northern lakes.

Game.—The forests of Indiana are abundantly stocked with game.   Great numbers of deer are annually destroyed by the inhabitants. In travelling seven miles through the woods of Dearborn county, I counted two bears, three deer, and upwards of one hundred turkies; more than half of the latter, however, were young ones, just beginning to fly. I will here relate an adventure which may serve to throw some light on the natural history of the deer. In the course of the day, I missed my way and wandered several miles in the wilderness, in my endeavors to regain the path I started a fawn, which I soon caught, in consequence of its becoming entangled in the herbage. It bleated and appeared greatly frightened. Conceiving myself to be near a settlement and unwilling to destroy it, I resolved to carry it to the first house; but after travelling half a mile its dam made her appearance, and seemed by her piteous demonstrations, plainly to reproach me for my cruelty; upon which I gave the fawn its liberty. But I was not a little surprised, to find it so much attached to me during our transient acquaintance, that it absolutely refused to leave me. I pushed it from me and pursued my course; but soon found it at my heels, apparently as docile as a pet lamb; and was compelled to frighten it before it would turn from me. Relating this fact to some old hunters, they assured me that such is the docility of fawns, that they can be as effectually tamed in an hour, as a year. Deer, it is said, are the mortal enemies of rattlesnakes; and often kill them designedly by jumping on them. They can scent them at considerable distance; and when pursued by dogs will avoid those which may happen to lie in their way, by suddenly inclining to the right or left. It is also reported that the turkey buzzard has the power of killing the rattlesnake by its intolerable stench—which it most powerfully emits by a violent fluttering in the air a little above the snake's head.

Farmers are greatly annoyed by the smaller animals, such as squirrels, moles and mice; for nature is as prolific in animal as vegetable productions. The mole is particularly troublesome to corn-fields while the seed is coming up, and injurious to meadows, as it bores the earth in every direction.

Minerals,—The surface of Indiana is too champaign to be rich in mines of gold or silver. It is, nevertheless, stated that a silver mine has been discovered near Ouitanan. Iron ore is found in many counties, probably in sufficient quantities for domestic use. Chalybeate springs are plentiful. The water between Whiteriver and New Lexington is in some places impregnated with copperas to such a degree, that linen washed in it turns black; and a few of the inhabitants have been induced to abandon their habitations in consequence of the supposed unwholesomeness of their wells.

Indian Claims.—Near two-thirds of this state belongs to the Indians. Their title is extinguished in the eastern part, from Fort Wayne to the river Ohio, on an average of about twenty-five miles wide, on the margin of the Ohio and up the Wabash and western line to a point N. W. of Fort Harrison, and from thence eastwardly to the eastern purchase, about thirty-five miles from the Ohio. Notwithstanding the greater extent of soil purchased from the Indians in the west, a meridian equidistant from the eastern and western boundary would pretty fairly divide the population; but the western section will populate fastest, owing to the extent of recently purchased lands.

KENTUCKY,

Is bounded north by the Ohio river, west by the Mississippi, south by Tennessee, and east by Virginia. Its length from east to west is 328 miles; breadth from north to south 183 miles. Its area is 40,110 square miles, or 25,670.000 acres. Its southern boundary is in 36 30—and its northern extremity, (which is in the north bend of the Ohio) 39 10 N. latitude.

FACE OF THE COUNTRY.

The bottoms of the Kentucky side of the Ohio, from its mouth to that of Big Sandy, will average one mile in width. The timber is beech, sugar maple, sycamore, cottonwood, hackberry, pawpaw, and honey locust. These bottoms are in some places subject to periodical inundation, but are nevertheless susceptible of cultivation; about one sixth part of this land is cleared.

Parallel to the Ohio, and in the rear of the bottoms, lies a strip of country from five to twenty miles wide, and as long as the state, which is cut into deep vallies and high hills, by the numerous creeks and runs entering the Ohio. This soil, however, is rich and the greater part capable of improvement. Between this strip, Big Sandy and Green rivers, and the eastern counties, lies the garden of the state, if not of the world. It is about 150 miles long, and from 50 to 100 miles wide, and comprises the counties of Mason, Fleming, Montgomery, Clarke, Bourbon, Fayette, Scott, Harrison, Franklin, Woodford, Mercer, Jessemine, Madison, Garrard, Logan, Casey, Lincoln, Washington, Green.

L

This extensive tract is intersected by Little Sandy, Licking, Kentucky, and Salt rivers, and their numerous forks. This district has the happiest surface; gradually rising and descending alternately. There are no swamps, and the hills are of such easy ascent, that the fields show to the best possible advantage.

The angles of ascent are from eight to twenty-four degrees; the vallies are very narrow, and what is quite singular, inferior in point of fertility to the uplands. The soil, is black and friable, generally, but sometimes of a deep vermillion hue, or of the color of strong ashes. These lands produce black walnut, black cherry, honey locust, buckeye, pawpaw, sugar tree, mulberry, elm, ash, cotton wood, white thorn, with a grape vine encircling almost every fourth tree. The depth of the soil is always the greatest on the summits of the ridges and hills, varying from one to twenty feet. There is little or no under wood; but its place was supplied, when the country was first settled by the whites, by the reed cane, which covered all the rich lands. In the woods the earth is not incumbered with the rubbish of fallen timber, nor the trunks of partially decayed trees, as is the case in the northern states. The trees are small and strait, and do not in many places average more than twenty to an acre, except near the principal streams, where the prevailing timber is oak, and the soil hard and sterile to the distance of two or three miles. This part of the state is not so well watered as the hilly strip near the Ohio and the broken country near the Virginia boundary line, yet almost every farm is blessed with a durable spring.

The counties bordering the Virginia and Tennessee frontiers, situated in the eastern and south-eastern parts of the state, are broken by the spurs and lateral branches of the Allegany and Cumberland mountains. Besides, it is in these sections of the state that the Big Sandy, Licking, Kentucky, and Cumberland rivers have their sources. The small streams are numerous; and have gullied the earth into sharp hills, long crooked ridges, deep glens, dark hollows, and frightful gulfs. The hills are covered with oak, chesnut, hickory, gum, and poplar, and the vallies with beech, sugar maple, elm, poplar, black walnut and hackberry. In the bottoms of the gulfs, or "*coves*" as the inhabitants call them, the trees are thickly planted, and grow to a most extraordinary size, particularly the poplars, which frequently measure eight feet in diameter, and of immense height. It is in these unfrequented recesses that solitude may be said to hold her court ; for the light of heaven is not able to penetrate the eternal gloom which reigns beneath the impervious foliage. What a scene for Scott! His description of the woods of Soignies is strikingly appropriate to the coves and gulfs of Kentucky and Tennessee.

> " Thy woods, dark Soignies, holds us now,
> Where the tall beeches' glossy bough,
>   For many a league around,
> With birch and darksome oak between,
> Spreads deep and far a pathless screen,
>   Of tangled forest ground."

The areas of these gulfs are from one to fifty acres, perfectly level at the bottom, and covered, when in a state of nature, with a thick growth of cane, they have gaps or outlets on one side through which flows the brook created by the numerous springs issuing from the base of the almost surrounding hills. The water of these springs is excellent and durable ; the sides of the hills, when not too steep for the plough, yield fine crops of corn, potatoes, &c. The soil is exceedingly rich, and the inhabitants often locate themselves in these peaceful retreats. They afford a pleasant residence in winter, but are too confined and sultry in the summer.

Between the Rolling fork of Salt river and Green river, in Nelson county principally, is a tract of country, about forty miles square, mostly barren, interspersed with plains and strips of good lands, which are advantageous situations for raising cattle, as the neighboring barrens, as they are improperly called, are covered with grass, and afford good pasturage. Small tracts of similar land are found upon Great and Little

Barren rivers. But the country between Green and Cumberland rivers is emphatically called "*the barrens*," by the inhabitants living north of Green river and the Knobs of Pulaski county ; not because the soil is unproductive, but because the timber is uniformly oak, chesnut, hickory, gum, lyn, poplar and cucumber. The "oak" or "knob" district, includes the counties of Pulaski, Wayne, Rocky Castle, Knox, Cumberland, Warren, Barren, Livingston and Christian.

In 1800, the Legislature of Kentucky made a gratuitous grant of this extensive tract to actual settlers. Every actual settler was entitled to a lot of four hundred acres. At the time, this land was considered of little value ; but time and settlement has given it a reputation. It proves to be excellent grain land ; and hogs and cattle are easily raised. In consequence of the great size of the lots, and the destitution of water in many places, the *range* cannot be destroyed, as has been the case in the *old* or northern settlements. There are no meadows or pastures to be seen in this quarter; all the domestic animals run in the woods. These lands will yield from forty to fifty bushels of Indian corn ; fifteen bushels of rye, twenty of wheat, and thirty of oats, an acre ; besides, tobacco does well in the swails and flats, which are sometimes very fertile ; cotton and indigo will do tolerably well. The gardens produce onions, cabbage, sweet and Irish potatoes. The bottoms of Cumberland, where it runs on the Kentucky side of the boundary line, are very productive, not so subject to inundation, nor so wide as those of the Ohio. The soil is a gravelly clay or loam of a vermillion color, except in the poplar timbered lands, where it is a deep, ash colored mould, rich, durable, and capable of producing one hundred bushels of corn an acre. The inhabitants make use of this soil for the culture of tobacco, of which they raised great quantities last season. I scarcely passed a plantation, which had not a tobacco field ; for which purpose they had uniformly cleared a piece of *new* ground. The country merchants were offering from twelve to fifteen dollars a hundred in advance. The chesnut trees are remarkably tall and handsome; and the inhabitants mostly use this timber for rails and shingles.

RIVERS.

The Ohio washes its northern margin for the space of 838 miles, and the Mississippi its western limit 74 miles. Most of the rivers have a northern direction and empty their waters into the Ohio.

The *Big Sandy*, rises in the Allegany mountains near the heads of Clinch and Cumberland, and forms the eastern boundary of the state for nearly 200 miles; it is 200 yards wide at its mouth, and branches into the north-east and south forks forty miles from its entrance into the Ohio. The south fork receives a great number of large creeks, among which are Shelby, Bear, Turkey, Bartle's, Paint and Blane's, all of which run east or north-east. It is navigable to the Ouascioto mountains.

Between the mouths of Big Sandy and Licking, the following creeks and rivulets enter the Ohio; they are from twenty to seventy miles long, and from fifty to twelve yards wide at their mouths.

	Miles.
Little Sandy, *(Below Big Sandy.)*	22
Tigers creek,	21
Connoconneque,	19
Salt Lick creek,	14
Sycamore,	18
Crooked creek,	13
Cabin creek,	2
Brooke creek,	6
Limestone, (small)	3
Bracken,	22

Licking river heads in the south-east corner of the state, near the sources of Cumberland river, pursues a north-western course and falls into the Ohio, at Newport, directly opposite Cincinnati. In high water it swells to a respectable size, but in long droughts nearly disappears beneath the limestone rocks, which constitute its bed.

The *Kentucky* rises in the mountains in the S. E. corner of the state, and interlocks with the head waters of Licking and Cumberland. It runs a N. W. course, and falls into the Ohio, at Port William, 77 miles above Louisville. It is 150 yards wide at its mouth, and has a boatable navigation 150 miles. It receives the north and south forks which are considerable streams, which enter the main branch about two miles apart in Madison county. These forks rise in the hills near Cumberland river and run nearly north. Dicks, a small river which rises in Lincoln county, and by running N. N. W. falls into the left bank of the Kentucky below the mouth of Hickman. It is about fifty miles long and fifty yards wide at its mouth; its current is very rapid, and its course confined by precipices of limestone and white marble, and in some places nearly 300 feet high. Elkhorn, which has two forks, the N. and S. the first heads near Lexington, and the second near Georgetown. These branches water Scott and Fayette counties, and are well calculated for driving hydraulic machinery. This river enters the Kentucky eight miles below Frankfort, and is fifty yards wide at its mouth. Eagle creek rises in Harrison county, and runs N. W. and empties into the Kentucky fifty miles above its mouth.

Salt river rises in Mercer county—has three branches all issuing from the same county, and enters the Ohio 20 miles below Louisville. It is 150 yards wide at its mouth, and navigable 150 miles. It waters Jefferson, Greenup, Washington and Mercer counties.

Green river has its sources in Lincoln county. It pursues a western course, and enters the Ohio, 200 miles below Louisville, and 50 miles above the mouth of Cumberland. It is 200 yards wide at its mouth, and navigable for boats nearly 200 miles—It receives in its progress a great number of tributary streams, the principal of which is Great Barren river, which also divides into numerous forks, heading near the Cumberland and Tennessee. Its course is N. E. Little Barren river heads in Bullett county, and enters the right bank of Green river, 50 miles below the mouth of Great Barren. *Rough* river rises from the S. E. enters Green river 50 miles above its entrance into the Ohio; and Panther's creek comes in from the S. E. 26 miles from the Ohio.

Tradewater river heads in the bend of Cumberland river, in Christian county, and running a N. W. course falls into the Ohio, 200 miles below the mouth of Green river, or about equidistant from the mouths of Green and Cumberland. It is about 70 yards wide at its mouth and 80 miles long.

Cumberland river rises near the south fork of Big Sandy, in the S. E. corner of the state; 80 miles below its head, it passes the Tennessee boundary line, and runs about 40 miles in that state, and then re-enters Kentucky, but by a curviture of 50 miles separates Wayne county from Pulaski; it then turns to the S. W. advances into the state of Tennessee. After meandering about 200 miles through that country, turns to the N. W. passes by Nashville into Kentucky, and unites with the Ohio in a W. direction, 1113 miles below Pittsburg. It is 300 yards wide at its mouth, and is navigable in large vessels to Nashville, where it is about 190 yards wide, and continues that breadth upwards of 200 miles. It is navigable more than 300 miles above Nashville in boats of 15 tons burthen. At Nashville it is 20 feet deep, from November to June, but frequently in freshes it is 40, 50, and sometimes 60 feet deep, overflowing a great part of the low grounds. From June to November, it is usually 10 and 12 feet deep. The current is very gentle from Nashville to the Ohio, about 200 miles, affording an easy navigation.

Red river heads in Cumberland county, and runs a S. W. course into Cumberland river. This stream is 60 yards wide and 50 miles long.

Tennessee river runs about 75 miles in Kentucky, before it enters the Ohio.

Kaskinampas river waters the western end of the state—it heads near the Tennessee and runs a western course, entering the Mississippi, about half way between the mouth of the Ohio and New Madrid.

POPULATION IN 1815.

Counties.	Population.	Chief Towns.	Population.
Adair	6,011	Columbia	175
Barren	11,286	Glasgow	244
Boone	3,608		
Bracken	3,451	Augusta	255
Breckenridge	3,430		
Bourbon	18,009	Paris	838
Butler	2,181		
Bullet	4,311		
Clarke	11,519	Winchester	538
Casey	3,285	Liberty	33
Campbell	3,060	Newport	413
Christian	11,020	Hopkinsonville	131
Cumberland	6,191	Burkesville	106
Clay	2,398		
Caldwell	4,268		
Estle	2,081		
Fayette	21,370	Lexington	4,326
Franklin	8,013	Frankfort	1,099
Fleming	8,947		
Floyd	3,485	Prestonville	32
Gallatin	3,307	Port William	120
Greenup	2,369		
Green	6,735	Greensburgh	132
Grayson	2,301		
Garrard	9,186	Lancaster	260
Henry	6,777	Newcastle	125
Harrison	7,752	Cyntheana	369
Henderson	4,703	Henderson	159

Counties.	Population.	Chief Towns.	Population.
Harden	7,531	Elizabeth Town	181
Hopkins	2,964	Madisonville	37
Jessamine	8,377	Nicholasville	158
Jefferson	13,399	Louisville	1,357
Knox	5,875	Barboursville	55
Livingston	3,674	Smithland	99
Lewis	2,357		
Lincoln	8,676		
Logan	12,123	Russelville	532
Mason	12,459	Washington	815
Mercer	12,630	Danville	432
Madison	15,540	Richmond	366
Muhlenbergh	4,181	Greenville	75
Montgomery	12,975	Mountsterling	325
Nicholas	4,893		
Nelson	14,078	Beardstown	821
Ohio	3,682	Hartford	110
Pulaski	6,897		
Pendleton	3,061	Falmouth	121
Rockcastle	1,731		
Scott	12,419	Georgetown	529
Shelby	14,837	Shelbyville	424
Wayne	5,430	Monticello	37
Washington	13,248	Springfield	249
Warren	11,937	Bowling-green	154
Woodford	9,659	Versailles	483
54	406,511		

RATIO OF INCREASE.

In 1790 the population, was 73,677; in 1800—220,960; in 1811—406,511.—It therefore appears that the population from 1790 to 1800 encreased at the rate of about eleven per cent; from 1800 to 1810, at the rate of about six per cent; and doubled itself in about eleven years.   Since 1810 it has

M

probably increased at the rate of three per cent. and will again
double in about twenty years. But Mr. Niles, editor of the
Weekly Register, says, that it is estimated on ascertained
facts and reasonable data that the present population of Kentucky is about 527,000—viz. 420,000 free white, and 107,000
slaves, which gives an increase of 125 per cent. in five years.

VILLAGES.

These are not so numerous as in the northern states ; yet
every county has its seat of justice. I shall only notice such
as I have seen.

Mayville stands on the bank of the Ohio, just below limestone creek, 500 miles below Pittsburgh, and 66 above Cincinnati. Its site though pleasant is confined, as the bottom on
which it stands is not more than 50 rods wide, and the hills
in its rear rise abruptly to the height of 450 feet. It contains about 400 houses ; there are three streets running parallel with the river and four cross ones, besides lanes and
alleys. There is a glass factory and a printing office. It is
a brisk place, being the principal *river* port for the north-
east half of the state, as Louisville is for the south-west. Boats
and waggons are continually arriving and departing ; and great
numbers of emigrants cross at this place for Ohio and Indiana. The taverns are well kept, and charges reasonable. The
great road from Lexington to Chilicothe, crosses the Ohio at
Maysville. Several vessels have been built above the town,
where the bottom expands to the width of a mile.

Washington is situated in a rich settlement, about three
miles south-west of Maysville—It has three parallel streets,
but the buildings are not thick ; many of them, however, are
large and handsome. There is a brick jail, a stone church
for Scotch Presbyterians, and a Baptist meeting house ; an
academy, post office, printing office, five taverns, and several
stores. Several new buildings were going up in May last,
and what is deserving of mention, I saw several waggons la-

den with boards sawed in Allegany county in the state of New-York, and rafted down the Allegany and Ohio rivers, as far as Limestone.   These boards are sometimes carried in waggons as far as Paris and Lexington.

Paris—The capital of Bourbon county, is situated upon a handsome ridge on the right bank of Stoner fork of Licking, at the mouth of Houston creek.   There are two merchant flowering mills, and several carding machines, two churches, and a printing office, besides a large number of well finished stores, mechanic shops, &c.   The greater part of the buildings are brick, and as large as any in the state.   It is twenty miles east of Lexington, sixty-five S. S. E. of Newport, and in N. lat. 38, 14.   The surrounding country is rich and delightful—and the road from thence to Lexington leads through a district surpassing in beauty, if possible, the brilliant description of Imlay.

Lexington.   I had occasion to visit this place in the summer of 1797; it then contained about 50 houses, partly frame, and hewn logs, with the chimneys *out side;* the surrounding country was then new ; a village lot could have been purchased for $30, and a good farm in its vicinity for $5 an acre.   The best farmers lived in log cabins, and wore hunting shirts and leggings.   In May last, (1816) business again called me to Lexington.   But how changed the scene !   Every thing had assumed a new appearance.   The beautiful vale of Town Fork, which in 1797, I saw variegated with cornfields, meadows, and trees, had in my absence been covered with stately and elegant buildings—in short, a large and beautiful town had arisen by the creative genius of the west.   The log cabins had disappeared, and in their places stood costly brick mansions, well painted and enclosed by fine yards, bespeaking the taste and wealth of their possessors.   The leathern pantaloons, the hunting shirts and leggings had been discarded, for the dress and manners of the inhabitants had entirely changed. The scenery around Lexington, almost equals that of the elysium of the ancients.   Philadelphia, with all its surrounding beauties scarcely equals it.   The surface resembles the gentle swell of the ocean, when the agitations of a storm have nearly subsided.   The roads are very fine and wide.   The grazing parks have a peculiar neatness; the charming groves, the small, square and beautiful meadows, and above all, the wide spreading forests of corn waving in grandeur and luxuriance, and perfuming the air with its fragrance, combine to render a summer's view of Lexington inexpressibly rich, novel, grand and picturesque.   The site of the town is in a *valley;* but the declivities are so gentle that some travellers, not scrupulously accurate, have described it as a *plain.* Town Fork creek waters the central parts of the town; it is narrow, and in severe droughts nearly dry.   The main street, which is one mile and a quarter long, runs parallel with the creek on the north side.   There are three other streets running parallel with the main street.   These are intersected at short intervals by cross streets; all of which are wide and mostly paved.   Main street presents to the traveller as much wealth, and more beauty than can be found in most of the atlantic cities.   It is about 80 feet wide, level, compactly built, well paved, and having foot ways, twelve feet wide on each side. I was surprised to see at every step, finely painted brick stores, three stories high, and well filled with costly and fanciful merchandize.   Near the centre of the town is the public square, lined on every side with large substantial brick houses, stores, hotels, &c.   In this square stands the market house, which is of brick, and well furnished on Wednesdays and Saturdays; but occasionally the scene of a barbarous practice; for it is here that incorrigible or delinquent negroes are flogged unmercifully.   I saw this punishment inflicted on two of these wretches.   Their screams soon collected a numerous crowd—I could not help saying to myself, "These cries are the knell of Kentucky liberty."   I had not leisure to count the buildings, and found no person capable of giving the requisite information. This town *appears* as large and populous as Cincinnati, which contained in 1816, 1000 houses and 6000 souls. The public buildings consist of several churches, belonging to methodists, presbyterians, baptists, seceders, episcopalians, and Roman catholics. The court house is a three story brick building, with a cupola rising from the middle of a square roof, and contains a bell and a town clock. The Masanoic Hall and the Bank, are fine brick buildings. There is a public library, and a university called Transylvania, liberally endowed, the terms of tuition are $200 per annum. There is a female academy, where the following branches are taught, viz. reading, writing, arithmetic, grammar, correspondence, elocution, rhetoric, geography, astronomy, ancient and modern history, chronology, mythology, music, drawing, embroidery, &c. The taverns and boarding houses are neat and well furnished. *Wilson's* hotel is excelled by none in America, for extensiveness, style and good living. The streets are often thronged with well dressed people. A prodigious quantity of European goods are retailed to the crowd of customers, who resort here from the neighboring settlements. There are two bookstores, and three printing offices, from which are issued as many weekly papers, viz: the Reporter, and Kentucky Gazette, both republican, and the Monitor, federal, and the only one of that political cast in the state. The inhabitants are as polished, and I regret to add, as luxurious as those of Boston, New-York or Baltimore ; and their assemblies and parties are conducted with as much ease and grace, as in the oldest towns of the union. The manufactories are extensive, and promise a continued growth of the town. There are four nail factories, which manufacture seventy tons of nails yearly—two copper and tin manufactories—several jewellers and silversmiths, ten sadler shops, five cabinet shops, and three painters, seven tailor shops, an umbrella manufactory, twelve blacksmiths, two gunsmith shops, several tobacconists, five chair makers, three dyers, six hatters, sixteen shoemakers, two stocking weavers; besides tanneries, breweries, distilleries, cooperies, brickyards, carding machines, &c. The rope walks are on a large scale, and its manufac·

tures of hemp in 1811, were valued at $500,000. There are several cotton and woolen manufactories—three steam grist mills, and two steam paper mills. The Lexington woolen manufactory, erected by Messrs. Prentis's & Co. and Mr. Sanders large cotton manufactory are built on the Town Fork, about a mile south-west of the town. They went into operation in June last. Mr. Sanders employed about 150 hands; the articles manufactured, consist of cotton yarns, sheeting, shirting, bedticking, counterpanes, table cloths, chambrays, cassinets, sattinets, woolen cords, &c. The woolen manufactory also employed 150 hands—it manufactures, broadcloths, cassimeres, blankets, and flannels. It has a steam paper mill connected with it, which produces paper of a fine quality. The other paper mill rivals any establishment of the kind in the United States.

There are between fifty and sixty *villas*, or handsome country residences in the vicinity of Lexington, and that of Henry Clay, Speaker of the House of Representatives, may be pronounced one of the most delightful. It is situated about one mile east of the town, on an agreeable rise, and is nearly surrounded with poplar and locust groves.

The inhabitants of Lexington have a healthful and sprightly appearance; there are several families from the New-England states, who have resided here for a number of years, and enjoyed good health.

There is nothing in the manners or morals of the people of Lexington, to justify the shameful calumnies of the British hireling, *Ash.* "The inhabitants (he says) shew demonstrations of civilization; but at particular times, on Sundays and market days, they give a loose to their dispositions, and exhibit many traits that should exclusively belong to untutored savages. Their churches have never been finished, and they have all the glass struck out by boys in the day, and the inside by rogues and prostitutes who frequent them at night."

Land is as dear around Lexington as it is in the oldest

settlement on the seaboard, whole farms have sold for $100 an acre ; and small parcels for a far greater sum ; town lots are exorbitantly high.

The cattle, horses and sheep are very fine. Great numbers of cattle are bought by the drovers for the Baltimore and Philadelphia markets. A first rate yoke of cattle can be purchased for fifty dollars ; and a horse worth one hundred dollars in New-York, could be bought for seventy dollars. Provisions are cheap, and abundant. Mechanics charges are high. A tailor will charge you from five to ten dollars for making a *coat!* Board $2,50 a week for laborers. Most of the mechanics are in prosperous circumstances.

Georgetown, the capitol of Scott county, is situated on Royal Spring, which empties its waters into North Elkhorn, nearly a mile from the town. It has several manufactory establishments, a court house, baptist meeting house, printing office, post office, and a rope walk. It is fourteen miles north of Lexington, and on the head of a flourishing settlement.

Harrodsburgh, a post-town of Mercer county, is pleasantly situated on both sides of Salt river, which is here a handsome rivulet, of good water, and affording a liberal supply for sevaral mills. This village is ten miles N. by W. of Dansville, and contains 76 houses, some of them of good size and appearance ; it has a meeting house and post office ; the country in its vicinity, is neither so rich nor so level, as around Dansville.

Dansville, the capital of Mercer county, is situated on the S. W. side of Dicks river, which is here a mere brook. 40 miles S. by W. of Frankfort, and 33 S. S. W. of Lexington. It has 200 houses, a court house, jail, presbyterian church, post office, and a printing office ; in which is published a newspaper called the "*Light House.*" The surrounding country is rich and closely settled. There are several mills, factories, and an extensive rope walk.

Stanford, the chief town of Lincoln county, is situated on a fertile and handsome plain, ten miles S. S. E. of Dansville ;

it has about 100 houses, a stone court house and jail, post
office, and a rope walk.   There are five plantations in its
neighborhood, abounding with good springs, which constitute
the sources of Green river.

Summerset—The seat of justice for Pulaski county, stands
on the side of a hill in a rich undulating country, twelve S. S.
E. of Stanford.—It contains about 70 houses, brick, framed,
and hewn logs; it has a post office, three taverns, six stores,
three blacksmith shops, and a grist mill.   Six miles beyond
Summerset on the Monticello road, the aspect, soil and timber of the country, changes instantly; for you pass almost at
a single step, from the deep, black, rich soil, covered with
honey locust, sugar maple, buckeye, &c. into the *oak* or *knob*
region, where the soft vegetable mould, the accacia, grape
vine, and rich pastures disappear, and you tread on a firmer
soil, and make your way through a lofty oak and chesnut forest.   The ascent from the rich lands to the summit of the
Knobs, is several hundred feet.

Monticello—the chief town of Wayne county, stands on a
dry ridge, about half way between Cumberland river and
the Tennessee boundary line.   It has about 50 inelegant
hewn log dwelling houses, a rude court house, and a place for
public worship, three taverns, four stores, three blacksmith
shops.   The country for several miles to the south, is broken,
and abounds with streams and saltpetre caves.   The waters
are remarkably pure and wholesome.   A lead mine was discovered in the mountains about twelve miles south of Monticello, in April last.   This discovery was made by a *water-
witch,* as the inhabitants informed me.   The proprietors, are
confident of making their fortunes; they have already expended a considerable sum in excavating the rock through which
the vein leads.   My curiosity lead me to visit the spot, and
procure a specimen of the ore, which was very fine, but the
vein was only a yard wide and six inches deep.   Improved
land is selling near the Tennessee boundary line, for ten, fifteen and twenty dollars an acre, according to quality.

Wayne county is the most healthy part of the state. Diseases and physicians are almost unknown to the inhabitants; but as a drawback on this blessing, they frequently experience the most tremendous thunder storms. In travelling from Limestone to Cumberland river, I scarcely saw a single tree which had been struck by lightning. But immediately on entering this county, I discovered frequent instances of the lightning's rage; and soon had an opportunity of beholding it exerting all its power on the forest which covers Poplar mountain. The storm overtook me several miles from any house, and upon the summit of the mountain. The claps came in quick succession and were distinguished for uncommon vividness of the lightning, and terrific severity of the thunder. There was but very little rain, and not the least appearance of wind. Several trees were struck within a short distance of the covert I had selected. A large chesnut tree was literally shivered into splinters, and scattered to the distance of several rods, in every direction. The fragments exactly resembled the strips of a basket-maker.

Frankfort, the metropolis of the state, and chief town of Franklin county, stands on the east bank of Kentucky river, sixty miles above its entrance into the Ohio. The site of the town is a semicircular, alluvial plain, two hundred feet lower than the table in its rear. The river which is here about 100 yards wide, with bold limestone banks, forms a handsome curve and waters the southern and western parts of the town. The bottoms on both side of the river are very broad, but subject to inundation. For several years after the settlements were commenced, the inhabitants were afflicted with bilious complaints. But the low situations have been drained, and they now enjoy good health. The town is but little inferior to Lexington in the size and number of its houses; but is neither so pleasant, nor so rich in its surrounding scenery. The public buildings are, the state house, penitentiary, two churches, court house, jail, market house, &c. The first is of rough marble, eighty-six feet front by fifty-four deep—it is a parcel

N

lelogram, with a cupola rising from the centre of a square
roof. The public offices are on the first floor, the hall of the
representatives on the second, and senate chamber on the
third. The court house is of brick—it is large and convenient, and in every respect worthy of the metropolis of Kentucky. The penitentiary covers one acre; the walls are of
stone, the work shops occupy the front. The labor of the
convicts and articles manufactured, after paying for the raw
materials, considerably exceed in value the annual appropria-
tions of the state. It contains from 70 to 100 convicts.

There are several valuable rope walks, two bagging manufactories, powder mills, a grist and saw mill (below the town)
tobacco warehouse, two book stores and three printing offices, in which are printed the *Palladium*, the *Argus* and the
Pulse. This town is in 38, 14, north latitude and 24
miles N. W. of Lexington. Several large brigs have been
built here and sent to New-Orleans. The public inns are
commodious, and conducted in the best manner.

Franklin county is bounded west by Shelby, north-west
by Henry, north by Gallatin, east by Scott and Woodford,
and south by Mercer. It is a rich county, but not so populous as Fayette, Scott, or Woodford. It has no poor land
except narrow strips along the banks of Kentucky river. It
is watered by Kentucky and Elkhorn rivers. It abounds with
excellent marble, freestone; and sand suitable for the manufacture of glass, which is found in the river. There is a substantial chain bridge across the Kentucky at Frankfort.

Versailles—the seat of Justice for Woodford county, is situated on a creek running into the Kentucky river. It contains about 100 houses, mostly large, of brick and stone. It is
thirteen miles S. W. by S. of Lexington. Its inhabitants
are distinguished for their politeness and hospitality. Woodford county is rich and populous; bounded N. by Scott, E.
by Fayette, S. E. by Jessamine, S. W. by Mercer, and N.
W. by Franklin.

The public were last summer amused with a description

of a *wonderful cave*, said to have been discovered in this county. I made particular enquiries respecting caves and caverns, but heard nothing of any corresponding in grandeur and dimensions, with the one described in our newspapers of August 1816.

Shelbyville—the principal town of Shelby county, stands on Brashau's creek, twelve miles above its junction with Salt river. It has a court house, meeting house, post office, printing office. It is about twenty miles south-west of Frankfort—Shelby county is bounded north by Henry, west by Bullitt, east by Franklin, and south by Nelson. It is fertile, and copiously watered by several creeks running into Salt river.

Cynthiana—The seat of justice for Harrison county, is a flourishing town, stands on the north-east bank of the South Fork of Licking, 20 miles on a strait line above its junction with Main Licking. It contains about 100 houses, of brick, stone, frame, and hewn logs; it has a brick court and market houses, stone jail, an academy endowed by the legislature with 6000 acres of land. There are ten grist and saw mills, within three miles of the town. The town is situated on a large and handsome bottom, in a healthful, rich settlement. It is 34 miles N. E. of Frankfort, and 26 N. by E. from Lexington. The road from Frankfort to Augusta passes through Cynthiana. Harrison is bounded north by Pendleton, south by Scott, west by Franklin, and east by Bracken. Its surface is in many places broken—it is very well watered by the South Fork of Licking, Eagle creek, and its head branches.

Augusta, the seat of justice of Bracken county, stands on the bank of the Ohio, on a spacious and pleasant bottom, 22 miles below Maysville. The margin of the river is beautifully ornamented with a double row of locust trees, and the streets and yards are also well shaded by locust and poplars. It was court week, and the day very hot and sultry, when I arrived here from Cincinnati, and proceeded by land to Washington. Slavery never appeared more odious to me

than on that day. The neighboring fields were filled with negroes, bear headed, toiling beneath the rays of a scorching
sun, and covered with sweat and dust, while the well dressed
whites, sat in groupes beneath refreshing shades, engaged
in reading newspapers, and beguiling the hours in the vivaci-
ty of coloquial intercourse. This town has a particular air
of neatness; but its trade is not very extensive. I omitted
counting the buildings, or making any topographical notes.
There is probably about 75 houses, a court house and meeting house. The flats above the town are more than one mile
wide. Bracken creek enters the Ohio about half a mile above
the village. This creek branches about a mile and a half
from the river; and affords water for several grist mills.
Bracken county is considerably broken, but it may be rank-
ed among the rich counties.

  Newport, the seat of justice for Campbell county, is situated immediately above the mouth of Licking, and directly
opposite Cincinnati; its site is a rich, elevated and beautiful alluvial plain, commanding a fine prospect of Covington,
Cincinnati, the opposite hills, and both up and down the Ohio
river. It is healthy and affords good well water at the depth
of 40 feet. It has enjoyed considerable political advantages,
being the point of rendezvous for most of the military expeditions from Kentucky against the British and Indians. The
United States have erected an arsenal immediately above
the confluence of the Licking with the Ohio; and make this
place a point of debarkation for such troops as are sent down
the river. Notwithstanding its early settlement and fine situation, it has not flourished until within the last two years—
It begins to assume the appearance of a handsome town.
There are several fine brick houses—it has a court house,
(building) a jail, market house, an academy (not yet in operation) endowed by the legislature of Kentucky with 6000 acres
of land; arrangements were made last season for the erection
of a brick school house, and the organization of a school on
the Lancastrian plan; there is a baptist and a methodist congre-

gation, but no permanent meeting houses—a post office, *no printing office*, but a fine vacancy for such an establishment.

The *arsenal* "consists of a capacious, oblong, two story armory of brick; a fire-proof, conical magazine, for gunpowder; a stone house for the keeper, and wooden barracks sufficient for the reception of two or three regiments of men, the whole inclosed with a stockade."

The proprietor of this town is Gen. James Taylor, who commenced building and laying out lots in 1791, and conveyed two acres to the county as a site for the public buildings. His title is indisputable, and his terms and policy liberal. He has introduced the culture of the vine; and his vineyard greatly embellishes the place.

Covington is a new town finely situated on the bank of the Ohio, immediately below Newport on the opposite side of Licking—the plain on which it stands is extensive and similar in soil and elevation, to the site of Newport. The proprietors are Messrs. Gano's and T. D. Carneal. "It is so planned and surveyed, as to make the streets appear to be a continuation of those of Cincinnati. Each block of lots has the advantage of two 16 feet alleys." They have made liberal donations for the erection of public buildings. This town is to be connected with Newport by a bridge across Licking— nay, some are so sanguine as to talk of a bridge across the Ohio, thereby connecting at a future period, "*the three cities.*" The great road to the Miami and Whitewater settlements, from the interior of Kentucky, Tennessee, Virginia and the Carolinas, passes through this place.

If the lover of the sublime and beautiful of nature, wishes to contemplate a ravishing panorama, let him embark at Columbia, on a fine summer's day, and suffer his boat to glide at leisure until he passes the mouth of Licking. His eye will fix itself alternately on the broad, placid "*belle riviere,*" rolling in grandeur, the extensive valley of the Ohio, clad in the rich luxuriance of its summer vestments, equalling in beauty, the fabled vale of Tempe, the hills, rising majestically from the bottoms, like two immense amphitheatres, the fine plantations, the vast assemblage of boats, the sites and buildings of Cincinnati, Newport and Covington—he will be charmed, and forcibly struck with the *tout ensemble* of so many interesting objects, and the striking proximity of three flourishing towns. Campbell county is generally hilly, being broken by Licking river, and several creeks—the soil, however, is tolerably good, and the growth of timber very heavy. The woods abound with vast quantities of genseng, and there are large tracts of land to be sold, on reasonable terms; they are well watered, and in a healthy part of the state.

" In the bed of Licking, within a mile of its mouth, when the river is low, several copious veins of *chalybeate* water burst out, and have occasionally been resorted to, by the citizens. In addition to the *carbonate of iron*, they contain the different salts common in the spring water of this region. They seem to be formed in the alluvial grounds which skirt the river, and may be mentioned as specimens of a numerous class of *chalybeate* springs, with which the alluvial formation abounds."

Newport and Covington will enjoy a large share of the interior trade of Kentucky; as Licking river, in high water, is navigable for more than one hundred miles, for boats carrying two hundred barrels of flour.

Port William, the chief town of Gallatin county, stands on the right shore of Kentucky, just above its *embouchure*. It contains about fifty houses, many of which are of brick—but although pleasantly situated at the mouth of a navigable river, the outlet of a fine country, it has not flourished.

Newcastle, the seat of justice for Henry county, is situated in a populous district, 18 miles nearly south of Westport. It contains about 70 houses, principally of hewn logs. The court house is a large convenient brick building, two stories high and about forty feet square.

Westport, is situated in Henry county, on a high bluff near the bank of the Ohio, 48 miles below the mouth of Kentucky river, and 17 above Louisville.   It has about 25 houses. The county of Henry was established in 1799 ; it is bounded north by the Ohio river, west by Jefferson, south by Shelby, and east by Kentucky river.   It is about thirty miles square, and obtained its name from the celebrated Patrick Henry of Virginia.   It is watered by the Little Kentucky, which has a sufficiency of water for mills the greater part of the year—Drennon's, Harrod's, Flatt, Six mile and Corn creeks, upon all of which are a number of grist and saw mills. A considerable part of this county is broken by the Ohio, Little and Great Kentucky rivers.   The soil is favorable to the growth of corn, rye, oats, wheat, tobacco, hemp, sweet and Irish potatoes.   Each family may easily raise cotton enough for its own use.   The hills afford a plentiful supply of oak timber suitable for ship building, and the county is rich in fossil productions.   There is a salt lick on Drennon's creek, 25 miles from the Ohio, at which salt has occasionally been made, and it is believed by many, that by proper management the whole state could be supplied with that necessary article from these works alone.   Lead ore is found near the lick ; and about three miles higher up the creek is a medicinal springs much frequented by the inhabitants in summer.   The grass fed beef of this county is said to possess a superior flavor, owing chiefly, it is supposed, to the many sulphurous licks on almost every little water course.   The tobacco crop for exportation in favorable seasons has exceeded 300 hogsheads.

Louisville—The chief town of Jefferson county, stands on an inclined plain, about one quarter of a mile above the Falls of Ohio.   The three principal streets run parallel with the river, and the view of the rapids, the opposite shore, Jeffersonville, Clarksville, and Silver Creek hills, is very fine.   For several years succeeding the first settlement of the town, the inhabitants were annually visited by agues and bilious fevers, but latterly, these disorders have in a measure disappeared. Louisville is at present in a state of rapid growth and im-

provement and nearly equals Cincinnati and Lexington in
size and beauty. It has many public buildings, several rope-
walks, manufactories—two printing offices, bookstore, &c. It
is 706 miles, by the windings of the Ohio, below Pittsburgh,
40 W. of Frankfort, and 481 above the mouth of the Ohio;
in north lat. 38 15. Beargrass creek enters the river at the
upper end of the town and affords a good harbor for boats.
Building lots are high; more houses were built last summer,
than during any season since the town was commenced. The
boards, plank and shingles used, are mostly brought in rafts
from the mills of Allegany county, in the state of New York.
The buildings extend from the mouth of Beargrass down the
Ohio to opposite the lower end of Corn Island, a distance of
upwards one mile; boats can lie with perfect safety at any
point of the shore, from the mouth of the creek to the middle
of the island, the river being deep, with little or no current in
the bend of the river abreast the town. The eminence on
which the town stands is seventy feet in height, and gently
descends to a narrow plain along the bank of the river—it is
along this plain that the contemplated canal, on the Kentucky
side of the rapids, is proposed to be cut; it is to commence a
little below the mouth of Beargrass creek, and discharge itself
below Shippingport, a distance of one mile and three quarters
and twenty-eight perches. The legislature of Kentucky have
incorporated a company for opening this canal. Mr. L. Bald-
win, an able engineer was employed in the winter of 1816, to
survey the ground; he bored through the various strata along
the route, and estimated the expence of a permanent canal
for keels or other vessels of 30 tons at $ 240,000. It is said that
a canal, sufficiently capacious for a vessel of 400 tons burthen,
could be opened by digging to the average depth of 20 feet
an 6 inches —the soil is generally a stiff clay, upon a bed of
limestone rock, which no where rises more than three feet and
a half above the floor of the canal. It is the opinion of many
that the completion of the proposed canal, on a scale large
enough to admit vessels of 3 or 400 tons burthen, would mate-

rially check the future growth of Louisville; but I can see no just reason for concurring in this belief—the canal will augment rather than diminish the already extensive business of this town; and the principal pillars of her prosperity is found in the great fertile district between Kentucky and Salt rivers. Jefferson county is bounded north and west by the Ohio, east by Bullitt and south by Nelson. It is one of the most populous counties in the state, of a rich soil and watered by creeks running into the Ohio and Salt rivers.

Shippingport—Is situated at the foot of the rapids, and about two miles below the mouth of Beargrass. Boats, which pass the rapids through the Kentucky channel generally stop here. Mr. Berthoud has a convenient shipyard and Mr. Terrasson one of the finest ropewalks in the United States, being twelve hundred and fifty feet long. A little above the harbor is a mill turned by the Ohio, by means of a race.

Russellsville, the chief town of Logan county, is nearly equidistant from Green and Cumberland rivers, or 35 miles from both. Red river approaches it within 15 miles on the south, and Muddy river a branch of Green, on the north, within 25 miles. Each of those rivers are navigable in freshes for large boats into Green and Cumberland rivers. This town contains upwards of 150 houses—it has a court house, college, a branch of the Kentucky bank, meeting-house, two printing presses, &c. It is 180 miles S. W. of Frankfort, and 85 S. of Louisville. Logan county is bounded N. by Ohio county, N. W. by Muhlenburgh, W. by Christian, E. by Warren, and S. by Tennessee. On the south it is watered by the auxiliary streams of Red river, and north by those that fall into Green river. There are a great number of grist and saw mills in this county and fine sites for the erection of water-works. There are several salt licks in the vicinity of Russellsville. To the north of this town the land is covered with a very heavy timber—to the south, barrens, or open prairie country: this strip is about 15 miles wide and extends from east to west 90 miles. These prairies are rich, finely watered, and adorned

O

with islets or intersected by groves of timber sufficient to maintain an immense population.   A vineyard has been planted two miles from Russellville, by a society organized for that purpose.   Cotton is raised for exportation, and wheat for domestic use.

Bairdstown,—The capital of Nelson county, is situated on the east side or Beech Fork, one of the principal branches of Salt river.   It contains nearly 200 houses, a stone courthouse and jail, church, market house, &c.   It is 35 miles south of Frankfort—and in north lat. 36 49.   Nelson county is bounded north by Shelby, north west by Bullitt, west by Hardin, east by Mercer, south east by Lincoln and south by Greene. This county is watered by the head waters of Salt and Green rivers.   It contains some good and much poor land.

Henderson—the county town of Henderson county, stands on the *red bank* of the Ohio, 75 miles below Louisville. The houses are principally built of logs, and its appearance is dull, but it enjoys a considerable share of the Orleans trade ; five hundred hogsheads of tobacco have been shipped at this place in a single year.   Henderson county is bounded north by the Ohio, east by Green and Muddy rivers, which separate it from Ohio and Muhlenburgh counties, west by Tradewater river which divides it from Livingston county, and west by Christian.   The staple of this county is tobacco ; but cotton is raised in considerable quantities.

Vangeville,—A *log city,* at the mouth of Salt Lick Creek, 36 miles above Maysville, has fifteen or twenty old log houses, situated near the margin of the Ohio, on low ground, subject to frequent inundation.   The water of this Saline is not very strong—yielding only one bushel of salt from 300 gallons of water.   The inhabitants have had as many as 200 kettles in operation.   It is thought that if the wells were sunk to a proper depth, water of a superior quality might be procured in abundance.   Yet owing to the cheapness of the Kanhawey salt, and the proximity of those works, it will probably be many years before the trial will be made.

EXTENT OF NAVIGABLE WATERS.

	Miles.
The Ohio navigable on the northern frontier, .	500
Mississippi, ...	75
Tennessee, ...	100
Cumberland and its branches, ...	700
Trade water, ...	60
Green river and forks, ...	350
Salt river, ...	150
Kentucky, ...	230
Licking, ...	100
Big Sandy, ...	60

Total, 2325,

ANTIQUITIES.

Ancient fortifications and mounds are found in Kentucky, and in almost every county. The only work of this kind which I have particularly examined, is situated on the second bottom of the Ohio, nearly opposite the mouth of the Big Scioto river. It is evidently the remains of a military posisition of great strength. It is about half a mile from the river. The walls, which are of earth, are yet standing; and enclose, as nearly as I could ascertain by pacing, fourteen acres of ground. It is of a square form. The officious hand of civilized man has not yet marred the woods which shade these venerable ruins; nor has any curious antiquary mutilated the walls, by digging in quest of hidden treasure. Time appears to have been their only enemy; and he seems in this instance, not to have manifested his usual rage for obliiteration. The walls are in many places sixteen feet high, and no where less than eight; they are about thirty feet wide at the base, and wide enough on the top to admit a horse team and

waggon.   There are seven gateways, three on the west, two
on the east, and two on the north; they are all about 29 feet
wide ; from the north west angle the ruins of a covered way,
extend to a creek which runs on the west side of the fort,
at the distance of 280 yards—the covering has fallen in, and
large trees are growing in the ditch, but the course can be distinctly traced, and no one in the least acquainted with military affairs, can hesitate for a moment to pronounce it the remains of a covered way.   From the west side of the fort are
two parallel walls, thirty feet apart, reaching to the creek,
which is there 220 yards distant.   These walls are as wide
and as high as the walls of the fort ; they appear to have been
carried to the bank of the creek, where they abruptly terminate.   There is no appearance of a head work beyond the
creek, to protect the water carriers ; but this defect was
probably supplied by strong *pickets.*   Another creek or run,
approaches within 150 yards on the east side of the fort, and
two parallel walls run from the fort to this stream, which also
is not defended by a head work.   Thus the garrison of this
ancient fortification had three avenues through which they
could safely procure water.   There are two large mounds a
few rods south of the fort.   The timber growing in and around
these works, consists of white oak, hickory, sugar maple and
beech ; many of the trees are very large, and these perhaps,
the third generation since the construction of the fort.

Travellers assert that several hundred mummies were discovered near Lexington in a cave, but which have been wholly despoiled by the first settlers.   Dr. Cutler, who has accu-
rately examined the trees on some old forts near the mouth of
Kentucky river, thinks from their appearances that they are
the *second* growth, and the fortifications " must have been
built upwards of one thousand years.   One fact is also clear ;
they must have been the efforts of a people acquainted with
some science, and capable of infinite labor ; and it is difficult
to conceive how they could be constructed without the use of
iron tools and the instruments we are compelled to employ in

works of much less magnitude and character.   At a small distance from each foot there stands a mound of earth thrown up
in the manner of a pyramid."

THE RANGE.

The reed cane, an evergreen, which in the first settlement,
of the state covered the country on all the rich lands from
Big Sandy to the Tennessee frontier, and which constitute
the principal food for horses and cattle in winter, has of late
years almost entirely disappeared.   But a still more valuable
succedaneum has sprung up in its stead, so that the woods
and commons in the best counties afford a rich and luxuriant
pasturage.   This is a short, nutritious grass called "nimble
will," which has completely overspread with astonishing celerity, almost every spot of waste or uncultivated ground.
The inhabitants affirm that the range is now better for horses
and cattle, than it was when the country was in a state of
nature.

DOMESTIC ANIMALS.

The horse, " noble and generous," is the favorite animal of
the Kentuckians, by whom he is pampered with unceasing attention.   Every person of wealth has from ten to thirty of
good size and condition; and upon which he lavishes his corn
with a wasteful profusion.   A common work horse is worth
$50, and a genteel saddle horse $100.   *Cattle* are raised in
great numbers in every part of the state; large droves are
annually bought up for the new Territories, and for the and
atlantic markets—oxen are very little used on the farm;
and are mostly reared for the *drovers*.   A large sized ox can
be purchased or 25 dollars; and a cow for ten and twelve
dollars.   Sheep have multiplied greatly since the *Merino*

mania of 1810.   Hogs are raised with great ease, and in vast numbers, on the oak and chesnut lands in the southern counties.   I have myself seen several farmers, who owned between two and three hundred.

POULTRY, WILD FOWL, GAME.

The farm yards swarm with domestic fowls, and hens lay and sit in winter as well as in spring and summer; they can be multiplied to almost any number and with a trifling expence. The quail is the most common of the feathered tribe—they are to be seen at every step, singly and in flocks.   Wild turkies are still numerous in the unsettled parts.   The robin of the northern states is almost a stranger in Kentucky and Tennessee.   Bear, deer, wolves and foxes are numerous in the eastern and southern counties.   Rabits and grey squirrels are very plentiful in the settlements.

NATURAL CURIOSITIES.

These are numerous and are to be found in almost every county in the state—they chiefly consist of *caves, sinks,* and *precipices*—Many of the most remarkable caves hitherto discovered, have been minutely described in our newspapers and geographical publications; they are a source of neverending wealth to their owners.   The earth which they contain is so strongly impregnated with nitre that the inhabitants often obtain from 100 lbs. of it, 50 lbs. of saltpetre ; and if returned to the caves after leaching, it will in a few years regain its original strength.   The richest counties in this article of commerce are Barren, Rockcastle, Montgomery, Knox, Estle, Warren, Cumberland, and Wayne; the last has produced from 50, to 70,000 lbs. a year.   The returns of 1810 for the state gave 201,937 lbs.   But during the war the quantity of saltpetre made exceeded 400,000 lbs. a year; and the amount of gunpowder manufactured for the last five years, will average 300,000 lbs. annually.

The precipices formed by the Kentucky are in many places awfully sublime—presenting perpendicular banks of 300 feet, solid limestone, surmounted with a steep and difficult ascent four times as high.   It is by descending this river from the mouth of Hickman Creek, to Port William, that one is enabled to form something like an adequate idea of the depth and extent of the immense calcareous rock upon which rests the soil of Kentucky.   To the geologist, these stupendous piles exhibit a most interesting spectacle of contemplation ; for it is here that nature has laid bare the very bowels of the earth.

The banks of Cumberland river are less precipitous, but its bed is equally depressed below the surface of the surrounding country.   The descent from the hills to the bottoms is abrupt, and the traveller sees with wonder alternate strata of limestone rock and earth, both from one to ten feet thick.   I counted at Coffee's ferry, in Wayne county, as I descended the hill, *sixteen* distinct layers of this rock, the aggregate thickness of which was 485 feet ; and the intermediate earth was collectively much thicker.   Surprising as it may seem, the lower strata of earth contained *pebbles* and *cylindrical* stones, smoothed by the action of water.   I leave it to philosophy, to explain *how* they came there, or rather what convulsion or revolution of nature has buried them beneath such an accumulation of sand and lime stone   They have apparently been entombed by the progressive growth of the earth.

SPECULATION.

The monster *speculation*, has fixed his eager grasp on some of the best tracts of land, to the great injury of the state, and with flagrant injustice to the poor.   I must confess

I felt indignant, when, after passing an extensive and fertile tract of beautiful land, of many thousand acres, and surrounded by rich and flourishing settlements, I enquired the cause why it was not *settled*, and received for answer, that it belonged to a rich gentleman in Virginia, or to some other opulent, non-resident land-jobber, who would not sell it for less than $ 80 dollars an acre. One often meets with these waste tracts in Kentucky, and the western counties of Virginia; and the evil is felt in Ohio, Pennsylvania, and New York, to the disgrace of our legislation, which grants every facility to the rich, without consulting the interests of the poor.

BANK CAPITAL, MANUFACTURES.

The *Bank of Kentucky* the only one in the state is established at Frankfort, with branches at Washington, Paris, Lexington, Dansville, Russellsville, Bairdstown, and Louisville.

Its capital stock is	-	$ 2,077,750 10
Debts due,	-	4,087,740 87
Deposits in cash,	-	1,864,326 11
Notes in circulation,	-	1,877,557 83
Cash on hand,	-	1,233,148 64

The notes of this bank are in excellent credit, but bills from the neighboring states, particularly those of Ohio, have a free and extensive circulation.

There are no data by which to determine the annual amount of manufactures. The returns of 1810 gave $ 6,182,010— since which they have probably doubled. They consist of cloths and stuffs, bagging for cotton and hemp, iron, castings, nails, earthenware, glass, leather, cordage, paper, distilled spirits, oil, salt, saltpetre, gunpowder, and maple sugar. There are about 60 rope walks, 7 paper mills, 5 furnaces, upwards of 20 powder mills. Between 2 and 300 bushels of salt are yearly made at the different licks. Almost every plantation has a sugar camp. The sap is sweeter than that produced from the sugar trees in the northern states ; besides, the quantity is actually greater from trees of the same diameter. The maple of Kentucky is a short, thrifty-looking tree, with numerous limbs and branches. The quantity of maple sugar annually produced in the state, is supposed to exceed two millions of pounds.

DWELLING HOUSES.

In the new settlements, the inhabitants uniformly live in log cabins, the logs being laid up round or hewn, according to the taste or convenience of the builder. In the old settlements of the rich counties, *log houses* have nearly disappeared, and stone, brick, or frame houses of good size and appearance have arisen in their places ; the first are most in vogue, but no matter what the material, the *chimney* is sure to be placed *out doors*.

CHARACTER, MANNERS, RELIGION.

It is almost superfluous to say that the Kentuckians are generally brave, patriotic, and hospitable. Their courage and love of country have been evinced in the marshes of Louisiana, in the wilds of Indiana, on the borders of Canada, and by the alacrity with which 20,000 volunteers, repaired to remote scenes of danger, during the late war. The godlike virtue of hospitality is still cherished by all classes, as well by those living on public roads, as by those resident in retired situations, and the stranger of decent deportment, is sure to find a cordial welcome at the firesides of private dwellings.

To reverse the picture, the rich hold labor in contempt, and frequently make the possession of slaves a criterion of merit; that is, most farmers, would make a marked distinction between two young gentlemen, one possessing slaves, the other

P

not, but equal in point of property, personal accomplishments, and moral endowment, who should pay their addresses to his daughter; the suit of the slaveholder would be favorably received, while that of his rival would be disdainfully rejected.

The climate of Kentucky, judging from the appearance of the inhabitants, must be highly favorable to the growth of the human species : they are well formed—have fine complexions, and teeth very little liable to decay. Their dispositions may be pronounced cheerful, and suicides are much less frequent than in the northern states. Coffee is a favorite beverage. Luxury begins to show herself on their tables, and in their best rooms.

Baptists, Methodists, Presbyterians and Seceders, are the prevailing sects ; they manifest a spirit of harmony and liberality towards each other ; and whatever may have been said to the contrary, it is a solemn truth, that religion is no where more respected, than in Kentucky. I last summer traversed the whole state ; and I had previously at two different periods passed from its southern to its northern frontiers ; and from my own observation can speak with confidence. In many places the inhabitants are not satisfied to attend divine worship on Sundays only, but meet in conference three times a week. In May 1816, five miles north of Harrodsburgh, I saw the greatest religious assemblage I ever witnessed. Our camp meetings in New-York bear no comparison to it in point of numbers. The day was favourable ; the minister stood on a scaffolding erected for the occasion, in the centre of a handsome woods free from brush or logs, the hearers to the number, as I judged, of at least 10,000, stood in concentric circles around the orator. The number of horses and carriages was absolutely incredible ; and I do not enlarge, when I say that they literally covered twenty acres of ground.

The Reverend Elijah Parish, whose book can be found in most of our *schools*, is very incorrect and unjust, when he says, " A large portion of the people are poor, and in a low state of society ; idleness and dissipation having been very prevalent, the frontier inhabitants commonly build a hut of logs, clear two or three acres for corn, depend on the woods for the pasture of one or two cows and to fatten a number of swine; the gun furnishes them with most of their meat. When the range, as they call it, is eaten up by the cattle, and the game scarce, like wild Arabs, they load their pack horses, take their families, cows, and swine, and seek a new settlement in the bosom of the forest."

HISTORY.

Kentucky remained unnoticed by the whites until 1766, " when John Finley, an Indian trader, travelled through it, and on his return to North-Carolina, represented to Colonel Boon, the beauty, and fertility of the country. In 1769, they, in company with some others, agreed to travel there, and explore it more fully ; but were unfortunately plundered, killed, and dispersed, except Colonel Boon, who remained a solitary inhabitant of the wilderness, until 1771, when he returned to his family on Yadkin river. In 1773 he finally resolved to take out his family, but was prevented on the way by the hostility of the Indians, until 1775, when he and his family, with 5 other families, that were joined by 40 men from Powell's valley, arrived on the banks of Kentucky river, and erected a fort, which they named Boonsborough; and so rapid has been the population since, that it was erected into an independent state by an act of Congress, Dec. 6th, 1790, and taken into the union two years after."

LOUISIANA

IS situated between 29 and 33 N. latitude, and is bounded north and west by the Missouri Territory, south by the Gulf of Mexico, and east by the Mississippi Territory. Its boundaries are thus defined by law: "Beginning at the mouth of the river Sabine; thence by line, to be drawn along the middle of said river, including all islands to the thirty-second degree of latitude; thence due north, to the northern-most part of the thirty-third degree of north latitude; thence along the said parallel of latitude, to the river Mississippi; thence down the said river to the river Iberville, and from thence along the middle of the said river and lakes Maurepas and Ponchartrain, to the gulph of Mexico; thence bounded by the said gulph to the place of beginning, including all islands within three leagues of the coast." By a subsequent law of congress, that part of West Florida, lying between the rivers Mississippi, Iberville and Pearl, and the 31st degree of north latitude, containing about 6,000,400 acres, has been annexed to Louisiana.

RIVERS.

The rivers of this state empty themselves into the gulf of Mexico, the Mississippi and lake Ponchartrain.

Pearl river heads in the Choctaw country, near lat. 33 N. and pursues a S. W. course for 60 miles, thence east 150 miles until it falls into lake Borgne, a little to the east of lake Ponchartrain.—It is said to be navigable 150 miles—it has 7 feet water at its entrance, but deepens at the distance of two miles from the lake; but the navigation is at present obstructed by logs and drift wood.—It flows through a fertile district, and separates Louisiana from the Mississippi territory.

Chefuncti, a small river, having its source near the parallel of 31 N. falls into lake Pouchartrain at Madisonville; it is boatable thirty miles: the *Pongipaho*, another small river runs nearly parellel with the Chefuncti, and enters the lake about ten miles further west. The bayous Castain, Lacombe, and Boucfouca are also tributaries of this Lake.

Amite river, heads in the Misssissippi territory, a little north of lat. 31, and runs south into the river Iberville.—It is navigable for boats and canoes nearly to its head. The road from Madisonville to Natchez crosses its head branches: the *Ticfah*, 35 miles long, heads to the east of the Amite, and runs south into lake Maurepas.

Iberville river, is properly one of the *decharges* of the Mississippi; it leaves the Mississippi 20 miles below Baton Rouge, and runs east into lake Maurepas. It is only about three months in a year that it is navigable, and then by vessels drawing less than three feet water; and is perfectly dry during the remainder of the year, from the Mississippi to the entrance of the Amite, a distance of twenty miles.

The *Mississippi* waters the eastern frontier of Louisiana, from lat. 33 to 31, where it enters the state through which it passes, by various channels, into the gulf of Mexico. The distance from lat. 31 to the Balize or mouth of the main branch of this river, is 354 miles.

The Bayous which leave the Mississippi and fall into the gulf of Mexico to the west of the Balize, are:

Bayou Atchafalaya, leaves the river three miles below the mouth of Red river, and enters the gulf near Vermillion bay. It is large, but rendered unnavigable by an immense floating bridge, or raft across it, formed by the gradual accumulation of drift wood. It is many leagues in length, and so firm and compact in some places, that cattle and horses are driven over it. It is the opinion of some travellers, that this bayou was anciently the only passage of the Mississippi to the sea; but Schultz has suggested a more probable hypothesis, which is, that it was formerly a continuation of Red river. The water which descends this channel passes under the bridge, and in many places may be seen whirling through small holes and crevices, and at last rushes forth with considerable violence. In times of inundation small boats can pass the bridge by keeping on the flats. Large boats drawn into the vortex of this Bayou, find it difficult to regain the Mississippi.

Bayou Placquemine, leaves the Mississippi eight miles below the outlet of the Iberville on the opposite shore, and communicates with the gulf, through Freshwater bay, Atchafalaya and La Fourche; it is about 70 yards wide, and navigable for boats.

Bayou La Fourche, leaves the Mississippi thirty-two miles below Bayou Placquermine, and communicates with the gulf by two mouths a short distance to the west of lake Wachas. In the old French maps this stream is called La Riveire des Catamaches. It is navigable at certain seasons for vessels of sixty tons burthen.

In addition to the above, numerous short bayous, canals and passes, leave the main branch of the Mississippi, between the outlet of La Fourche and the Balize.

Bayou Sara and *Thompson's Creek*, water the Feliciana district, between Baton Rouge and fort Adams. They are about forty miles long, and sixty yards wide at their mouths— they run parallel with each other and enter the Mississippi twelve miles apart; the first a little above point Coupee, and the last seven miles below.

The small rivers, *Teche, Vermillion, Mermanto,* and *Calcasu*, water the *Attacapas* and *Opelousas* countries, and fall into the gulf between Atchafalaya and the mouth of the *Sabine.*

The *Sabine* forms the boundary between Louisiana and the Spanish province of Texas—enters the gulf 250 miles west of the Balize, and is navigable 280 miles. About 35 miles from its mouth and a little above the Sabine lake it receives the river *Natchez.*

Red river rises in Mexico, near the sources of Rio del Norte, and meanders in a south-eastern direction from the north-west corner of the state to the Mississippi, which it enters in N. lat. 31, 5, and where it is 400 yards wide. Its waters are brackish, of a redish color, tinged by the red soil of its banks high up the river. It is navigable 1500 miles, and although never departing but a few miles from the line of its general course, is nevertheless crooked. The banks are overflowed in spring to a great extent, and in some places to the depth of ten or fifteen feet. The *Rapide* 135 miles from its mouth is impassible in dry seasons with loaded boats. This rapid is occasioned by a ledge of soft rock, which crosses the river. This rock is soft, and of the consistence of pipe clay ; so that the obstructions could be easily removed.

Its bottoms, or rather prairies, are wide and rich. Thirty miles from its mouth it receives Black river, a large and navigable stream which winds 200 miles through the state, nearly equidistant between the Mississippi and Red river. This river branches 50 miles from its mouth into the Barchelet and Washita forks. The north fork of Red river is a considerable stream, and joins the main branch about one hundred miles above the entrance of Black river.

The Dacheet and Saline are the most remarkable branches of Red river proper. The first waters a great range of rich soil, which forms the north-west angle of Louisiana. The Saline is a valuable salt flat, from which any quantity of that mineral could be produced, that the population of the state could require.

About three hundred miles above Natchitoches, the navigation of this river is totally obstructed by rafts or coverings of driftwood, at intervals, for seventeen leagues, and so exactly do these bridges resemble the common bottoms, in soil, brushwood, and trees, that the traveller could cross them, unconscious of their existence. Towards its head its current narrows to the width of a small creek, in consequence of the rocks and precipices, which prevent its expansion.

Black river is large and winding—its course is nearly parellel with the Mississippi, at the distance of about 40 miles;

the name of Black river, at the distance of 60 miles is changed, and is then called the Washita river; here its course
bends to the westward.   The Washita receives the Tensaw
from the east, and the Occatohoola from the west at the same
place.   In 1799, the fish of Black river perished in consequence of the stagnation of its waters, caused by an inundation
of the Mississippi.

LAKES.

The chain of lakes which wash the eastern side of the island
of New-Orleans, consist of Maurepas, Ponchartrain, and
Borgne.   Lake *Maurepas* lies about 20 miles north of New-
Orleans, and is twelve miles long and eight wide.   It receives
and discharges the river Amite and the little river of Ticfah,
nine miles further east is lake Ponchartrain, which lies immediately behind the city of New Orleans.   It is about 35 miles
long and 25 wide, and generally from ten to fifteen feet
deep.

This lake receives the little rivers Pongipaho and Chefuncti, as well as the bayous Castain, Lacombe, and Boucfouca. Lake Borgne lies still further east, but by a deep bay approaches to within a few miles of the Mississippi, with which
it communicates by means of a bayou and Vilere's canal.   It
was by this route that the British approached to the banks of
the Mississippi in the winter of 1814.   The margins of all
these lakes are in most places low and marshey.   Lake Wachas lies to the west of the Mississippi, and 22 miles from
New-Orleans.   It is 23 miles long and six miles wide, and
communicates with the gulf by several outlets. *Colcasu* lake
lies near the mouth of the river of the same name, and is 35
miles in circumference, 40 miles below Natchitoches is lake
Occasse; and near this town are two large lakes, one a mile,
and the other six miles distant.   One of these lakes is 30 and
the other 50 miles in circumference—they communicate with
Red river by means of bayous.   When the river is high the

water flows back into the lakes. " The immense number of fowl which abound in these lakes, during the winter, almost exceeds credibility. The air is darkened with the large flights, especially near the close of the day ; and the ear almost stunned with the noise they make. One man may kill many hundreds in an afternoon. The hunter takes his station on a convenient spot, and loads and fires as fast as possible, without taking particular aim, until he finds he has killed a sufficient number to load his horses. These fowl are swan, geese, brant, and several species of ducks. In the summer, several kinds of fish are said to be equally plenty. The Indians, in taking fish, frequent'y make use only of the bow and arrow. With this instrument an Indian will often load his horse in a very short time. The fish consist principally of the cat, pike, buffalo, sucker, and white and black perch, and are generally of a very large size."

Lake Noiz lies ten miles above Natchitoches, and is 50 miles in circumference. It discharges its waters into the bayou Rigula de Bondieu, a tributary of Red river, which comes in three miles above Natchitoches. All the salt used by the inhabitants of the Red river settlements, is made near lake Noiz. The water is so highly impregnated with salt as to require very little boiling. The conveyance of the salt to market is easy, as the outlet of the lake is navigable for boats most of the year. Eight miles farther up, is *Spanish* lake. also about 50 miles in circumference, which rises and falls with the river. Above this, at the distance of twenty leagues is Lake *Bistineau*, sixty miles long, extending parallel with the river, at the distance of from three to fifteen miles. This lake is situated opposite of the driftwood raft, and has *double outlets*, called the Bayou *Channa*, and the Bayou *Dacheet.* It receives numerous tributary streams.

Sabine lake is twenty-five miles long and twelve wide—it receives and discharges the river of the same name ; and lies about twelve miles from the gulf. Cattahoola lake near the mouth of Washita, is a pleasant body of water, 40 miles in circumference. Barataria lake lies west of the Balize.

Q

EXTENT, SURFACE, SOIL, ISLANDS.

Louisiana is 300 miles in length, from east to west, and 240 miles broad from north to south, having an area of 41,000 square miles, or 26,240,000 acres. Its surface is champaign from the gulf of Mexico, to Baton Rouge, and Red river, which includes a vast alluvial tract extending from lake *Borgne* to the *Sabine*, 250 miles long, and from 70 to 140 miles wide. This extensive district is intersected by numerous rivers, bayous, creeks, lagoons and lakes, dividing the country into a great number of islands, very unequal in size and figure. The island of New-Orleans, formed by the Iberville and lakes on the east, and the Mississippi on the west, is 150 in length, and those formed by the bayous La Fouche, Placquemine, and Atchafalaya, are very large. The country about the Balize for 30 miles, is one continued swamp, destitute of trees, and covered with a coarse species of reeds four or five feet high. Nothing can be more dreary than the prospect from a ship's mast head while passing this immense Sabornœian waste, where the eye gains no relief, but ranges over a boundless horizon of pestilential marsh.

The soil gradually becomes firmer as we ascend the streams; all of which have narrow strips of rich tillable land, from half a mile to a mile and a half wide ; but these bottoms uniformly incline from the Mississippi and its bayous; consequently, where they overflow their banks the waters recede to the low grounds in the rear of the bottoms, where they either stagnate and thereby perpetuate the empire of swamps, or form for themselves distinct channels to the gulf—hence the origin of the numerous bayous. This country, therefore, instead of having dividing ridges between the streams, has a surface considerably depressed below the level of the river banks, to receive the superabundant waters.

The country between the Mississippi, Iberville and Pearl rivers, and N. lat. 31, is an important part of the state ; the southern half of this extensive district is a level, fine country ; yet highly productive, for cotton, sugar, rice, corn and indigo.   The banks of all the streams are low, and the current of the water sluggish ; and good springs are scarce ; but from Baton Rouge to Pinckneyville, about 50 miles in a direct line, the country presents an undulating surface, and covered with a heavy growth of timber, consisting of white, red and yellow oak, hickory, black walnut, sassafras, magnolia and poplar. The district of Feliciana is considered by many as the garden of Louisiana.   Planters residing on Bayou Sara and Thompson's creek, and in the rear of Baton Rouge, are very rich—some of them have as many as 600 acres of land in a state of cultivation.   The cotton raised here is of superior quality ; and the culture of the sugar cane has been introduced.   The hills, in a state of nature, are covered by thickets of reed cane, of the most luxuriant growth.   A New-England farmer can hardly form an adequate idea of the wealth of these planters.

Their plantations consist of from three hundred to one thousand acres ; and some of the most opulent frequently have 300 acres of cotton in one field.   They all have slaves, and some as many as 300.   The soil is of the richest kind, similar in quality and appearance to the best lands of Kentucky, but the hilly parts are more liable to be washed and gullied by heavy rains.   Between Thompson's creek and Baton Rouge there is a rich savanna six miles long and one wide, bordered alternantely by woods and plantations.   All the creeks which enter the Mississippi above Baton Rouge are liable to be suddenly swelled to the size of rivers during heavy showers.   The tract of country between the old demarkation line and Thompson's creek, is watered by bayou Sara, and its tributary streams.

At the distance of 20 miles from Baton Rouge to the east, the fine lands commence, and forming a barrier between the white settlements and the Choctaw nation, extend to Pearl river.   These lands are the most healthful for settlements of any in Louisiana. They have a pretty undulating surface ; and although the soil is light and sandy, is highly product-ive.

Bartram's description of the soil of an island at the mouth of Pearl river, will answer for a considerable district border-ing the Iberville, lakes Maurepas, Ponchartrain and Borgne, and Pearl river.

" The interior and by far the greatest part of the island, consists of high land ; the soil to appearance a heap of sea sand in some places, with an admixture of sea shells, this soil, notwithstanding its sandy and sterile appearance, when di-vested of its natural vegetative attire, has, from what cause I know not, a continual resource of fertility within itself ; the surface of the earth, after being cleared of its original veget-able productions, exposed a few seasons to the sun, winds and triturations of agriculture, appears scarcely any thing but heaps of white sand, yet it produces corn, indigo, batatas, beans, peas, cotton, tobacco, and almost every sort of escu-lent vegetable, in a degree of luxuriancy very surprising and unexpected, year after year, incessantly, without any addi-tion of artificial manure or compost ; there is, indeed a foun-dation of strong adhesive clay, consisting of strata of various colours, which I discovered by examining a well, lately dug in Mr. Rumsey's yard ; but its lying at a great depth under the surface, the roots of small shrubs and herbage, cannot reach near to it, or receive any benefit unless we may sup-pose, that ascending fumes or exhalations, from this bed of clay, may have a vivific, nutritrive quality, and be received by the fibres of the roots, or being condensed in the atmos-phere by nocturnal chills, fall with dews upon the leaves and twigs of these plants, and there absorbed, become nutritive or exhilerating to them."

As an instance of the salubrity of the atmosphere on this island, Mr. Bartram observes, " The French gentleman (proprietor of the plantation) was near eighty years old, his hair almost white with age, yet he appeared active, strong and muscular, and his mother who was present, was one hundred and five years old, active and cheerful, her eyes seemed as brisk and sparkling as youth, but of a diminutive size, not half the stature and weight of her son ; it was now above fifty years since she came into America from old France."

The northern coasts of the lakes Maurepas, Ponchartrain and Borgne, are generally dry and healthful; the land east and west of Madisonville, along the borders of the lakes is a sandy plain, extending in some places twenty miles from their shores, and nearly as level as the ocean, which appears to have receded from it. The bottoms of these lakes are even and sandy, and appear to be a continuation of the great inclined plane between the Mississippi and Pearl rivers. The southern banks are low and marshy. Madisonville is handsomely situated on the right bank of the Chefuncti, two miles above its entrance into lake Ponchartrain, and about 26 miles south east of New Orleans. This place has not yet attained much importance in point of wealth and population, but is unquestionably destined to become a great commercial city. It is favorably situated for the coasting and West India trades, having about two days sail in going out, and about two weeks in coming in, the advantage of New Orleans. It lies more convenient for the necessary supplies and materials for repairing and building vessels, and such are the local advantages of this place, that government have fixed on the site of a navy yard near the mouth of the Chefuncti, where the keel of a light frigate was laid down in 1812, intended for the defence of the lakes. It is believed to be a more healthful situation, and less infected with musquetoes, than New Orleans. The wild lands are finely timbered with pine, live oak, cypress, magnolia, plum, gum, bay, cottonwood, ash, willow, and occasionally impervious cane brakes. These cane brakes are sometimes improperly called *swamps*, but the reed cane is never found on wet, marshy ground, always grows in a rich, deep, dry soil. The pine timber is remarkably tall and strait, with trunks from 70 to 80 feet high before coming to the limbs. The pine of Louisiana and Florida, is more sappy and yields more turpentine than the pine of the north ; and a considerable part of the inhabitants gain a livelihood by making tar and pitch, which they sell at New-Orleans. The vast forests of pine between lake Ponchartrain and the Choctaw territory, will furnish an inexhaustible supply of these articles for a century to come. The beach of the lakes are lined with a species of muscle shells, called by the French *des coquilles,* from which lime of the best quality is produced. The fish of the lakes and rivers, and the game of the forests, is plentiful but inferior in quality. The soil is found to be highly favorable to corn, cotton, sugar, indigo, rice, sweet potatoes, pumkins, plums, cherries, figs, peaches, grape vines, and most kinds of garden vegetables. Sugar plantations are becoming numerous ; and the settlements extending. The country above Madison-ville, is peculiarly adapted to the rearing of hogs and cattle ; for they neither require salt, nor attention in winter ; and no where in the United States are they raised in greater numbers than in the district under review ; the reed cane, and the grass of the prairies constitute their principal food. The most natural grass of this country is of a very harsh nature, and the cattle not at all fond of it. It is known by the name of wire grass, and they only eat it while young. For the procuring it young, or renewing this kind of pasture, the woods are frequently fired, and at different seasons, in order to have a succession of young grass, but the savannas that are interspersed in this kind of land furnish a more plenti-ful and more proper food for the cattle.

"Some high pine hills are so covered with two or three varieties of the oak, as to make an underwood to the lofty pines ; and a species of dwarf chesnut grows here ; another species, of a larger growth, is also found in the lower parts, particularly in the edges of the bay or cypress galls.

"The sandy and most sterile soil, in wet seasons, bears many things far beyond expectation, and is very useful for the cultivation of peach and mulberry orchards. This land might also be rendered useful for many other purposes ; but either the people do not choose to go out of the old beaten track, or content themselves with looking elsewhere for new land, improveable with less cost. The method of meliorating it, is certainly obvious to the meanest capacity, as it every where, at a greater or less depth, covers a stiff marly kind of clay, which I am certain, was it properly mixed with the land, would render it fertile ; and this might be done with little expence, the clay lying in some places, within half a foot of the surface : in most places it is found at the depth of three, four, or five feet, consequently not very hard to come at. This land is also frequently found rocky, with an iron stone, especially near where the pines are found growing in a gravelly tract, which is frequently the case.

" The hammock land, so called from its appearing in tufts among the lofty pines : some small spots of this kind, if seen at a distance, have a very romantic appearance. The large parcels of it often divide swamps, creeks, or rivers from the pine land ; this is indeed its most common situation. The whole of the uplands, remote from the sea in the northern parts, is this kind of land : its soil is various, in some places a sand of divers colours ; but the hammock soil is a mixture of clay and a blackish sand, and in some spots a kind of ochre. On every kind of this land lies a stratum of black mould, made by decayed leaves, &c. of the wood and other plants growing upon it. The salts contained in this stratum render it very fruitful, and, when cleared, this is the best, nay, the only fit land, for the production of indigo, potatoes, and pulse ; the first crops, by means of the manure abovementioned, generally are very plentiful ; but the salts being soon evaporated, if the soil over which it lay should prove to be sand, it is not better than pine land ; the other sort bears many years planting : its natural produce is so various in this climate, that the complete description of all would be more work than one man's life-time would be sufficient for."

Pearl river, like the Mississippi, has its bayous, and enters lake Borgne through various channels. The swamps skirting this river for eight or ten miles from its mouths, are too subject to inundation to admit of extensive settlements, until protected by levees, when the banks of its channels will no doubt present flourishing sugar and cotton plantations.   The lowest grounds are covered with a heavy growth of cypress trees. In the rear of the cypress groves are found strips of the richest land, rendered almost impassable by the reed cane, which is much thicker on the ground than our best nurseries, of all sizes, from half an inch to two inches in diameter, and from six to thirty-five feet in height.   It is thought that this river might be rendered navigable for sloops, by the removal of the rafts of driftwood, as high up as the ford near Ellicott's line, which crosses the river about 75 miles from its mouths ; this ford in dry summers is little more than ancle deep. At this point the country has assumed an uneven surface, which it maintains, with the exception of a few savannas, to the Mississippi.   The savannas are in this country of two very different kinds : the one is to be found in the pine lands, and notwithstanding the black appearance of the soil, they are as much white sand as the higher lands around them.   True it is, that clay is very often much nearer to their surface than in the higher pine lands ; they are a ki   sinks or drains to those of higher lands, and their low situation only prevents the growth of pines in them.   In wet weather, the roads leading through them are almost impassable.   On account of their producing some species of grass, of a better kind than the wire grass, they are very often styled meadows ; and I believe, if they could be improved by draining them, without taking away all their moisture, very useful grass might be raised in them ; but on draining them completely, they prove to be as arrant a sand as any in this country.   These savannas often have spots in them more low than common, and filled with water : they are overgrown with different species of the *cratægus*, or hawthorn, as also very often a species of shrub much resembling the *laurus* in appearance, but as I never had an opportunity of seeing it in blossom, I cannot describe it, so as to ascertain the genus to which it belongs. In its fruit it is widely different from any of the laurel kind, that have fallen under my inspection; it is a bacca, with several cells, full of an agreeable acid, like the common lime from the West Indies; it is of the size of a large pigeon's egg, but more oblong. The other savannas differ very widely from these; they consist of a high ground, often with small gentle risings in them. There is generally a rivulet at one end, and often at both ends of them. The soil is here very fertile; and in some I have seen fossil shells in great numbers, in others flint, in others again some chalk and marl. It is remarkable, that the cattle are very fond of the grasses growing here. In these savannas, if a well or pond is dug, the water has a very strong nitrous taste." *

The banks of the Boguechitto, a respectable tributary of Pearl river, and which heads near the sources of Tongipaho, are in many places bordered by rich and extensive prairies, which afford an inexhaustible pasturage to vast droves of cattle belonging to the White settlers and to the Choctaw Indians. These prairies are remarkable chiefly for the immense number of strawberries, which they produce, of superior size and flavor.

The great valley of the *Washita*, is nearly in the form of a semi-elipsis, and extends far beyond the northern confines of the state, with an average width of 50 miles. This river winds above 300 miles through an alluvial region, and together with its numerous bayous, lakes, and tributary streams, chequers 6,000,000 of acres, into a net-work of natural canals, affording in the aggregate more than 1500 miles of easy internal navigation. Between the Washita and the Mississippi the little rivers Ox, Bricklayers, and Providence, meander at the distance of five, ten, and fifteen miles from each other, and parellel with the Washita. The country is alluvial and flat, from Red river to the beautiful lake Occatahoola the

* Bernard Romans.

R

water sluggish and the currents of the streams less than one mile an hour. The floods of the Mississippi have been known to cause a regurgitation of the Washita's current above one hundred miles. Above lake Occatahoola the waters have a brisker motion, and it is there that the high land and permanent strata of soil commence. Above the alluvial tract the timber is chiefly pine and oak, the soil sandy or clayey, and the rocks principally slate ; some of it alluminous, but none fit for covering houses ; there is a kind of argillaceous composition, resembling oil-stone or turkey-stone, but too brittle for flints ; and a kind of sandy aggregate, which seemed as if it might be employed for grindstones. Mineralized and carbonated wood is found in several places. There are no certain indications of fossil coal.

The plains of the Washita, like those of the Mississippi, have a slight inclination from the river ; and the inundations of the Mississippi have been known to approach to within a short distance of the Washita, threatening to break through its banks ; this, however, is not a common occurrence. Some writers have represented the country between the Mississippi and the Washita to be one entire cypress swamp; but late discoveries prove that there exists large tracts of fine cotton and sugar lands between those rivers ; especially above Bayou Barchelet.

The garden of the Washita bottoms includes Bostrop's grant, twelve leagues square, lying on the bayous Siard, Berthelemi, and the Washita. This grant was made by the Spanish governor general, the baron Carondelet, on conditions that Bastrop's colony should confine themselves to the cultivation of wheat ; and that he should erect several grist mills upon the bayous. This tract is mostly high prairie, interspersed with woodland ; the soil is exceedingly rich and the country delightful ; yet the inhabitants are mostly poor and indolent, and frequently intrude on the public lands.

The wealth which annually floats out of Red river to New-Orleans market, is absolutely incredible—even at this early period of the settlements, when it may be said that the capacity of the country to produce is but imperfectly understood ; when not the tenth part of its natural resources are put in requisition by the hand of industry ; and when a great proportion of the inhabitants are poor and all are comparatively indolent, yet the trade of this river is already astonishing. About six miles from its mouth is a bayou leading from *Long* lake ; this lake is three miles wide and fourteen long.

Red river pursues a very serpentine course. The country at short intervals on both sides from its mouth to the Missouri boundary, is interspersed with lakes, a part of which have been described ; but the total number of them exceeds forty. They all communicate with the river by bayous, and rise and fall with it . these lakes, bayous and tributary rivers and creeks, canal the country in every direction and greatly facilitate the transportation of goods, produce, lumber, &c. The bottoms are from one to ten miles wide ; very rich in soil and productions. The timber of the bottoms is willow, cotton-wood, honey locust, pawpaw, and buckeye ; on the rich uplands, elm, cucumber, ash, hickory, mulberry, black-walnut, where the grape vine greatly abounds ; upon the second rate or sandy uplands, white, pitch and yellow pines, and most kinds of oak. The settlements extend from the mouth of the river, generally on both sides, as far as the great jam of driftwood, a distance of nearly two hundred miles. These settlements are distinguished by the names of Baker's Station, Avoyelles, Holmes' Station, Rapide, Gillard's Station, Cane river, Natchitoches, and Bayou Pierre. Above Baker's Station is a prairie nearly forty miles in circumference. It is entirely destitute of trees or shrubs, but produces an excellent grass for fattening cattle. The beef is said to be of a fine quality ; and hogs find in the roots and nuts an abundant food. The inhabitants are settled in the outer skirts, on the border of the woods. The inhabitants are Spanish, Irish, French, and Americans. A few miles above this prairie, the land becomes moderately hilly. The pine

woods are here between thirty and forty miles wide, extending
to the great prairies of Opelousas. Holmes' station is 40
miles above Baker's. The land produces sugar, cotton, corn
and tobacco in perfection. On the south side of the river is
a large body of rich land reaching to Opelousas, which is watered and drained by two large bayous called Bayou Robert
and Bayou Au Bœuf. Their waters are very clear, and
take their rise in the high pine hills between Red river and
the Sabine. These afford a safe communication with the
gulf of Mexico, for an extensive range of country. It is believed that this body of land which is about forty miles square,
for richness of soil, growth of timber, excellence of water, salubrity of climate, extent and convenience of navigation, is not excelled by any tract of land in Louisiana. From
Holmes' Station to the Bayou Rapide is thirty miles. The
lands on this bayou are nearly of the same quality with that
on the Bayous Robert and Au Bœuf. These lands feed vast
herds of stock. This Bayou has two mouths, which enter
Red river about twenty miles apart, forming a curviture
somewhat in the shape of a *half-moon.* A large creek of
pure water enters the stream upon which are several sawmills,
and groves of pine timber. Boats cannot pass round this
curviture on account of obstructions formed by rafts of driftwood, but can ascend from the lower part more than half
the distance. On both sides of the lower mouth of this bayou, are situated the richest part of the Rapide settlement.
Few countries exhibit more beauty or greater indications of
wealth. The plantations are in a high state of cultivation,
the soil rich, and the cotton raised here is of the best quality
in the state. The sugar cane flourishes. The cotton and
tobacco are very good, as are all kinds of vegetables. The
orange and figtrees grow luxuriantly; to complete these bless-
ings, the climate is healthful and the inhabitants in a manner exempted from the diseases usually incident to warm climates.
This country furnishes immense quantities of lumber for the
New-Orleans and West India markets; and is capable of

continuing the supply for ages.   From the Rapide to the Indian villages is about 24 miles ; the bend is fine and susceptible of every kind of cultivation the whole distance.   These villages are situated on both sides of the river in a very productive soil.   Just above the Indian towns, the rich and populous settlement of Gillard's station, commences.   Six miles higher up is the Baluxa Indian village, where the river divides into two branches forming an island of fifty miles in length, and three or four in breadth, very fertile.   The east stream is called *Rigule de Bon Dieu ;* on the left hand is the *boat channel* to Natchitoches.   On this branch for forty miles, there are thick settlements, rich lands, and the inhabitants wealthy.   This is called the River Cane settlement.

A little above this settlement, the river divides into three channels, and forms the Brevel islands, the largest of which is thirty miles long and three or four wide.   The central division is lined with settlements and is the boat channel ; the western channel, called Fausse Riviere, is navigable but is uninhabited, owing to the lowness of the banks.   This channel passes through lake *L'Occasse,* above which the three channels separate, where is situated the town of Natchitoches, and fort Claiborne, which stands on a hill elevated about thirty feet above the banks of the river.   This town contains about 100 houses ; it was originally settled by the French. The land has here a handsome swelling surface, yielding a rich and spontaneous pasturage to prodigious herds of cattle, and droves of horses, which give beauty and animation to the prospect, and croud the earth in every direction.   Cattle can be purchased for six dollars a head ; horses, for fifteen or twenty dollars.   Swine run wild and are raised with little or no expence, in immense numbers.   The planters commence their cultivation about the first of March.   During the growth of vegetation they have sufficient rains to keep the earth moist, but in September and October, severe droughts are experienced.   Although the dews are very heavy and powerful, yet the sun's rays lick up this moisture before it descends to the roots, and only gives it time to cool the withering stalk. The dews are known to fall so profusely as to be seen running in little streams on the ground.

From Natchitoches a road leads to the Sabine, Nacogdoches and San Antonio. The Bayou Bon Dieu enters the river about three miles above this town. Another bayou communicates with Bon Dieu and lake Noiz; above this lake the river continues in one channel, passing through the fine settlement of Grand Ecorce, seven miles long; at the upper end of which comes into the river a bayou or decharge of Spanish lake. The river again divides a short distance above this lake; after which, the course of the west branch is westerly for nearly 80 miles, when it turns to the eastward and communicates with the right branch, forming an island 100 miles long, and thirty wide. Boats cannot ascend by the west branch in consequence of collections of driftwood, which choak up its current, in several places. The French settlement of Bayou Pierre extends nearly the whole length of this branch; the land is of the best quality, and the inhabitants possess large herds of cattle, and are good livers. The face of this part of the country is agreeably hilly; and the water very good. On the main or eastern branch, are several settlements. The land on this branch is very rich; but much cut up by bayous, lakes and islands.

The bottoms are several miles wide. The plantations reach up to the commencement of the driftwood bridges.— Bayou Channo, leading into lake Besteneau, affords a pretty good navigation; and by passing through the lake and bayou Dacheet, boatmen gain several miles, as the meanders of the river are very tedious. The medium depth of this lake, is from fifteen to twenty feet, and never less than twelve, though the remains of cypress trees of all sizes, now dead, most of them with their tops broken off, are yet standing in the lake. From bayou Dacheet to the mountains, the river is free of obstructions. Eighty miles above Dacheet, is the Caddo Indian towns. The lands for this distance, are high, rich bottoms, widely extended from the river. Twenty miles below these towns, the river changes its direction, and turns to the west.

The great range of pine forests that occupy the space from the prairies of Opelousas to the Red river, wind along the Sabine. The general surface of this region rises gradually from prairies into hills; the principal range of which pursues nearly the same course as the Sabine, at the distance of twenty or twenty-five miles from the river, and divide the waters that flow into it from those that flow into the Red river and Calcasu. Along the creeks, through this tract of country, are found spots of productive soil. Pine and oak are the prevailing timber on such situations, and pasturage is abundant during the months of spring and summer; but want of water during the dry seasons is the greatest defect of that country. The Prairie grand Chevreuil begins betv een the overflown lands of the Atchafalaya and the Teche rivers, on the west of the former, following the direction of the Teche, nearly north—sometimes north west, terminates eight miles east of Opelousas. Most of the prairie is extremely rich, particularly on the borders of the Teche. The timber consists of several species of hickory, sycamore, sweet gum, black oak, willow oak, American elm, magnolia, sassafras, &c. with some live oak below lat. 30 15. The soil is a rich, friable, black loam, from a foot to 18 inches deep—and the climate, though the place be surrounded with swamps and lagoons, is mild and healthful.

The country between the Mermentau and Atchafalaya, extending 115 miles along the gulf, and about 90 north, is called the Attacapas. Within this there is a great prairie, bearing the same name. Considerable tracts are subject to inundadation, but many parts possess the highest degree of fertility.

North and east of this lies the great Opelousas prairie, extending to the Sabine, and forming the south west corner of the state. It has several large prairies, such as the Opelousas

prairie—on the north of that the Grand prairie, the prairie
Mamon, prairie Calcasu, and the Sabine prairie.   The first
of these contains upwards of 1,120,000 acres.   Rich soil, and
good timber are found along the southern and eastern parts of
this district ; but the rest is wild and the most of it barren,
occupied only by great herds of cattle and buffaloe.

LEVEES.

These are embankments formed on the margin of the Mississippi ; and those of its bayous, to prevent their currents
overflowing the plantations during the periodical floods.   The
principal levee commences at the head of the island of New-
Orleans, and extends to Fort Placquemines, a distance of 130
miles.   It is in some places lined with two rows of orange
trees.

   "The levee is commonly constructed in the following manner, and is indeed but a trifling work, considering the importance of its object :—At a distance, seldom exceeding thirty
or forty yards from the natural bank, a mound of earth is raised about five feet high, and twelve at the base, with a sufficient width at the top for a foot path ; in general, resembling
very much the embankments on the Delaware, erected to
keep out the tide from the marshes on its borders.   The size
varies considerably ; in some places, particularly on the points,
where the land is higher, and against which the current of
the river strikes with less violence, the levees are very trifling ; but in bends, where the current acts with greater force,
it is found necessary to oppose a more considerable mound ;
on some of the bends, where the force of the current is very
great, the embankment is a work of considerable consequence.
The levee of M'Carty's, a few miles above New-Orleans, is
almost fifteen feet high, by thirty at the base, and six feet at
the top ; this is the most considerable on the river, excepting
that immediately in front of the city.   As there is no stone
to be had, the only material is a soft clay, with cypress staves

placed on the outside, that is, next the river, and the whole covered with earth and sodded. On the inside a ditch is made, for the purpose of receiving and carrying off the water, which weeps through the embankment in the season of the floods. The road lies between the ditch and fences, and is crossed at intervals of half a mile, by drains from the ditch just mentioned, and covered like the sewers of a city; these drains pass through the fields, and carry the water to the swamps. A vast quantity of water is continually oozing through the porous embankments, and in many places gushes through holes made by crawfish, which often increase so rapidly as to cause a breach in the levee. It requires several years for the levee to become perfectly solid and firm; previous to this, it is liable to be injured by rains. The embankment runs in a very irregular line; in many places it changes its direction every twenty or thirty yards, for its zig-zag course is not only suited to the sinuosities of the river, but also to its smaller indentations, for being too slight a work to compel the river to hold a regular course, it is obliged to yield to its caprices: and as the river encroaches or recedes, another levee is constructed nearer the river or behind the first; from which circumstance, there are in many places what are called double-levees. A person standing inside of the levee, during the flood, seems to be considerably below the surface of the water, or as some have expressed it, "the water appears to roll over his head." There is, however, something of a deception in this; for there are in few places more than two or three feet of water against the levee, as the ground between it and the river is much higher than on the inside; this may be accounted for, from the quantity of sediment there deposited, and the circumstance of the road having been worn down by constant use. What is considered a good levee, may in most places be made for five hundred to a thousand dollars per mile; but in many it would cost several thousands. Every individual is required to keep up the levee in front of his own land, and before the

S

season of high water it is inspected by commissioners appoint-
ed for the purpose, in each parish, and if found insufficient
it is made at his expense. But this is by no means adequate
to ensure safety; for during the continuance of the floods
the levees demand the most vigilant attention; they must be
continually watched, and all hands are often drawn from the
fields to guard them for whole days and nights. The action
of the current discovers defective parts, before unobserved;
here earth must be added and slabs placed, to prevent it
from crumbling in; and often, after the rains, which prevail
at this season, it becomes spongy and lose in its texture, and
the holes made by crawfish at this time are particularly to
be dreaded. It not unfrequently happens, that from the
want of strength, or from the negligence of some individual,
both he and his neighbors are ruined.*

CREVASSE.

A *crevasse* is a breach formed in the levee by the waters
of the river in time of inundation. The one which broke
through the levee, six miles above New-Orleans, on the 7th
of May, 1816, was 140 yards broad, and received a volume
of water six feet deep. A *crevasse,* says Mr. Breckenridge,
"rushes from the river with indescribable impetuosity, with
a noise like the roaring of a cataract, boiling and foaming, and
tearing every thing before it. To one who has not seen this
country it is almost impossible to convey any idea of the ter-
rors excited by a *crevasse,* or breaking of the levee. Like
the breaking out of fire in a town where no one knows when
his own dwelling may be assailed, it excites universal con-
sternation; every employment is abandoned for miles above
and below, and all hasten to the spot, where every exertion
is made day and night to stop the breach, which is sometimes
successful, but more frequently, the hostile element is suffered to take its course. The consequences are, the destruc-

* See Breckenridge's Views of Louisiana.

tion of the crop, the buildings, and sometimes the land itself
is much injured where the current rushed over, carrying
away the soil, or leaving numerous logs and trees drawn int
the vortex as they floated down the river; these must be
destroyed before the land can again be cultivated.   The effects of a breach of the levee are even more desolating than
those of fire.

The first view which the traveller has of the levee on descending the Mississippi, is at Point Coupee, 172 miles above
New-Orleans by the courses of the river.   It is here that the
country assumes a new aspect ; and it is here that the navigator emerges from a gloomy wilderness, presenting detached
settlements, at long and tedious intervals, into charming and
finely cultivated plantations.

Here the beauty of the Mississippi and prospect of the
country exhibit a view so enchantingly delightful, as scarcely
to admit of description.   On the side of this elevated, artificial bank, is a range of handsome, neatly built houses, appearing like one continued village, as far as the city of Orleans.
They are one story, framed buildings, elevated on piles six or
eight feet high, and well painted; the paint generally white.
The houses for slaves are mostly placed on straight lines and
nicely white-washed.   The perpetual verdure of numerous
orange trees, intermixed with fig trees surrounding the houses,
and planted in groves and orchards near them, highly beau-
fy the prospect ; while the grateful fragrance of constant blos-
soms, and the successive progress to plentiful ripened fruit,
charm the eye, and regale the senses.

In the rear of Point Cupee, is the settlement of Fausse
Riviere, bordering on the ancient bed of the river, which is
now impassible for boats except in the highest floods.

The high land terminates at Baton Rouge in an elevated
bluff, 30 or 40 feet above the greatest rise of the water in the
river.   And here commences the eastern embankment
which is continued, like that on the western side, to Orleans ;
and a range of houses, ornamented with orange and fig trees,

the same distance, perfectly similar to that on the opposite bank. Baton Rouge settlement extends about thirty miles on the river, and to a considerable distance back, in an eastern direction.

At a point a little below the Iberville, and sixteen miles below Baton Rouge, commences an uninterrupted series of plantations, which are continued, upwards of one hundred miles, to the city of Orleans. These plantations are all cleared in front, and under improvement. Some of them are planted with sugar cane, but the greater part with cotton. They are narrow at the bank, and extend back to the swamp ground, which is incapable of cultivation ; the land no where admitting of more than one plantation deep.

The settlements of Bayou la Fourche extend about 50 miles on both sides of that stream, one plantation deep. From the outlet of this bayou, to the city of New-Orleans, the land will admit of only one plantation deep, and is rarely capable of cultivation, more than one mile from the bank of the river. It then becomes low and swampy to the lakes and the sea. The swamps are immense, intersected by creeks and lakes ; but the swamps generally abound with large cypress trees. Great quantities of this timber is sawed by mills, erected on streams formed by cutting sluices through the Levee. These mills are worked with great rapidity nearly half the year.

Concord settlement lies between Tensaw river and the Mississippi, opposite to Natchez, and contains about 400 families. Contrary to the statements of most travellers, who have pronounced this district an uninhabitable swamp, Mr. Darby affirms, that the wide space between the Washita and Mississippi, is either a cane brake along the water courses, or a hard, dry surface, when the flood has subsided, of course first rate corn, sugar or cotton land.

Fifteen miles below the city of New-Orleans, and at the head of the English bend, is a settlement, called Saint Bernardo, or Terre au Bœuf, containing two parishes. The inhabitants are nearly all Spaniards from the Canaries, who improve a narrow strip of land, principally for raising poultry and garden vegetables, for the market at New-Orléans.

BARRATARIA,

Is a bayou, or or a narrow arm of the gulf of Mexico, west of the Balize.   It communicates with the lakes which lie on the south-west side, and these with the lake of the same name, and which lies contiguous to the sea, where there is an island formed by the two arms, or *decharges* of this lake and the sea. Both ends of this island were fortified in 1811, by the pirates under M. La Fitte.   This island is situated in N. lat. 29 ; and is remarkable for its health, strength as a military posi- tion, and the vast quantity of shell fish with which its waters abound.   In time, this may become a place of weal h and im- portance, as by a late survey of the country in its rear, it is found that there is a district of half a million of acres, very fertile, and sufficiently high to constitute a healthful settle- ment, of the first rate sugar lands.   Barrataria affords a safe and capacious harbor for light ships of war and merchant vessels.

ALLUVIAL SOIL.

The alluvial soil of Louisiana, independent of its intrinsic fecundity, finds in the annual floods a perpetual renewal of its strength, from the fertilizing slime and mud deposited by the overflowing current of the Mississippi.

" The deterioration of the alluvial lands of the Mississippi is scarcely perceptible, even on fields which have been under cultivation 60 or 70 years, or more."[*]

When the river, says Dr. Dunbar, by disruption, alters its course, and new accumulations of slime, sand and marl are laid upon this very compact earth, a false belief might be in-

---

[*] Extract of a letter from Mr. Robertson, member of Congress from Louisiana, to the author, dated Feb. 19, 1817.

duced that this solid soil is not the offspring of the river, but the original parent earth coeval with the Mississippi itself, upon which this great river afterwards deposited the rich spoils of the northern regions, borne down by its mighty tide. This compact soil I have found at the depth of from ten to thirty feet; and in other situations no appearance is to be seen of any other than the common soil formed of the mud of the river. The soil near the river is sandy, particularly that which has been lately formed. From a quarter to half a mile from the margin of the river the sand is less apparent, and loses its name of " terre sablonneuse," acquiring that of " terre grasse," being the richest black marl, with a moderate admixture of sand. At greater distances, and frequently at some depth under the last mentioned soils, is found the above mentioned compact earth, called glaise (potter's earth) : it is no doubt eminently adapted to the use of the potter, though hitherto not much applied to the manufacture of earthern ware. Upon all lands long subject to culture, and defended from the inundation, although near to the margin, the appearance of sand is almost lost; but it is evident, from the friability of the soil, and the facility with which it is cultivated, that a large portion still remains intimately mixed with it; whereas the terre grasse (unmixed or pure marl) yields with difficulty to the plough : it exhibits proofs of the richest marl, a slight shower causing it to crumble into powder after being turned up.

SUGAR CANE, COTTON, RICE.

Late experiments prove that the sugar cane can be successfully cultivated in any part of Louisiana, except in the swampy or " unripe" alluvial soils.

Sugar lands yield from one to two hogsheads of a thousand weight and 50 gallons of rum, per acre; the value is about $100 a hogshead.

It is confidently stated, that two young French gentlemen made in one season with 28 hands, 200 hogsheads of sugar—and the same letter states that an old man, assisted only by his two sons, carried 30 hogsheads to market, the produce of their own hands, in one season.

The planters, in order to guard against the effect of an early frost, regularly finish about the 15th of October pulling up the canes intended for next year's planting. This is done by putting them into stacks *(morasses)* with all their leaves on, in such a manner as to expose the smallest possible quantity of the stalk to the weather. Early in the spring, those canes are laid along in plough furrows, the large end of one cane nearly touching the small end next to it, and the furrows distant from each other about three feet. The plant is cultivated as we cultivate the Indian corn, and with equal ease. The cutting and grinding are commenced whenever the seed canes are put up, and continue frequently till the latter end of December; and long after the canes has been killed by the frost.

A mill which grinds 300 gallons per hour and will deliver upwards of two tons of sugar per day, costs in workmanship and materials 1000 dollars, besides the expense of a rough cover for it, 40 feet square. The cost of three pestles of sufficient size to keep pace with the mill, is 350 dollars, and that of the mason work in bedding them and making the furnaces, is 250 dollars; which with the price of 30,000 bricks, a proportionable quantity of mortar, a rough building to cover the boilers, and six draft beasts to impel the machine, constitute the whole expenses of an establishment sufficient for the manufacture of 200 hogsheads of sugar.— It must, however be recollected, that the Lonisiana hogsheads contain a little more than 1000 cwt.

"The cotton lands of Louisiana yield from 500 to 2000 pounds weight of seed cotton per acre. A hand will cultivate ten acres."* Several of the planters assured me that the land from Pinckneyville to New Orleans will produce an average of

* Mr. Robertson's Letter

200 lbs. in the seed from each acre. The profits of a good slave may be estimated at $240.

Rice is cultivated with the greatest facility, as water is easily diverted from the rivers and bayous into the fields. *The use of water on rice is more to suppress the growth of noxious weeds and grass,* which would otherwise stifle the grain, than for promoting the growth of the rice itself; for none of the grasses can stand the water, but rice does, as long as it is not totally immersed. Therefore it is, that after weeding, the planter, if he has it convenient, lets on water to about half the height of the grain.

Table of profits resulting from the employment of fifty workmen on a farm in Louisiana.

STAPLE.	AMOUNT.	PRICE.	Nett Value.	Annual revenue from each hand.	Acres.	No. of acres in the state suited to each staple.
Sugar,	150,000 *lbs.*	$,03 *per lb*	$12,000.	$240	150	250 0 0
Rice,	700 *bbls.*	6 *per bbl.*	4,000.	84	100	250 00
Cotton,	60,000 *lbs.*	.15 *per lb.*	9,000.	120	250	2,400,000
Indigo,	7,000 *lbs.*	1, *per lb.*	7,000.	140		2,000,00
Tobacco,	60,000 *lbs.*	10. *p. cwt.*	5,375.	107		1,000,000

NOTE.—The whole extent of the state of Louisiana, after deducting one-fifth for the swamps, rivers, lakes, pine barrens and other irreclaimable tracts, extends over 23,480,320 acres. The one-tenth of that quantity may be assumed for cotton. Indigo, which demands a richer soil, but similar climate, is allowed another tenth. Tobacco can be raised in all parts of the state, but the soil best suited for it is nearly the same as that required for sugar cane. [*Niles.*]

TREES, SHRUBS, PLANTS.

The forests of Louisiana, Florida and a part of the Mississippi Territory, are festooned in many places, with a greyish vegetable moss, called *Spanish beard.* It grows from the limbs and twigs of all trees in the southern regions, from north lat. 35 deg. down as far as 28 deg. and I believe every where within the tropics. Wherever it fixes itself, on a limb or branch, it spreads into short and intricate divarica-

tions; these in time collect sand and dust, wafted by the
wind, and which, probably by the moisture of it absorbs,
softens the bark and sappy part of the tree, about the roots
of the plant, and renders it more fit for it to establish itself;
and from this small beginning it increases, by sending down-
wards and obliquely, on all sides, long pendant branches,
which divide and subdivide themselves, *al infinitum.* It is
common to find the spaces betwixt the limbs of large trees,
almost occupied by this plant; it also hangs waving in the
wind like streamers, from the lower limbs to the length of
fifteen or twenty feet, and of a bulk and weight more than
several men together could carry; and in some places cart-
loads of it are lying on the ground, torn off by the violence
of the wind. Any part of the living plant torn off and
caught in the limbs of a tree, will presently take root, grow,
and increase in the same degree of perfection, as if it had
sprung up from the seed. When fresh, cattle and deer will
eat it in the winter season.

The laurel magnolia is the beauty of the forest, and rises
100 feet and often much higher; the trunk is perfectly erect,
rising in the form of a beautiful column, and a head resembling
an obtuse cone; the flowers which are on the extremity of
the branches are large, white and expanded like a rose; and
when fully expanded they are from six to nine inches in diameter; and have a most delicious fragrance.

The cypress of Louisiana and Florida, is a tree of the first
magnitude and utility: often measuring from six to ten feet
in diameter, and from 40 to 50 straight shaft. It occupies many parts of the swamps, frequently to the exclusion of any
other timber; and is *never* found on high dry land. Axmen
are sometimes obliged to erect scaffolds before they fall the
tree; in consequence of a number of conical excrescences rising from its base to the height of eight or ten feet, called cypress knees, and being hollow are used for beehives. The
sugar maple is rarely seen south of N. lat. 31. Sassafras,
persimon, holly, buckeye, mulberry, wild cherry, pawpaw,

T

myrica incdora, (from the berries of which the green wax is made) chinquapin, chesnut, all the species of the oak family; all the varieties of pine, red cedar, sweet and sour oranges, the latter are indigenous, hawthorn, ozier, plum, *bois d'arc*, is found on the Washita; its bark dies a beautiful yellow. The China root and passion flower are abundant on the rich grounds. The sensitive briar is common to the poor and sandy lands. Several species of the beautiful plant, *saracinia* in the margins of swamps and wet grounds; and three or four handsome species of the water dock; poke, very large and luxuriant. Sumac, along the water courses, and in the swamps where the land is good, several species of well tasted grapes are found in great plenty. Many of the trees in the low grounds are loaded with a variety of vines, the most conspicuous of which are the creeper, and ivy. The *Misletoe* is very abundant and saucily attaches itself to almost every kind of tree, not excepting fruit trees.

BIRDS, BEASTS.

Most kinds of water fowl found in the northern lakes frequent the waters of Louisiana in winter. Those of the feathered tribe which may be considered as local, consist of the white pelican, white eagle, swan, sandhill crane, great white owl, wild turkey, crested bittern, paroquet, prairie hen, tufted woodcock, ivory woodpecker, great bat, rice bird, red bird. The pelican is the largest, measuring from wing to wing seven feet. Its pouch or reservoir contains its food, and will hold six or eight quarts. The prairie hen is something larger than a partridge.

Deer, bear, wolves and a species of the tyger, abound in the hills and prairies. Buffaloe are found in the prairies to the west of Opelousas and north of Red river. The tyger resembles the spotted leopard of Africa. They have been frequently killed between Natchez and Baton Rouge. Wild horses are frequently seen in large droves between Red river

and the Sabine; and small game abound in all the upland
forests.

POPULATION.

The population according to the census of 1810, was
76,556; but may now be safely estimated at 120,000 souls, of
all colors. The following estimate was given in 1814:

This state is divided into three great natural sections, viz:
the north-west, Red river and Washita section; 21,649 sq.
miles, and 12,700 inhabitants. The south-west, Opelousas
and Attacapas section, 12,100 square miles and 13,800 inhabitants. South-east, New-Orleans and West Florida section,
12,120 square miles, and 75,200 inhabitants.

NEW-ORLEANS.

This city stands on the left bank of the Mississippi, 105
miles fr m the gulf of Mexico. The city is regularly laid
out; the streets are generally forty feet wide and cross each
other at right angles. The houses are principally brick on
the streets near the river; but on the back part of the town
mostly wood. The population is at present 30,000 souls,
which are rapidly increasing by accessions from all the states
in the union, and from almost every kingdom of Europe. It
it is above one mile and a half long, and half a mile deep.
A great number of new buildings were erected last year, distinguished for size and the improved style of the architecture.
The public buildings consist of three banking houses, two
handsome churches, custom house, town house, market house,
arsenal, convent, jail, theatre, governor's palace, built by the
Spanish government. These are all fine buildings. The
place des armes is a beautiful green, which serves as a parade.
Most of the houses in the suburbs have beautiful gardens
ornamented with orange groves. The great cathedral church
and town house are in the centre of the town, fronting the

square.* There are five newspapers printed in this city, two in French and English, viz : The *Courier*, and *Ami des Lois*, (friend of the laws) and three in English, the *Louisiana Gazette*, the *Orleans Gazette*, and Price Current or Commercial Register, by *Dubourg.* The buildings have no cellars, except the vacancy formed between the ground and the lower floors ; which are raised five or six feet from the earth.   The tornadoes to which the country is subject, will not admit of the houses being carried up several stories, like those of New-York and Philadelphia ; but they have terraces and walks on their tops *a la mode Francoise.* The market is plentifully furnished with the necessaries and luxuries of every clime.   It is upon the levee fronting the city that the universe is to be seen in miniature.   It is crowded with vessels from every part of the world; and with boats from a thousand different places in the "upper country." Here in half an hour you can see, and speak to Frenchmen, Spaniards, Danes, Swedes, Germans, Englishmen, Portuguese, Hollanders, Mexicans, Kentuckians, Tennesseans, Ohionians, Pennsylvanians, New-Yorkers, New-Englanders and a motley groupe of Indians, Quadroons, Africans, &c. Here are boats from Chatauque lake in New-York ; from La Bœuf, Connemeugh, Brownsville, in Pennsylvania; from the heads of Holston and Clinch ; Cumberland, Licking and Green river, Muskingum, Scioto, Tuscarawa, Wabash, Kaskaskia, Missouri, Washita, Red river, Vermillion, Ponchartrain, Amite, and an hundred other rivers.

---

* The chapel of the convent of the Ursuline nuns is small, but very neat within, being chiefly calculated for the accommodation of that sisterhood. Public service is performed here regularly. The nuns are separated from the audience by a partition of lattice-work, through which they may barely be distinguished   Their whole number at present does not amount to more than forty or fifty. A summer residence in New-Orleans must be extremely disagreeable, as even at this early season I find it intolerably hot and sultry. The evenings however are cool and pleasant, and as this city has no public gardens or promenade, the levee after sunset is crowded with company, who having been confined all the day to their houses, seldom miss this favorable opportunity of breathing a little fresh air. That unfortunate class of females, the mulattoes, who from their infancy are trained in the arts of love, are far from being considered in the same humiliating light with those white ladies to whom they are nearly allied in profession. Since custom has planted an insurmountable barrier to their ever forming an honorable connexion with white men, necessity has compelled them to resort to the practice of forming tem-

COMMERCE, WEALTH.

The exports of Louisiana already exceed those of all the New-England states by more than $150,000 a year. Between 3 and 400 sea vessels arrive and depart annually.—Nine hundred and thirty-seven vessels of all denominations departed during the year 1816, from the Bayou St. John, a port of delivery in the district of Mississippi; the tonnage of these vessels is calculated at sixteen thousand; they are chiefly employed in carrying the produce of that part of the Floridas belonging to the United States, consisting in barks, coals, cotton, corn, furs, hides; pitch, planks, rosin, skins, tar, timber, turpentine, sand, shells, lime, &c. The receipts of this city from the upper country is beyond conception. Five hundred and ninety-four flat bottomed boats and three hundred barges have arrived within the last year from the western states and territories, with the following articles of produce viz:—Apples 4253 bbls; bacon and hams 13000 cwt. bagging 2579 pieces; beef 2459 bbls. beer 439 do. butter 509 do. candles 358 boxes; cheese 30 cwt. cider 646 bbls. cordage 400 cwt. cordage bailing 4798 coils; corn 13775 bushels; corn meal 1075 bbls. cotton 37371 bales; flaxseed oil 85 bbls. flour 97419 do; ginseng 957 do; hay 356 bundles; hemp yarns 1095 reels; hides 5000; hogs 500; horses 375; lead 5500 cwt. white lead 188 bbls. linens, coarse 2500 pieces; lard 2458 bbls. oats 4065 bushels; paper 750 reams; peltries 2450 packs; pork 9725 bbls; po-

porary engagements with those whom they may fancy. Engagements of this kind are every day formed, for a month or a year, or as much longer as the parties may be mutually pleased. During any engagement of this kind, it is in vain to solicit improper favors: they are generally as strictly continent as the marriage ceremony could possibly make them. When the time is expired, or the lover gone, they accept of the next best offer that may be made to them. This class of the society of this city is so generally esteemed, that no gentleman hesitates a moment in paying his compliments to those females belonging to it, whom he may meet with in the street or elsewhere. A far greater degree of distinction prevails among this class than even among the whites. They who are so many degrees removed from the black that the connection is no longer visible in the skin, consider themselves as the " best blooded;" and so down to those who are only one degree superior to the blacks, whom they all treat with more contempt than even the whites do.
[*Schultz.*]

tatoes 3750 bushels; powder, gun 294 bbls. salt petre 175 cwt. soap 1538 boxes; tallow 160 cwt. tobacco 7282 hhds. do. manufactured 711 bbls. do. carrots 8200; whiskey 320,000 gallons; bear skins 2000. Besides a quantity of horned cattle, castings, grind stones, indigo, muskets, merchandize, pacan nuts, peas, beans, &c. The schedule of the above produce is independent of what is furnished by Louisiana, consisting of cotton, corn, indigo, molasses, masts and spars, planks, gunpowder, rice, sugar, shingles, soap, taffia, tallow, timber, bees wax, &c. which are generally brought to market in planters crafts, or taken from off the plantation by foreign bound vessels.

The quantity of sugar made on the Mississippi alone, is estimated by a late writer, at *ten millions of pounds.* Twenty thousand bales of cotton were exported in 1812.

Perhaps there is no country in the globe where so much wealth is divided among so few individuals as in Louisiana. Its resources are immense, while its population is comparatively small. The yearly income of many of the planters, amounts to 20,000 dollars : and it is said to be not uncommon to mark from one to three thousand calves in a season, and to have from ten to twenty thousand head of fine cattle.

MILITARY TOPOGRAPHY.

New-Orleans was fortified by the Spaniards more for the purpose of defending it against the inroads of the Mississippi, than the approaches of an enemy. It is unquestionably invulnerable to a naval attack; as the late improvements at Fort St. Philip, at the English turn, will prevent the ascent of ships of war. Mr. Stoddard thinks that a fleet wholly unobstructed by land batteries, would find it extremely difficult to ascend against the rapidity of the current.

About 12 miles below New-Orleans is a narrow extent of land, never overwhelmed, which runs towards the Lakes, reaching about twenty miles; this tongue of land is called the

Terre au Bœuf, (ox land) about a mile in length, and divided in the centre by a creek, having swamps on each side. An enemy might land upon this tongue from lake Borgne, which approaches it on the north-east. The British army under Packenham gained the Mississippi, through the swamps between Au Bœuf and bayou St. John, near Velere's canal. South-west of the city is an other narrow elevated tongue of land. The road from the back of the city divides at two miles from it, and the one road proceeds northeastly on a tongue of land about half a mile in width, known by the name of Chantilly ; this terminates in marshes and swamps at the distance of twenty miles. The other road on the left westerly crosses St. John's creek over a draw-bridge, and intersects the river road about fifteen miles above the city. This St. John's creek heads in a swamp south-west of New-Orleans, and after meandering about six miles in a north by east direction, falls into lake Ponchartrain. At the mouth of this bayou there is a fort which protects the city against the approach of an enemy. It was expected that the British in 1814 would have attempted to gain the city by this route. The depth of water in it varies from three to nine feet, as the water may rise or fall by the winds, or by the waters of the lake. From the bar to the canal of Carondolet, are usually from nine to ten feet of water. This canal rises in a basin directly behind the Charity Hospital of New-Orleans, and is large enough for several small vessels. It extends in a direct line about two miles to St. John's creek, and is about twenty feet wide. Several handsome country seats, a village, and orange groves adorn its banks. It has already been of great advantage to the inhabitants. Articles for transportation are conveyed by Lake Ponchartrain to the mouth of the creek of St. John, and thence pass up the creek six miles and then pass through the canal to the walls of the city. It has been proposed to extend the canal to the Mississippi, and it has been contemplated to deepen the whole canal for military and commercial purposes.

INDIANS.

The Indians of Louisiana chiefly reside on the Red river. *Natchitoches* tribe formerly numerous and much attached to the French, who highly respect these Indians, and a number of decent French families at Natchitoches have a mixture of their blood in them. This tribe anciently dwelt in a large village near the site of the present town of Natchitoches. They have been reduced by war and small pox to about 30 souls, and reside at present at lac de Muire, 25 miles above Natchitoches. The *Boluxas* from Pensacola live at the mouth of Rigulet de Bondieu. They are reduced to thirty warriors—are harmless and friendly. The *Appalaches*, consisting of 14 families reside on bayou Rapide. The *Alibamies*, consisting of 70 families reside at Opelousas and near the Caddo towns. The *Conshattas* live on the Sabine, and have about 400 souls. The *Pacanas* live on the Quelquechose river, and consist of thirty warriors besides women and children. The *Tunicas* reside principally at Avoyelles; and are reduced to 140 souls. The *Pascagolas* reside on Red river; have only 24 warriors. The *Tensaws* live on Bayou au Bœuf; and are equally reduced in numbers and spirit. All the preceding tribes, except the Natchitoches, are emigrants from West-Florida. The *Chactoos* inhabit the branches of Bayou au Bœuf and are the aborigines of the country where they live. The *Wachas* are reduced to half a dozen souls and are servants in French families. The *Choctaws* frequent the state, and have two or three fixed villages. The Opelousas, consist of about 150 souls, and reside near the church of the same name. The *Houmas* and *Attacapas* are united and amount to about 200 souls: the former were original proprietors of the soil of the island of New-Orleans. These Indians, as well as the Tunicas and Choctaws, are to be seen at all times, near the suburbs in groupes, men, women, and children, reeling under the influence of the bottle.

EXTENT OF NAVIGABLE WATERS.

	Miles.
The Mississippi proper, is navigable in Louisiana,	712
Iberville and the lakes east of New-Orleans,	250
Amite river,	100
Pongipaho, Chefuncti, and the bayous Castain, Lacombe, and Baucofuca,	300
Pearl river and Boguechitto,	100
Bayous Atchafalaya, Placquemine, La Fourche, and others leaving the Mississippi,	300
Red river (in Louisiana)	450
Bayous and lakes of Red river,	500
Washita and its tributary lakes and rivers,	1500
Teche, Vermillion, Sabine, &c.	550
Gulf coast, bays and lakes,	1000
	5762

U

MICHIGAN TERRITORY,

IS situated between 41 50 and 45 20 N. latitude, and 5 12 and 8 16 W. longitude. Its boundaries, established by law in the winter of 1804–5, are a due N. line from the southern most point of Lake Michigan, thence S. E. by the divisional line which separates the British possessions in Upper Canada, passing through Lake Huron and St. Clair, to Lake Erie, and south by a due E. and W. line, which divides it from the states of Ohio and Indiana. As this southern line has never been run, it is uncertain where it would intersect lake Erie. An observation of a British traveller, makes the latitude of the southern extremity of lake Michigan, a degree and a half south of Detroit, which would carry the line entirely south of lake Erie. However, the mouth of the Miami-of-the-lakes has been assumed as the line, until an actual survey shall remove the ambiguity.† This territory is 256 miles long from north to south; breadth from east to west 154 miles—contains 34,320 square miles, 22,284,000 acres. It is a large peninsula, of a triangular form, with its base resting upon Ohio and Indiana.

RIVERS.

These are numerous and mostly navigable for boats and canoes, nearly to their heads. Those running into lake Michigan are,

1. The *St. Josephs*, which heads in Indiana and interlocks by its several branches, with Black river, St. Josephs

---

† It is not yet ascertained which lies furtherest south, Green bay or lake Michigan.

of Miami, Eelriver, and Tippecanoe. It enters the S. E.
end of the lake—it is rapid and full of islands, but navigable
150 miles, and is 200 yards wide at its mouth. The Potta-
wattimie Indians, who reside on the shore, catch prodigious
quantities of fish in its waters.   It runs about forty miles in
the Michigan Territory.   On the north bank of this river
stands the old fort St. Josephs, from which there is a bridle
road to Detroit.

2. *Black river*, called Le Noir, in the French maps, heads
near the Miami-of-the-lakes, in small lakes, interlocks with
the two St. Josephs, Raisin and Grand river, and enters the
lake 14 miles north of the mouth of St. Josephs, with which
it runs nearly parallel for seventy miles. The land on its
banks are said to be of an excellent quality. It is a fine navigable stream for boats ; there are several Indian towns upon
its head branches.

3. *Marame*, a short river, heads about 45 miles from the
lake, runs west and empties into the lake about ten miles north
of Black river, and forms a capacious bay at its mouth.

4. *Barbue*, which falls into the lake a few miles north of
Marame, is nearly similar in size, course and appearance.

5. *Raisin*, a short river, having its source about 50 miles
from the lake, discharges its waters into a bay 16 miles north
of Barbue.   Great quantities of grapes are found on its banks,
from which circumstance it derives its name.

6. *Grand river*, the largest tributary of lake Michigan
heads in lakes and ponds in the S. E. corner of the territory, interweaves its branches with those of Raisin, Black river, Mastigon and Saganaum, and falls into the lake about 20
miles north of Raisin.   This river is described as running
through a country, consisting alternately of wood lands and
prairies, abounding with most kinds of wild game.   It is navigable for small craft to its source ; in high water boats and
perogues pass from lake Michigan into lake Erie, through
this and Huron rivers. The general course of this river is
W. N. W.   A canal connecting it with the Saganaum, run-

ning into lake Huron, could be opened, it is reported, at a small expence. This canal is among the number recommended by judge *Woodward*, of Detroit, in his able report on the subject of internal navigation.

7. The *Mastigon* has its sources in ponds and marshes, near the centre of the territory—its course is nearly west, and the bay into which it falls, lies 20 miles north of the mouth of Grand river.

8, 9, 10. *White*, *Rocky*, and *Beauvuis*, all short rivers, running a westerly course, and emptying themselves into the lake in the order named, at the distance of from ten to fifteen miles apart.

11. *St .Nicholas*, 50 miles long, and 50 yards wide at its mouth, is the next stream worthy of notice, as we proceed northwardly ; it enters the lake about half way between Michilimackinac and *St. Josephs*.

12. *Marguerite*, a handsome boatable river, interlocks with branches of Saganaam, St. Nicholas and Grand rivers. A voyageur in the service of the North West Company, who spent a winter hunting and trafficing on this stream, informs that the country is considerably broken and well timbered, a few miles from the lake.

13, 14, 15. *Monistic*, *Aux Sables*, *Lasiette*, and *Grand Terverse*, small rivers, which enter the lake between Marguerite and the straits of Michilimackinac.

The greater part of the rivers just described expand and form circular bays or small lakes, behind the sand hills near the lake. This effect is produced by the frequent conflicts between the currents of the rivers and the surf of the lake ; for the latter not only *repels*, as it were, the tributary streams but at the same time washes the sand of the shore into their mouths, causing the smaller ones to contract at their entrances into mere brooks.

These basins are from two to three miles across, and are, at certain seasons literally covered with ducks, wild geese and other water fowl, which resort here to harvest the folle avoine,

profusely sown by nature's hand. The pious and benevo-
lent *St. Pierre* could have found in these bays materials for
an eloquent chapter on the beneficence of the deity.

The rivers which fall into lake Huron between Mickilimack-
inac and the straits of St. Clair, have a northern or north western direction. *Chagahagun* river enters the lake about 35
miles east of Michilimackinac.

2. *Thunder river*, falls into the bay of the same name,
about half way between Michilimackinac, and the outlet of
lake Huron.

3. *Sandy river* runs into Saganaum bay.

Saganaum river, which is next in size to Grand river, and
with which it interlocks, heads near the centre of the territory.
The land on this river is of a good quality, and sufficiently extensive to form at some future day a rich and populous settlement. It enters the bay of the same name. The Chippewa Indians have several villages on this river ; and there
are two *salines* running into it, which it is believed will be
able, when properly worked, to supply the territory, if not
all the settlements on the upper lakes. Sugar river and several considerable creeks run into the lake between Saganaum
and the strait of St. Clair. At the upper end of this strait,
on the American side stands fort *Gratiot*, built by Capt.
Gratiot in the summer of 1815.

The straits of the St. Clair are 26 miles long. The land
on both sides is partly prairie interspersed with strips of lofty
woodland, of oak, sugar, poplar, black walnut, hickory, honey
locust, and white pine. Nature has here planted groves of
white pine suitable for boards, shingles, and masts ; and which
is increased in value by the scarcity of this valuable wood,
since it can be easily transported to distant parts, destitute of so
useful a material. In the strait are several valuable islands,
and there is water sufficient for a 20 gun brig.

The rivers and creeks running into St. Clair, from the
American territory are, *Belle* river which heads near the
Saganaum, and enters the lake nine miles below the strait.

There are good situations for settlements, and some pine groves upon this river. About fourteen miles further down the lake is the river *Huron*. On the banks of this stream is found some of the best land in the territory. Here is a considerable French settlement, which was commenced more than 20 years ago.

A little above the mouth of this river, the Indians have a reservation three miles square, on which is *Machonee's* village. The white settlements on this river are rapidly increasing by reason of numerous emigrants from Oxford and the settlements on the river Thames, in Upper Canada; who are disgusted at the colonial administration of the British government. Several mills were erected last summer; and the lands are rising in value. The bottoms of Huron, are wide and rich; the principal timber on the bottoms, is sycamore, hickory, elm, locust, poplar, maple; on the upland, oak, ash, hickory; there are considerable quantities of white pine. Below Huron at the distance of eight or ten miles is *Buttermilk* creek upon which the land is susceptible of admitting a pretty handsome settlement. Between this and Detroit is Tremblee, and another creek, the name of which I do not recollect.

The strait of Detroit, connecting lake Erie and St. Clair, is 24 miles long, and like the strait or river St. Clair, navigable for large vessels and studded with islands; it is about half a mile wide, with a current running nearly three miles an hour. This strait receives the rivers *Rouge, Ecorce, Magvago* and *Brownstown* creeks. The river Rouge heads about 40 miles south-west of Detroit, near the head branches of Huron; it enters the strait five miles below Detroit, expands to the width of 600 yards at its mouth, forming a considerable bay, and is navigable to Conley's ship yard, five miles from its mouth, for vessels of 150 tons burthen; and it is navigable for canoes and light boats thirty-five miles. Ten or twelve miles from the strait commence wide and fertile black walnut and sycamore bottoms. I have been 15 miles up this stream, and was surprised to find so large a body of rich land, so cheap and so little cultivated, within eight or ten miles of a town settled nearly a century ago.   The corn, wheat and potatoes raised on the banks of this river, yield as abundantly as the best soils of the state of Ohio.   These lands belong to the United States, with the exception of two sections, one mile square each, at *Seginsavin's* Indian village, on the river; and two sections at *Tonquish's* village; and can be purchased at two dollars an acre.   The river *Ecorce* (Bark river) falls into the strait three miles below the mouth of Rouge, and nearly resembles that river in the width of its mouth, slowness of current, and the great quantities of folle avoine growing in its waters.   Maguaga creek comes into the strait opposite to *Grosse isle,* and about one mile below the village of the same name.   *Brownstown* creek is crooked, deep, sluggish, and winds through the Wyandot reservation and empties into the strait against Malden, behind Bois Blanc island. I was told that neitheir of these four streams afforded mill seats.   Between Brownstown village and the mouth of the Miami-of-the-lakes, we cross the following streams in the order named, viz:

Huron river, called by some little Huron, enters the lake seven miles south of Malden; it heads in the vicinity of the principal source of Grand river, and between which and it, there is said to be a navigable communication for canoes, through a chain of ponds and marshes.   Before reaching the open lake, it winds its way two or three miles through a vast meadow of *folle avoine,* in which the water is from five to seven feet deep; and it is with much difficulty, that boatmen unacquainted with its entrance, mazy sinuosities, find its mouth, a harbor, fuel, and a resting place, when overtaken by night or menaced with a storm.

Six miles south of Huron, Swan creek or river Aux Cignes into the lake ; its banks near the lake are low, but the meadow or prairie is susceptible of cultivation ; a few wretched French families are the only human beings that have had the courage to brave disease and rattle snakes. Their wheat, corn, pumpkins and gardens do well, indeed there is very little of the *meadow* but what might be ploughed; corn, flax, and hemp would do best; the pond lilly, folle avoine and other aquatic plants almost choak up the channel of the river, giving the water an offensive and putrid smell; it will rope in summer like molasses, yet the inhabitants make a free use of it for cooking and drinking. Why it does not produce almost instantaneous death I cannot conceive; their children near the lake look miserably. This is by far the worst looking stream tributary to lake Erie. The timbered land here, approaches within a mile of the lake; four miles from which this stream has a brisk current, and afford situations favorable to the erection of water machinery. The trees are lofty—the land high and arable.

Three miles farther south is Rocky creek, dignified by the French, with the title of " la riviere aux Rochers." It has higher banks and a swifter current than any of the neighboring streams, and furnishes sites for mills. The rocks found in its bed and on its banks are calcareous. The Little river *Aux Sables*, (or Sandy creek) falls into the lake two miles S. of Rocky creek. The lake here forms a considerable bay, which receives the waters of these streams. A few French families are settled on their banks. The soil of the upland bordering on these creeks, is sandy.

Seven miles south of Sandy creek following the road, but not half that distance by the lake coast, enters the river Raisin. It interlocks with the St. Joseph of Miami, and Black rivers, running into lake Michigan, and heads in swamps and small lakes. Its general course is a little south of east. Fifteen miles from its mouth it receives the river Macon. The Raisin is about 45 yards wide and boatable to within a few miles of a branch of Black river. There is an extensive prairie at its mouth, and several hundred acres of folle avoine. The settlements extend from within two miles of the lake to the mouth of the river Macon, a distance of 15 miles. The

lots are surveyed in the French mode, being only three Paris-
ian arpents wide on the river and extending back far enough
to contain one hundred acres, more or less. This river
owes its name to the vast quantities of grapes which are found
on its banks. The inhabitants are mostly French, who raise
wheat, corn, and potatoes, more than sufficient for their own
consumption. The soil proves to be rich and durable, and
the settlements have been blessed with unusual health. The
bottoms are equal to those of the Miami; but the soil of the
upland is in many places light and sandy. There are several grist and saw mills on the river. The country has been
settled about thirty years; and the orchards already yield an
abundance of apples. Cider and peach brandy are made
for exportation. The French settlers, until very lately,
did not set a proper value on their improvements; but would
often dispose of them, for comparatively, a trifling sum.—
From the river Raisin to the mouth of the Miami of the-lakes
is 18 miles. The first stream is Otter creek, or river Le
Loutre, 4 miles from Raisin. It affords several situations for
mills, upon which there are already a number erected. Wa-
poo creek flows into the lake about two miles north of Miami
bay. Swan creek, which rises near the head of Otter creek,
falls into the Miami-of-the-lakes or Maurice, four miles
from its mouth. This is a brisk stream, abounding with mill-
seats. The Miami will particularly be noticed in the description of the state of Ohio.

ISLANDS, BAYS, LAKES.

Michilimackinac island is important in a military and political point of view, being the Gibraltar of the North West.
It is of an elliptical form, about seven miles in circumference,
rising gradually to the centre; its figure suggested to the
savage mind, its appropriate name, *Michi Mackina*,* (Great

* The Indian tradition concerning the name of this little barren island is curious.
They say that Michapous, the chief of spirits, sojourned long in that vicinity.—
They believed that a mountain on the border of the lake was the place of his

X

Turtle.) The greater part of the island is almost an impenetrable thicket of underwood and small trees, which contribute
materially to the defence of the garrison. *Fort Holmes* stands
on a summit of the island several hundred feet above the level of lake Huron, and is now one of the most formidable positions in the western country. The French were the first
settlers; and, their descendants to the number of about 300
reside near the garrison. *Manitou* island is situated near
the eastern coast of lake Michigan, south of L'Arbre Cruche.
It is six miles long and four wide. The *Castor islands,* are
a chain of islets extending from Grand Traverse bay nearly
across the lake. They are low and sandy; but afford a shelter for light boats in their passage to Green bay. *Grosse Isle*
already named is a valuable alluvion of several thousand acres,
being five miles long, and from one to two wide. It divides
the river Detroit into two channels, commencing two miles
above Malden. *Bois Blanc* (White Wood) island is situated directly in front of Malden, and at the distance of 200
yards; but south of the ship channel, which circumstance
gives the United States an indubitable claim to its possession,
although the English have in contempt of Mr. Jay's treaty
kept military possession for the last fifteen years. The most
considerable bays on the east side of lake Michigan, are those
of Sable and Grand Traverse. The last is about twelve
miles deep, and four or five broad. Those on the Huron
coast are Thunder and Saganaum bays. The last is forty
miles deep, and from eight to twelve wide. Miami bay,
which resembles a lake, is situated at the mouth of the river
Miami-of-the-lakes, and is about eighteen miles in circumference. The interior of the Michigan peninsula contains a great number of small lakes and ponds, from half a
mile to twelve miles in length—from which issue many of the
rivers. The strait connecting lakes Huron and Michigan, is

above; and they called it by his name. It was here, say they, that he first in-
structed man to fabricate nets for taking fish, and where he has collected the greatest quantity of these finny inhabitants of the waters. On the island he left spirits, named Imakinakos, and from these aerial possessors, it has received the ap-
pellation of Michilimackinac.   [*Heriot.*]

salled *Lac des Illinois*; is fifteen miles long, of an oval figure, and subject to a flux and reflux.

SURFACE, SOIL, TIMBER.

There are no mountains in this territory; the interior is table land, having a western and northern inclination, interspersed with small lakes and marshes, from which issue the head branches of the rivers. Prairies exist, from the banks of the St. Josephs to lake St. Clair; some are of an excellent soil; others, sandy, wet and sterile. There are, nevertheless, extensive forests, of lofty timber, consisting of oak, sugar maple, beach, ash, poplar, white and yellow pine, cucumber, buckeye, basswood, hickory, cedar, plum, crab apple, cherry, black and honey locust. The last flourishes as far north as the margin of lake Huron—yet east of the Allegany mountains, it is never found north of the Delaware. The bottoms, and high prairies are equal to those of Indiana. A considerable part of the coast of lake Michigan consists of a range of sand-hills, thrown up by the surf and "eddying winds." The timbered uplands are well adapted to the production of most kinds of grain; and appear to bear a long series of crops, as is the case with the ridge in the rear of Detroit.

EXTENT OF CEDED LANDS.

At a treaty held at Detroit in November, 1807, between Gen. Hull and the chiefs of the Pottawattamie, Ottawa, Wyandot, and Chippawa tribes, all the lands within the following limits, except the reservations hereafter described, were ceded to the United States, viz: "Beginning at the mouth of the Miami river of the lakes, and running thence up the middle thereof, to the mouth of the great Au Glaize river; thence running due north until it intersects a parallel of latitude, to be drawn from the outlet of lake Huron, which forms the

river Sinclair ; thence running north-east, the course that may
be found, leading in a direct Lne, to White rock, in lake
Huron ; thence due east, until it intersects the boundary line
between the United States and Upper Canada, in said lake ;
thence southwardly, following the said boundary line, down
said lake, through river Sinclair, lake St. Clair, and the river Detroit, into lake Erie, to a point due east of the aforesaid Miami river, thence west to the place of beginning.''

Within these limits, the United States have about four millions of acres at their disposal ; and the Indians the following
reservations, viz : one tract of land six miles square, on the
Miami, above *Roche de Bœuf,* including *Tendaganee's* village ; three miles square, (immediately above the United
States' twelve miles square, ceded by the treaty of Greenville ;) four miles square at the mouth of the Miami, including
Waugau's and *Mishkemau's* villages ; three miles square
near the junctions of the rivers Raisin and Macon ; four sections of one mile square, each on the river Rouge, including
Seginsavin's and *Tonquish's* villages ; three miles square
on lake St. Clair, above the river Huron, including *Machonee's* village ; considerable reservations at *Maguaga** and
Brownstown ; besides six sections of one mile square each,
to be located by the Indians, so as not to interfere with the
claims of white settlers.

INDIANS.

There are two small villages of Ottawas near Miami bay,
and another of the same nation near *Roche de Bœuf,* six miles
above Fort Meigs. The Miamies have four or five towns on
the head branches of Black river. The Pottawattamies have
an establishment on the river *Macon,* a little above the French
settlement on the river Raisin. They have also two villages
on the river Rouge, and several on the St. Josephs, and one

---

* The famous chief *Myeerah,* or *Walk-in the water,* resides in this village. Although a savage destitute of science and civilization, he may be pronounced one
of '' nature's nobles.''

on the river Huron, about fifteen miles from Brownstown.
The Wyandots reside at Brownstown and Maguaga ; the
first village contains twenty-five houses and the last nineteen.
There is a large Ottawa village on the river Huron, under
the ferocious chief Makonee : * the Chippewas have villages
on Saganaum river ; and the Ottawas are also established at
L'Arbre Cruche ; the Indians of this village raise large quantities of corn ; and have made greater advances towards civilization, than any of their aboriginal neighbors ; they profess
the Roman Catholic system of worship, and have a chapel
and a missionary priest.   The Indians of this territory have
been estimated at 3000 souls ; this number has doubtless
been considerably diminished by the battles which they
fought, and the uncommon sufferings which they endured,
during the late war.   Their trade is very valuable to
their white neighbors ; they all cultivate Indian corn, and
some of them *n heat*, as well as most kind of garden vegetables and fruit—raise horses, cattle, hogs and poultry, but
nevertheless derive a principal part of their subsistance from
the waters and forests.

SETTLEMENTS.

The white settlements are chiefly on the strait of Detroit,
the rivers Miami, Raisin, Huron, and lake St. Clair ; but
extend from Fort Meigs to lake Huron, separated, however,
at short intervals, by woods, or Indian reservations of from
three to ten miles in extent.   Where the French inhabitants
are seated, the lots are narrow, houses thick ; only one plantation deep, always fronting the creeks, rivers, and lakes.
Hitherto, this territory has not enjoyed the character to which
its soil, climate, and advantageous situation for trade, justly
entitle it.   Time, and the enterprising emigrants, who are

* In 1808, this monster finding one of his tribe drunk, and asleep, a short distance above Detroit, deliberately cut off his head. with his tomahawk, and kick-
ed it along the street for several rods.   The cause of his displeasure was jealousy ;
he suspected the victim of his vengeance with having had an illicit connexion with
one of his numerous wives.

now rapidly encreasing in numbers, will place its reputation in a proper point of view. Settlements are now beginning on lakes Huron and Michigan, and promise to become extensive and permanent.† From the river Rouge to lake St. Clair, a distance of twelve miles, the country resembles the suburbs of a large town, the houses being no more than twenty rods distant from each other, and the greater part of the way much thicker.

The United States' troops under the command of Gen. M'Comb, were employed last summer in opening a road from the river Ecorce to the rapids of the Miami, a distance of sixty six miles. Upon this road may be found many eligible situations for farms and stands for taverns; and no where north of the cotton and sugar climate, could agriculturalists find a finer field for enterprize, or a surer prospect of reward.

DETROIT.

This city stands on the western side of the strait, eighteen miles above Malden, and six below the outlet of lake St. Clair. The buildings approach close to the river bank, which is from thirty to twenty feet high; abrupt at the lower end of the town, but subsides into a gentle slope near the upper limits, where the plain on which it stands becomes about 500 yards wide. There are three streets, running parallel with the river; these are intersected by six cross streets, besides several lanes. The situation of the town is agreeable and romantic. The buildings are brick, stone,

---

† Capt. Price, of the U. S. army, passed from Michilimackinac to Detroit, by land, in March last, a distance of 450 miles. He coasted the shore of lake Huron on the ice, to Saganaum bay, and thence by land. Capt. P. describes the lands on the Saginaum, "of an excellent quality, and most beautifully situated; the river bold and navigable for 21 miles, with large prairies from 4 to 6 miles deep. From Saganaum to Flint river, 15 miles, a level country, lands excellent and well timbered: from thence to Flint river, a waving country, not broken, nor high hills; from thence to the river Huron, 30 miles from Detroit, the face of the country and soil very much resemble that of the county of Cayuga, in New-York, principally cloathed with Oak, a very open country, and no underwood, interspersed with small beautiful lakes abounding in fish of a superior quality: from Huron to Detroit, generally a low flat country, susceptible of being drained and cultivated, the soil deep and rich.

frame, and in some instances, hewn logs; but two thirds are frame; some very fine and painted; there are about three hundred buildings of all descriptions, exclusive of the suburbs, or " *Cotes*," extending above, as far as lake St. Clair, and below, as far as the river Rouge, which appear to be a continuation of the town. The principal streets are wide, and most of the houses have picketed gardens in the rear. The inhabitants are more than half French; the balance consists of emigrants and adventurers from various parts of Europe and America.

Before the great fire in 1806, the town was surrounded by a strong stockade, through which there were four gates; two of them open to the wharves, the others to the land; this defence was intended to repel the attacks of the Indians. Gen. Hull, while governor of the territory, planted a long line of pickets; but the length of the line to be defended, and the interstices, which were left, render them nearly useless.— Several wooden wharves project into the river; the U. S. wharf is about 140 feet long, and a vessel of 400 tons burthen can conveniently approach its head. The public buildings consist of the council house, jail, and United States' store. The last is a fine brick building, situated near the water in the rear of the public wharf, 80 feet in length, 30 feet wide, and three stories high. It was filled in November 1813, with the trophies of the Thames. Lots are rising in value; the French are now preparing to build an elegant Roman chapel, 150 by 50. Government are about commencing the building of a state-house, which is to be a large and handsome brick building. There are a number of stores which appear to have a brisk trade; the owners know how to extort an exorbitant price for their merchandize. The streets of Detroit are generally crowded with Indians of various tribes, who collect here to sell their skins. You can hear them whooping and shouting in the streets the whole night. There is a kind of nunnery, a Roman chapel for devotion and singing; a wretched printing office in which re-

ligious French books are printed in a rude style.   A newspaper, entitled the " Michigan Essay," was issued from this
office by *James M. Miller*, from Utica, in 1809, but the
proprietor was obliged to relinquish the undertaking for want
of an adequate patronage.   A new paper, however, will appear in the course of the present year, which, will, no doubt,
be permanent.   Learning is at a low ebb; yet there is a large
number of men of genius and education resident in the city.
The French are dexterous watermen, and will navigate a
small bark, in a rough sea with incredible skill.   They have
nothing like enterprize in business ; are very fond of music,
dancing, and smoking.   The women have generally lively and expressive countenances.   The complexions of the
lake-faring men have approximated almost to the savage hue.
" At Vincennes and Detroit," says Volney, " I met with faces
that reminded me of Bedwins and Egyptian fellahs. In the hue
of their skin, quality of hair, and many other circumstances,
they were alike.   They likewise resemble in having a mouth
shaped like a shark's, the sides lower than the front, the teeth
small, regular, white, and very sharp, like the tyger's. This
form may perhaps arise from their custom of biting from a
large piece when they eat, without the use of knives.   This
motion gives the muscles a form, which they at length retain,
and the solid parts are modified conformably to it."

   The fort stands on a low ridge, in the rear of the town, at
the distance of about two hundred yards.   From the summit
of this ridge, the country gradually subsides to a low swampy
plain from five to nine miles across, covered with thick
groves of young timber.   Beyond this plain, commences
a surface moderately hilly, and a soil more congenial to the
growth of grain, and fruit, if not of grass.   The inhabitants
have to draw their wood a mile and a half, from the United
States' lands, in the rear of the town.   It sells in market for
three dollars a cord ; almost every farm has an orchard ; apples, pears and peaches do well—several hundred barrels of
cider are annually made, which sells at a high price.

FISH, WILD FOWL, GAME.

There is no state or territory in North America, so bountifully supplied with fish, aquatic fowls, and wild game; all the rivers from the Miami-of-the-lakes to the St. Josephs of lake Michigan, afford an inexhaustible supply of fish, to say nothing of the vast lakes, which wash 600 miles of its frontier. The trout of Michilimackinac have a superior relish; and unlike most kinds of fish, never cloy the appetite by use; they weigh from ten to seventy lbs.—and are taken at all seasons. White fish are caught in prodigious numbers with seines, in the strait of Detroit and lake St. Clair; and there are situations, where a person, with a hook or a spear, may soon catch as many as he can carry. Sturgeon are common to lakes Erie, St. Clair, Huron and Michigan; they are a size less than those of the Hudson, and are doubtless a distinct species.

Myriads of ducks and wild geese frequent the rivers, bays, and lakes, and can be easily shot; for their fears seem to be drowned in the constant din of vociferous quakings and in the incessant thunder of their wings. Wild turkies, quails, grouse, pigeons, hawks, are numerous; the latter, are, perhaps, the most common *land* bird, the black bird excepted, which in autumn appear in swarms, and are injurious to corn and new sown wheat.

Wild game is plentiful; bears, wolves, elk, deer, foxes, beaver, otter, muskrats, martin, raccoon, wildcats, rabbits, and squirrels are found in the forests. The beaver frequents the rivers running into lake Michigan.†

† To kill the beaver, the hunters go several miles up the rivers before the approach of night, and after the dusk comes on, suffer the canoe to drift gently down the current, without noise. The beaver, in this part of the evening, come abroad to procure food, or materials for repairing their habitations; and as they are not alarmed by the canoe, they often pass it within gun-shot. The most common way of taking them, is by breaking up their houses, which is done with trenching-tools, during the winter, when the ice is strong enough to allow of approaching them; and when, also, the fur is in its most valuable state. [Henry]

Y

ANTIQUITIES.

On the river Huron, thirty miles from Detroit, and about eight miles from lake St. Clair, are a number of small mounds, situated on a dry plain, or bluff near the river. Sixteen baskets full of human bones, of a remarkable size, were discovered in the earth while sinking a cellar on this plain, for the missionary. Near the mouth of this river, on the east bank, are ancient works representing a fortress, with walls of earth thrown up, similar to those of Indiana and Ohio.

At *Belle-Fontaine,* or Spring-Wells, three miles below Detroit, are three small mounds, or tumuli, standing in a direct line, about ten rods apart. One of these having been opened, bones, stone-axes, arrow-heads, &c. were found in abundance. About one fourth of a mile below these, are still to be seen the remains of an ancient fortification. A breastwork, in some places three or four feet high, encloses several acres of firm ground, in the centre of an extensive marsh.

EXTENT OF NAVIGABLE WATERS.

	Miles.
Lake Michigan navigable	260
Lake Huron,	250
Lake St. Clair and Straits,	56
Detroit river,	26
Lake Erie,	72
Rivers running into lake Erie,	175
Do. entering the straits of Detroit and St. Clair river and lake,	100
Rivers emptying into Huron,	150
Streams entering Michigan,	700
	1789

POPULATION, DISEASES, CLIMATE.

There is no data to determine with accuracy the present population; however, it probably exceeds 12,000 souls, exclusive of Indians. The census of 1810, gave 4642 souls, distributed as follows :

Counties.	Whites.	Slaves.	Total.
Detroit, . . .	2114 .	17	2131
Erie, ...	1327 .	4	1331
Huron (of St. Clair) .	578 .	2	580
Michilimackinac, .	599 .	1	600

The diseases of this territory, are chiefly fevers, bilious and intermittents, agues, jaundice and dysentery ; the last is often fatal to children. Consumption is unfrequent. The fatal epidemic of the winter of 1813 traversed this territory like a destroying angel ; and swept off above 100 men, besides Indians.

The climate of the eastern part of this territory is nearly similar to that of the western counties of New-York and Pennsylvania ; towards the Indiana territory, milder ; but upon the coast of lake Huron, and even that of St. Clair, it is more severe ; and winter-like weather is felt at least two weeks earlier than at Detroit. Lake St. Clair is frozen over every year from December to February. Observations made by Gen. Wilkinson in 1797, show that from August 4, to Sept. 4, the thermometer in several places between St. Clair and Michilimackinac, was never higher at noon than 70 degrees, and that in the morning and evening it often sunk to 46 degrees. The northwest wind sweeps with great force across lakes Huron and Superior. I shall close the account of this territory with an extract of a letter from Gen. Hull to his correspondent in Auburn.

" There is very little settlement on the west part of lake Huron, or on the east part of lake Michigan. While I was at

Detroit, I made a treaty with the different nations of Indians, and purchased their lands for the U. S. from the Miami of lake Erie, nearly to Saganaum bay, including all the lands, between that distance on lake Erie, the river Detroit, lake St. Clair, the river St. Clair, and lake Huron; and extending back to the westward about eighty miles. I believe the Indian title has not been extinguished to any other lands, within the territory of Michigan; excepting some small tracts in different situations.

"Within this tract, are the rivers Miami, Raisin, Huron, Rouge, Huron of lake St. Clair, Trent, and some branches of the Saganaum river, besides many other smaller streams.— There is supposed to be included within this tract, about seven millions of acres. The lands on all those rivers are fertile, and capable of abundant productions. The country is generally level, and easy to be cultivated. While I was in Detroit, I sent in the fall of the year, a number of oxen, cows, and in company with others, amounting probably to 2 or 300, with one man to take care of them, give them salt, &c. on the upper branches of the river Rouge. In the spring when they returned, the cows had fine calves, and the whole were in excellent order; they looked better than those fed on hay. I consider that country, after it is cleared, a very healthy country. My family were at Detroit eight years, and were more healthy than when they lived in this town, [Newtown,] which is thought to be as healthy as any in Massachusetts. The climate is much milder, than in the same latitude in the Atlantic. We rarely have sleighing many days, excepting on the ice. I believe there is no part of the world where the soil is better for wheat, and fruit of all kinds."

MISSOURI TERRITORY,

IS situated between 29 and 49 N. latitude, and 12 50 and 36 W. longitude ; and is bounded north by Upper Canada, south by Louisiana and the Gulf of Mexico, east by the North West and Illinois Territories, Indiana, Kentucky and Tennessee ; west by Spanish possessions, Indian Territories, &c. Its computed length from north to south is 1494 miles—breadth 886 miles—its area is about 985,250 square miles, or 630,560,000 acres.

RIVERS.

Red river and the *Washita,* both wind several hundred miles through this territory ; the tributaries of the Washita, north of Louisiana, are Bayous Cerne, Cypress, Saline, and Hachios. The Hot Springs constitute its extreme sources.

The *Arkansas,* † after the Missouri and Mississippi, is the most considerable river of this territory. It takes its rise near the 41st degree of north latitude, with the Rio del

---

† The Arkansas river, taking its meanders agreeably to Lt. Wilkinson's survey of the lower part, is 1981 miles from its entrance into the Mississippi to the mountains, and from thence to its source 192 miles, making its total length 2 173 miles, all of which may be navigated with proper boats, constructed for the purpose ; except the 192 miles in the mountains. It has emptying into it, several small rivers navigable for 100 miles and upwards. Boats bound up the whole length of the navigation, should embark at its entrance, on the 1st of February ; when they would have the fresh quite to the mountains, and meet with no detention.— But if they should start later, they would find the river 1500 miles up nearly dry. It has one singularity, which struck me very forcibly at first view, but on reflection I am induced to believe it is the same case with all the rivers which run through a low, dry, and sandy soil in warm climates. This I observed to be the case with the Rio del Norte, viz : for the extent of 4 or 500 miles before you arrive near the mountains, the bed of the river is extensive, and a perfect sand bar, which at certain seasons is dry ; at least the water is standing in ponds, not affording sufficient to procure a running course. When you come nearer the mountains, you find the river contracted, a gravelly bottom, and a deep navigable stream. From these circumstances it is evident, that the sandy soil imbibes all the waters which the sources project from the mountains, and renders the river (in dry seasons) less navigable *five hundred miles* ; than 200 miles from its source.　　　[*Pike.*]

Norte, and the Platte and Roche Juane of the Missouri, and the Colorado of Caliaforna, in an immense ridge of mountains which gave rise to the Red river of the Mississippi, and runs in a S. E. and N. W. direction across the province of New Spain. The Arkansas is about two thousand miles in length; the navigation, however, cannot be said to be good; the channel is wide and shallow, and is interrupted by a considerable number of rapids. Its principal tributaries, are,

1. The *Nagracka*, from the N. W. upwards of 100 yards wide. 2. *Neskalonka*, about 120 yards wide, shoal and narrow at its mouth, but deepens and spreads above its outlet. 3. *Grand Saline*, or *Newsewketonga*, from the north, which interlocks with the Kansas river; about 50 miles from its mouth the prairie grass is encrusted with salt; the Indians collect it by scraping it off the prairie with a turkey's wing, into a trencher. 4. *Strong Saline* 75 yards wide. 5. *Verdigris*, 100 yards wide, bears north-west. 6. *Grand River*, interlocks with the Osage 130 yards wide; the two last enter within a quarter of a mile of each other. Below the mouth of Grand river commence the rapids which continue for several hundred miles below, down the Arkansas. 7. *Des Illinois*, which enters from the N. E. side. 8. *Canadian* river, comes in from the S. W.; the latter river is the main branch of the Arkansas, and is equally as large. 9. *Pottoe*, a deep narrow stream, which puts in on the S. W. 10. *River au Millieu*, falls in from the N. E. 11. *Bayou Marcallin*; besides numerous creeks, bayous and small rivers.

White river, waters the country between the Arkansas, and the St. Francis—it is a noble stream, and occupies with its numerous tributaries, a vast extent of country. The Westernmost branch, or more properly White river, rises in the Black mountains, which separate it from the Arkansas; the Northern and Eastern, take their waters from the vicinity of the Osage, the Gasconade, the Maremeg and the western branch of the St. Francis. It enters the Mississippi, about twenty miles above the Arkansas; thirty miles up, it communicates with that river, by a channel with a current setting alternately into the one stream, and into the other, as either happens to be the highest. By computation it is navigable eleven or twelve hundred miles, though it is exceedingly crooked. It is interrupted by no shoal or rapid; its waters are pure and limpid, and its current never becomes low, even in the dryest season. Four hundred miles from its mouth it receives Black river, its principal eastern branch; it afterwards receives a number of others which are known by various names. Rapid, John, James and Red rivers, are each navigable from one to three hundred miles. Black, or Le Noir river, is navigable four or five hundred miles; receiving a number of tributary streams of considerable size. The Current, Elevenpoint and Spring rivers are principally spoken of. The last deserves a more particular description. It rises suddenly from a number of springs, which uniting within a short distance of the place from whence they issue, form a river two hundred and fifty yards in width, affording a navigation from thence, for laden batteaux to the Mississippi : contracting its width however, to fifty or sixty yards. This immense spring is full of the finest fish; bass, perch and pike mingle here indiscriminately. In the winter, it is the resort of swarms of ducks, swans, and geese. It is about two hundred miles west of Cape Girardeau.*

These rivers are all remarkable for the navigation which they afford; most of them having sufficient water to carry a boat without any interruption, almost to their very sources. Springs, creeks, and rivulets are very abundant. Every one who has traversed it agrees, that the country occupied by the waters of White river, perhaps two hundred and fifty miles square, is one of the finest for settlements in western America. It is interspersed with what are called knobs; hills or ridges, the summits are strewed with horn stone, but generally the land is of the first rate quality; in most places

* See Breckenridge's Sketches of Louisiana, published at St. Louis in the autumn of 1811.

finely wooded, and the prairies of small extent.   The description of Kentucky, at first deemed romance, would be applicable to this country.

The St. Francis, enters the Mississippi 75 miles above White river, and affords a navigation of six hundred miles. Its western branch rises with the waters of White river, and its eastern one with Big river, a branch of the Maremeg. It is very erroneously laid down on the common maps; its general course must be at least sixty or seventy miles further east.   After pursuing a course nearly south, and uniting with its western branch, it suddenly turns S. W. so as to correspond with the course of the Mississippi, and runs nearly parallel with that river four hundred miles.   The St. Francis is navigable from a point sixty miles west of St. Genevieve. Before it makes the sudden turn to the west, it is a beautiful limpid stream, passing through a charming country; but afterwards encreased in size, and entering the low lands, flows with a slow and lazy current.   It communicates with the lakes that lie to the east, between it and the Mississippi; which are formed by rivulets flowing from the upland country, and the springs which lose themselves in the level commencing at Cape Girardeau.   On the south side it overflows its banks considerably; so that when high, a person may easily lose the channel, unless well acquainted with its course.   The channel is, in many places, much impeded with driftwood. The north bank is less subject to inundation, and in many places produces quantities of cane.

Between the St. Francis and the mouth of the Ohio there are no large streams; two bayous leave the Mississippi and enter the St. Francis many miles from its mouth, forming several large islands.   The Chepousa river heads in a lake, and after running about seventy miles falls into the Mississippi ninety miles below the mouth of the Ohio.

Between the mouth of the Ohio and that of the Missouri, we successively pass, the Tywawatia creek, Riviere de la Pomme, Obrazo, Amite and St. Lora rivers; this is a handsome stream ; Saline river or creek, on which is made great quantites of salt. Gabourie and Platine creeks, and the river Maremeg. These streams, except the last, are necessarily short, by reason of the proximity of the St. Francis.

The Maremeg river, enters the Mississippi about forty miles below the Missouri. Although extremely crooked, it is a fine river, and navigable two hundred and fifty miles to its very source ; for like Spring river, it issues forth suddenly from a large fountain. This appears to be a circumstance not unusual with the rivers of this country. It rises near the waters of White river. The Maremeg is remarkable for the quantities of fish with which it abounds ; large quantities are caught and salted up.—The White fish is considered one of the best fish of the fresh water, and is found in abundance in this river. A considerable branch called the Negro fork navigable forty or fifty miles with canoes, rising near the Mine-a-Burton and the Big river ; a branch of this, has its source at a very short distance from the St. Francis, and in a circuitous course of forty miles almost includes the Mine-a-Burton. The Maremeg has no considerable branches on the north, owing to its proximity to the waters of the Missouri on that side.

The *Missouri*, is the largest branch of the Mississippi ; the sources of this river are still undiscovered. It was navigated by Captains Lewis and Clark 3090 miles, where it was inclosed by very lofty mountains. Its breadth is various, from 800 to 300 yards wide ; 1888 miles from its mouth it is 527 yards wide ; at this distance from its mouth, it is larger than the Illinois ; from its mouth to *Fort Mandan* in lat. 47 21, a distance of upwards of 1600 miles, the navigation is good, the current deep and rapid, and the water muddy ; at its entrance into the Mississippi, in lat. 38, 45 ; it is 700 yards wide. In lat. 47 3, two thousand five hundred and seventy-five miles from its confluence with the Mississippi, are the grand rapids ; these falls are eighteen miles long, and in that distance descend 362 feet. The first great pitch is 98 feet,

Z

the second 19, the third 48, the fourth 26 ; smaller rapids make up the balance of the descent. The rivers entering from the right bank of the Missouri, are,

1. *Bonhomme* river flows into the Missouri about 70 miles above its mouth. This stream interlocks with branches of the Maremeg, waters a fine district of territory, has a northern direction, and is about 100 yards wide at its mouth. 2. *Gasconade*, heads near the St. Francis, runs north and enters the Mississippi about 40 miles above the Bonhomme. 3. *Osage* river, rises in the Black mountains, which separate its waters from those of the Arkansas. It is said to be navigable 600 miles; but it does not afford a good navigation, being full of shoals and ripples. It has a great number of tributary rivers, besides large creeks, among which are, *Mary's* river, heads near the Gasconade, runs N. W. and falls in twenty miles from the Missouri. *Little Gravel*, heads near the Missouri, and pursuing a S. E. course enters from the left bank, nearly 100 miles above the mouth of the Osage. *Great Gravel*, from the south, interlocks with the St. Francis, enters the Osage, east of Little Gravel, but thirty-six miles above, and according to Pike, is 118 miles above the confluence of the Osage with the Missouri. The Pottoe, a small river. The Yungar, heads between White river of the Mississippi, and the Grand Fork of the Osage, pursues a north-east course, and joins the Osage about 25 miles above Great Gravel river : the Indians call it *Ne-hem-gar;* it derives its name from the vast number of springs at its source ; it is supposed to be nearly as extensive as the Osage river, navigable for canoes 100 miles, and is celebrated for the abundance of bear, which are found on its branches. On it hunt the Chasseurs du Bois of Louisiana, Osage, and Creeks (or Muskogees) a wandering party of which have established themselves in this territory ; between whom and the French hunters, frequent skirmishes take place. Above this river are the Park, Cardinal, Buckeye, and Grand Fork from the south ; and Grand river, East Fork, and Vermillion from the S. W.

Little Saltwater, abounding with salines, is the next stream entering the left bank of the Missouri. *Mine* river, heads between the great Osage and branches of the Kanzas, and is the largest flowing into the Missouri between the Osage and Kanzas. The main branch of the Mine river, called Salt Fork, is generally impregnated with salt as thoroughly as the sea water, from June to November. A small creek runs into it, from fifteen to twenty feet wide, and from six to twelve inches deep formed entirely of salt springs, without its current encreasing or decreasing during the whole season. *Blue water* river, 80 yards wide. *Kanzas* river, is large and navigable, heads near the sources of the Arkansas, is 230 yards wide at its mouth ; empties itself about 650 miles above the mouth of the Missouri. The Kanzas nation of Indians claim the lands bordering on this river and its extensive branches ; the country is rich but destitute of timber, except on the water courses ; grapes are found in abundance and the country back from the streams is almost one continued prairie. Independence, 120 yards wide. Wolf river. Great Nemahaw, 130 yards wide. Weeping river. *Platte* river is the next important stream ; it heads to the west of the *Arkansas*, winds several hundred miles through an open prairie country, and enters the Missouri 330 miles above the Kansas. Its banks are much frequented by white and red hunters. Quicam river 1026 miles from the mouth of the Missouri, 150 yards wide, not navigable, heads in the black mountains, and waters a broken country. Teton river falls into the Missouri 132 miles higher up ; it is small, and heads in the plains. *White* river, comes from the south, is 150 yards wide at its mouth, and navigable 100 miles. *Chien*, or *Dog* river, is nearly half a mile wide according to the Indians, flows through a plain level country, for several hundred miles, mostly destitute of timber, but settled along the bottoms with Indians, towards its head. *Warrica*. *Batteaux* river, on which are several Indian villages ; it has several branches, is about 100 yards wide and a hilly broken country. *Little*

Missouri, falls into the Missouri 90 miles above Fort Mandan; it resembles its namesake, exactly in the color of its water, current and taste. Some of the tops of the hills here, are as white as chalk. *Yellow Stone,* or *Roche Jaune,* nearly half a mile wide, rapid, rather shallow but not fordable; the water clear, excepting when rain falls, and then it becomes immediately thick from the earth which is washed into it from the barren hills. Many of these hills are so washed, and become so steep, that no animal can ascend them, except the cabree, and mountain ram. The bottoms are rich; timber mostly cotton-wood. The mouth of this river is 278 miles above the Mandane villages; 186 above the little Missouri, and 1888 miles from the mouth of the Missouri. *Big Horn* river, 300 yards wide, has several forks. *Muscleshell* river, empties itself 660 miles above Fort Mandan; it is 110 yards wide—its mouth is in N. lat. 47 24. The Missouri is here 522 yards wide. Above the Muscleshell in lat. 47, 24 12, Captains Lewis and Clark, arrived at the Forks of two rivers; doubts arose, which of these rivers was the Missouri. Parties ascended both branches about 50 miles; the *south* branch was found to afford the best navigation, and was accordingly assumed as the true Missouri; it is 372 yards broad; and the other, which they named *Maria's* river, 586 yards wide; both streams abound with fish. The south branch had for two or three days, the appearance of claret, but again assumed its usual muddy color. At the distance of 250 miles from the great falls, and in the rocky mountains, the Missouri divides into three nearly equal branches at the same point. The two largest branches are so nearly alike in magnitude, measuring sixty yards across, that captain Lewis did not conceive that either of them, could with propriety, retain the name of *Missouri,* and therefore, called the north branch *Jefferson,* the west or middle branch *Madison,* and the south branch *Gallatin* river. The confluence of these rivers is 2848 miles from the mouth of the Missouri, by the meanderings of that river, and in lat. 45, 22 34. He ascended the

Jefferson, or most northerly fork, 248 miles to the upper forks, where the navigation become impracticable ; making the total distance from the mouth of the Missouri, *three thousand and ninety* miles.

The rivers which flow into the Missouri from the left or northern bank, beginning at its mouth, are, *Femmeosage, Cherette, Otter* and *May* rivers, which enter between the mouths of the Bonhomme and the Osage : Cedar river; Great Manitou, Little Manitou, Goodworman's river ; Chariton, Grand river, Tyger river, Little Platte, Soldier's river, Little Sioux rivers ; the last rises in lake Esprit fifteen miles from the river Moyen, and is sixty-four yards wide ; here commences the Sioux country ; the next river of note is the big Sioux river, which heads with the St. Peters and waters of lake Winnipique in a high wooded country ; about ninety miles higher up, the river Jacque falls in on the same side, and about 100 yards wide, this river heads with the waters of lake Winnipique, at no great distance east from this place ; the head of the river Moyen is in Pilican lake between the Sioux rivers and the St. Peters ; above this, are Three rivers, Ball river, Chuss-chu, Maria, &c.

The rivers entering the right bank of the Mississippi, above the mouth of the Missouri, are, 1. *Buffaloe* river, comes from the north-west, 190 yards wide at its outlet ; it bears from the Mississippi S. 30 W. 2. *Bar* river, about 20 yards wide. 3. *Oahahah,* or Salt river, bears from the Mississippi N. 75 W. and is upwards of 100 yards wide at its entrance, of a mild current ; about one day's sail up this river there are salt springs, at which salt has been made for several years past. 4. *Jaustioni,* 30 yards wide, bears from the Mississippi S. W. and constitutes the boundary line between the United States and Sac nation on the west side of the Mississippi. 5. *Wyaconda,* 100 yards broad at its junction with the Mississippi ; bears from the latter nearly due west. 6. *De Moyen* river, very large, 200 yards wide, and seven or eight hundred miles long ; heads to the north-west of the Sioux branch of the Missouri; its chief tributaries are, Rustand, Tetone, Buffaloe, Point, Grand and Village rivers, all running in from the south and south-west, and north Fork.   7. *Iowa* river, 150 yards wide, bears from the Mississippi S. W. This river is navigable for batteaux near 300 miles, where it branches out into three forks, called the Turkey's foot. These forks shortly after lose themselves in Rice lakes. Thirty-six miles from its mouth it divides into two branches; the right fork is called Red Cedar river, from the quantity of that wood on its banks.   8. *Wabisisinekan*, runs nearly parallel with Red Cedar Fork of the Iowa; and has very little wood on its banks.   9. *Great Macoketh*.   10. *Little Macoketh*: these rivers have no remarkable characteristics; though it is said that lead mines exist on their banks.   12. *Cat Fish* river.   12. *Turkey* river, 100 yards wide, bears from the Mississippi about S. W.   The Renard Indians who reside on this river supply Prairie des Chiens with corn. 13. *Yellow* river, bears from the Mississippi nearly due W.   14. *Upper Iowa*, about 100 yards wide, enters the Mississippi about 35 miles above Prairie des Chiens; bears N. W.   15. *Racine*, or *Root* river, bears due west, navigable for canoes 60 miles.   16. 17. *Le Claire*, and *Embarras* rivers, which join these waters just as they form a confluence with their grand estuary.   18. *River* of the *Montaigne qui trompe dans l'eau*, a small stream in the rear of the hill of that name. 19. Rivière *Au Bœuf*, 30 yards wide, bears N. W. and falls into the lower end of lake Pepin.   *Cannon* river, enters the Mississippi 40 miles above lake Pepin.   St. Peters river which has several large large forks, the principal is the river Sauteaux; 15 miles up this river commence fine prairies and the Sioux villages.   Great and Little Sac rivers, the first is two hundred yards wide; and joins the Mississippi a little above St. Anthony's falls; about 45 miles higher up is Pine creek, where Lt. Pike wintered in 1805; on its margin are large groves of *Red* and *White* pine; in the rear of these, prairies.   *Elk* river; this stream affords a communication with the river St. Peters ; they first ascend it to a small lake, cross it, then ascend a small stream to a large lake, from which they make a portage of four miles west, and fall into the Sauteaux river, which they descend into the St. Peters. *River de Corbeau,* about 375 miles above the falls of St. Anthony, has a mild current, and empties itself into the Mississippi by two channels.

Lieut. Pike thought that the junction of these streams should be called the forks of the Mississippi, as it is of equal magnitude and heads not far from the same source. This fork affords the best and most approved communication with *Red river,* a tributary of Hudson bay, by ascending the De Corbeau 180 miles, to the river *Aux Feuilles,* running N. W. which must also be ascended 180 miles, where there is a *portage* of one mile into the Otter Tail Lake, which is a principal source of Red river. The other branch of the river De Corbeau, bears S. W. and approximates with the St. Peters. The mouth of the De Corbeau is in lat. 45, 47, 50 N. *Pine river,* bears N. 30 E. is eighty yards wide at its mouth, and communicates with *Lac Le Sang Sue,* or Leech lake, through a chain of lakes, ponds, &c. by a short portage. *Pike river,* is the next stream entering from the west ; it bears nearly due north ; running at the distance of from twenty to forty miles from the Mississippi. *Lake Winnepique* river, bears northwest, rises near that lake ; *Leech lake* river, running out of Leech lake, one of the main sources of the Mississippi.

The northern frontier of this immense territory is watered by streams flowing into Hudson bay. The principal of which constitute the head branches of Red river and the Pasquayah Assinnibion.

At present, it is not known how far this territory extends westwardly beyond the Sabine, along the coast of the gulf of Mexico. The Spaniards contend that their province of Texas reaches to the Sabine. The rivers which water the disputed territory, are Rio Toyac flowing into Sabine lake, Rio Trinity, running into Galveston bay, Rio Brassos, Rio

Colorado, and Rio Guadaloupe, all emptying into the gulf; the last at the distance of 170 miles from the Sabine. The country between the Sabine and Colorodo is in many parts rich, and capable of producing sugar and cotton to almost any amount, besides it is a very good stock country, agreeably variegated with prairies and forests of heavy timber.

LAKES.

The country north of the Missouri abounds with lakes and ponds. Lake Despice forms the grand reservoir of the *Little Sioux*, and is seventy miles in circumference. West of the head branches of the Mississippi are Packagamau, remarkable for the wild rice which grows in its water. Lake Winnipique, of an oval form, thirty-six miles in circumference, Leech, and Otter Tail lakes. In the south along the vallies of the Washita, Arkansas, White river, St. Francis. Small lakes are numerous.

MOUNTAINS.

The Masserne ridges, extend westwardly from near the Mississippi to the sources of the Red river, and give to the country west of the Washita, a rugged surface. The Black mountains run nearly parallel to the Missouri, from the head of the Kanzas. The rocky mountains form a formidable natural boundary on the west and northwest.

SALINES.

The country between the river Platter and Fort Mandan, on both sides of the Missouri contains a number of small lakes, many of which is said to be so much impregnated with saline properties, of the nature of glauber salts, as to produce similar effects. It is certain that the water of some of the smaller streams possess this quality. Sabine, Chalybeate, and Sulphur springs are numerous; particularly the first, which are useful in many diseases. The *Hot Springs*, at the head of the Washita, are a great natural curiosity; they are six in number, issuing from the side of a hill, the body of which is silicious, partly flint, and partly free-stone; the soil overflowed by the waters of the springs is incrusted with a calcareous matter. Their heat is too great for the hand to bear; the highest temperature is about 150 deg. and is greatest in dry seasons. Meat has been boiled in them in a shorter space of time than could be accomplished by a culinary fire. The water is soft and limpid, without smell, and of an agreeable taste. It is drunk after it becomes cool, and used for every other purpose in preference to the water of the cold springs in the vicinity. The Indians have from time immemorial resorted to them on account of their medicinal virtues. The land around them is called by them the "*Land of Peace;*" for hostile tribes frequent the waters at the same time with perfect harmony. Dr. Hunter, who visited these springs, found a *green plant* growing in the hot water, which seemed to be a species of the *conferva;* but what is more remarkable, a small testaceous animal adhered to it and lived in a temperature approaching the boiling heat. He beheld plants, shrubs and trees, and a species of wild cabbage, absolutely growing and appearing healthy, while their roots were exposed to a heat of 130 degrees. He, and his companion, Mr. Dunbar, cooked the cabbage and found it to be mild and good for food. These waters have effected surprising cures in chronic pains, paralysis, &c. Persons, who, by exposure to the vicissitudes of climate and season, have been restored by the use of these springs, from a state of entire inability of motion, to complete health and activity. A careful analysis of these waters, by evaporation and precipitation, indicated the presence of a small portion of carbonic acid, some of the muriate of soda, a small quantity of calcareous matter, and a scarcely perceptible portion of iron. Invalids in great numbers frequent these springs; they find relief not by drinking the water, but by exposure to the steam, which the springs constantly emit, and which in very dry weather is too hot to be endured. Volcanic productions are found in the neighborhood of the springs. It is stated that severe explosions have been heard and lava seen in the fissures caused by the irruption.

The salines have uncommon strength; and they are so abundant that almost every county, and in some districts every township will forever have an inexhaustible supply of salt; particularly, south of the Missouri. One of the head branches of the Kanzas, (20 yards wide) which Lieut. Pike crossed on his route to the Arkansas, was so salt that the water sufficiently seasoned the soup of the meat, which his men boiled in it. In many places the earth was so strongly impregnated with nitre and saline qualities that the bare spots at noon day were covered with a thin layer of congealed salt. Lieut. Wilkinson found the water of the Grand Saline running into the Arkansas, so strong as to render unpalatable the corn which his party boiled in it. "Every day," they "passed strongly impregnated salines and perceived the shores of the river completely frosted with nitre." The grass of the prairies in the vicinity of the Grand Saline, resembles that of the salt marshes of the seaboard. Lt. Pike found rock salt in the banks of a stream west of the Arkansas.

Mines of sal gem or Rock Salt exist towards the head branches of the Arkansas, and sometimes approach to the very surface of the earth. The Indians employ levers to break it up and loosen it, some is white and some of a reddish hue. Upon the south-western head branches of the Arkansas is another remarkable saline :

" On the declivity of a small hill, there are five holes about a foot and an half in diameter, and two feet deep. They are always full of a very salt water, but never run over. Dip out as much as you please, there is no diminution; the deficiency is instantly supplied. and about ten feet lower down the hill there issues a spring of pure and fresh water.—When these regions become peopled, the transportation of this rock-salt will be perfectly easy, by means of the Arkansas. Experience has proved it to be preferable to every other kind in curing provisions." The intelligent Dr. Sibley says, that the " Grand Saline is situated about 280 miles southwest of Fort Osage, between two forks of a small branch of the Arkansas, one of which washes its southern extremity, and the other, the principal one, runs nearly parallel, within a mile of its opposite side. It is a hard level plain of a reddish colored sand, and of an irregular or mixed figure; its greatest length is from north-west to south-east, and its circumference full 30 miles—from the appearance of driftwood that is scattered over, it would seem that the whole plain is at times inundated by the overflowing of the streams that pass near it. This plain is entirely covered in dry hot weather, from two to six inches deep, with a crust of beautiful clean white salt, of a quality rather superior to the imported brown salt; it bears a striking resemblance to a field of brilliant snow after a rain, with a light crust on its top. On a bright sunny morning the appearance of this natural curiosity is highly picturesque. It possesses the quality of looming or magnifying objects, and this in a very striking degree, making the small billets of wood appear as formidable as trees. Numbers of buffaloes were on the plain. The Saline is environed by a strip of marshy prairie with a few scattering trees, mostly of cotton wood. Behind, there is a range of sand hills, some of which are perfectly naked, others thinly clothed with verdure, and dwarf plum bushes, not more than thirty inches in height, from which we procured abundance of the most delicious plums I ever tasted. The distance to a navigable branch of the Arkansas is about 80 miles, the country tolerably level, and the water courses easily passed."

MINERALS.

Lead is the most abundant mineral hitherto discovered in this territory. It is the opinion of a late traveller that the mines

on the river Maremeg and Gouberie, are alone capable of supplying the whole world.   About 1000 tons have been smelt-
ed at the several furnaces annually.   These mines are numerous, and extend over a large district of country, being fifty
miles long and twenty-five broad.   The most noted, are
Mine Le Burton, Mine la Motte, New Diggings, American
Mine, &c.   The ore can be found in almost every direction.
The price of lead is from four to five dollars a hundred, and
shot nine dollars.   Most of the mineral is so exceedingly
rich, that 100 pounds of ore will produce from eighty to ninety of pure lead.*   Lead mines are said to exist on the waters
of the Washita and the St. Francis.   Iron, tin, zinc, copper,
salt-petre, and fossil coal, are found in abundance.

SOIL, SURFACE.

There are extensive alluvial tracts on all the rivers. This
land, where it is not subject to inundation, is of the first quality, and apparently experiences little or no deterioration from
producing a long series of crops.   Between the bayous of the

---

* The mineral at Mine le Burton is generally found in veins of almost every
size from three feet in circumference and under, and from six to twelve feet beneath
the surface of the earth.   At the New Diggings it is found from four to thirty feet
under ground, where they are obliged to discontinue their work on account of the
water coming in upon them.   They have no contrivance to draw it off, except a
single bucket, suspended from an arm in a crochet, after the manner of most of
our country wells.   The workmen are ill provided with instruments, having no
other tools than a pick-ax and shovel, with which they open a hole about six or
seven feet deep, and four or five in length and breadth; if they are successful they
enlarge the hole, but if not they abandon it and open another, either along side
of the former, or in any other spot where their fancy may direct. I have no
doubt that those grounds or mines which have apparently been exhausted, or abandoned on account of the water flowing in upon them, will eventually be found the
richest discoveries yet made.   I am of opinion, that in no instance have they yet
fallen upon the main bed of ore, which probably lies at such a depth as will require the sinking of a shaft to a considerable depth, to enable them to work it.—
Hitherto they have been contented with the small spurs or veins which are found
near the surface of the earth.   When the mineral is collected for smelting, they
build up in the woods a back wall with two sides, about sixteen feet in front, eight
wide, and six in height, with the floor a little inclining towards the back, where
a few small holes are left for the lead as it melts to run into the moulds.   Here
they pile up wood and mineral in alternate layers, and setting fire to the whole,
the operation of smelting is quickly performed.   There is but one regular built air-
furnace throughout this country, which is at the Mine le Burton.   The expense
of such a building is so great, and the mineral so plenty, that the miners prefer an
open furnace, which in all probability cannot cost them more than forty or fifty
dollars; whereas a proper air-furnace, like the one just mentioned, would cost
them 5 or 6000 dollars.   [Schultz.]

St. Francis and the Louisiana boundary line, the Mississippi, St. Francis and Arkansas annually overflow considerable tracts, which in many places produces irreclaimable swamps.

The country may be said to be fertile from the mouth of the Missouri, westwardly, as far as the Kanzas, and northwardly, up the Mississippi, as far as the Great Sac river. Beyond these limits the soil gradually deteriorates, until you reach the morasses of the north, and the sterile prairies and barren hills of the west.

Never having travelled in this territory, except from the mouth of the Ohio to St. Genevieve, I shall chiefly confine myself to extracts from writers of well known authenticity. In the first place I will introduce the testimony of Mr. Brown, the surveyor, who was employed by government, to run the Osage boundary line extending from the Missouri to the Arkansas.

"The Boone's Lick country no doubt is the richest considerable body of good land in the territory. I think it very similar to the good land of Kentucky, and as it has no bed of rock as is in Kentucky it is perhaps superior. Between Boone's Lick and the fort, the land south of the river is one extended prairie, except perhaps a hundred sections or so of tolerable good wood land, extending more or less, say twenty miles down the river from the fort. One or two creeks pass through this timber from the prairie, sufficient for small machinery or grist mills. The prairie lies well and in general is scarcely inferior in point of soil to the river bottom. The fort is in latitude thirty-nine degrees five minutes north, and stands on the brow of a hill with a rocky base and within a hundred yards of the river. It commands a full view of five miles east down the river and two miles north up. The square of two leagues reserved for the fort was so laid off as to have the fort near the north east corner; about half this square is timbered land of good quality.

"Proceeding on the boundary line at seventy-six miles from the fort, we crossed the Osage river, some three or four miles

below the Osage village.   Thus far the land is prairie altogether, except some little spots and strips on the creeks, not
any where sufficient for a settlement.   A great proportion of
the land, so far, is of good quality and lies well.   There is a
very extensive bottom on the north side of the Osage river of
the finest quality, and on the south side of secondary bottom.
There rises on this plain, south of the river, some high mounds
or insulated hills, near the Indian village, and about two miles
west of the line; I ascended them and am persuaded, that
turning round I could survey 500 square miles, and nearly all
of the first quality ; timber and springs only are wanting to
make this the finest part of the world I have yet seen : About
a hundred and thirty miles took us to the timbered land ; we
observed the land to be poorer as we approached it.   About
this we found the first running streams except the Osage river ;
they ran west and were waters of the Grand river of the Arkansas.   Having entered the timbered land we saw but little
more prairie.   At 200 miles we crossed the head water of
the Buffaloe fork of White river, it was inconsiderable and
hardly ran.

Two hundred fifty-four and a half miles took us to the Arkansas river, at a point some twenty miles below a stream on
the other side called the Pottoe and near the mouth of a creek
called Frog Bayou.   It is a piece below the settlement which
is above the Cherokee village.   The woodland we passed
through was oak timbered, poor, stony and perhaps should
be called mountainous.   There is but little exception to this
remark.   This high land separates the head waters of White
river from those of Grand river.   As to game we found plenty for use, though not so much as I expected ; I saw no buffaloe until near the waters of White river.   Having completed the boundary line, which is about 140 miles due west
from the meridian run from the mouth of the Arkansas, we
started down the river at some little distance off.   The land
is poor, stony, and broken, oak and pine timber, down to the
Cherokee village, say sixty miles, east of the line.   About

twenty miles further east to the mouth of the Quadrant, the land is less broken and stony, though still rather poor. The river bottom is generally rich, I believe, though not very extensive where I was and somewhat subject to inundation.—From the Quadrant we came the usual way to St. Louis. On our return found the land generally poor, broken and stony, yet there is some very good bottom land on the tributary streams of White river and the St. Francis, and many spots might be selected fit for cultivation, though not enough to give a character to the country. Near the little village of St. Michael, is some very good land, and some little further on the way toward the Mines is a small settlement of very fine land.

Lieut. Pike states that "the country round the Osage villages, is one of the most beautiful the eye ever beheld. The three branches of the river, viz: the large east fork, the middle one (up which he ascended,) and the northern one, all winding round and pass the villages, giving the advantages of wood and water—and at the same time, the extensive prairies crowned with rich and luxuriant grass and flowers—gently diversified by the rising swells, and sloping lawns—presenting to the warm imagination the future seats of husbandry, the numerous herds of domestic animals, which are no doubt destined to crown with joy those happy plains. From the Osage towns to the source of the Osage river, there is no difference in the appearance of the country, except that on the south and east, the view on the prairies becomes unbounded, and is only limited by the imbecility of our sight. The waters of the White river and the Osage, are divided merely by a small ridge in the prairie, and the dry branches appear to interlock at their head. From thence to the main branch of said river, the country appeared high and gravelly ridges of prairie land.—On the main White river is large timber and fine ground for cultivation." Lt. Pike found valuable bottom land on White river. But from the Verdigris to the Arkansas he passed over gravelly hills and a prairie country, in some places well watered, but deficient in timber, except for a limited number

of inhabitants for a few years. He frequently met with salines, spa.springs and iron ore. All the country, between the
forks of Kanzas river, a distance of 160 miles, may be called
prairie, notwithstanding the borders of wood land which orna-
ment the banks of those streams, but are no more than a line
traced on a sheet of paper, when compared to the immense
tract of meadow country. As he approached the Arkansas,
the country appeared low and swampy for the space of fifteen
or twenty miles. From thence, about half way to the mountains, is a continued succession of low prairie hills, badly watered and nearly destitute of timber.

BOONE's SETTLEMENT.

"Boone's lick, now Howard county, begins at the mouth of
the Great Osage river, and runs up said river to the Osage
boundary line; thence north with that line to the Missouri;
thence up the Missouri to a point opposite the Kanzas river;
thence northward 140 miles; thence eastward to the main dividing ridge of high ground between the Mississippi and Missouri rivers; thence along said ridge to the head of the main
fork of Cedar river; thence down this river to the Missouri,
and down the Missouri to Osage river, or place of beginning;
containing about 30,000 square miles; one half of which is
first rate land, and but little that is not fit for cultivation;
three fifths are prairie.

" The first settlement of this county was made in 1805, at
Boone's lick, Mackay's saline, by Maj. Nathan Boone, son of
the celebrated Col. Daniel Boone, for the purpose of making
salt, and has since been occupied for salt works. Farmers
did not settle until the fall of 1811, when about twenty settled Boone's lick bottom. This settlement increased slowly
on account of the Indians, during the late war. In November, 1815, the population amounted to 526 free white males,
and it was formed into a separate county of the above boundary and name. It now, [August 24th,] contains about 1,050

free white males.   A site is fixed upon for a town by the county commissioners, on the bank of the Missouri, in a very eligible situation.   The lots will shortly be put in market.

The face of the country is neither mountainous nor hilly, yet a great part of it is uneven, or rolling ground.   There is great uniformity throughout the county, and but little diversity of soil, stone, or timber.

The river Missouri runs through the county.   The other navigable streams are the Great Osage, Mine river, and Kanzas from the south; the Charlatan, Grand river, and Little Platte from the north, besides numerous small streams.

Salt springs are found in abundance in some parts of this county.   The main branch of the Mine river, called the Salt fork, is generally impregnated with salt as strongly as the sea water, from the month of June to November.

Minerals of various kinds are found here.   Iron in abundance, lead, tin, copper, zinc, silver rare, sulphur, alum, copperas, saltpetre, &c.   To the botanist this country will afford a rich harvest.   It abounds in medicinal plants, from among which the aborigines select those capable of curing the most inveterate *syphilis*.   The natives also cure the bite of the rattlesnake, and rheumatisms of long standing.   They are also remarkable for their treatment of gun-shot wounds.   The Great Osage Indians, or, as they call themselves, *Wassashsha*, are the most skilled in medicine.   Agriculture is but little attended to, although the country is extremely fertile.   One acre of land will produce 160 bushels of prime corn, fifty do. of wheat, sixty lbs. to the bushel, and 1000 lbs. of Carolina cotton in the seed.   Hemp, flax, and every article of agriculture, except tobacco, in greater abundance than any county near the same latitude in the United States.   Tobacco does not do well; nor can any farmer with us tell the reason.   A public road is now opening from Potosi, the lead mines, in Washington county, to this settlement, and is already cut to the Osage river, which will greatly facilitate the intercourse with the States.   The air in this climate is less liable to sudden changes than the country more eastward. We seldom have chilling cold, unless the north-west winds break across the vast extent of prairies which lies between us and the northern regions ; that wind, however, seldom continues longer than eight hours. The spring season opens with heavy rains, which continue, with short intervals, until the first of May, and from that month to the first of August there is but little rain ; weather hot, with frequent thunder and lightning. Diseases are but little known in this agreeable climate ; those most frequent are remittent fevers. The greatest scourge is the influenza. It is probable that diseases will be introduced with wealth and dissipation.

The place selected for a town is nearly in the centre of the great body of rich land in this Territory, and is situated in about 38 deg. 43 min. north lat. It is 150 miles west of St. Louis, 158 from the mouth of the Missouri by land, and 180 by water, from St. Charles 130, from *Cote sans dessire* 60, from the Grand river* 24, from the Great Osage town 100, the same distance from the nearest point on the Mississippi, and 130 from the town of Potosi, Washington county. The principal articles of trade are salt, live stock, beef, pork, beaver, tallow, beeswax, honey, peltries, saltpetre and grain. The inhabitants are composed of different religious persuasions. The state of education is very deplorable : yet the mass of our citizens are perhaps not as ignorant as the same class of men in the States. We are in the first stage of our political existence, and expect to emerge from our darkness and obscurity very rapidly.†

On the west bank of the Mississippi, there is a continued line of settlements except at short intervals, of low bottoms, or barren hills, from the mouth of the Missouri to the confluence

* The mouth of the Grand river will, at some future day, be the capital of the Missouri country. It is at the centre of all the flat lands and is the most delightful spot in the western territory. From this spot to the Mississippi, at the nearest point, it is only 25 leagues across a delightful country, dry and open.

† Extract of a letter from John G. Heath, Esq. published in the National Register.

of the Ohio ;   there are also considerable settlements at New-
Madrid, and below the St. Francis, extending to the mouth
of the Arkansas.   There are likewise, a few insulated settlements up the St. Francis, Arkansas, Whiteriver, and Washita.

BANKS OF THE MISSOURI.

The banks of this immense river, are lined with mineral
and vegetable riches.   Fifteen miles above its entrance into
the Mississippi, on the southern bank, is a coal hill, called by
the French, la Charboniere.   This hill is one solid mass of
stone coal, and is supposed to afford an inexhaustible supply
of that valuable species of fuel.   The northern shore, as far up
as the Gasconade, is generally a low, rich bottom, from one to
two miles wide, covered with ash, sycamore, pecan, black
walnut, honey locust, &c.   On the south hills, rivulets and a
small number of small creeks, with a rich soil, fine timber,
grape vines, and a luxuriant growth of cane.

From the Gasconade to the entrance of the Osage, the
south side of the river is hilly, but well timbered.   Thus far
the soil is well suited to the cultivation of the grain and agricultural products of the middle and western States.   The
timber is of various sorts, but the cotton-wood predominates
on the made bottoms.   "To give," says Mr. Soulard, "a
precise idea of the incalculable riches scattered along the sides
of the Missouri, would require unlimited knowledge.   The
low bottoms are covered with large trees, especially the poplar and cotton trees, large enough for first rate canoes, the
sugar maple, the red and black walnut, so useful to joiners ;
the red and white elm, the three-thorned acacia, of which
impenetrable hedges can be made ; the osier, the red and
black mulberry, the limetree, the horse chesnut, all of which
are very plentiful ; red and white oak, fit for vessels, and all
other sorts of timber, pine, and on the Rocky mountains, cedar are common productions.   I find it impossible to enume-

rate all the trees, which are yet unknown in other countries; and with whose uses and qualities we are as yet unacquainted. The smaller plants are still more numerous. The Indians know the virtues of many of them; some are used to heal wounds, others to poison arrows, some again for dying colors, and they employ certain vegetable simples to cure radically and promptly the venereal disease. They conceal from us, with great care, a plant which renders them for some instants insensible to the most vehement fire. I have seen them take hold of red hot irons and burning coals without suffering any inconvenience.

"The lands in the neighborhood of the Missouri are excellent, and when cultivated are capable of yielding all the productions of the temperate climates, and even some of the hot ones; such as wheat, maize, and every kind of grain; common and sweet potatoes; hemp, which seems to be an indigenous vegetable; even cotton succeeds here, though not so well as further south; and the raising of it answers a good purpose for the families already settled on the river: for from a field of about two acres, they obtain a crop sufficient to clothe a family. The natural prairies are a great resource for them. These afford excellent pasture, and require but little labor to clear them. After one year's exertion, a man may enjoy his fields duly prepared for crops. Brick and potter's earths are very common, and the true Chinese Kaolin is reported, by good judges, to be here, that substance to which porcelain, owes its peculiar fineness. And there exist on the borders of this grand river, salt springs enough to furnish salt for the country when it shall become inhabited, and a great deal to spare.

"Saltpetre is found very abundantly in numberless caverns near the Missouri. The rocks are generally calcareous; though there is one which is peculiar to this river. It is of a blood-red colour, compact, yielding to a tool, hardening in the air, and receiving the neatest polish. The natives make their pipes of it. The strata are so extensive that there is any quantity that may be wanted for other purposes. There are also quarries of marble; but we know as yet little more than its colour, which is veined red. It is said there is a body of gypsum; and this would not be very difficult to explore "

Captain Lewis relates that he for several days saw burnt hills, furnishing large quantities of *lava* and pumice stones; of the last he observed several pieces floating on the Missouri as low as Milk river.

BANKS OF THE MISSISSIPPI.

The bottoms of the Mississippi afford suitable situations for settlement, from the mouth of the Missouri to the falls of St. Anthony, except at certain bluffs, where the soil is too barren to invite settlers. The alluvial bottoms are generally composed of a rich, sandy soil, yielding a pretty heavy growth of pecan, poplar, sugar-maple, honey-locust, ash, cotton-wood, black walnut, and cucumber. The prairies in many places approach close to the river; they are sometimes visible through the skirts of the woods. Above the Wabisipinekan, the land bordering the river is three-fourths prairie, or rather " bold hills, which instead of running parallel with the river, form a continual succession of high, perpendicular cliffs, and low vallies: they appear to head on the river, and to traverse the country in an angular direction.— These hills and vallies give rise to sublime and romantic views. But this irregular scenery is sometimes interrupted by a wide extended plain, which brings to mind the verdant lawn of civilized life; and would almost induce the traveller to imagine himself in the centre of a highly cultivated plantation. The timber above this, is chiefly ash, elm, cotton-wood, birch and sugar-maple."†

Above the falls of St. Anthony the pine country commences; this timber borders all the streams, except occasional tracts of sugar maple, basswood, beech, &c.

† See Pike's Journal, Appendix No. 1, page 50.

ANIMALS.

Nature has been bountiful to her red children resident on
the waters of the Missouri and Missi sippi. The buffaloe
abounds from the plains of Assinuibion to the confines of
Louisiana, and from the Mississippi to the Rocky Mountains.
Their hides and tallow, are important articles of the commerce of the territory. Lieut. Pike, whose route was up
the Osage river to the Great Osage village, from thence across
the head streams of the Kanzas and Whiteriver to the Arkansas, and thence up that river to the Mexican Mountains,
found no difficulty in supplying himself and party with an
abundance of meat, by laying the immense herds of buffaloes
under contribution. He affirms that he does not think it an
exaggeration to say, that he saw 3000 buffaloes in one drove,
and " the face of the earth appeared to be covered with
them." In one of his hunting excursions, a scene took place
which "gave a lively representation of an engagement ; the
herd of buffaloes, being pursued by his horsemen, divided into separate bands, and covered the prairie with dust, and first
charged on the one side, and then to the other, as the pursuit
of the horsemen impelled them ; the report and smoke from
the guns, added to the pleasure of the scene, which in part
compensated for our detention. The cow buffaloe was equal
to any meat I ever saw. I will not attempt to describe the
droves of animals we now saw on our route, [up the Arkansas to the Mexican Mountains ;] suffice it to say, that the
face of the prairie was covered with them on each side of the
river ; their numbers exceeded imagination."

" The borders of the Arkansas river may be termed the
paradise (terrestrial) of our territories, for the *wandering
savages*. Of all countries ever visited by the footsteps of
civilized man, there never was one probably that produced
game in greater abundance, and we know that the manners
and morals of the erratic nations, are such (the reasons I leave

to be given by the ontologists) as never to give them a numerous population ; and I believe that there are buffalo, elk, and
deer sufficient on the banks of the Arkansas alone, if used
without waste, to feed all the savages in the United States'
territory one century."

The Indians have several methods of taking the buffaloe ;
they sometimes drive them down precipices ; whole droves,
are often killed or dashed to pieces, by the violence of the
fall ; they frequently attack them on horseback, with bows
and arrows.   This is a dangerous sport, as the assailants are
sometimes vanquished, pursued, and overtaken by these animals, rendered furious by the anguish of numerous wounds.
The usual mode with the Sioux is to make a fence of stakes,
wattled with small branches.   A small party is sent out to
decoy the animals into the pound ; they are dressed in ox-
skins, with the hair and horns, and by their gestures so completely resemble the buffaloe that they readily lure them to
destruction ; the decoyers bellow and paw the earth, gradually retreating to the enclosure, which they enter, and are followed by the herd or drove, until the animals find themselves
enclosed in a pound, which the utmost force cannot break
down.   At this moment the Indians, women, children and
dogs, rush from their hiding places, and fall upon the rear of
their unsuspecting prey, and commence the slaughter, sometimes killing as many as 100 at a time.   The affrighted animals make desperate efforts to escape, by retreating, or forcing
the fence, but are deterred, by the fierce assaults of the dogs,
a shower of arrows, and by the activity of the Indians on
foot and on horseback, who to their discordant yells, inspire
additional terror, by the shaking of skins, beating of drums
and all the dread-exciting devices of which savage ingenuity
is susceptible.

The great brown bear of the Upper Missouri, is a terrible
animal ; and the extreme difficulty with which they are killed
render them a dangerous and formidable enemy to man.   In
an encounter with two of these beasts, above *White or Milk*

river, Captain Lewis was pursued by one of them after being wounded, a considerable distance before he could reload his rifle, when a shot from the hunter who accompanied him, brought him to the ground. Nothing but a shot through the brains will stop their career, and this is a very difficult operation, on account of two large muscles which cover the side of the forehead, and the sharp projection of the centre of the frontal bone, which is also very thick.

One of his men who was afflicted with biles, was suffered to walk on shore; but late in the afternoon, he came running to the boats with loud cries, and every symptom of terror and distress; for some time after we had taken him on board, he was so much out of breath as to be unable to describe the cause of his anxiety; but he at length said that about a mile and a half below, he had shot a brown bear, which immediately turned and was in close pursuit of him: but the bear being badly wounded, could not overtake him. Captain Lewis with seven men, immediately went in search of him, and having found his track followed him by the blood for a mile, and found him concealed in some brushwood, and shot him with two balls through the skull. Though somewhat smaller than that killed a few days ago, he was a monstrous animal, and a most terrible enemy; our man had shot him through the centre of the lungs, yet he had pursued him furiously for half a mile, then returned more than twice that distance, and with his talons had prepared himself a bed in the earth two feet deep and five long, and was perfectly alive when they found him, which was at least two hours after he had received the wound.

A few hours afterwards, the men in the hindmost canoes discovered a large brown bear lying in the open grounds, about three hundred paces from the river; six of them, all good hunters immediately went to attack him, and concealed themselves by a small eminence, came unperceived within forty paces of him; four of the hunters now fired, and each lodged a ball in his body, two of them directly through the lungs: the furious animal sprang up and ran open-mouthed upon them; as he came near, the two hunters who had reserved their fire, gave him two wounds, one of which breaking his shoulder, retarded his motion for a moment; but before they could reload, he was so near that they were obliged to run to the river, and before they reached it, he had almost overtaken them; two jumped into the canoe, the other four separated, and concealing themselves in the willows, fired as fast as each could reload; they struck him several times, but instead of weakening the monster, each shot seemed only to direct him towards the hunter, till at last he pursued two of them so closely, that they threw aside their guns and pouches, and jumped down a perpendicular bank of twenty feet into the river; the bear sprang after them, and was within a few feet of the hindmost, when one of the hunters on shore shot him in the head and finally killed him; they dragged him to the shore, and found that eight balls had passed through him in different directions: the bear was old and the meat tough, so that they took the skin only.†

Wild horses are found in droves on the prairies, between the Arkansas and Red river; they are very fleet and difficult to be taken, and of various colors; they are taken by expert riders, on swift domesticated horses, who throw a noose over their necks with inconceivable dexterity.‡ Deer, elk, bear, wolves, panthers and antelopes are numerous. Wolves

† See Lewis and Clark's Travels, Vol. 1, pages 214, 216.

‡ The Spaniards of Texas are the most skilful people in the world, in pursuing and noosing the wild horse. They adopt the following method:—" They take a few fleet horses and proceed into the country where the wild horses are numerous. They then build a large strong enclosure, with a door which enters a smaller enclosure; from the entrance of the large pen they project wings out into the prairie a great distance, and then set up bushes, &c. to induce the horses when pursued, to enter into these wings. After these preparations are made they keep a look out for a small drove, for, if they unfortunately should start too large a one, they either burst open the pen or fill it up with dead bodies, and the others run over them and escape; in which case the party are obliged to leave the place, as the stench arising from the putrid carcases would be insupportable; and, in addition to this, the pen would not receive others. Should they, however succeed in driving away a few, say two or three hundred, they select the handsomest and youngest, noose them. and take them into the small enclosure, then turn out the remainder, after which, by starving, preventing them taking any repose, and continually keeping them in motion, they make them gentle by degrees, and finally break them to submit to the saddle and bridle." [Pike]

C c

and panthers follow the buffaloe herds, and feast on the calves. The grizzly or white bear, is found on the head branches of the Missouri, and is equally ferocious as the great brown bear, and often attacks the Indians. Cabree and moose are plentiful. Rocky Mountain Sheep are the most common animal. Their horns are a natural curiosity, shaped like those of the common sheep, but enormous in size, full of knobs and measuring three feet in length, five inches in diameter near the head, and weighing twenty pounds and upwards. This animal is taller than a deer, and has a larger body; it is covered with soft, dun-colored hair, except on the belly, which is white. Its legs and feet resemble those of the domestic sheep. It possesses uncommon agility, and climbs cliffs and steep mountains with such ease that no other animal can follow it. Its flesh is considered equal to that of a deer.— Beaver abound from the Missouri throughout the Sioux country, and in most parts of the territory.

There are several species of wildcats. They are small, but very fierce, and often kill sheep and cabree, by leaping on their necks and eating away the sinews and arteries, until they fall, when they suck their blood. One species is very beautiful, being ornamented with black and white spots, on a bright yellow ground. The lynx, marten, muskrat and ermine, are common.

The prairie dogs reside on the prairies south of the Missouri, in towns and villages, having an evident police established in their communities. The sites of these towns are generally on the brow of a hill, near some creek or pond, in order to be convenient to water, and to be exempt from inundation. Their residence is in burrows, which descend in a spiral form. Lieut. Pike caused 140 kettles of water to be poured into one of their holes, in order to drive out the occupant, but failed. They never travel more than half a mile from their homes, and readily associate with rattlesnakes.— They are of a dark brown color, except their bellies, which are red. They are something larger than a grey squirrel, and very fat—supposed to be granivorous. Their villages sometimes extend over two or three miles square, in which there must be innumerable hosts of them, as there is generally a burrow every ten steps. As you approach their towns, you are saluted on all sides by the cry of *wishtonwish*, uttered in a shrill and piercing manner. See Pike's Journal, page 156.

INDIAN CESSIONS.

The Indian title, by various treaties, has been extinguished to about 70,000 square miles, or about 45,000,000 acres a tract of country as large as the states of Vermont, New-York and New-Jersey.

The line between the whites and the Indians begins three hundred miles up the Missouri river, at the mouth of the Kanzas, in lat 39 deg. 5 minutes north, and runs north over a rich country, one hundred miles, to the head of the little river Platte, then east over naked sterile ridges one hundred and fifty miles and a half, to the des Moines, (river of the Monks) then down that river 16 miles to the Mississippi. South of the Missouri, the line begins at Prairie de Feu (fire prairie) thirty miles below the mouth of the Kanzas, and runs south 254 miles down that river to Arkansas; then down that river supposed 250 miles to the Mississippi.

TOWNS, VILLAGES, FORTS.

Belle-Fontaine is pleasantly situated on the south side of the Missouri, four miles above its mouth. The head quarters of the ninth military department, are established here. There is a palisade work, with quarters large enough for the reception of about 300 men. The barracks, officers' quarters, magazine, &c. are built of logs. The garrison is situated on the river bluffs, at the distance of about 450 yards from the water. The inhabitants are chiefly French.

Florissant, a flourishing French village, is situated on the north side of the Missouri, about twelve miles above Belle-Fontaine.

St. Charles, is a handsome village, settled by the French, but at present containing many American families. It contains about 1000 inhabitants. It is twenty-one miles from the mouth of the Missouri, and eighteen from St. Louis, by land—over an excellent road and through a rich country, principally prairie land. The main street of St. Charles, is on the first bank, the second on the top of the hill. On this street is situated a round wooden tower, formerly occupied by the Spaniards as a fort or guard house.

The villages and settlements of Femme Osage, Cherette, Bonhomme, Gasconade, and Cote sans Dessire, embellish the banks of the Missouri, above St. Charles.

St. Louis, the largest town of the territory, and at present the seat of government, stands on a high bank, fifteen miles below the entrance of the Missouri, and in N. lat. 38, 39.—The buildings are scattered along three parallel streets, extending upwards of two miles along the river, and each rising above the other, which gives to the town a neat and romantic appearance. Most of the houses are built of stone, and whitewashed on the outside. Almost every house has an extensive garden or park, around which high stone walls are built. Some of the buildings are very large and costly, and surrounded with galleries. The population exceeds 3000 souls. It has a bank, printing-office, post-office, and Roman chapel. It already enjoys a handsome trade, and from its local advantages, promises to become a rich and populous city. The country, around and west of St. Louis, is for fifteen miles, one extended prairie, of a very luxuriant soil and in a high state of cultivation. There is a ferry from this town to the Illinois side of the Mississippi : from hence passes the main road to Kaskaskia.

Carondelet, is a small French village, six miles west of St. Louis, in the direction of the mines.

Villepuche, a French village of sixty or seventy houses, is situated on the margin of the Mississippi, nineteen miles below St. Louis, and just below the mouth of *Bigolua* creek.

Herculaneum, stands near the Mississippi. It is settled by Americans, and has a fine manufactory of shot; the proprietor, Mr. Matlock, has a fall for the shot, of 200 feet perpendicular. The lead mines are about forty-five miles due west from this place.

St. Genevieve, is situated on the second bank of the Mississippi, about one mile from the river, and twenty-one miles below Herculaneum, in lat. 37 51, N. It was commenced about the year 1774, and is at present the principal depot for most of the mines on the waters of the Maremeg; and the storehouse from whence are drawn the supplies of the miners. Its site is a handsome plain of about 100 acres; the little river Gouberie, the two branches of which form a junction between the town and the river, water it on its upper and lower margins. In front of the town there is a fine bottom, extending from the mouth of the Gouberie, eight or nine miles along the Mississippi, and the greater part of the distance three miles wide. The *common field,* enclosed and cultivated by the citizens, contains about 7000 acres. The surrounding country is broken, but yields good crops. The town contains about 350 houses, an academy and eight or ten stores. A road runs from this town to the lead mines, and the greater part of the inhabitants have an interest in, or are employed in some way, in the lead trade.

New-Bourbon, is situated on a bluff, two miles lower down the river, and contains about seventy buildings. The inhabitants of both villages, are principally French, and a gay and hospitable people.

Cape Girardeau, stands on an eminence 20 miles above the mouth of the Ohio, and seventy-two below St. Genevieve; it is settled by Germans and a few French. The country to the west of the village, is uneven, but of a good soil, for several miles. The bottoms are deep and capable of producing the greatest crops of corn, cotton and tobacco.*

New-Madrid, is situated on a rich plain near the river bank, about seventy miles below the mouth of the Ohio. This place has been finely described, and appears to better advantage on paper, than when under a *coup d'œil*. The soil is very rich, producing cotton, indigo and corn; but the back country for several miles is reported to be swampy and sickly. There is a creek entering the Mississippi just above the town, which affords a good harbor for boats, and a pleasant lake in its rear. The river is constantly making encroachments upon the banks in front of the place.

INDIANS.

The Knisteneaux, Chippewas, Sioux, Foxes, Sacs, and Iowas, reside between the Missouri and the British possessions.

The *Knisteneaux* chiefly reside in the British possessions north of lake Superior; yet some bands have established themselves south of the boundary line, as determined by the treaty of Paris, and reside on streams running into Red river, [of Hudson bay, which heads south of the sources of the Mississippi,] Moose river, Pasquayah, &c. They are of a moderate stature, well proportioned, and of great activity. Examples of deformity are seldom to be seen among them.— Their complexion is of a copper color, and their hair black. Their eyes are black, keen, and penetrating; their countenance open and agreeable, and it is a principal object of their vanity to give every possible decoration to their persons. Of all the nations which I have seen on this continent, says Mac-

* *Christian Schultz*, an American, and an agreeable writer, who travelled in this country in 1808, counted the *layers* of the alluvial bottom, where a large part of the bank had newly broken off and fallen into the Mississippi. He found the whole height of the bank to be forty three feet and a half, and ascertained, with tolerable accuracy, that the total number of the *layers*, was seven hundred and ninety-eight. The *strata* were generally distinct and easily indicated, and from less than a quarter to three inches in thickness. He infers from these *data*, that it has taken at least 800 annual inundations to raise the bank to its present elevation.

kenzie, the Knisteneaux women are the most comely. Their
figure is generally well proportioned, and the regularity of
their features would be acknowledged by the more civilized
people of Europe. Their complexion is not of so dark a tinge
as is common to those savages who have less cleanly habits. It does not appear, that chastity is considered by them
as a virtue; or that fidelity is believed to be essential to the
happiness of wedded life, for a temporary interchange of
wives is not uncommon; and the offer of their persons is considered as a necessary part of the hospitality due to strangers.

A part of the *Chippewa* nation reside in this territory—
they inhabit the head branches of the Mississippi, Leech, Ot-
tertail, Winnipique and Red lakes, the river De Corbeau,
and Red river. They claim an immense extent of territory,
and are a numerous nation. They speak a copious language,
which is very difficult to be attained, and furnishes dialects
to the various emigrant tribes. They are not so warlike as
their Sioux and Knisteneaux neighbors. They are sober,
timorous, and vagrant, with a selfish disposition which has
sometimes created suspicions of their integrity. Their stature has nothing remarkable in it; but though they are seldom
corpulent, they are sometimes robust. Their complexion is
swarthy; their features coarse, and their hair lank, but not
always of a dingy black; nor have they universally the piercing eye, which generally animates the Indian countenance.—
The women have a more agreeable aspect than the men, but
their gait is awkward, which proceeds from their being accustomed, nine months in the year, to travel on snow-shoes and
drag sledges of a weight from 2 to 400 pounds.

The *Sioux*, claim a tract of territory, equal in extent to
some of the most powerful empires of Europe. Their boundaries "commence at the Prairie des Chiens, and ascend the
Mississippi on both sides, to the river De Corbeau, up that
river to its source; from thence to the source of the St. Peters; from thence to the Montaigne de la Prairie; from thence
to the Missouri, down that river to the Mahas, bearing thence

to the source of the river de Moyen; and from thence to the place of beginning." They also claim a large territory south of the Missouri. The country east of the Mississippi from Rum river to the river De Corbeau, is in dispute between them and the Chippewas, and has been the source of many a sharp encounter for 150 years past." These Indians are the dread of all the surrounding tribes: for they are unquestionably the most warlike.

Their best lands, and most populous villages, are on the St. Peters. This nation are divided into 6 bands, viz. 1. *Minowa Kantong*, who extend from Prairie des Chiens to Prairie des Francois, thirty-five miles up the St. Peters.— This is a very warlike band. 2. The *Washpetong*, who inhabit the country from the Prairie des Francois to Roche Blanche on the St. Peters. 3. *Sussetongs*—they extend from the Roche Blanche to lac le Grosse Roche, on the St. Peters. This band hunt on St. Peters and upper portions of Red river of lake Winnipie, which is a level, plain, fertile country, free of stones, and intersected with small lakes. It abounds with fur animals, the beaver, otter, and marten, which enables them to purchase more merchandise, in proportion to their number, than their neighbors. 4. *Yanktons* of the north inhabit a country which is almost one entire plain, destitute of wood, but a good soil and well watered. 5. Yanktons Ahnah are considered the best disposed Sioux, who rove on the banks of the Missouri. Their country is very fertile, consisting of wood land prairie. 6. Tetons Bois Brule. 7. Tetons Okandandas. 8. Tetons Minnakineazzo. 9. Tetons Sahone are four bands which rove over a country almost entirely level, where a tree is scarcely to be seen, unless it be by water courses, or steep declivities of a small number of hills. It is from this country that the Missouri derives most of its colouring matter; the earth is strongly impregnated with glauber salts, allum, copperas, and sulphur, and when saturated with water, large bodies of the hills are precipitated into the river. On this account the waters of the Missouri have a purgative effect on those who are not accustomed to use them. These four bands are the pirates of the Missouri, and considered the vilest miscreants of the savage race. 10. Wahpacootas band rove in the country W. of St. Peters, from a place called Hardwood to the mouth of the Yellow Medicine river: never stationary only when their traders are with them, which is not at any fixed time; a great portion of their country is open plains, and tolerably fertile.

The Assinnibions, (Osinipoilles,) are a revolted band of the Sioux; they inhabit a prairie and champaign country, situated between the Pasquayah or Sascatchiwine and the Rocky Mountains; they live by the chase, and have very little commerce with the whites, and can muster now upwards of 1500 warriors. Their lodges are tents formed of buffaloe hides.

" The Iowas reside on the rivers De Moyen and Iowa, in two villages. They hunt on the west side of the Mississippi, the river De Moyen, and westward to the Missouri; their wars and alliances are the same as the Sacs and Reynards; under whose special protection they conceive themselves to be. They cultivate some corn; but not so much in proportion as the Sacs and Reynards. Their residence being on the small streams in the rear of the Mississippi, out of the high road of commerce, renders them less civilized than those nations."

" The Reynards (or Foxes) reside in three villages. The 1st. on the W. side of the Mississippi, six miles above the rapids of the river De Roche. The 2d. about twelve miles in the rear of the lead mines, and the 3d. on Turkey river, half a league from its entrance. They are engaged in the same wars, and have the same alliances as the Sacs, with whom they must be considered as indissoluble in war or peace. They hunt on both sides of the Mississippi from the river Iowa, (below the Prairie Des Chiens) to a river of that name above said village. They raise a great quantity of corn,

D d

beans, and melons; the former of those articles in such quantities, as to sell many hundred bushels per annum."*

The Sacs (or Saukies) and Reynards (or Foxes) claim
the land from the mouth of the Jaustioni, on the W. side of
the Mississippi, up to the upper Iowa river, above the Prairie des Chiens, and westwardly to the Missouri; but the
limits of their respective claims are undefined.

"The river St. Peters, or St. Pierre, according to Carver,
flows through a most delightful country, abounding with all
the necessaries of life, that grow spontaneously, and with a
little cultivation it might be made to produce even the luxuries of life. Wild rice, (folle avoine) grows here in great abundance, and every part is filled with trees bending under their
loads of fruits, such as plums, grapes, and apples; the meadows with hops, and many sorts of vegetables; whilst the
ground is stored with useful roots, with angelica, spikenard,
and ground-nuts as large as hens' eggs. At a little distance
from the sides of the river are eminences, from which you
have views that cannot be exceeded even by the most beautiful of those I have already described; amidst these are delightful groves, and such amazing quantities of maples, that
they would produce sugar sufficient for any number of inhabitants.

"A little way from the mouth of this river, on the north
side of it, stands a hill, one part of which, that towards the
Mississippi, is composed entirely of white stone, of the same
soft nature as that I have before described; for such, indeed,
is all the stone in this country. But what appears remarkable is, that the colour of it is as white as the driven snow.
The outward part of it was crumbled by the wind and weather
into heaps of sand, of which a beautiful composition might be
made; or, I am of opinion, that when properly treated the
stone itself would grow harder by time, and have a very noble
effect in architecture.

* See Pike, Carver, &c.

"Near that branch which is termed the Marble River, is a mountain, from whence the Indians get a sort of red stone, out of which they hew the bowls of their pipes. In some of these parts is found a black hard clay, or rather stone, of which the Naudowessies (Sioux) make their family utensils. This country likewise abounds with a milk white clay, of which China ware might be made equal in goodness to the Asiatic ; and also with a blue clay that serves the Indians for paint; with this last they contrive, by mixing it with the red stone powdered, to paint themselves of different colours."

South of the Missouri are the following tribes, viz : The Great and Little Osage tribes, who reside principally on the Osage river and the Arkansas ; they are next to the Sioux in point of population ; both bands can assemble a combined force of 2500 warriors.   They are remarkably tall, large, and ferocious—erect and well proportioned ; their complexion is between an olive and a copper color ; their eyes dark brown, their noses large and acquiline ; they usually wear a dressed buffaloe skin over their shoulders.   They are expert warriors, and generally engaged in war with the Sioux and western nations.   Their chief villages are on the bank of the Osage river—the houses stand in two rows on a straight line, with a wide street between them.

The Kanzas reside on the river of that name about 240 miles from its mouth.   They have a fine country, rich in game and vegetable productions.   They hunt on the head branches of the Kanzas and Arkanzas, can muster 460 warriors, are similar in form and manners to the Osage.

The Pawnees reside on the Kanzas, Great Nimmehaw, and Arkansas ; they are divided into three bands, the Pawnee Loups, Pawnees proper, and Pawnee republicans ; they can raise 2500 warriors ; and trade with the Spaniards and Americans : they are said to be friendly to white people, but the treatment which Pike's party received at their hands, was such as to give no very favorable idea of their morality. There are colonies of Creeks, Cherokees, and Choctaws settled on the Arkansas and Whiteriver, who are drawn thither by the facility with which game is hunted.

The Ottoes and Missouris, whose tribes are consolidated, live on the river Platte, 45 miles from its mouth, and are reduced to about 650 souls.

The Wetepahatos, live on the Padouca fork of Platte river, are agreeable and well disposed people.

The Kiawas are neighbors to the Wetopahatos, and are two thousand strong.

The Kenenavish, or Cow Indians, live on the head branches of the Padouca, and have about 1500 souls.

The Kites, frequently associate with the Kenenavish, and have about 550 souls.

The Mahas, once a formidable nation, residing in villages on the west bank of the Missouri, 235 miles above the mouth of river Platte, but now a wandering, feeble tribe, reduced by war and the small pox, to about 650 souls.

The Poncars have been reduced by the Sioux, from a respectable nation to about 250 souls—they live on the river Poncar, west of the Missouri.

The Ricaras reside in fortified villages between the river Tetone and Mandan villages. They were once powerful; and are of Pawnee origin.

The Mandans are described as a friendly and hospitable nation—they have been reduced by war and the Sioux, to about 1250 souls. Their towns are defended by a strong stockade, and are situated in the Great bend of the Missouri, 35 miles above the Ricaras.

The Ahwahawas, are a small nation, live three miles above the Mandans, whom they resemble in their persons and manners; they have about 55 warriors and 250 inhabitants.

The Minetares, or *Grosse Ventres*, (big bellies.) They claim no lands except what they occupy. Their villages are on Knife river, five miles above the Mandan towns. There is a great scarcity of wood in the neighborhood of these towns, which induces them to leave their homes in cold seasons, and seek a shelter on the bottoms of Roche Jaune and the Missouri.

The Chiens, or Dog Indians emigrated from the borders of Red river of Hudson bay, but now wander on the banks of Chien river. Their numbers are about 1250 souls.

The Katas, 350 strong, reside on the north and south forks of Chien river.

The Nemausins are a small tribe inhabiting the south forks of Chien river.

The Datomes live on the head waters of Chien river, and have only 50 warriors.

The Castahanas, are very strong, and roam in an open country between the head waters of Roche Jaune (Yellow Stone) and Platte rivers, and raise great numbers of horses and mules, are friendly to whites, but maintain a defensive war with the Sioux.

The Quehatsas or Gens de Corbeau, (Crow Indians) are a peaceful nation; they live on both sides of Roche Jaune river; and are divided into four bands.

The Gens de Panse, (Paunch Indians) reside on the heads of Roche Jaune and Bighorn rivers, and can count 850 warriors.

The Snake Indians inhabit the Rocky mountains, from the head waters of the Missouri to the sources of the Arkansas. They are an inoffensive people, and greatly oppressed by their neighbors.

The Aliatons, *of the west*, live south of the Snake Indians, near the Spanish frontier; they have very few arms; but often attack the Spaniards successfully, only with bows and arrows.

The Tutseewas or Flat-heads, live on the west side of the Rocky Mountains; little is known of their habits and villages.

South of the Arkansas, on the head branches of Redriver, and beyond the Sabine are the following nations, viz:

The Caddoquies, a small, but martial tribe residing on Red river of the Mississippi.

The Yatasees live on the same river, below the Caddo towns; the Spanish government claim jurisdiction over them.

The Nandaquies live on the Sabine and Rio Toyac.

The Adaize live on lake Macadon; their language is so difficult to understand, that no nation it is said, can speak ten words of it.

The Aliche reside near Nacogdoches on Rio Brassos.

The Keychies inhabit the eastern shores of the Rio Trinity, near the road from Natchitoches to St. Antonio.

The Tachies reside on a branch of the Sabine.

The Nebadaches are settled on the same stream.

The Bedies live to the south of Nacogdoches.

The Mayes live on the bay of the St. Bernard near the mouth of Guadaloupe river. They are at perpetual war with the Spaniards, but friendly to the French.

The Carankouas, live on a peninsula in the bay of St. Bernard; they are enemies to the Spaniards, but kind to the French.

The Tetaus or Comanches, a powerful vagrant tribe, roam at will over the immense prairie region, stretching from the head waters of the Arkansas to the Rio del Norte. They never reside at the same place but a few days; the buffaloe is their principal food. They travel on horseback.

The above nations, except the last, which resides between Red river and the Rio Guadaloupe, inhabit a country abounding in deer and buffaloe, and wild horses. They cultivate the richest soil and are generally harmless and friendly; they are reduced in numbers from thirty to two hundred warriors.

RECAPITULATION.

Names of Tribes.	Warriors.	Total No. souls.	Villages.
Assinibions, about . .	1,250	6,500	7
Knisteneaux, . . .	550	2,450	
Chippewas, . . .		3,200	
Sioux, ...	3,835	21,675	6

Names of Tribes.				Warriors.	Total No. souls.	Villages.
Reynards,	.	.	.	440	1,750	4
Sacs,	.	.	.	750	2,850	4
Iowas,	.	.	.	300	1,400	3
Osages,	.	.	.	2,500	10,500	4
Kanzas,	.	.	.	465	1,650	2
Pawnees,	.	.	.	2,500	7,500	4
Ottoes, &c.	.	.	.	250	600	2
Mahas,		.	.	350	750	
Poncars,		.	.	50	250	
Ricaras,		.	.	550	2,500	
Mandans,		.	.	350	1,200	
Ahwahawas,		.	.	50	250	
Minatares,		.	.	620	250	
Chiens,		.	.	350	1,250	
Wetapahatoes and Kiawas,				5,250	11,850	
Kenenavish,		.	.	450	1,570	
Kites,	.	.	.	120	470	
Katas,	.	.	.	75	250	
Nemausins,		.	.	50	220	
Dotames,		.	.	30	120	
Castahanas,		.	.	1,300	5,005	
Quehatsas,		.	.	960	3,550	
Gens de Panse,		.	.	860	2,850	
Tut-see-was,		.	.	Unknown.		
Alliatans of the west,			.	Unknown.		
Caddoquies,		.	.	150	350	
Yattasees,		.	.	150	350	
Nandoquies,		.	.	40	150	
Adaize,		.	.	20	190	
Aliche or Heiche,		.	.	.	25	
Keychies,		.	.	60	220	
Tachies,		.	.	80	350	
Nebedaches,		.	.	80	350	
Bedies,		.	.	.	350	
Accokesaws,		.	.	85	350	
Mayes,		.	.		250	

Corankouas,	.	550	2,500
Tetaus or Comanches,	.	.	5,500
Total,		30,920	103,025

BOUNTY LANDS.

Two millions five hundred thousand acres of bounty lands are surveyed in the Missouri territory, between latitude 38 and 40 degrees north, and longitude 10 and 12 degrees west from the city of Washington. This tract is watered by the Missouri, Gasconade, John's river, Gravel, Great Osage, &c. and is chiefly of the first quality, prairie and woodland interspersed; the timbered land is covered with tall canes, a sure indication of a warm and productive soil. These lands are capable of sustaining a numerous population; and from their advantageous local situation, will rapidly enhance in value.*

ANTIQUITIES.

The Sioux country, on the Wabisipinekan, St. Peters, and Yellow river, abounds with ancient entrenchments, mounds, and fortifications. Similar works were discovered by Lewis and Clark, and by later travellers on the Missouri, Osage, Platte, &c. Six miles west of St. Louis, is a place called the "valley of bones," where the ground is promiscuously strewed with human and animal bones; some of the latter have been discovered of an enormous size.

---

* " The emigration to this country continues to an unparalleled extent. This is probably the easiest unsettled country in the world to commence farming in. The emigrant has only to locate himself on the edge of a prairie, and he has the one half of his farm a heavy forest and the other half a fertile plain or meadow, covered with a thick sward of fine grass: he has then only to fence in his ground and put in his crop. The country abounds with salines and salt works sufficient to supply the inhabitants with good salt: a navigation to almost every man's door, which will give him a market for all his surplus produce, and bring to him all the necessary articles of merchandise. The soil and climate are favorable to the growth of Indian corn, wheat, rye, oats, cotton, tobacco, hemp, flax, and almost all kinds of vegetables which grow in the United States. Take the country for all in all, I believe there is no section of the U. States has ever opened such a great and advantageous field for enterprise, either for the industrious laboring man or for the steady, professional character."
[Extract of a letter from Fort Osage, Feb. 22, 1817.

THE NEW STATE,

Formed from the western part of the Mississippi Territory, *(not yet named*)* is bounded as follows : Beginning on the river Mississippi at the point where the southern boundary line of the state of Tennessee strikes the same, thence east along the said boundary line to the Tennessee river, thence up the same to the mouth of Bear creek, thence by a direct line to the northwest corner of the county of Washington, thence due south to the Gulf of Mexico, thence westwardly, including all islands within six leagues of the shore, to the most eastern junction of Pearl river with lake Borgne, thence up said river to the thirty-first degree of north latitude, thence west along the said degree of latitude to the Mississippi river, thence up the same to the place of beginning.

It is situated between 30 and 35 N. lat. and 8, and 14 W. longitude. Length from North to South, about 340 miles, breadth about 150, containing about 45,000 square miles, or 30,000,000 acres.

RIVERS.

All the principal streams of this state have a southern direction, flowing into the Mississippi, the Tombigbee, and Gulf of Mexico.

The Mississippi winds along its western frontier, 572 miles. The streams which join it from the south in this distance are,

The Yazoo river which heads near the Tennessee boundary line in lat. 35. It has numerous head branches of excellent water. It joins the Mississippi at right angles, 112 miles

---

* The convention will probably adopt that of " *Mississippi.*"

E e

above Natchez. It is 280 yards wide at its mouth, of a gentle current, and navigable about 100 miles. It waters that part of the state lying between the Tennessee boundary, the Mississippi and the road leading from the Muscle shoals to Natchez. Big Black river enters the Mississippi about 50 miles above Natchez, heads in the Chickasaw country, and is navigable about 70 miles in wet seasons. Bayou Pierre flows into the Mississippi 40 miles above Natchez; the next streams are Cole's creek, and Catharine's creek, each about 40 yards wide. Between Natchez and the line of demarcation are Homochitto river, about 60 yards wide, heads south-east of Natchez near Pearl river, and is a handsome stream of pure water. Below this a few miles is Buffaloe creek, about 40 yards wide; these streams are not fordable except in seasons of drought. Proceeding to the east along the Louisiana or old West Florida boundary line, run by Andrew Ellicott, we successively cross branches of bayou Sara, Thompson's creek, Amite, Ticfou, Pongipaho, Chefuncti, and Boguechitto, before we reach Pearl river; all of which have been noticed in the description of the rivers of Louisiana. Pearl river, is the largest stream between the Mississippi and Mobile, and runs through the Choctaw territory. Between Pearl river and the Pascagola, is the Benasouah and several other small streams tributary to the bays of St. Louis and Biloxi; east of this bay the first river is the Pascagola a large and navigable river. It rises near lat. 33, and runs south parallel to the Tombigbee and Mobile 250 miles, expanding near the gulf, into a broad bay, but too shoal at its entrance to admit vessels drawing more than four feet water; above this bay, there is a good boat navigation 150 miles; twenty miles from the gulf it receives from the west the river Hatcha Leecha. Fifteen miles north of the old Florida line, it receives the Chickasaka river, which heads near the head branches of Pearl river, and waters a part of the Choctaw territory. Chickasaka receives from the west Chabol river, besides numerous creeks. Pascagola receives from the north-east Cedar, Pine Barren, and Red Bank creeks, &c. Between the Pascagola and Mobile is the bayou Batrie. The Mobile river is only 45 miles in length, deep, broad, and navigable for vessels of considerable burthen; the bay of the same name, however, which is 30 miles long, may be considered as an extension of the Mobile, which gives 75 miles from the gulf of Mexico to the confluence of the Tombigbee and Alabama, whose united waters form the Mobile river and bay. The only remaining river to be particularly noticed, is the Tombigbee, which will be probably found to run nearly on the line, or will be assumed as the boundary, between the newly erected state and the Alabama territory. This is a large navigable river rising in the Cherokee country, within a few miles of the Tennessee river, a few miles below the Muscle Shoals, being 450 miles long, by its meanderings, from its source to its junction with the Alabama.

The Tombigbee receives a great number of creeks and small rivers from the west; such as Chickasaw creek, which enters five miles below Dog creek, flowing in four miles above fort Stoddert. Bassa Bagrie, entering near the confluence with the Tombigbee and the Alabama. Opalee river comes in about 40 miles above the mouth of Alabama; after which, among others, it receives Senelee, Nooxabba, Noisy creek, Swan creek, Salabamaby, and Black Warrior.

Vessels drawing twelve feet water can ascend as far as Fort Stoddert, and frequently as far as St. Stevens, a little above which are rapids, but which in a good pitch of water, do not oppose many obstructions to boats. Six miles below the junction of the Tombigbee with the Alabama, the Mobile divides into two branches, the easternmost of which is called the river Tensaw; this falls into the east side of Mobile bay, about nine miles below the town of Mobile.

A subsequent division gives to each of these channels two mouths; and whilst the mouths of the western channel are designated by the names of Mobile and Spanish river; those of the eastern are called the Tensaw and Appalachee rivers.

Indeed the whole of the eastern channel from its first severance from the rest of the river is often designated by the name
of the Tensaw river; but certainly with no propriety, as it is
no distinct river at all; but merely the eastern channel of
the main Mobile river. These different channels are connected by intervening streams ; the most remarkable of which
is called Lizard's creek, and unites the western channel with
an offset from the eastern channel now called Mobile river,
but formerly the bayou Matthieu. It is by the western channel and Lizard's creek, and the bayou Matthieu or Middle
river, that vessels usually ascend the Mobile, especially when
the wind is favorable, as this route is more direct than the
main western channel. Lizard's creek is about twenty miles
above the town of Mobile, and the distance through it from the
western channel to the Middle river, is about three miles.
After getting up the bay, over what is called the bar, there is
no difficulty in ascending the Mobile by any of the channels.
That which passes immediately by the town of Mobile, is not
so deep as that at the mouth of the western channel, which is
called Spanish river; but vessels frequently go up Spanish
river into the main western channel, and then drop down six
or seven miles, to the town of Mobile. If you leave the bay,
and proceed up Spanish river, and then continue up the main
western channel to Fort Stoddert, you will generally find from
four to five fathoms of water in the middle of the river, and
about twelve feet near the bank. The shallowest part of the
river is near Simon's bluff, where there is only 7 feet of water. The population from the town of Mobile to the junction
of the Mobile, or Tombigbee, with the Alabama, is very trifling indeed : and the lowness of the land adjacent to the river for thirty miles above the town, with the indifferent quality of the high lands contiguous to it, forbid the expectation
of any rapid increase of population. The high land approaches the river at seven places in the space of forty miles, and
at each of these places a family or two reside. The country behind is generally uninhabited. The distances of the

several bluffs or highlands near the river, are as follows: From Mobile to the Bayou St. Louis, four miles; thence to Dubroca's bluff, seventeen; Chast ng's, or the old French fort, six; Simon's bluff, six; Bazil Chastang's, three; Cedar creek, two; Fort Stoddert, six; total 44 miles.

The entrance of Mobile bay is in N. lat. 30 15; the aver- erage width of the bay is about twelve miles. Opposite its mouth is Dauphin island extending from east to west about seven miles. The coasters from Lake Ponchartrain and bay- ou St. John enter the bay, through the strait between the west end of the island and the main land; the water in this pass is very shoal, and is incapable of receiving vessels draw- ing more than five feet of water. Vessels from Pensacola, the West Indies and other places, enter the bay between Dauphin Island and Mobile Point, or the extremity of the main land on the eastern shore. Between Dauphin Island and Mobile Point, there are eighteen feet of water, and the channel is so near that you may throw a biscuit on shore. Proceeding up the bay, you find three fathoms of water for about ten miles. Then you have thirteen feet for about eight miles further, or to within nine or ten miles of Dog river, which is three leagues below the town of Mobile. From the place last mentioned below Dog river to the upper end of the bay, the depth of water is about twelve and a half, except at the shoal which extends across the bay, and is called the bar, over which you cannot calculate on more than eleven feet of water. From one end of the bay to the other, the water is very shallow for a considerable distance from the shore. The bay appears well adapted to vessels of about 150 tons bur- then; but the cotton and lumber, which will become the sta- ple articles of the country, would render vessels of 300 tons more eligible.

The Tennessee river forms the north eastern boundary of the state for about 50 miles: thus it will be seen by reference to the Map of the late Mississippi territory, that the new state is peninsulated by the Mississippi, Gulf of Mexico, Mobile,

Tombigbee and Tennessee rivers.   The northern half of the
state may be said to be well watered by pure and wholesome
streams, more especially that part drained by the head creeks
of the Natarchucky, [main branch of the Tombigbee] Black
Warrior, [eastern branch of the Tombigbee,] and Yazoo rivers, which interlock at numerous points.   The southern
part of the state abounds with an abundance of navigable
streams, but having sluggish currents, the water is neither
so pure nor so wholesome.

VIEW OF THE GULF COAST.

The distance from the mouth of Pearl river to the entrance
of Mobile bay is about one hundred miles.   The coast is in-
dented with numerous bays and lined with a great number
of islands. The navigation from lake Borgne to Mobile is safe
and easy for light vessels.   The bay of St. Louis is 25 miles
east of the mouth of Pearl river ; is about ten miles long and
four wide, timbered by a low country of pine forests, and cypress swamps, except where the ground has been cleared by
the few French inhabitants who have settled on its margin.
Two miles east of the bay is Pass Christian ; the coast for
a short space is high, commanding, and healthy, and is resorted to in autumn by many of the inhabitants of New-Orleans,
who here find an airy and healthful situation during the sickly
season. From Pass Christian to the bay of Biloxi, is 24 miles ;
this bay is ten or twelve miles deep, but narrow ; a number of
French are settled on its borders.   Pascagola bay is the next
harbor, but only for light vessels.   It is about four miles
across the several branches of the Pascagola, and the intervening marshes, intersected by bayous and cut-offs ; from
thence to Mobile, a distance of 45 miles, the coast presents
low, sandy banks, covered with pine forests, with very few
settlements, to cheer the way and relieve the fatiguing same-
ness of the prospect.

SURFACE, SOIL, TIMBER.

In order to form a correct idea of the surface, soil and timber of this state, it would be necessary to travel from the mouth of Pearl or Pascagola rivers, northwardly, to the Tennessee boundary line ; the first hundred miles would be through forests of the long leaved pine, interspersed with cypress swamps, bay galls, and open prairies—the surface generally champaign ; but occasionally swelling into hills of moderate elevation, and receding into vast prairies, inundated marshes and pestilential swamps. A considerable proportion of this part of the country is susceptible of successful cultivation. The soil is generally sandy—sometimes gravelly and clayey. It will, nevertheless, produce several kinds of fruit, plums, cherries, peaches, figs, sour oranges and grapes ; cotton, corn, indigo, sugar and garden vegetables. It has a subsoil of clay, from which it is supposed to derive its fertility. This section of the state so nearly resembles in soil, surface and timber, that part of Louisiana, lying between lake Ponchartrain and the old West Florida line, that a reference to page 126, &c. will render further description unnecessary.

Proceeding northwardly, through the Choctaw, Chickasaw and Cherokee territories, we perceive a gradual change of timber, improvement of soil, and elevation of surface, passing from a level, pine, sandy country, to forests of poplar, hickory, oak, black walnut, sugar maple, buckeye, elm, hackberry, &c. —a soil of deep vegetable mould of surprising fertility ; and a surface agreeably undulating.

In soil, the country bordering on the Tennessee frontier resembles that of the best parts of Kentucky—in surface, more rolling and broken—in productions, more various and luxuriant. The country bordering on the Tennessee river, for 100 miles above and below the Muscle Shoals, and for forty miles north and south, I consider as the garden of North America, and unquestionably the best adapted to longevity and human enjoyment. Here is a soil happily congenial to corn, sweet potatoes, indigo, cotton, garden vegetables and fruit. Even *wheat* will yield a productive crop. But it is the excellence of the water, mildness and healthfulness of the climate, and proximity to the navigable waters of Tennessee and Tombigbee, that render it the most desirable to new settlers of any of the states or territories, within the limits of the Union.

The long leaved pine prevails from the Gulf coast to the northern boundary of the Choctaw territory. This timber is tall, straight, and majestic, running frequently from sixty to eighty feet clear of a limb—some probably go as far as 100 feet. The Choctaw and Chickasaw countries abound with rich prairies: the largest is on the road from the Choctaw to the Chickasaw nation—and is in length near forty miles over, from north to south, with a horizon, in that direction, *apparently* as boundless as the ocean.

Almost every foot of the land from the banks of the Yazoo, to the Mississippi on the west, and the Tennessee on the east is incomparably rich and beautiful, well watered and healthful. A great proportion of this tract, however, belongs to the Chickasaw Indians. The pine lands do not approach within twenty or thirty miles of the Mississippi, even as low down as Ellicott's line, forty-five miles below Natchez; in the interior, between the Mississippi and Tombigbee, it extends north to the Yellow Fork of Yazoo, in N. lat. 33 30.

The soil of the richest uplands is nearly of the color of ashes—deep and capable of long series of crops without manure; the rocks and stones are calcareous, intermixed with flint, sandstone and slate. Canebrakes cover the whole face of the country, wherever the soil is deep. Swamps are almost unknown for one hundred miles south of Tennessee river.

The cypress galls, which is the poorest species of land, contains veins of a very fine clay, fit for manufacturing; it is very white, soft and tenacious, and free from gritty particles. There is also a great variety of nitrous and bituminous earths;

fossils, marls, iron ore, lead, chalk, slate, free stone : amber-
gris has been found on the coast.   Coal is found on the Tombigbee, Tennessee, Black Warrior, and several other streams.

On the navigable waters of the Chatahouchee, Conecah,
Mobile, Tombigbee, Pearl, and Mississippi, are immense
supplies of all kinds of timber suitable for foreign markets ;
white oak, live oak, pine, cypress, cedar, black walnut, locust,
magnolia, hickory, of great size, and conveniently situated for
hauling to the waters.   Vast quantities of lumber are shipped at Mobile.

CLIMATE, PRODUCTIONS.

The best lands produce cotton of a fine quality ; the average quantity of cotton raised on an acre of land in the Mississippi Territory, has been estimated at one thousand pounds
in the seed ; but I think one thousand two hundred may be
safely calculated on in good seasons.

I have before me several letters on the subject of the climate and productions.   Mr. Lattimore, delegate to Congress,
from the late Mississippi Territory, considers the climate as
not unfavorable to northern constitutions ; he admits that there
are certain situations in the southern parts, which are rather
sickly ; but speaks favorably as to the general healthfulness of
the country.   The following letter of James M'Guffin, Esq.
a long and respectable inhabitant of St. Stephens, may, perhaps, represent the country in a too favorable point of view,
if applied to the country south of the demarcation line ; but
he certainly does not draw a picture too highly colored for
the upper part of the state, say from the sources of the Yazoo to the Tennessee.   The letter was addressed to a gentlemen in Louisiana ; the reader will perceive that his observations relate to the country on both sides of the Mobile.

" I believe it [the Mobile country] to be the most agreeable climate I ever experienced south of my native state, (Pennsylvania).   The diseases are less violent and fewer in num-

F f

ber, more easily removed by medicine than in any country north, or even west or south. In this country, we find the natives of almost every climate or country. And although they expose themselves to severe labor during every month of the year, an unusual portion of health is found universal. Notwithstanding the southern latitude, it is an universal remark, that the heat of summer is found less oppressive than in the *middle states.* The constant prevalence of the sea breeze during the summer, from the Gulf of Mexico, together with the elevation of the surface of our country, satisfactorily accounts for this circumstance; however extraordinary it may appear, we have neither the climate of the Mississippi, nor that of the Atlantic in the same parallel of latitude.

The rapid improvement of the sheep of our country, and the perfection to which the apple and cherry are brought, completely fix the fact, however extraordinary. The Mississippi and Georgia, both refuse these products.

" On the same plantation I have seen the apple, cherry, orange, fig, quince, Irish potatoe, wheat, rye, buck-wheat, flax, cotton and sugar cane, grow well, nearly all of which excel. The productions of our country, that we find on the surface of the earth, merit an early attention. The lumber of our rivers are a source of wealth sufficient to enrich the country, had we no other ; the groves of white oak are immense, immediately on the margin of our rivers, the lumber of which is highly prized in the foreign markets. The groves of red cedar are extensive, also live oak, a variety of pines, cypress, &c. calculated to execute commercial enterprize. The cotton of our country was the first that was sold in the New-Orleans market last year, for the enormous sum of *thirty five* dollars per hundred.

It ought never to be forgotten that when our produce or lumber is on hand, it is at once at market. The ease with which stock of every description is raised, is alone a source of wealth, when attended to. The farmer may calculate for years to come on having no other trouble in raising his cattle, hogs, sheep, &c. than that of looking after. The mutton, veal and lamb of our country is certainly superior to any animal food I ever tasted. The fowling of our rivers is not surpassed by any country in the United States. The oysters and fish of the bay of Mobile have been much admired by the citizens of even New-York ; and, were I to point out a situation best calculated to meet every source of advantages and furnish the best access to enjoyment, I have no hesitation in giving the vicinity of St. Stephens and Fort Claiborne as affording it ; lying in the high country, affording high and river bottom land of the first quality, within two days ride of the margin of the Ocean from Mobile to Pensacola, over an excellent level road between these two places, are found situations capable of giving all the gratifications expected from a residence in the vicinity of the Ocean ; amongst those the bay of Perdido has arrested much attention, and has been announced by many intelligent travellers and persons of taste, as one of the most desirable on any continent explored; its scenery productions and uncommon salubrity of climate, has caused many to call it the Montpelier of America. The constant prevalence of the sea breeze,tempers the heat of summer so as to make these situations very desirable. The ease with which southern fruits are obtained at all seasons, the flavor of fish, oysters, crabs, and lobsters, would court the residence of the most voluptuous epicures of our country. As to the valuable productions of our country brought to perfection by common day laborers ; the profits are not to be surpassed by the agriculturalists of any country.

Another writer speaking of the Mobile district says : No country can have a more delightful climate. Though some particular places may be considered rather sickly, owing to local causes, yet generally speaking, it is a healthy country. If bilious complaints are more prevalent than in higher latitudes, still, consumptions, pleurisies, rheumatisms, asthmas, and the long catalogue of the diseases of cold climates, are rarely ever witnessed in the Mississippi and Mobile country.

ANIMALS.

Game is scarce; but deer, bear, wolves, tigers,* panthers, wild cats, foxes, ground hogs, and squirrels, are found in the forests skirting the Mississippi.   There is a small animal called the " *salamander*," of the size and form of the common rat, the head and teeth like the squirrel, and the eye small, like the mole.   The hair is fine and of a fox color.   It burrows in the ground, but horizontally.   Where it enters the ground, it throws up a small hill about six inches high and eighteen inches diameter.   It is supposed to live upon the bark of fine roots, and roams abroad only at night in search of food and water, which it sips from the dew on the grass ; it is extremely shy, and retreats to its hole on the smallest alarm, something like the Guinea pig.   The jaws are very strong, the teeth sharp, and the bite very severe.   They are to be found near the gulf coast.   The alligator inhabits the streams, south of lat. 32 ; they are destructive to hogs, dogs, and other animals, which venture into the water, or approach the margins of rivers, lakes and bayous.

When full grown, the alligator is about 15 feet long ; the scales upon the skin of the head and back are so hard that a rifle ball will scarcely penetrate them.   The female scratches a hole in the sand or dry soil, where it is exposed to the heat of the sun, where she deposits and covers her eggs, which are hatched by its warmth.   When the young is hatched it takes care of, and provides for itself.   The teeth of this animal are short, strong and irregular, and the jaws remarkably strong. If they once get hold of their prey, they never suffer it to

---

* Schultz relates that in traversing the streets of Natches, he noticed leopard skins hanging at the doors of several stores, which he concluded had been imported ; but happening to mention this circumstance to a number of gentlemen assembled at the hotel, who informed him, that they were animals killed in the country —one within twelve miles of the city, the skin of which measured five feet three inches in length, and four feet in breadth.   They appear in every respect like the leopard of Africa, except having a darker stripe along the back from the head to the tail.   They are called the spotted tiger in this country, and although not numerous, yet of late years they are frequently met with.

escape : if large, it is carried into the water and drowned : if
small, it is devoured on the shore.   When a deer or grown
hog is killed by them, it is suffered to float in the water until
it becomes putrid, and is then eaten.   They often bask on the
shore or on logs, where they sleep.   On the approach of rainy
weather, they make a bellowing noise resembling the bull, or
rather like snoring in sleep, which may be heard at the distance of half a mile.   They seldom leave the banks of rivers
and deep ponds, from which they retreat to the water on the
approach of danger.   When they are found at a distance
from the water, they defend themselves to the last extremity ;
and when wounded, they will hold a stick so fast between the
teeth as to be carried by it a considerable distance : the jaws
of the lion but little exceed those of the alligator in strength.
In many instances, knots of lightwood of the size of a goose
egg, have been found in the stomach ; whether to aid the power of digestion, or for what other purposes, is not known.   It
disappears in cold weather in autumn, and returns in the
spring ; except in warm days, when it rises and basks in the
sun beams.   It is believed that they have no regular winter
habitation, but burrow into the mud at the bottom of lakes,
ponds and still water, where there is a portion of warmth produced by a mixture of mud and vegetable matter.

The Murena Siren is troublesome to rice planters.   It
cuts holes through their dams in the night and lets off the
water.   The body is about two feet long, and in its form resembles the eel.   The skin is thin and tough, and covered
with fine scales of a dark brown color.   The mouth is small
and well furnished with sharp teeth.   It has two short legs
which come out near the head ; each furnished with four toes
and claws, which enables it to pass through mud and water
with great facility.   It has three gills on each side, and when
they are opened, resemble ears.   When the male and female
are separated, they make known their distresses by a noise not
unlike the howling of a young puppy, from which it is probable they they have taken the vulgar name.   They are said to

live upon frogs, water lizards, and mud worms, and are remarkable for the length of their intestines.

The Gouffre is the resident of the pine barrens : it lives principally under ground, except when it wants food and water, and is said to live upon vegetables. The shell is about 15 feet long, and 12 inches wide. It is remarkable for its strength, being able to move without much difficulty upon the ground, with a man standing upon its back. It digs a hole in the ground, the direction of which is a depressed angle of about thirty degrees and ten feet deep. In the bottom, a nest of young rattle-snakes is often found in the early part of the summer. The gouffre generally remains some time at the entrance of its cave, before it ventures abroad; and on the appearance of danger retreats. It resembles the logger-head turtle, and brings forth its young in the same way. It shields itself from danger by closing up its shell, and is rarely seen any distance from its den.

THE RANGE.

The pine country, which is about one half of the state, will probably forever remain an excellent range for hogs, cattle and horses ; but in the northern or best part of the country, when thickly settled, enclosed pastures may become necessary. The cane gives milk and butter a fine flavor and uncommon richness. Horses, which feed on it do well, if salted frequently—otherwise it is apt to scour them, especially, if not bred in the country ; besides the reed cane, the native or buffalo clover and the rye grass enrich the range. The rye grass, when full grown, is from two to three feet tall—the head and beard resemble the real rye : the native clover has a larger leaf, and grows more luxuriantly than the common white clover, which it closely resembles in every thing but size ; the leaves are about as large as a shilling piece, and the blossom as large as that of red clover.

A CONVENTION,

Is to meet at the town of Washington on the first Monday of July 1817, for the purpose of forming a constitution and state government ; the delegates are to be elected in the several counties, in the following proportion, viz:

FROM THE COUNTY OF

Warren,	2	Rep.
Claiborne,	4	
Jefferson,	4	
Adams,	8	
Franklin,	2	
Wilkinson,	6	
Amite,	6	
Pike,	4	
Lawrence,	2	
Marion,	2	
Hancock,	2	
Wayne,	2	
Greene,	2	
Jackson,	2	
Total,	48	

TOPOGRAPHICAL.

The parallel of 35 deg. of north latitude, which is the dividing line between the state of Tennessee, and this state, crosses the Mississippi, a little below the mouth of Wolf river ; one mile below which is fort Pickering, where there was formerly a small garrison : there are about a dozen houses ; the bank, which is called the fourth Chickasaw Bluffs, is from 60 to 100 feet high, sloping in places, but perpendicular at the points. The inhabitants raise corn and cotton, the soil is good, and this bluff from its elevated and airy situation, may become the site of a handsome town.   The period of the existence of the future city must necessarily be remote, since the Chickasaws, own the country immediately in the rear of the fort, and will not willingly dispose of the soil; as they have a considerable town within five miles of the river, in an eastern direction.   This bluff has a front of ten miles on the river, part in Tennessee, and part in the newly erected state. Between this and the mouth of the Yazoo, are only a few detached settlements; the greater part of the way wilderness; the view up this river is about five miles.   The 34th deg. of latitude which crosses the Mississippi a few miles above White river, entering from the west, appears to be the boundary of the alligator region; they are rarely seen north of the entrance of the Arkansas.   The forests, the foliage and drapery of the trees, begin here to present a new and interesting aspect, and Nature attires herself in habiliments of richer hues—the articles of her toilette and wardrobe, here become more brilliant and diversified.   The laurel magnolia, the pride of southern forests, the stately cypress, unkown to the middle states, raise their lofty heads, with proud preeminence above their humble neighbors.   The cane and cotton greatly increase in size, and vegetation every where acknowledges the genial influence of a milder sun, as well as the boundless fertility of the soil.   The trees are curiously ornamented and festooned with the Spanish beard, waving to the winds, and the earth covered with impervious and wide-spreading canebrakes.

Ten miles below the mouth of Yazoo river, are the Walnut hills: the situation is pleasant, the land high, waving and fertile.   Here are fine cotton plantations, and the ruins of Fort M'Henry.   Twenty-five miles below the Walnut hills, is the settlement of Palmyra, settled by New Englanders; and twenty-seven miles below this is Big Black river.   There are several settlements on this river, extending forty miles up; the inhabitants are subject to bilious complaints, owing to the inundations caused by the back current of the Mississippi setting up twenty miles. Two miles further down is the Grand Gulf, which excites great terror in the breasts of inexperienced boatmen, but is little regarded by old navigators; it is nothing more than a large eddy, into which, if a boat be drawn, it is very difficult to regain the current of the river. Ten miles below is the mouth of bayou Pierre; the settlements bordering on this stream are rendered unhealthy by the Mississippi's damming up its waters in times of floods. The traveller here finds himself in the proper region of the paroquets—indeed the woods appear alive with birds of various sorts. Pigeons at certain seasons are seen in darkening clouds; and wild turkies in frequent flocks. Water fowls are numerous in winter. About thirty miles up this stream, by its windings, is port Gibson, the chief town of Claiborne county; it is a pretty thriving place, and contains about sixty houses; it has an academy under good regulation; the country is hilly, with rich plantations. Two miles below the mouth of bayou Pierre, is Bruinsburg, a hamlet of four or five houses. The next object worthy of the traveller's notice, is Cole's creek; this is a handsome, transparent sandy bottomed stream, except when disturbed by heavy rains, when it swells to a frightful torrent; impassable, at times for several days. Fifteen miles from the river it divides into the North and South Forks. Between these branches is the town of Greenville, the capital of Jefferson county. It is very handsomely situated on a dry sandy plain, on what is called the middle branch of Cole's creek, and consists of one wide straight street, half a mile long, and intersected by two cross ones; the number of buildings is about 65; the surrounding country rich and well cultivated; roads bad, and travelling often interrupted by the swelling of the several branches of Cole's creek. It has a court house, church, post-office, several stores and taverns. Water of a good quality is produced by digging about thirty feet. A few miles S. W. of Greenville is the little village of Uniontown, of half a dozen houses. A few miles further in the direction of Natchez, is the village of Sulzerstown, of fifteen or twenty houses. The country continues hilly, plantations large, and the produce chiefly cotton. Ten miles below Cole's creek, is Fairchild's creek, a handsome stream, subject to sudden swells, and heading near Washington. Ten miles further brings us to *Natchez*, which is situated on the east bank of the Mississippi, about 300 miles above New-Orleans, in lat. 31 33. The greater part of the town stands on a bluff upwards of 150 feet above the surface of the river; the intercourse between the *hill* and the *bottom* is carried on over a dug way, rendered tolerably easy by its length. The houses have an air of neatness though few are distinguished for elegance or size. To enable the inhabitants to enjoy the evening air, almost every house has a piazza and balcony. There is a considerable inequality in the surface of the hill, which prevents handsome streets, and extensive views through the surrounding country. The soil is rich, and vegetation of most kinds attains to uncommon luxuriance ; the gardens are ornamented with orange trees, figs, plums, peaches, and grape vines. The number of houses is about 300 ; the inhabitants are distinguished for their wealth, luxury and hospitality ; this remark is only applicable to the merchants and rich planters ; for there are great numbers of poor dissipated wretches ; of all nations, and of all colors. The greater part of the business is transacted on the bottom, where there is a large eddy which enables boats to land with safety and convenience. Two weekly newspapers are published, and learning begins to receive attention. Cotton is the grand staple of the Natchez settlement ; the income of the first planters is princely ; from 5000 to 30,000 dollars per annum ; some have as many as 300 acres in a single field, solely devoted to cotton ; they commence planting it about the middle of February ; corn is planted from March to July, according to the convenience of the cultivator. The sugar cane is sometimes planted as high up as Natchez, but not with the same success as is experienced at Baton Rouge. There is no doubt, however, but that it will eventually succeed ; at least to a degree equal to the demand for home consumption. Labor is almost exclusively performed by slaves. A good negro, from 20 to 30 years of age, will command from 800 to 1200 dollars. A prime slave will attend about three acres of cotton, which will yield an annual nett profit of from 230 to 260 dollars ; the clear profit of the full grown male slaves will average about 200 dollars, after deducting the expence of food and clothing. Sea vessels come up the Mississippi as far as Natchez; but the voyage is tedious and of late years not often attempted. The market of Natchez is well supplied with fish ; most of the flour and grain is purchased from the Kentucky boats. The country for the space of 20 miles in the rear of this town is settled ; but not thickly, by reason of the extensiveness of the plantations, which generally contain from 400 to 1000, and upwards of acres. Natchez is much resorted to by the Choctaw Indians, whose possessions are within less than one day's ride to the east. Great numbers of squaws, boys and girls, are employed by the planters to assist in gathering the cotton crop. Land is very high in the settlements along the Mississippi from Yazoo river to the line of demarcation ; say from $40 to 50 for whole farms.

From Natchez to the old West Florida line the surface and scenery remains unchanged, excepting the sugar plantations, which begin to show themselves below the Homochitto. The first stream you pass, after leaving Natchez, is Catherine's creek, about 40 yards wide, and boatable several miles during high water. About 20 miles up this creek is situated the town of Washington, which contains about 150 houses ; it is at present the seat of government, has a jail, court house, several stores, and taverns. One mile below Catherine's creek, are the White Cliffs, composed of white clay, and strongly resembling chalk. Twenty-seven miles further is the entrance of Homochitto, a beautiful little river 60 yards wide, having its branches interwoven with those of the Amite. This river may at present be considered as the northern boundary of the sugar region, though it will probably arrive to perfection as far north as the Arkansas. Most kinds of tropical fruits flourish here, such as the sweet orange, guinea corn, Indian kail, pomegranate, ginger, &c. The country is settled on both sides the Homochitto, nearly to the Choctaw boundary. Six miles below the Homochitto is Buffalo creek, a deep, still stream, about 40 yards wide and 30 miles long. Two miles below this creek are Loftus Heights, about 150 feet above the level of the Mississippi ; Fort Adams is situated on this bluff, and is now going to decay. There is a small village of 20 houses near the fort ; but villages and towns do not appear to flourish in a country so exclusively devoted to the culture of sugar and cotton. Five miles below is the line of demarcation, run by Andrew Ellicott in 1796, as the boundary between the United States and West Florida, but at present the limit between the new state and Louisiana, from the Mississippi to Pearl river ; it was cut out 40 feet wide, but is at present filled with brushwood and small trees. Pinckneyville, a village of 30 or 40 houses is situated about ten miles from the river, on a sloping plain in the centre of a rich settlement, and about one mile and a half from the line. The country is thinly settled along the line to the Amite, and indeed through to the Mobile. The town of Mobile stands on the head of the bay and west of the river of the same name ; in lat. 30 12 north ; regularly laid out, of an oblong figure. In consequence of the marshes to the north-west of the town, the inhabitants are sometimes visited with fevers and agues. There are many fine brick houses; the whole number of buildings are about three hundred ; there are about twenty stores. It has greatly improved since the beginning of 1816,—six new dry goods stores, one hardware store, and several lumber houses have been recently established ; in short, improvements of all kinds are going on with spirit, and its foreign trade fast increasing. The inhabitants principally consist of French, Spaniards, and Americans ; towards the lower end of the town stands Fort Charlotte, taken by Gen. Wilkinson in 1812 ; it is a regular built fortress, with commedious barracks.   The trade of Mobile is already considerable; the chief articles of export are lumber, pitch and tar, fur, cotton, beef and pork, rice and corn.   Ascending the Mobile the first place is St. Stephens, which stands on the west side of the Tombigbee, 80 miles above Mobile, and at the head of sloop navigation; it contains about 250 houses, a printing-office, academy, and fifteen stores; and is a thriving healthy place, advantageously situated for trade.   The valley or rather alluvion of the Mobile, is from five to ten miles wide, and is cut into numerous islands by the several branches of the river and the bayous, leading from one channel to the other; these islands are from five to thirty-five miles in length, and from one to five in width; the soil is of the best quality, but subject to be overflowed in spring and fall; they are best adapted to the growth of rice and indigo.   The sugar lands are extensive, and are found equal, if not superior to those of the Mississippi.

Eighty miles above St. Stephens is the entrance of the Black Warrior, a fine stream from the east; this is the largest above the confluence of the Alabama—it holds out to adventurers very superior advantages; because it is destined to become the channel of communication, between the immense fertile country on both sides of the Tennessee river, and the several sea ports which will at no remote period embellish the bays of Mobile and Perdido.   The fact appears clearly established, that goods can be brought from Europe, New-York, or even New-Orleans, to Huntsville in Tennessee, by way of the Mobile, Tombigbee and Black Warrior, in about half the time and for less risk and expence than by any other route, hitherto used or known.

From Mobile to the falls of the Black Warrior, is about 500 miles by water; boats that do not draw more than three feet of water can ascend it thus far at all seasons; and the portage from the falls to the Tennessee river is about 40 miles.

Mr. James O. Crumb, an enterprising merchant of Huntsville, I believe was the first to make the important discovery that European goods could reach the Tennessee river, from Mobile in thirty days, when it would require 100 days by ascending the Mississippi, to arrive at the Muscle Shoals. An extract from Mr. Crumb's letter will explain the facility with which he executed his enterprize.

"I left home about the first of September for Mobile, and on my way engaged with captain Bacon to take charge of my boat, &c. which I procured at Mobile, drawing about two feet water when loaded ; at St. Stephens the cargo was completed of some articles that could not be purchased below. I accompanied the boat about eight miles, to see her safe over Megrois Shoals, a place said to be dangerous in passing over loaded boats ; there was at that time a flood in the river, and we had little or no difficulty in getting through. Captain Bacon states that he was 20 days coming from Mobile to the falls of Black Warrior, including five or six days of delay. The impediments in the rivers are trifling to such a boat as mine, which is about 35 feet in length. The cargo consisting of brown and Havanna white sugars, coffee, rum, wine, oranges and a few dry goods, arrived at the falls in good order : two waggon loads of sugar, wine, coffee and oranges I brought to Huntsville ; and it is remarkable that out of one thousand oranges not more than half a dozen spoiled. In eight days the waggons reached this place from the falls of Black Warrior, over a road three fifths of which is level and the balance not much broken ; not more than three hills of consequence are recollected, and a four horse team can easily draw two thousand weight up either of them. There has been very little labor bestowed in cutting out the road, and I discovered that by turning it a little from its windings, it could greatly be improved ; the distance I suppose from Huntsville to the falls of the Black Warrior is about 120 miles. It is evident the distance can be much shortened by straightening the road."

From Thompson's creek, near Fort Deposit, to the highest navigable point of the Black Warrior is about forty miles ;

the last stream at this point is between 40 and 50 yards wide, and not easily forded at a common pitch of water, and the current very gentle.   There are shoals below, for the distance of about 30 miles, but it is not rough water for more than four miles, and there, boats have no difficulty when there is a moderate swell in this river.   A road could easily be made along the portage, capable of admitting waggons carrying 3000 weight, as the intervening country is a firm level valley of excellent white oak and poplar, land well watered and capable of sustaining a numerous population.   It is thought that a canal uniting the Tennessee and the Tombigbee could be constructed without meeting very formidable obstacles.

Very important cessions were obtained from the Cherokees, Chickasaws, and Choctaws, by the commissioners Jackson, Meriwether, Coffee and Rhea, in September last ; the whole together, contain about 13,000 square miles, or 8,320,000 acres, of land of the first quality, and delightfully situated on both banks of the Tennessee above and below the Muscle Shoals ; on Duck, Elk river, Buffalo, Beech, Caney and Bear creeks, Blackwarrior, Natarchucky, Tombigbee, Cahaba, &c. Thousands of adventurers in the southern states, Kentucky, and Tennessee, have their eyes upon this favorite tract ; the Muscle Shoals may be considered as the focus of emigration, for two or three seasons, in the course of which, every lot will unquestionably be settled or at least purchased.

There is at this moment a population of upwards of 15,000 souls in Madison county ; which six years ago was a howling wilderness.   The new purchases will admit of at least six new counties, as large, and fertile as Madison.

The Muscle Shoals are about 100 miles south of Nashville ; a town will, in the course of the present year, be laid out near them ; there is a good bluff for a town, and a large convenient spring, on the south side of the river, three miles below the shoals ; and four miles below the shoals on the north side of the river there is a good bluff for a town, with a large good spring, called Sweet Water ; but which of these places will have the most important town, may depend on circumstances that have not yet occurred.

Madison county is about 20 miles square, and is reported to have " produced ten thousand bales of cotton for market last year ; and if the report is true, that that county nearly doubled any county of its size in the United States, in the production of cotton, and if the late purchase in the Mississippi territory on both sides of the Tennessee, is six times as large as Madison county, and was in an equal state of cotton cultivation, then the produce of both together would be *seventy thousand* bales of cotton, which is as much as is manufactured at all the manufacturing establishments in the United States of America ; which quantity of cotton, with the other produce of that country, would support an extensive and brisk trade at a town or towns near the lower end of the Muscle Shoals, where there would be a double demand for cotton ; one for the upper country trade, for the settlements in the middle and upper parts of the Ohio country, as well as for the settlements on the upper Mississippi and Missouri ; the other at New-Orleans for exportation."

Mr. Crumb, whom I have quoted in a preceding page, and who is well acquainted with the country from Huntsville to Mobile, represents the cotton of the Tombigbee, Cahaba and Alabama to be of a most extraordinary size and luxuriance : " I cannot describe the cotton fields unless I compare them to a neglected peach orchard with branches projecting from bottom to top, with a stem about the size of a man's wrist, from eight to ten, eleven and twelve feet high." The cotton of East Tennessee, not a degree and a half north of the shoals, rarely grows to more than four feet in height, with a feeble stem of about an inch diameter.

The Muscle Shoals are about twenty miles in length, and three broad ; and full of islands. In low water they are serious obstructions to the navigation of the river. The descent is gradual but rapid ; the various channels will afford convenient situations for an almost indefinite number of mills or other hydraulic establishments. A good boatable channel could be easily opened through the shoals, for a trifling expence, considering the importance of the object. Boats of thirty tons burthen, ascend and descend without risk, when there is a moderate swell in the river.

EXTENT OF NAVIGABLE WATERS.

	Miles.
Mississippi navigable,	572
Tennessee,	250
Yazoo and branches,	270
Big Black river,	150
Homochitto, Amite, &c.	170
Pearl and branches,	229
Pascagola and do.	250
Bayous of bays St. Louis, Biloxi, Pines, &c.	100
Gulf coast,	120
Tombigbee and western branches,	600
Total	2902

NAVIGABLE WATERS,
(OF THE ALABAMA TERRITORY.)

	Miles.
Tombigbee and eastern branches, Tensaw, Mobile, Fish river, &c.	750
Alabama and branches, including Cahaba, Coosa, Tallapoosa, Kiowee, &c.	800
Perdido, Conecah, Escambia, Yellow-water, Choctaw and Pea rivers, and Gulf coast,	370
Chatahouchee and western branches,	550
	2470

H h

INDIANS.

There is only three tribes resident in the western part of the late Mississippi Territory; the Chickasaws, Cherokees and Choctaws. The Chickasaws have about 1800 warriors, and 4000 women and children—they own several millions of acres of excellent land, between 38 and 34 north lat. and the Tennessee and Mississippi rivers, besides four reservations from one to four miles square: these Indians have always been the warm friends of the United States, and distinguished for their hospitality. Some of the Chickasaw chiefs possess numerous negro slaves, and annually sell several hundred cattle and hogs. The Colbert family are the most opulent; George Colbert is the proprietor of the ferry, where the road from Nashville to Natchez, crosses the Tennessee river; it is worth two thousand dollars a year; his charge is fifty cents for a footman, and one dollar for a man and horse—the travel is already great, as all the boatmen who descend the Mississippi to New-Orleans, return by land through the Choctaw and Chickasaw nations, and cross at this ferry. Colbert has a fine tract of land four miles square, and it is said that his bill against the United States for provisions, horses, ferriage, &c. furnished during the war, to the Tennessee militia, was 75,000 dollars. The Chickasaws reside in eight towns, and like their neighbors, are considerably civilized.

The Cherokees are a powerful nation, having a population of 14,580 souls, and 4000 warriors. They still own an extensive district, chiefly on the south side of the Tennessee river, to the east of the Chickasaw possessions, and extending from the head branches of the Tombigbee to above the Hiwassee east, and south as far as the Estenaury. The following extracts, from the pen of Return J. Meigs, sen. who has long resided in the nation as Indian agent, will best illustrate their character and present habits.

"In the year 1809, I had a census taken of the number of the Cherokee nation, which amounted to 12,359. The number of males and females were nearly equal—they have considerably increased since that period, so that including a colony of Cherokees that went to settle on the river Arkansas, their number is about 14,500 souls—those who emigrated to Arkansas, as well as those on their ancient grounds, have made considerable advances in acquiring the useful arts, particularly in the manufacture of cotton and woolen cloth. They raise the cotton, and the indigo for dying their yarn; they are good weavers, and have at this time upwards of 500 looms: most of the looms are made by themselves; they have more than 500 ploughs—this greatly increased the tillage of their lands; they have large stocks of black cattle and horses, swine and some sheep; they have domesticated poultry in plenty: and having now an abundance of the necessaries of life, their population proportionably increases. By means of some schools, many of their young people read and write. A great part of the men have adopted our modes of dress; and the females without exception dress in the habits of the white people. Some of them, who are wealthy, are richly dressed. They are remarkably clean and neat in their persons: this may be accounted for by their universal practice of bathing in their numerous transparent streams of water which in almost every direction run through their country. Men, women and children practise bathing, which undoubtedly contributes to their health. All can swim, and this is often of great convenience, as no river can impede their way in travelling. When the females bathe, they are never exposed : any improper conduct towards them would be held in detestation by all. Since I have been first in that nation, a young white man solicited the hand of a young Cherokee woman. She refused his offer, and objected, as a principal reason, that he was not clean in his appearance, that he did not as the Cherokees do—bathe himself in the rivers. Ablution with these people was formerly a religious rite. It is not now viewed by them in this light, but it is nearly allied to a moral virtue.

"I have not been an inattentive spectator in viewing these
people in various situations; in their forests, in their houses,
in their schools, and in their public councils. The progress
of their children in their schools has been as great as that of
any other children, in acquiring the knowledge of letters and
of figures. Nature has given them the finest forms; and can
we presume that God has withheld from them correspondent
intellectual and mental powers of mind. No man who has
had public business to transact with them, can have a doubt
of the capacity of their minds. Their hospitality in their
houses is every where acknowledged; their bravery in the
field is also acknowledged by those who acted with them in
the late war against the hostile Creeks. If a statuary should
want models for the human figure, he will find the most perfect amongst the southern Indian tribes south of the Ohio river. About one half of the Cherokee nation are of *mixed*
blood by intermarriages with the white people. Many of
these are as white as any of our citizens. There are some
of the aboriginal Cherokees, who have never used any particular care to guard their faces from the action of the sun
who have good complexions. I have frequently attended at
the schools for the instruction of the Indian children; seen
them by classes go through their exercises. On these occa-
sions I have seen tears of joy steal down the cheeks of be-
nevolent men—men who rejoice at the diffusion of knowledge
amongst this long-lost part of the human race. The Cherokees universally believe in the being of God; they call him
the Great Spirit; they mention him with reverence; with
them, his attributes are power and goodness. They never
profane the name of God in their own language. They have
no series of words that they can combine to profane the name
of God.

"The Choctaws are still more numerous than the Cherokees,
their lands are situated between the Yazoo and Tombigbee,
and the parallels 34 and 31 north. They reside on the
Chickasaka, Yazoo, Pascagola and Pearl rivers; they are

friendly to white travellers for whose accommodation, while
sojourning in their nation, they have established a number
of public inns, which for neatness, accommodations and mod-
eration of charges, actually excel many white taverns in the
northern states.   A considerable part of their lands are pine
timbered ; but much of it rich waving, hickory and poplar
land.   Some of them have large farms, in a good state of
culture, and many of them spend much of their time in agricultural improvements.   Many years ago they had forty-three
towns and villages, containing 4,041 warriors, and 12,123
souls.   Since that time they have no doubt considerably increased in numbers."

POPULATION.

The white population of the proposed state amounted in
December, 1816, to 23,644 souls, distributed through the
several counties as follows, viz :

Counties.				Whites.	Slaves.	Total.
Adams,	.	.	.	3,608	6,394	9,998
Jefferson,	.	.	.	2,548	2,358	4,906
Claiborne,	.	.	.	1,716	1,790	3,506
Wilkinson,	.	.	.	3,218	4,057	7,275
Amite,	.	.	.	3,365	1,694	5,059
Warren,	.	.	.	799	768	1,569
Franklin,	.	.	.	1,696	1,013	2,708
Marion,	.	.	.	1,015	686	1,701
Pike,	.	.	.	2.078	540	2,618
Hancock,	.	.	.	667	333	1,000
Lawrence,	.	.	.	1,367	417	1,784
Wayne,	.	.	.	1,566	517	2,084

	Total,	23,644	20,547	44,208

There are besides 191 free blacks, the greater part of
whom reside in Adams county.

NORTH-WESTERN TERRITORY,

Is situated between 41 50, and 49 N. lat. and 8 20 and 18 30 west longitude ; and bounded south by the parallel of the south end of lake Michigan, (in N. lat. 41, 50) which divides it from the Illinois Territory ; west by the Mississippi river, which separates it from the Missouri Territory ; north by the straits of St. Mary, lake Superior and a part of Upper Canada ; east by lakes Huron, Michigan, and Green bay.*

RIVERS.

The rivers of this territory have three different directions ; a part run northwardly into lake Superior : others westwardly into the Mississippi ; some eastwardly into lake Michigan and the Illinois.

The following streams water the eastern side of the territory, and fall into the Illinois, lake Michigan, Green bay and lake Huron.

Fox river which heads in the south-eastern corner of the territory, is noticed in page 22.

Plein river, or Des Planes, enters the Illinois 55 miles south of the Chicago portage. According to Major Long, Topographical Engineer in the U. S. service, it is a " small stream rising in the low lands bordering upon the west side of lake Michigan, and has its general course in a south-westerly direction. The valley of this river has an average width of about one mile, and is terminated, on both sides, by regular

* Should it hereafter be found that the south end of Green bay, is situated *south* of the southern extremity of lake Michigan, then, according to the boundaries of the Michigan Territory, as defined by law, that Territory will include the peninsulas formed by parts of lakes Superior, Huron, and Michigan, Green and Noquet bays, and the river Manistique, over which the Michigan Territorial jurisdiction at present extends.

banks, nearly parallel to each other, extending along the river about thirty miles from the head of the Illinois. In ascending this river, also, the banks or bluffs gradually decrease in height, being, as before mentioned, about one hundred feet high at the mouth, and only twenty or twenty-five at the distance of thirty miles higher up the river, where, instead of maintaining their parallel direction, they form nearly right angles with the course of the river—that on the right taking an easterly, and that on the left a north-westerly course; but being gradually inflected from these courses, they form an extensive curve, encircling a large tract of flat prairie, in no part elevated more than twelve or fourteen feet above the common level of the water in this vicinity. The river throughout the above mentioned distance has four or five short rapids or ripples, that make their appearance only in times of very low water. In every other part it has the appearance of being a chain of stagnant pools and small lakes, affording a sufficient depth of water for boats of moderate draught.

Ascending the Illinois about 70 miles further, we arrive at the mouth of the Depage; this stream closely resembles the Plein in the height of its bluffs, width of its valley, soil and timber. It takes its rise a few miles west of the Plein, and has a course nearly parallel with it.

"Chicago river," says Mr. Long, in his report to the acting Secretary of War, "is merely an arm of the lake dividing itself into two branches at the distance of one mile inland from its communication with the lake. The north branch extends along the westerly side of the lake about 30 miles, and receives some few tributaries. The south branch has an extent of only five or six miles, and receives no supplies except from the small lake of the prairie above described.—The river and each of its branches, are of various widths, from fifteen to fifty yards, and for two or three miles inland, have a sufficient depth of water to admit vessels of almost any burthen. The entrance into Lake Michigan, however, which is eighty yards wide, is obstructed by a sand bar about seventy yards broad; upon the highest parts of which the water is usually no more than two feet deep. The difficulty of removing this obstruction, would not be great.— Piers might be sunk on both sides of the entrance, and the sand removed from between them. By this means, the river would be rendered a safe and commodious harbor for shipping : a convenience which is seldom to be met with on the shores of Lake Michigan.

" The water course, which is already opened between the river Des Planes and Chicago river, needs but little more excavation to render it sufficiently capacious for all the purposes of a canal. It may be supplied with water at all times of the year, by constructing a dam of moderate height across the Des Planes, which would give the water of that river a sufficient elevation to supply a canal extending from one river to the other. It would be necessary, also, to construct locks at the extremities of the canal; that communicating with Chicago river being calculated to elevate about six feet, and that communicating with the Des Planes about four feet.

" To render the Des Planes and Illinois navigable for small boats and flats, requiring but a small draught of water, nothing more is necessary than the construction of sluices of a width sufficient to admit the boats to pass through them. This may be effected by clearing away the loose stones from the bottom, and forming banks erected with stone, two or three feet high, on each side of the sluice. There are but few places, however, where works of this kind would be necessary : the extent of the whole probably would not exceed two miles.— Thus a water communication between the Illinois and Lake Michigan may be kept open at all times, sufficient to answer all the purposes for which a canal will be wanted for many years to come."

Between Chicago and the entrance of Green Bay, the following rivers empty into Lake Michigan from the west, in the order named, viz. Tauahan, Wakayah, Masquedon, Cedar, Roaring, Milwakee, Saukie, Skabayagan, Maurice, and

Fourche. These streams have all an eastern course, running generally parallel with each other at the distance of from ten to twenty miles, and heading from thirty to sixty miles from the lake. *Roaring river,* so called from a " rumbling noise, like distant thunder, which is heard every two or three days during the warm season, occasioned, it is thought, by the vast quantities of copper, which attract the electric fluid to that place."* The Indians, in consequence approach this river, with religious awe, as the residence of the Great Spirit. The banks of this river are high near its mouth, where the earth appears to have been rent asunder by some great concussion. The Indians never eat the fish of this river, as they are of a poisonous nature, the water being strongly impregnated with copper.

Green bay is about 120 miles in length, and from six to thirty wide, extending north and south parallel with lake Michigan, at the distance of from twenty to forty miles, according to the indentions and projections of their shores.— It receives several rivers, the principal of which, are Fox river, which interlocks with the Ouiscousin, and falls into the south end of the bay. Twenty miles north of the mouth of Fox river is a small stream called Riviere Rouge. North of this are Gaspard, and Menomonie rivers: the last interlocks by a short portage with the Rufus branch of the Chippawa, running into the Mississippi at the lower end of lake Pepin. Sandy river falls into Noquet's bay, by which name the north end of Green bay is usually designated.

Between the Detour, or entrance of the bay and Michillimackinac, are the rivers Manistique and Mino Cockien: the first falls into lake Michigan thirty miles north of the mouth of the bay ; it is a large river: it takes its rise from a large lake, and nearly communicates with lake Superior; its banks are high and sandy, and abound with pine timber. The Mino Cockien is also a large and deep stream, heads near lake Superior and flows into lake Michigan about thirty-five miles

* Gen. Hull

south-west of Michilimackinac. Between Michilimackinac
and the strait of St. Mary, the rivers Bouchitaouy and St.
Ignace empty into lake Huron.

The strait or river St. Mary connecting lakes Superior and
Huron, is about fifty miles in length; and is divided into several channels, which form a variety of islands. The largest
of which is St. Josephs, 75 miles in circumference. Nibish
island intervenes between St. Josephs and the western shore.
Sugar island is long and narrow, bending towards the north in
form of a crescent, and causing an enlargement of the waters
between it and the continental coast. This is called lake
George. Ships of great burthen can approach to the sault or
rapides. The rivers Minaston, Miscoutinsaki and Great
Bouchitaouy falls into this strait from the south; the last interlocks with branches of the Manistique.

That part of the territory stretching along the southern
borders of lake Superior, is well watered by about thirty rivers; the principal of which, commencing at the east end of
the lake, are Grande Marais, Corn, Dead, Carp, Great and
Little Garlic, and Porcupine rivers, all of which fall in
east of the Great peninsula of Shagomigon, which projects into the lake upwards of sixty miles; between this peninsula,
(which is 370 miles west of Sault de Marie) and the Fond du
Lac, are the rivers, Ontonagon, Fair, Montreal, Bad, Burnt-
wood, Goddard's, and Strawberry rivers. The river St.
Louis, falls into West Bay, at Fond du Lac; it is large, and
navigable one hundred and fifty miles, and heads near the
eastern head branches of the Mississippi. The North-West
Company have several trading houses established at its mouth
and on its banks towards its source.

A prodigious number of streams pay their tribute to the
Mississippi, from the east, between its source and Rocky-
river, which discharges its waters in the Illinois Territory.

Le Croix and Deer rivers, the extent of whose navigation
is unknown, and whose branches are interwoven with those of
the St. Louis, enter the Mississippi below the forks of that
river.

Meadow river, falls into the Mississippi three miles below the Falls of Packagamau, (in N. lat. 46 20) bears N. E. and is navigable for Indian canoes one hundred miles, winding through prairies, with pine and spruce swamps in their rear. Below this is Swan river, bears east from the Mississippi, and is navigable for canoes ninety miles, to Swan lake.

Sandy Lake river, is forty miles below Swan river; it is large, but short, connecting the lake of the same name with the Mississippi by a strait only six miles in length. This lake is about twenty-five miles in circumference, and receives a number of small rivers, the most important of which is Savanna river, which by a portage of about four miles, communicates with the river St. Louis, emptying into Lake Superior at the Fond du Lac, and is the channel by which the N. W. Company convey their goods.

Muddy river, twenty yards wide, falls into the Mississippi about twenty miles below Sandy lake outlet. The next stream is Red Cedar river, issuing from the lake of the same name, and is nearly equidistant between the river De Corbeau from the west and Sandy Lake river. Between this and the Falls of St. Anthony, are Shrub-Oak, Lake, Clear, Elk, St. Francis, and Rum rivers, all emptying in from the east. Clear river is a beautiful little stream of about eighty yards in width, and heads in swamps and rice-lakes towards Lake Superior. Rum river is about fifty yards wide, and heads in Le Mille Lac, which is thirty-five miles south of Lower Red Cedar lake. Indian canoes ascend quite to the lake, around which is the best hunting ground for a space of several hundred miles.

St. Croix river joins the Mississippi several miles below the falls of St. Anthony; it is 80 yards wide at its mouth, 500 yards from which commences Lake St. Croix, two or three miles wide, and thirty-six long. This river communicates with Burnt-wood river, "by a portage of half a mile only, and in its whole extent has *not one fall or rapid* worthy of notice."† This, with the mildness of its current and

---

† Pike.

its other advantages, render it by far the most preferable communication which can be had with Lake Superior, from the
waters of the Mississippi.

Riviere de la Montaigne, and another small river, fall into
the upper end of Lake Pepin.

Chippeway, or Sauteaux river, enters the Mississippi at
the lower end of Lake Pepin. It is a deep, wide, majestic
stream, interlocking with the Montreal, flowing into Lake Superior, and with the Menomonie running into Green Bay.—
Its branches are numerous ; the most considerable of which
are Rufus, Vermillion, and Copper rivers. It divides into
the east and north branches about thirty miles from its confluence with the Mississippi.

Between Lake Pepin and the Ouisconsin, the Buffaloe,
Black, and Prairie Le Croix rivers, enter the Mississippi
from the east and north-east. Black river is about two hundred yards wide, heads near Fox river of Lake Michigan, and
pursues a course nearly parallel with the Ouisconsin.

The Ouisconsin joins the Mississippi at Prairie Des Chiens,
where it is about half a mile wide. It heads east of the
sources of Fox river, and is the grand channel of communication between Prairies Des Chiens and Michilimackinac.

Rocky river takes its source near Green Bay of Lake Michigan, more than 450 miles from its mouth, and is navigable
upwards of 300 miles. It runs across the N. W. corner of
the Illinois Territory, and enters the Mississippi two hundred and ten miles below Prairie Des Chiens, and three hundred and ninety above St. Louis.

The interior of this Territory, is watered by innumerable
small lakes and ponds, from which issue the head branches of
all the principal rivers. These lakes generally abound with
folle avoine, water fowls and fish—each in such prodigious
quantities, that the Indians are in a manner exempted from
the contingence of famine.

SOIL, SURFACE, TIMBER.

The alluvial bottoms are as rich as those of Ohio and Michigan, as is proved by the excellence of the corn crops at Green Bay, Prairie Des Chiens, and even on the banks of the Ontonagon, on the southern shore of Lake Superior.— The uplands and prairies south of the parallel of St. Anthony's falls, are generally good, interspersed, however, with tracts of wet land, rocky prairies, and shrub-oak ridges, and extensive strips of a light, sandy soil, only suitable for the culture of barley and the smaller grains. High, bald hills present themselves, in places, along the banks of Rocky river and the Ouisconsin.

Lieut. Pike, in ascending to the source of the Mississippi, found a gradual deterioration of soil and climate from the falls of St. Anthony, as he proceeded northwardly. The pine, or fir region, may be said to commence at the falls; "but there are some exceptions, where you meet with small bottoms of oak, ash, maple, and lynn:" the woods, however, are full of elk, deer and buffaloe, as far up as the river De Corbeau, (in lat. 45 50.) From thence to Pine river, the shores of the Mississippi in general " presented a dreary prospect of high, barren knobs, covered with dead and fallen pine timber. To this there were some exceptions of ridges of yellow and pitch pine; also some small bottoms of lynn, elm, oak, and ash. The adjacent country is (at least two-thirds) covered with small lakes, some of which are three miles in circumference. This renders the communication impassable in summer, except with small bark canoes."† Above Pine river, he saw but few situations fit for cultivation, game scarce, and the country a succession of pine and hemlock ridges, with here and there a prairie, and small bottoms of elm, beech and basswood. Finally, from Leech Lake, upwards, to the extreme sources of the Mississippi, " the whole face of the

† Pike.

country has the appearance of an impenetrable morass or boundless savanna."

Within a circle of country, of less, perhaps, than fifty miles diameter, rise the sources of three immense rivers, viz. the Mississippi, the St. Lawrence, and Red river of Hudson bay—all running in different directions, and discharging their waters into three distinct seas. This circumstance clearly proves this tract, wet and swampy as it is, to be the most elevated land on the continent of North America. The river St. Louis of Lake Superior, may be considered as the head branch of the St. Lawrence.

The dividing ridges, between the Mississippi and Lake Superior, which in some maps are erroneously represented as mountains, are chiefly covered with forests of pine, spruce, and hemlock, giving to the country a cold and dreary aspect. Towards the shores of Lake Superior, the country improves in fertility and appearance, and affords, in places, rich bottom and upland—whose forests, in time, will no doubt resound with the noise and bustle of a " *Yankee*" colony.

From the Fond du Lac to Point Shagomigon, the banks of the lake are in general of strong clay, mixed with stones, which render the navigation irksome and dangerous. From this point, or rather peninsula, to the outlet of the lake, the shore is almost one continued straight line of sandy beach, interspersed with rocky precipices of limestone, from twenty to an hundred feet high, without a single bay, and but few good harbors: timber, oak, sugar-maple, pine—uplands of a sandy soil—bottoms rich.

The country on the southern shore of the strait St. Marie, will admit of extensive settlements ; the easternmost channel, called Miscoutinsaki, has a *rapid*, well adapted for mill seats. The lands on the southern shore of the river of the same name, are excellent; prairies on its margin, and at a short distance back are groves of sugar-maple, in which the Chippeway Indians have numerous sugar-camps. From the the Sault de St. Marie, to this river, is almost one continued meadow.

The North West Company's factory, is at the foot of the rapids on the British side of the strait. The whole establishment consists of store-houses, a saw-mill, which supplies lumber for all their posts on Lake Superior, a batteau-yard, stockade and garden. Nine miles above, at Pine Point, is a dock-yard for constructing vessels, where reside a ship-carpenter and several artificers. At the factory there is a canal, with a lock at its lower entrance, and a causeway for dragging up the batteaux and canoes, and a good road for the transportation of merchandize.

FISH.

An abundance of white-fish, are at all times to be found on the rapids. Henry, who spent several winters at the Sault, subsisted almost wholly upon them.

"The method of taking them is this : each canoe carries two men, one of whom steers with a paddle, and the other is provided with a pole, ten feet in length, and at the end of which is affixed a scoop-net. The steersman sets the canoe from the eddy of one rock to that of another; while the fisherman, in the prow, who sees, through the pellucid element, the prey of which he is in pursuit, dips his net, and sometimes brings up, at every succeeding dip, as many as it can contain. The fish are often crowded together in the water in great numbers ; and a skilful fisherman, in autumn, will take five hundred in two hours." He caught five hundred, with his own hands, in the course of a few days, weighing from four to six pounds, and of a very superior flavor. Fish of various species, but particularly white-fish, crowd up to the foot of the rapids in such amazing shoals that many thousands of inhabitants could be supplied throughout the year. In the river Ontonagan, at the rapids, three leagues from the lake, where he wintered in 1785, he affirms that sturgeon are so abundant, that a month's subsistence for a regiment, could have been taken in a few hours. With the assistance of his men, he soon caught two thousand trout and white-fish, the former averaging about fifty pounds each.

The three great lakes, Superior, Huron, Michigan, and Green Bay, in short all their tributary rivers, afford bound-less supplies of sturgeon, carp, trout, black bass, &c.

MINERALS.

Dubuque's lead-mines, situated between the Ouisconsin and Rocky rivers, and approaching to within five or six miles of the Mississippi, are between twenty-seven and twenty-eight leagues long, and from one to three broad. Mr. Du-buque's claim to these mines is supposed to be spurious, in which case they become the property of the United States. At present they yield from 20 to 40,000 pounds of lead a year; and are deemed equally inexhaustible as those of the Maremeg, near St. Genevieve.

Very specious accounts have been published, respecting the abundance of copper ore, to be found in various parts of this Territory. Carver states, that he discovered several mines of virgin copper, on both sides of the St. Croix, which was as pure as that found in any other country. This wri-ter was of the opinion that this mineral would become an im-portant article of commerce; "as the metal which costs no-thing on the spot, and requires but little expence to get it on board, could be conveyed in boats and ships to Quebec.—The cheapness and ease with which any quantity of it may be procured, will make up for the length of way that is ne-cessary to transport it, before it reaches the sea coast; and enable the proprietors to send it to foreign markets on as good terms as it can be exported from other countries."

Alexander Henry, Esq. in speaking of the Ontonagon, states, that he found that river "chiefly remarkable for the abundance of virgin copper, which is on its banks and in its neighborhood. The copper presented itself to the eye in masses of various dimensions. The Indians showed him one of twenty pounds weight. They were used to manufacture this metal into spoons and bracelets for themselves. In the perfect state in which they found it, it required nothing but to be beat into shape." Upon a second visit to the mouth of that river, he took the opportunity of going ten miles up its banks with Indian guides, where he discovered a mass of copper of the weight, according to his estimate, of no less than five tons. Such was its malleable state that with an axe he was able to cut off a portion weighing an hundred pounds. On viewing the surrounding surface, he conjectured that the mass, at some period or other, had rolled from the side of a lofty hill which rises at its back. Upon the island of Nanibojou, between Point Mamance and Michicopoten, upon the north eastern coast, our adventurer found several pieces of virgin copper, of which many were remarkable for their form,—some resembling the leaves of vegetables, and others animals. Their weight was from an ounce to three pounds.

Capt. Norburg, a Russian gentleman, acquainted with metals, and holding a commission in the British service, was employed by a company of adventurers, to explore the borders of Lake Superior, in quest of copper-mines. He examined the coast of Nanibojou, and found several veins of copper and lead. He erected an air furnace at Point aux Pins, and ascertained that the lead ore contained silver in the proportion of forty ounces to a ton ; but the copper-ore in very small proportion indeed. Near Point aux Iroquois on the south side of the lake, fifteen miles from the Sault St. Marie, he discovered a *shod* of eight pounds weight—of a blue color and semi-transparent. This he carried to England, where it produced in the proportion of sixty pounds of silver to a hundred weight of ore. It was deposited in the British Museum.

The agents of the Company, among whom were Henry and Norburg, repaired to the Ontonagon, where besides the detached masses of copper, formerly mentioned, they saw much of the same metal bedded in stone. They built a house, and commenced operations. In digging, they found frequent masses of copper, some of which were of three pounds weight. A green colored water issued from the hill, which tinged iron of a copper color.*

---

* See Travels and Adventures in Canada and the *Indian Territories*, &c.

K k

Mackenzie observes, that he should not be surprised to hear of the Americans employing people to work the copper mines. " Indeed," he adds, " it might be well worthy the attention of the British subjects to work the mines on the north coast, though they are not supposed to be so rich as those on the south."

Near the mouth of Roaring river, pieces of copper have been found, weighing from seven to twenty-five pounds : and on Middle Island, near the western coast of Lake Michigan, and not far distant from the above river, are found great quantities of pure copper.*

If it really be true that copper ore exists on the shores of Lake Superior, to the extent stated by Carver, Henry, Mackenzie, &c. the fact insures the future commercial consequence of this territory.   I must confess that I was sceptical until I consulted a highly valued correspondent, when the following answer in a manner dissipated my doubts :—" The existence of the *virgin copper* is beyond doubt.   My late friend, Gen. Pike, who was incapable of aught of fraud or insincerity, assured me he had been on the spot. Gen. Wilkinson, not knowing of Pike's information, gave me the description of the position, and every particular, corresponding with Gen. Pike's account.   I know that a company is about to be formed at this moment, [November 7, 1816,] the object of which, is to *work these mines.*"

Iron ore, copperas, limestone and allum, are found along the shore of lakes Huron and Superior; and lead abounds on the Depage.

---

* Gen. Hull, to the Rev. Jedediah Morse.

GREEN BAY, FOX RIVER, OUISCONSIN.

As the route from Michilimackinac to Prairie Des Chiens, by way of Green Bay, Fox river, and the Ouisconsin, is much frequented by American and British traders, and as it is yearly becoming more important, I will devote a few pages to a description of the navigation, and the country through which it passes. The distance between Michilimackinac and the French settlement is about 175 miles. The western coast of Lake Michigan, from Michilimackinac to the entrance of Green Bay, affords several good harbors, such as the islands of St. Helens, Epouvette, Mino Cockien river, Souchoir rock, and the Manistique. The entrance into Green Bay, will admit vessels of 200 tons burthen. The best harbors on the traverse of the bay, are the Petite Detroit, and isle Roche ; the last inaccessible to all winds : Sturgeon Bay and the mouth of Rouge river—nevertheless, the voyage is dangerous in boisterous weather, as the coast is in several places lined with rocks. The navigation of the bay is safe and easy, for large vessels.

Fox river falls into its south western extremity. It is about 400 yards wide, with three fathoms water at its mouth, and navigable one hundred and sixty miles, to the *portage.*—Half a mile from its mouth, commences a French settlement, extending the distance of five miles on both sides of the river, occupied by forty French families, who emigrated from Canada and France in the year 1720. They have small farms, and raise corn, wheat, peas, potatoes, horses, cows, hogs, &c. Before the late war, this settlement was well stocked with cattle and horses; some of the inhabitants having from 140 to 150 head of cattle. By frequent intermarriages with the Indians, and a long residence among them, nine-tenths of their women are of Indian origin. They are said to be modestly diffident, and preserve a tolerable share of the ease and courteousness of French politeness ; their costume very grotesque, wearing printed calico short gowns, stroud petticoats and mocasins. The inhabitants have been frequently oppressed by the Indians, particularly since the commencement of the late war.

A fort, under the direction of Capt. Gratiot, is erected on the ruins of the old French fort Le Bay ; it is a stockade with strong pickets, a bastion at each angle, with a piece of artillery on each. It is situated about one mile from the mouth of the river, on the left bank. and commands it completely. The country between the Fox and Menomonie rivers, is inviting to settlers : the soil is good, the climate much milder than at Michilimackinac, as the trees are clothed with verdure at least one month earlier. The sturgeon, trout, white-fish, and bass, of the bay, rivers and creeks, are equal in flavor and delicacy to any in America, and can be taken, with case, in almost any quantity. The soil on both sides of Fox river, is very fine, and the wheat fields and gardens give it the appearance of a rich and fertile country. The timber is oak, walnut, sugar-maple, poplar, elm, honey-locust, and pine. The shores of the bay and rivers, are agreeably diversified with prairies, islets of woodland, and thick forests. The inhabitants have always been remarkably healthy—and the U. S. soldiers in garrison, are even said to enjoy a better share of health than the troops at Michili-mackinac. The banks of Fox river continue low for two or three miles up, when they gradually rise eighty or an hundred feet above the water, from whence commence forests of oak, pine, hickory and maple. The shores of this river upwards, to Winnebago lake, is said to be of the same nature ; to which cause, and the preva-lence of the south-west wind in summer, may be attributed the healthiness of the country. There are several villages of Fols Avoines, Sauteaux and Pottawattamies, on the islands and shores of Green Bay ; a small Menomonie village of fifteen houses, is established about a mile up Fox river, where a great number of Sauteaux and Ottowas assemble in spring and fall. Nine miles further up, is another Menomonie or Fols Avoine village, and another at the Kakalin portage. This portage is about one mile long, the ground even and rocky ; the fall about ten feet, which obstructs the navigation for nine miles, there being an almost con-tinued rapid to the fall of Grand Kenomic, where there is a fall of five feet ; a little above this the river opens into Winnebago or Puant lake, at the distance of thirty miles.—This lake is ten leagues long, and from two to five wide.* At its entrance, is the first Winnebago village of ten or twelve lodges. About midway of the lake, is a Fols Avoines town of fifty or sixty warriors; and near the head of the lake is another Winnebago village, of fifteen or twenty houses. At the south-west corner of the lake, the Crocodile river enters from the direction of Rocky river, with which it communicates with the interval of two or three portages. The land bordering on the lake, is very fertile, abounding with grapes, plums, and other fruits which grow spontaneously. The Winnebagoes raise great quantities of corn, beans, pumpkins, squashes, &c. The lake swarms with fish, and ducks, geese, and teal. Fox river falls into the lake about twelve miles from the outlet of the lake, and is here 100 yards wide. Six miles higher, is a small Winnebago village, and a lake about ten miles long; about three miles above this lake, the river De Loup joins Fox river.— The banks of the river are here diversified with woods and prairies; " any quantities of hay may be made, and is as fine a country for raising stock as any in the same latitude through all America."† From the river De Loup to Lake Puckway, is about eighty miles; here is another Winnebago village of eight or ten lodges. This lake is nine miles long. Twelve miles further up, is Lac du Bœuf, which is four leagues in length, and full of *folle avoine*, and fowls in spring and autumn. Ten miles above Lac du Bœuf, the river forks into two nearly equal branches; but is so choaked with wild rice, as to be almost impassable. Thirty miles above the forks, is Lac Vaseux, which is a perfect meadow of wild rice. From this lake to the portage, is fifteen miles; the river becomes more and more serpentine, and is so choaked with wild rice, as almost to prevent the use of oars. At the portage, it is only five yards wide, except where it expands into small lakes and rice ponds, and so crooked that in navigating it five miles, you only approximate the portage one quarter of a mile. The length of the portage is two miles in ordinary seasons, but is much reduced by heavy rains; and it is stated by Gen. Pike that loaded boats have passed over when the waters are high. " Near one

---

* Carver says, fifteen miles long, and six wide.

† Dickson.

half of the way between the rivers, is a morass, overgrown with a kind of long grass, the rest of it a plain, with some few oak and pine trees growing thereon."*

In wet seasons the portage road is very bad—the soil being of a swampy nature, there is for nearly half way a kind of natural canal, which is sometimes used; a canal between the two rivers could be easily opened. The Fox and Ouisconsin, rise from the same height, in this manner:

The ground, at the head of Fox river, is often inundated by the Ouisconsin, so as to form one great lake at the head of the two rivers. This portage is about 350 miles east of the Falls of St. Anthony. There are two or three French families established at the portage. Goods are transported for 33 cents per hundred weight—a canoe $5, and a boat $8, paid in goods at an enormous profit. It is said that government have it in contemplation to establish a military post at or near the portage.

The Ouisconsin is about 100 yards wide at the portage, and flows with a smooth but strong current; in a low stage of water, the navigation is obstructed with sand bars. Its water is remarkably transparent, and the bottom sandy: the distance from the portage to Prairie Des Chiens, is about 240 miles. Its banks are pleasant and fertile, skirted by high hills at the distance of ten or fifteen miles. The Saukies (or Sacs) and Ottigaumies formerly resided on its shores, in several large and well built towns. The great Saukie village, about one day's travel below the portage, contained, in 1767, ninety houses, each large enough for several families, built of hewn planks neatly jointed. The streets were regular and spacious, their fields and gardens well laid out, in

---

* Carver.

which were cultivated large quantities of Indian corn, beans, melons, squashes, &c. The lands near these towns are of the first quality; the valley of the Ouisconsin is from two to ten miles in width, and covered in places with valuable groves of white pine. The hills or mountains cover an extensive tract, the soil of which is generally poor, and the timber a stinted growth of oak and hickory; stones mostly calcareous. Lead mines exist on the south side; the most important one, is near the Detour de Pin.*

The Fox and Ouisconsin rivers, is the route through which the traders of Michilimackinac convey their goods for the trade of the Mississippi, from St. Louis to the river De Corbeau, as well as all the tributary streams between those limits.

Prairie Des Chiens, is situated on the east bank of the Ouisconsin, about a mile above its junction with the Mississippi. There are about sixty houses, principally in two streets, (Front and First streets) though some are scattered along the bottoms for the distance of four or five miles; the ordinary population amounts to about 400 souls, except in spring and autumn, when the assemblage of white traders doubles this number, besides several hundred Indians. The inhabitants are chiefly French; a great part of whom have a mixture of Indian blood in their veins. The village is bounded by high, bald hills, the bottom about one mile and a half wide. The United States have erected a strong fort here. The mouth of the Ouisconsin, is in lat. 43 20.

---

* The mountains to the south of the Ouisconsin were examined by Carver, and found to abound in lead ore—and so plentiful was lead, in the great Saukie town, about forty miles below the portage, that he saw large quantities of it lying about the streets.

EXTENT OF NAVIGABLE WATERS.

	Miles.
Coast of lake Michigan, ...	280
East and west coast of Green bay, . . .	235
Coast of lake Huron, ...	50
Strait of St. Mary, ...	55
Coast of lake Superior from its outlet to the Grand Portage, } . . .	800
Plein and Depage, ...	200
Chicago, Wakayah, Masquedon, Milwakie, Saukie, &c. all entering the lake between Chicago and the mouth of Green bay, } . . .	400
Fox river, Crocodile and De Loup, . . .	250
Menomonie, Rouge, Gaspard, and Sandy running into Green bay, } . . .	350
Manistique and Miuo Cockien, . . .	150
St. Ignace and Little Bouchitaouy, . . .	120
Great Bouchitaouy and Minaston, . . .	140
Rivers flowing into lake Superior, American side,	1500
Mississippi, from the Red Cedar lake to the Illinois boundary, (in lat. 41, 50.) } . . .	1000
Tributaries of the Mississippi, above the falls of St. Anthony, } . . .	550
Chippewa, Buffalo, Ouisconsin, &c. . . .	1300
Part of Rocky river, and branches, . . .	570
Interior Lakes, ...	150

Total,	8,100

INDIANS.

The Menomonies, (Fols Avoines) and the Winnebagoes are the only nations who reside exclusively in this territory : the first have eight or ten villages, which are situated on the Menomonie river, (fifteen miles from Green bay;) on Fox river near its mouth; at the Kakalin and Grand Kenomic portages, on Winnebago lake, behind the But de Mort, and near *Les Milles Lacs* [Thousand Lakes.] This tribe is reduced to about 250 warriors; they are brave and much respected by their neighbors, and are permitted by the Sioux and the Chippewas to hunt on the Mississippi and lake Superior. They are remarkably handsome, have fine eyes and an animated delivery; their language has no resemblance to that of any of their neighbors, and is very difficult to be learned. Their temporary lodges, of which they have vast numbers, are in the form of an ellipsis, thirty or forty feet long and fifteen or sixteen wide, covered with rushes plaited into mats, and capable of sheltering sixty people from the storm.

The Winnebagoes or Puants of the French, reside on the Ouisconsin, Rocky river, Fox river and Green bay, and have nine villages, situated as follows : two on Green bay, one on an island in lake Michigan, two on Winnebago lake, one six miles above that lake, one on lake Puckway, one at the Portage of the Ouisconsin, and two on Rocky river. They can raise about 300 warriors.

The remnant of the Ottigaumies reside between the Ouisconsin and Rocky rivers. The Chippewas or Sauteaux, inhabiting the southern shores of lake Superior, head branches of the Chippewa, and other streams running into the Mississippi, are estimated at 1000 warriors. Parts of the Kickapoo, Pottawattamie and Ottawa tribes reside in the eastern part of this territory near the shores of lake Michigan. The Sioux claim a considerable tract of country on the east side of the Mississippi, above Prairie des Chiens.

ANTIQUITIES.

A little below lake Pepin, on the east bank of the Mississippi, are the remains of an ancient fortification ; the walls are about four feet high, extending nearly a mile, and sufficiently capacious to cover 5000 men; its form is circular and its flanks reach to the river ; the angles are distinguishable and fashioned with perfect regularity : the plan is extensive and no rising ground within cannon shot distance to command it.—Mounds of considerable height are to be seen on the banks of the Menomonie and Gaspard rivers.

CARVER'S PURCHASE.

The territory claimed by the heirs of the late Capt. Jonathan Carver, includes about 8,000,000 acres, and has the following boundaries, viz : " Beginning at the falls of St. Anthony on the east bank of the Mississippi, running south-east as far as the south end of lake Pepin, where the Chippeway river joins the Mississippi, and from thence eastward five days travel, accounting twenty English miles per day, and from thence north six days travel, accounting twenty English miles per day; and from thence again to the falls of St. Anthony, on a direct straight line."

This territory is watered-by the Chippewa river and its numerous branches, by the rivicre de la Montaigne, and St. Croix rivers, besides several smaller streams. Carver is the only traveller, who has traversed the interior of this tract.—The country adjoining the Chippewa river, as far up as the falls, which are about sixty miles from its mouth, is very level and almost without any timber; and on its banks lie fine meadows;—where, as our traveller informs us, larger droves of buffaloes and elks were feeding than he had observed in any other parts of his travels; above the falls he found the country very uneven and rugged, and closely wooded with pine, beach, maple and birch. At the heads of the Chippewa and St. Croix rivers, he saw " exceeding fine sturgeon." ".The country around St. Anthony's Falls is extremely beautiful. It is not an uninterrupted plain where the eye finds no relief, but composed of many gentle ascents, which in the summer are covered with the finest verdure, and interspersed with little groves, that give a pleasing variety to the prospect. Towards the heads of the river St. Croix, rice grows in great plenty, and there is abundance of copper."

Carver mentions that the northwest wind is much less powerful in the interior of this territory, that in the Atlantic states, and adduces as an argument in support of his position, the fact that the wild rice (oats) attains to perfection in this region, while it scarcely ripens in lake Erie, and is not found east of that lake.

There is a cave of great magnitude on the eastern bank of the Mississippi, about thirty miles below the falls of St. Anthony, which was visited by Carver in his tour through the northwestern regions.   The Indians term it *Wa-kon-teebc*, that is the Dwelling of the Great Spirit.   " The entrance into it is about ten feet wide, the height of it five feet.   The arch within is near fifteen feet high and about thirty feet broad.   The bottom of it consists of fine clear sand.   About twenty feet from the entrance begins a lake, the water of which is transparent, and extends to an unsearchable distance—for the darkness of the cave prevents all attempts to acquire a knowledge of it."   A pebble thrown into this subterraneous lake produces an " astonishing and horrible noise ;" Indian hieroglyphics are visible on the walls.

FOLLE AVOINE.

This productive and highly valuable aquatic plant *(avena fatua)* is found in all the lakes, rivers and bays of this territory. The Fols Avoines call it *Menomen*, and living almost entirely upon it, the French gave them the name of Fols Avoines, or wild rice eaters.   It grows in water of from four to seven feet depth; but always rejects a hard sandy bottom.   A meadow of wild rice strongly resembles an inundated cane-brake ; the plants extend from four to eight feet above the surface of the water—and are often so thick that they wholly prevent the progress of canoes and boats ; they are about the size of the red cane in Tennessee, full of joints, and of the color and texture of bullrushes ; the stalks above water and the branches, which bear the grain, resemble oats.   The Indians in order to prevent the geese and ducks from devouring the whole crop, sometimes run their canoes into the midst of it, while in the milky state, and tie the stalks just below the heads, into large bunches, in which state it remains three or four weeks, until perfectly ripe.   When the heads become ripe, they pass through it with their canoes lined with blankets, and bending the stalks or branches over the sides, beat off the grain with sticks—and such is the abundance of the harvest, that an expert Indian or squaw will soon fill a canoe.   After it is gathered, it is dried and put into skins for future use.   It is singular that this plant has never been found south of the Illinois, nor east of Sandusky bay; but is found north nearly to Hudson bay. The rivers and lakes of this territory alone, no doubt, annually produce several millions of bushels; and in time it may become an important article of commerce and agriculture. Some think that it might be successfully planted in the Atlantic rivers. The duck has become singularly expert in plucking her food from this plant; being unable to reach the highest branches, she presses her breast against the stalk and with a violent effort of her feet causes it to yield to her strength, which it readily does by reason of its slender fibrous roots—having forced the top of the stalk into the water, she keeps it under her body until she has finished her repast. It is equally nutritious and palatable as the common rice.

OHIO,

IS situated between 38 30 and 42 N. lat. and 3 32, and 7 43 W. longitude; bounded north by the divisional line between the United States and Upper Canada (passing through the middle of Lake Erie) and Michigan Territory; west by Indiana, from which it is separated by a meridian line running from the mouth of the Big Miami to the parallel of the southern end of Lake Michigan; south and south-east by the river Ohio, which separates it from Kentucky and Virginia; east by Pennsylvania, from which it is separated by a meredian line running from the mouth of Little Beaver creek to the northern boundary line of the United States in Lake Erie; containing, according to Mr. Drake, an erea of 40,000 square miles, or 25,000,000 of acres, including water. Its length, from north to south, is 228 miles—mean breadth, about 200.

RIVERS.

The rivers of this state, run north into Lake Erie, and south into the Ohio.

The *Ohio* washes the south-eastern frontier of the state, for the distance of 509 miles.

The *Great Miami* waters a large and interesting portion of the state. It is 200 yards wide at its mouth, rises between 40 and 41 N. latitude, and interlocks with the Massissinway branches of the Wabash, the St. Marys and Auglaize branches of the Miami-of-the Lakes, and the Scioto. Its current is generally brisk, but unbroken by rapids. The wide and fertile valley through which it flows, is sometimes subject to partial inundation. Its chief tributaries on the west, are Loramie's creek, which empties into it 130 miles above its *embouchure ;* Stillwater, entering it about 50 miles below, and Whitewater, which it receives within 7 miles of the Ohio.—The first of these is navigable for batteaux near thirty miles. On the east, Mad river is the only tributary deserving the name of river. It rises in the prairies north of the Indian boundary line, as established by the treaty of Greenville, and a few miles east of Gen. Hull's road to Detroit. It is bounded by some of the finest lands in the state; has a brisk current, pure water, and affords numerous mill-seats. It joins the Big Miami, a short distance above Dayton, and nearly opposite the mouth of Stillwater. About 100 miles from its mouth, are rapids, where the descent in a short distance is said to be 200 feet.*

The Little Miami heads south of the sources of Mad river, and west of those of Paint Creek, a considerable branch of the Sciota; from the east it receives the East Fork, Todd's Fork, and Cæsar's and Massie's creeks; it meanders through an extensive valley and abounds with valuable mill-seats. It enters the Ohio seven miles above Cincinnati, and in high water is 150 yards wide—its course is nearly parallel with the Big Miami, being no where more than twenty miles distant. The intervening country is watered by Mill creek, which empties into the Ohio, two miles below Cincinnati.

Between the Little Miami and the Scioto, a distance of 126 miles by the courses of the Ohio, are the following large creeks, from twenty to fifty yards wide and from twenty to fifty miles in length, viz. Big Indian, fourteen miles above Cincinnati, White Oak, Straight, Eagle, Bullskin, Brush, and Turkey creeks; the last is four miles below the Scioto.

The *Scioto* joins the Ohio in N. lat. 38, 34, 28, heads near the sources of the Sandusky, between the navigable branches of which there is a short and convenient portage of only four miles. It is navigable for large keel boats to Columbus, nearly 200 miles from its mouth, and for canoes almost to its head. Its principal branches

* The British hireling traveller, Ashe, has the following wonderful description of this river, which by the magic powers of his pen, he causes to *flow out of Lake Huron !!* " Mad river is remarkable for the fine quality of the water and the great purity of the stream. It received its name in consequence of its perpetual impetuosity, it being the only river in the Western country which does not subside in the summer and fall of the year. All the other rivers owe their great periodical volume to the effusion of ice and mountain snows, whereas, the Mad river issues out of *Lake Huron,* which affords it an equal supply without variation or end. It abounds with fish, and is so transparent, that they are driven with great facility into nets and snares; and are besides, often speared."

are Paint creek, which enters from the west four miles below Chillicothe; Darby's creek; from the east Salt, Walnut, Alkum, and
Whetstone forks.

The *Great Hockhocking* waters the country between the Scioto and the Muskingum—it enters the Ohio 150 miles above the
Scioto, and is navigable to Athens, forty miles from its mouth for
large keel boats.   Six miles above Athens are rapids which prevent the ascent of boats.

The *Muskingum* heads near the sources of the Cayahoga of
Lake Erie, and enters the Ohio immediately below Marietta.—
It is 250 yards wide at its mouth, and navigable for large keels
to the Three Legs, and from thence for small boats to within a
few miles of the Cayahoga.   It has several large branches, such
as Licking, Tuscarawa, Whitewoman, and Watomika, which will
be more particularly noticed hereafter.

Several large creeks water that part of the state lying between
the Muskingum and the Pennsylvania boundary line; such as
Will's creek, which falls into the Muskingum; Pawpaw, Little
Muskingum, Wheeling, Capteena, Stoney, and Sunfish creeks,
which fall into the Ohio.

The following streams water the northern portion of the state,
and pay their tribute to Lake Erie:

The largest and most westerly stream, is the *Miami-of-the-Lakes,*
sometimes called the Maumee, or Maurice.   It is formed by the
junction of the St. Marys and Little St. Josephs.

This river is 105 miles in length, and is navigable for batteaux
and perogues, throughout its whole extent, in all seasons, and for
vessels of sixty tons burthen as far as the rapids nearly opposite
Fort Meigs, eighteen miles from the lake.—These rapids oppose
no very serious obstacles to the navigation.   The Wolf rapids are
ten miles higher up.   At the several rapids, a portion of the stream
could easily be diverted into races for the supply of water works.
The rapids of the Miami, near the Fort, afford fine situations for
fishing, as the river at certain seasons is alive with fish of various
sorts.   They are often killed with sticks and stones, and caught
with the hands.   The course of this river is north-east; its banks
are regular—high, but not abrupt—sloping gradually to the wa-

ter's edge, and covered with a beautiful luxuriant verdure. The channel of the river from the rapids, to within three miles of the bay, is composed of limestone rock, formed into regular strata by parallel fissures, which sink perpendicularly into the rock, and run transversely across the river. The face of the bank, for ten or twelve feet above the water is also composed of solid rock, and from its appearance it is evident that the current has worn the channel many feet deeper than it was in former ages.

The *St. Josephs* heads in Indiana, and is navigable about fifty miles. The St. Marys in wet seasons is navigable for perogues to old Fort St. Marys, about 150 miles from its confluence with the St. Josephs, by the course of the river. It is very crooked, and the land in its margins generally of a good quality. Its head branches include three creeks which unite near Fort St. Marys. The *Auglaize* heads ten or twelve miles north-east of the source of St. Marys, and after passing by Wappaukenata, Tawa town, and several other Indian villages, falls into the Miami-of-the-lakes at Fort Winchester, fifty miles below Fort Wayne.

The *Toussaint* river, which enters the lake twenty miles east of the Miami, is little more than an arm of the lake winding through the prairies and forming a vast number of impassable sloughs; its extreme head is not more than ten or twelve miles from the lake, although at its mouth it is 100 yards wide; its current is lazy and choaked with wild rice, pond lilies and grass. It is covered at certain periods with geese and ducks, and abounds with otters and muskrats.

Portage river is an inconsiderable stream, heading in flat swampy lands, two miles south of Hull's road from Urbanna to Fort Meigs. It is navigable almost to its head, as the current is sluggish and the water deep. It is 140 yards wide, for six or seven miles from the lake, and affords a safe and easy harbor for boats of two tons burthen. Great numbers of ducks and geese frequent its water in autumn. The land along its borders for several miles is rich and easily cleared.

The *Sandusky* has its source in the same plain with the principal branch of the Scioto river, and winding its course through a rich, flat country, in a north-eastern direction, passing the posts of Upper Sandusky, several Indian villages and Fort Stephenson.

falls into the bay of the same name, two miles east of the mouth of Portage, or Carrying river, across the neck, but forty seven by the coast of the Great Penninsula formed by Portage river, Lake Erie, and Sandusky Bay. It receives in its course several large creeks; and is navigable almost to its head. Its banks for twelve or fifteen miles up, are low, and lined with wet prairies. *Pipe* and *Cold* creeks, fall into the bay a few miles east of the Sandusky river. These streams water a fine tract of country, have brisk currents, pure water, and frequent sites for mills; the last issues from a large, durable spring, with sufficient water to turn a grist-mill immediately at its source.

The *Huron* falls into the lake eleven miles east of Sandusky bay. It is about fifty yards wide at its mouth, and navigable about eighteen miles, to the forks. It has numerous head branches, which water a fertile and healthy district.

Ten miles further east, is the *Vermillion*, similar in course, size, extent, and other general features, to the Huron.

Black river empties into the lake twelve miles east of the Vermillion, which it closely resembles in its course and magnitude.

Rocky-River flows into the lake eighteen miles further east. It is more rapid than any of the neighboring streams, has higher banks, and is considerably larger than the three last named rivers. It has numerous forks, and waters a rich and thriving settlement.

Seven miles east of Black river, is the *Cayahoga*, the largest stream entering Lake Erie east of the Sandusky. Its course is south-east—current brisk, banks high and romantic. It heads in a large swamp, in which also rises the Turscarawa branch of the Muskingum.

Chagrin river runs nearly parallel with the Cayahoga, and enters the lake twenty miles east of Cleveland. It is about forty miles long, rapid, abounding in mill-seats, and subject to sudden swells.

Ten miles east of the Chagrin, is *Grand* river, a fine bold stream, which rises near Warren, and interlocks with branches of the Chagrin, Cayahoga, and Tuscarawa. Its course is circuitous, current rapid, banks elevated, and often precipitous, water pure and wholesome, and well calculated for hydraulic uses. It is not

M m.

navigable : there are several mill-dams across its stream—one within half a mile of the lake.

The *Ashtibula* interlocks with the Big Beaver of the Ohio, and falls into Lake Erie 20 miles east of Grand river. Its banks are high, and its stream too brisk to admit of easy navigation; course, north-west and north.

The *Conneaut* enters the lake ten miles east of the Ashtibula. It heads in the state of Ohio, near the eastern branches of the Ashtibula, and enters Lake Erie in Pennsylvania, about two miles east of the boundary line between the two states. Its waters are remarkably clear and healthful. It is not navigable, but affords a great many fine mill-seats.

SURFACE, SOIL.

That portion of the state which lies between the Pennsylvania line and the Muskingum river, bordering on the Ohio river, and extending northwardly for the distance of fifty miles, has an uneven surface, rising in places into high hills and subsiding into deep vallies ; some of them terminate in elevated peaks, and afford prospects bounded only by the powers of vision. Yet most of these hills have a deep, rich soil, and are capable of being cultivated to their summits.

The country along the Ohio, from the Muskingum to the Big Miami, continues broken ; but the hills gradually diminish in size as we proceed westwardly. The bottoms of the Ohio are of very unequal width. The bases of some of the hills approach close to the river, while others recede to the distance of two and three miles. There are usually three bottoms rising one above the other, like the glacis of a fortification. The river bottoms bear a heavy growth of beech, sugar maple, buckeye, elm, honey locust, black walnut, hackberry, sycamore, and ash, with an underwood of pawpaw, spicewood, dogwood, plum trees, crab apple, and grape vines. The hills are covered with oak, chesnut, hickory, sugar maple, poplar, sassafras, black ash, and black locust. In the western counties, and in the north-western and northern portions of the state, there is a leveller surface, and a moister soil, interspersed however with tracts of dry prairie, and forests of a sandy or gravelly soil. The north-western corner of the state, contains a considerable district of level, rich land, too wet and swampy to admit of healthy settlements: the soil is a black, loose, friable loam, or a vegetable mould, watered by sluggish and dark colored streams.

COUNTIES.

In describing this state by counties, I have preferred the geographical to the alphabetical order. I shall therefore commence with Hamilton, the oldest settled county in the state: those counties which have not many wild or unsettled lands to invite the attention of emigrants, will be briefly noticed.

HAMILTON COUNTY.

This county is situated in the south-western corner of the state; has the Ohio river south, Clermont county east, Butler north, and Indiana west. It is about 30 miles long and 20 wide, and is watered by the Ohio, Whitewater, Great and Little Miami, Mill, Deer, Taylor's and Dryfork creeks. It has a hilly surface in the vicinity of the large streams; in other parts level or gently waving. The vallies are broad and rich, and generally cultivated.— The price of unimproved lands, is from 10 to 25 dollars— cultivated farms near Cincinnati, from 30 to 70. Mills are numerous on Mill creek, and the Little Miami. There are few wild lands, and those of a second quality. This is the most populous county in the state.

The traces of an ancient population, and strong military positions, are found along the banks of the Miami, from its confluence with the Ohio to the limits of Butler county.

Cincinnati is the chief town, which from its present importance and certainty of future grandeur, deserves a minute description. There are, besides, the villages of Columbia, Newtown, Reading, Montgomery, Springfield, Colerain, Harrison, Crosby, and Cleves.

Cincinnati.—At present the largest town in the state of Ohio, is situated on the north bank of the Ohio River, directly opposite

the mouth of Licking, a considerable river of Kentucky, and in
north latitude 39, 6, 30, west from Washington City 7, 24, 45. It
is nearly under the meridians of Lexington and Detroit ; and
nearly parallel with St. Louis, Vincennes and Baltimore.   Its
distance (by land) from Pittsburgh is 300 miles—by water 524 ;
from Detroit 275; from Baltimore 400; Lexington 85, Chillicothe 84, Louisville 105, New-Orleans (by water) 1736.   It is
built upon two plains of unequal elevation : the first called *the bottom*, extends from the mouth of Deer to that of Mill creek, with a
medium width of 800 feet and about seventy feet above low water
mark.   The western or lower end of this bank is the lowest, and
in the highest floods subject to inundation.   The second is called
the hill, about fifty feet higher than the first ; its medium width is
one mile, bounded on the north by the adjoining hills.   The
streets most of them 66 feet wide, and intersect each other at right
angles.   There are no alleys nor diagonal streets.   The blocks or
squares are mostly divided into eight lots, 99 by 198 feet.   There
are 81 out-lots, of four acres each.   The streets which intersect
the river, are nine in number, their course is north 44 deg. west.
The first, or *uppermost*, called Broadway, strikes the river about
sixty feet below the steam grist-mill ; the names of the others are
Sycamore, Miami, Walnut, Vine, Race, Elm, Plum and Western
streets.   The names of the cross streets are Water street, Front,
Second, Third, Fourth, Fifth, Sixth and Northern.   The town
plat covers one entire and two fractional sections, and was originally surveyed by the patentee. John Cleeves Symmes, excepting
the reservation around old Fort Washington, which now constitutes a part of the town.   The number of public buildings and
dwelling-houses, in July, 1815, was 1100; the population was
at the same time estimated at 6000.   I visited this town in June
last, and from the number of houses then erecting, or about to be
commenced, and the great influx of emigrants, the number of
buildings are probably augmented to *thirteen hundred*, and the inhabitants to *eight thousand.*   About thirty of the houses are of
stone, 300 of brick, and the remainder of wood.   Most of them
are handsomely painted, which gives to the town an air of neatness.   The public buildings are spacious and elegant.   The first
court house was 42 by 54, and 84 feet high, but was unfortunate-

ly burnt down during the late war. The new court house is a stately edifice, and stands near the intersection of Main and Court streets; and is 56 by 66, with fire proof apartments, for the different county offices. The Baptist church in Sixth street is a neat brick building, forty by fifty-five feet, finished with taste.— The Presbyterian church is also of brick, sixty-eight by eighty-five; its aspect is low and heavy. The Methodist church is only one story high, but capacious. The Friends' meeting house is a temporary wooden building. The Lancastrian seminary, in the rear of the Presbyterian church, is an extensive brick building of a novel construction; it is composed of two parallel wings, eighty-eight feet deep, thirty wide, and thirty feet distant from each other, connected near the front by apartments for staircases, out of which arises a dome-capped peristyle, designed for an observatory. One wing of this edifice is designed for male and the other for female children. When completed, the whole building can receive 1100 scholars. In less than two weeks after the institution was opened upwards of four hundred children were admitted. It is a fact honorable to the liberality of the people of Cincinnati and its vicinity, that upwards of twelve thousand dollars were subscribed towards defraying the expenses of the building. There are three brick market houses; the largest is upwards of three hundred feet long. The Cincinnati Manufacturing Company have extensive stores above the mouth of Mill creek; the largest, an irregular building, is 150 feet in length, and from two to four stories high. The Steam Mill, finished in 1814, reflects honor upon the enterprising genius of the west. It is literally founded upon a rock; for it rests upon a horizontal bed of limestone, upon the beach of the river. In high water, it is completely insulated, and rises majestically from the bosom of the flood with the strength and firmness of a rock in the ocean. At its base, it is 62 by 87 feet; its walls are here ten feet thick. The height of this stupendous pile is 110 feet; the number of stories, nine, two of which are above the eaves. To the height of forty feet, the walls are *drawn in*, and gradually diminish in thickness—above they are perpendicular. In its construction, it swallowed up " 6620 perches of stone, 90,000 brick, 14,000 bushels of lime, and 31,200 cubic feet of timber. Its weight is estimated at 15,655 tons.* This mill was built under the direction of William Green, an ingenious stone-cutter. The model was furnished by George Evans, one of the proprietors : the building cost 120,000 dollars. The machinery is on the plan of Oliver Evans, and driven by an engine of seventy horse power. When in complete operation, it will grind 700 barrels of flour a week. The Steam Saw-Mill, erected on the bank of the river below the town, is a wooden building, thirty-six by seventy feet, and three stories high. The engine, which possesses twenty horse power, drives four saws in separate gates : the product of the whole is about 800 feet an hour. The logs are chiefly brought in rafts to the mill, and hauled up the bank by power from the engine. There is a cotton and woollen factory, which carries 3,300 spindles for cotton, and about 400 woollen. Besides this, there are four cotton spinning establishments, which together contain about 1500 spindles. A woollen manufactory, calculated to yield sixty yards of broadcloth per day, went into operation in the winter of 1815. Wool carding and cloth dressing, are performed in several places. Cables and cordage are produced for exportation, from two extensive rope-walks. White and red lead, free from alloy, is manufactured, sufficient for the supply of the whole state—the quantity is six tons per week. There are two glass factories, which produce window glass, hollow ware and white flint glass. A beautiful white sand is found near the mouth of the Scioto. Clay, for crucibles, is brought from Delaware ; but might be procured in the state of Ohio. I have seen a bed, in every particular corresponding with the Delaware clay ; white and tenacious, when moist, but perfectly *impalpable*, when dried and pulverized. A foundery for iron castings has been recently established. The mechanical arts, in all their various branches, are carried on to an extent and perfection scarcely credible, considering the youthfulness of Cincinnati, and the surrounding settlements. Nor are the fine arts neglected. Painting and engraving are executed with elegance. The inhabitants have a taste for music. There are at present two weekly newspapers published : the oldest paper is called the " *Western Spy*," and the other " *Cincinnati Gazette, and Liberty Hall*;"

* See Picture of Cincinnati, page 130.

each issue about 1500 papers a week. Several respectable books have been printed. Spirits and cordials are distilled for domestic use; beer, porter and ale, are made in great quantities, and of good quality, as well for exportation as home consumption. *Forty thousand* bushels of barley were consumed last year. The exports of Cincinnati, consist of flour, corn, beef, pork, butter, lard, bacon, whiskey, peach-brandy, beer and porter; pot and pearl-ashes; cheese, soap, candles; hats, hemp, spun yarn; saddles; rifles; cherry and black ash boards; staves and scantling; cabinet furniture and chairs. East Indian and European goods, are imported from Baltimore and Philadelphia, by the way of Pittsburgh. Lead is procured from St. Louis. Rum, sugar, molasses and some dry goods, are received in keels and steam boats from New-Orleans. Salt is easily obtained from the Kenhaway salt-works. Coal, of which vast quantities are consumed, is brought down the Ohio from Pittsburgh and Wheeling, in flat bottomed boats. White pine boards and shingles, are brought in rafts from Hamilton, on Alleghany; and afford, by the abundance of the supply, great facilities to building. There are three banking companies. " The Miami Exporting Company," was incorporated in 1803, for forty years. Its capital is 450,000 dollars; its paper is in excellent credit; its dividends have for several year fluctuated between ten and fifteen per cent. " The Farmers' and Mechanics Bank," was incorporated in 1813, for five years; the capital prescribed by law, is two hundred thousand dollars. Its dividends have varied from 8 to 14 per cent. " The bank of Cincinnati" is unchartered. Its shares are fifty dollars. Eight thousand eight hundred have been sold, to 345 persons. Its notes are in excellent credit, and its dividends good.

The Cincinnati University, is a mere nominal institution. At present it languishes in embryo. The public library contains upwards of eight thousand volumes, among which are many valuable works. The " School of Literature and the Arts," is principally composed of young men, and promises to become the nurse of genius and taste.

There is a land office for the sale of U. S. lands. Nine mails arrive every week.

Seven public roads enter Cincinnati; the Columbia road from the east; the Lebanon road from the north-east, the Hamilton from the north-west, and the Dayton from the north, unite at the head of Main street. The North Bend and Lawrenceburgh roads, enter the western side of the town. The Columbia road, leading up the valley of the Ohio upon a pleasant dry bottom, is the most used by parties of pleasure.

The price of town lots is high—and rents difficult to obtain.— The lots in Main, First, and Second streets, are now selling for more than $ 200 per foot, measuring on the front line. Those possessing less local advantages are sold from fifty to ten. Out-lots and lands adjoining the town, bring from 500 to 1000 dollars per acre. Farms below and above the creeks, and beyond the range of hills on the north, will sell for 50, 80, and 100 dollars an acre, according to quality and proximity to the town.

Cincinnati has four market days every week—two in the morning, and two in the afternoon. Beef, mutton, pork, venison, poultry, and fish, are plentifully supplied. Native and cultivated fruits, can be easily procured.

Several small vineyards have been planted in the vicinity of the town, which promise success. Grapes, either from Vevay or Newport, are often for sale in the markets during the proper season.

The remains of ancient works within the precincts of the town, consisted of—

1. A circular embankment eight hundred feet in diameter, thirty feet broad at the base, and from three to six feet high. It is composed of loam. There is no appearance of a ditch on either side; on the east side there is an opening ninety feet wide; on each side of this *gateway*, there is a broad elevation, or kind of parapet; from one of these extends a very low wall to the distance of five hundred feet, where it terminates in a mound. Near the other parapet, are two shapeless and insulated elevations about six feet high.

2. Two circular earthen enclosures of greater extent, but so defaced by time that it was difficult to trace them. One of these was on the bottoms, the other on the hill.

3. A circular bank of sixty feet diameter, formed by throwing up the earth from the inside.

4. Two parallel convex banks, 760 feet long, and forty-six feet asunder for two-thirds of the distance, when they converge to forty, and are finally connected at each end. There appears a perfect mathematical exactitude in the construction of this figure. The direction of these walls, is nearly east and west. There is an opening to the south, 30 feet wide.

5. An excavation fifty feet in diameter, and twelve feet deep.— Curiosity has not prompted an examination of its contents, to ascertain whether it was designed for a *well*, a cellar, or a military defence.

6. Four mounds of unequal dimensions. The largest is situated near the west end of the town, and is at present twenty-seven feet high. The late Gen. Wayne caused about eight feet of its summit to be cut off for the purpose of stationing a centinel thereon. Its figure is elliptical; its circumference at the base, is 440 feet.— From the depression of the earth's surface around its foot, it was no doubt formed by scooping up the soil—which was not the usual practice among the aborigines. Five hundred feet from this, in a northern direction, there is another, ten feet high, of a circular figure, and nearly flat on the top. North-east of this, is another, of less diameter and height. The last and most important, is situated at the intersection of Third and Main-streets, and is connected with the circular embankment by the low bank before described. Its venerable antiquity has not been respected; only a small part of it remains. When first discovered it was 120 feet long, sixty wide, ten high, and of an oval form. The order of the strata, was gravel, pebbles, loam, soil.*

---

* The author of the " Picture of Cincinnati," has given the following catalogue of articles taken from the above mound, at various times, viz : " 1. A piece of jasper, rock chrystal, granite and some other stones, cylindrical at their extremities, and swelled in the middle, with an annular groove near one end. 2. A circular piece of cannel coal, with a large opening in the centre, as if for an axis; and a deep groove in the circumference, suitable for a hand. It has a number of small perforations, disposed in four equidistant lines which run from the circumference towards the centre. 3. A small article of the same shape, with eight lines of perforations, but composed of argillaceous earth, well polished. 4. A bone, ornamented with several carved lines, supposed to be hieroglyphical. 5.

Columbia, is situated on a handsome plain, near the bank of the Ohio, a little below the mouth of Little Miami—it contains thirty or forty houses, and is settled principally by farmers. *Newtown*, is situated on the Chillicothe road, two miles east of the little Miami. *Montgomery*, is eighteen north-west of Cincinnati, in the Lebanon road, and about equidistant between Mill creek and Little Miami. *Reading*, lies ten miles north of Cincinnati, near Mill creek. *Springfield*, lies on the Hamilton road, one mile south of Mill creek, and eleven miles north of Cincinnati. *Cleves*, is a very small village, situated near the intersection of the Lawrenceburgh and Brookville roads, two miles north of Gen. Harrison's seat, at the north bend of the Ohio, and near the Miami river.— *Harrison*, is situated on the left bank of White water, seven miles from the north bend of the Ohio. It has been already described, (see page 120.) *Colerain*, stands on the left bank of the Great Miami, about twenty miles from its mouth. *Crosby*, is situated directly opposite Colerain, on the right bank of the same river; all, except the first, new and flourishing villages.

BUTLER COUNTY,

Lies north of Hamilton, south of Preble, east of Indiana, and west of Warren, and is about twenty-four miles square, It is watered by the Big Miami, which passes diagonally through it from north-east to south-west, as also by several handsome creeks, such

---

A sculptural representation of the head and beak of a rapacious bird, perhaps an eagle. 6. A mass of lead ore, (galena) lumps of which have been found in some other tumuli. 7. A quantity of isinglass, (mica membranacea) plates of which have been discovered in and about other mounds. 8. A small ovate piece of sheet copper with two perforations. 9. A larger oblong piece, of the same metal, with longitudinal grooves and ridges. 10. A number of beads, or sections of small hollow cylinders, apparently of bone or shell. 11. The teeth of a carniverous animal, probably those of the bear. 12. Several large marine shells, belonging perhaps to the genus *buccinum;* cut in such a manner as to serve for domestic utensils, and nearly converted into the state of chalk. 13. Several copper articles, each consisting of two sets of circular concavo-convex plates ; the interior one of each set connected with the other by a hollow axis, around which had been wound a quantity of lint : the whole compassed with the bones of a man's hand. 14. Human bones. These were of different sizes ; sometimes enclosed in rude coffins of stone, but oftener lying blended with the earth—generally surrounded by a portion of ashes and charcoal."

as Dryfork. running into Whitewater; Indian creek, Four Mile creek, Seven Mile creek, Elk and Dick's creeks, running into the Big Miami. The soil of two-thirds of this county is fertile ; but there are tracts of poor land in the south-east and north-west.

Hamilton, the seat of justice, is situated twenty-five miles north-east of Cincinnati, on the east bank of the Miami. Its site is elevated and beautiful : it has about seventy-five buildings, principally of wood ; a post-office, and a printing-office issuing a weekly newspaper, entitled, the " *Miami Intelligencer.*" In 1816, there were 2877 male inhabitants, over twenty-one years of age in this county.

Rossville, situated on the bank of the Miami opposite Hamilton, is a small place.

Middletown, is situated on the east side of the Miami, two miles from the river, and twelve miles above Hamilton.

Oxford, stands near the northern confines of the county, has few houses, but in time will probably become a respectable town —as a college is to be established in it, according to the provisions of a law passed in 1810. This seminary is endowed with an entire township of land, which has been chiefly leased to settlers ; the leases extend to 99 years, renewable for ever.

Two miles below Hamilton, there is an extensive ancient fortification on the top of an elevated hill; the walls are two or three feet high, and enclose eighty acres of land, being highest where the ground is most favorable to an attack. Three-fourths of its circumference are bordered by deep vallies; the remainder lies across a level ridge, and here the lines are triple."* There are a few openings in the wall, one or two piles of limestone, and a mound twenty feet in diameter at the base and seven feet high, near it.

PREBLE COUNTY.

Is bounded south by Butler, east by Montgomery, north by Darke and west by Indiana. It is twenty-four miles long and eighteen wide, and is watered by the head branches of Four and

---

* See Picture of Cincinnati, page 210.

Seven Mile creeks, Franklin creek, Bushy fork, Twin creek, and small branches of the north fork of White water, all affording excellent mill seats. The surface of this county is pretty level, soil rich and highly productive; timber, poplar, ash, black walnut of great size, and some oak.

Eaton, is the chief town; it is situated near the site of old Fort St. Clair, on 'a beautiful plain, inclined to the south, and watered by Seven Mile creek. It has about thirty-five houses, stone jail, and post-office—and is distant from Cincinnati about sixty miles, in a northern direction. This county contains several valuable tracts of unsold United States' lands.

DARKE COUNTY,

Is bounded south by Preble, east by Miami county, north by Indian lands, and east by Indiana, being thirty miles long and twenty-four wide. and is watered by Panther, Greenville and Stillwater creeks, and by the Mississinway; surface level, soil rich, but wet in places; barrens and prairies abound in the northwestern parts, timber, principally oak; but walnut, sugar maple, buckeye, &c. are common on the bottoms, and large tracts of vacant land, belonging to the United States. The sites of old Forts Jefferson, Recovery and Greenville, are in this county: the last has been fixed on as the county seat; but at present it is only a village of cabins: the population is now rapidly augmenting.

MIAMI COUNTY,

Has Montgomery south, Champaign east, Indian lands north, and Darke on the west. It is about thirty miles in length, and twenty broad; and is abundantly watered by the Big Miami, which divides it from north to south; by the South-West, or Stillwater branch, Panther and Greenville creeks; Loramie's creek, and Fawn, Lost, and Honey creeks; the surface is level, soil moist and rich.

Troy—the seat of justice for Miami county, stands on the west side of the Great Miami, twenty miles above Dayton, and 72 north of Cincinnati. It has a post-office and a public library.— Its site is a handsome plain, which, however, terminates in swamps, about one mile from the rear of the town.

Washington, eight miles above Troy, and situated on the same side of the river, on the site of an old Indian settlement. It has a post-office, and valuable mills and advantageous situations for other hydraulic establishments.

I am indebted to *John Johnston*, Esq. Indian Agent, for the following interesting description of this county.

Piqua-Town, is a post town, situated on the west bank of the Miami river of Ohio, in the county of Miami; and although not the seat of justice, is by far the place of the greatest notoriety and importance within the county. This is owing to the beauty of its situation, being the site of the old national town of the Shawanœse Indians, who named it after one of their principal tribes, viz. the Piqua tribe. The falls in the river at the town, afford many sites for water works. The Shawanœse were routed and driven from this place, about the year 1780, by the Kentuckians. It is seventy-seven miles north from Cincinnati, about eighty miles west from Columbus, the permanent seat of government of the state, 125 miles south of Fort Meigs, at Miami bay of Lake Erie, three miles below the mouth of Loramie's creek, the principal navigable stream of the Miami, and which affords a navigation for keel boats, batteaux and perogues, within twelve miles of the St. Marys, which with the St. Josephs, forms the Miami of the Lake at Fort Wayne, and thence running a north course enters Lake Erie at Fort Meigs. Piqua-Town, is thirty miles by land from St. Marys, and the same distance from Wapaghkanetta, at the head of navigation, on the Auglaize river. Another principal branch of the Miami-of-the-Lakes, which enters it at Fort Defiance, fifty miles by land from Wapaghkanetta. The navigation of the Auglaize is not considered so safe as that of the St. Marys, but it is the shortest route of the two, by five or six days, to the lake. Both routes are much used by flat boats, keels and perogues, in transporting the surplus produce of the country to the different military establishments on the lake. A canal to connect the waters of the Ohio, with those of the lake, between the heads of Loramie's creek, St. Marys and the Auglaize, is quite practicable; and is an-

ticipated at no very distant period.   It is probably no where else
so practicable within the limits of this state.   Piqua has five mercantile stores, two taverns, a market house, cabinet maker, several
house carpenters, two blacksmiths, two boot and shoemakers, two
saddle and harness makers, two Windsor chair makers, two house
painters, one tannery, a grist and two saw mills ; two prac-
tising physicians, and one apothecary shop; two taylors, two hat-
ters, a clock and watch maker, and one silversmith; two wheel-
rights, one blue dyer, one carding machine ; one Seceder meeting
house in the town, and a Methodist meeting house in the vicinity ;
an association for manufacturing and banking, with a capital of one
hundred thousand dollars, was established in 1815.   The Legislature not having thought proper to charter it, the association was
dissolved.   The country around Piqua, is settled by emigrants,
chiefly from Pennsylvania, New-Jersey and Kentucky ; they are
an industrious, moral and religious people ; and many of them
possessed of considerable wealth.   Religious denominations are
Methodists, Presbyterians, Seceders, Baptists and New-lights.—
The country is healthy and fruitful, abounding with springs of
the purest water.   The lands generally of the first quality.   Timber—the different kinds of ash, the oak, walnut, hickory, beech,
maple and sugar tree ; cherry, buckeye, honey locust, &c.

All the unsold lands belong to the United States, and they are
to be purchased at the land office in Cincinnati, at two dollars
per acre; one fourth of the purchase money to be paid down at the
time of entry or purchase, one fourth in two years after, one fourth
in three years, and one fourth in four years ; and at the expiration
of the fifth year, if not paid out for in full, the land reverts to
the United States, and is offered at public auction, and sold to the
highest bidder.   But such is the force of public opinion, that none
is found hardy enough to come forward and bid against the original claimant. He, in almost every instance, is permitted to re-enter
his land, and in this way ultimately redeems it.   By the act of
congress, there is in every township three sections, or 640 acres,
reserved for future sales, and these are held at four dollars an acre.
A whole section, a half or a quarter, may be purchased ; but the
government will not dispose of a lesser quantity than a quarter
section, or 160 acres.   When the land is paid for, patents issue

from the Department of State, signed by the President, and returned to the land office, where the claimants will receive them, on paying the postage from the seat of government. These titles are of the best kind, entirely safe and indisputable. In every township there is one section of public land set apart for the support of schools. No country can offer greater inducements to the industrious, enterprising emigrant, if we regard the soil, the climate, the low price of lands, the goodness of the title, and certain prospect of a market for the surplus produce; for the outlet to the sea is both ways, viz. by the lakes and the Ohio. Improved land sells from 4 to 25 dollars an acre.

As in all new countries, manufactures are in their infancy, all the handicraft arts of the first necessity are in use. The farmers in a great degree manufacture their own clothing.—Sheep are found to answer well, and there are great numbers for a new country. Half-blood and quarter Merinoes are common. Great numbers of horned cattle and hogs are raised and drove to market. The price of produce the present year [1817] is as follows : corn, 33 cents per bushel, wheat, 75 cents; buckwheat, 37 1-2 cents; oats, 33 cent; pork, $4,50 per hundred; beef, $3,50; whiskey, 62 1-2 cents per gallon; a good milch cow, $15; a good working horse, $40; sheep, $3,50 each; butter, 12 1-2 cents per lb.; cheese, 12 1-2; flour for market, delivered at St. Marys and Wapaghkanetta, $6,50 per barrel. The prices of produce the present year are higher than usual, the last season being very unfavorable for crops of wheat, corn and grass. Corn is usually purchased here in the fall for 25 cents, buckwheat and oats the same, wheat, 50 cents, pork and beef 2 50 to $3.

In the county of Miami there are no slaves, and very few free blacks. Slavery in every shape is prohibited throughout the state : and our laws interdict the residence of free blacks, unless under very special circumstances. There is not any prospect that the constitution of this state will ever be altered so as to allow of slavery.

In the county of Miami there have been several new towns laid off: none are improved but Piqua and Troy. The latter is the seat of justice, seven miles lower down on the same side of the Miami. Having been located in a low situation, contiguous to swamps and marshes, it has proved sickly, and does not offer ever to become a place of any importance.

The average produce of lands in this county, is about as follows; corn, 50 bushels to the acre; wheat, 25 bushels; oats, 30 bushels; hemp grows remarkably well, but there is little raised. Crops of hay are very heavy, and the country is well adapted to grass of all kinds.

In the land district of Cincinnati, there remains yet to be sold, about a million and a half of acres. These lands lie chiefly in the counties of Champaign, Miami, and Darke. These three counties extend northward to the Indian boundary. Persons purchasing, for prompt payment, reduces the price to $1 64 the acre. A discount of 8 per cent is allowed on all payments made before they are due. The lands still occupied and owned by the Indians, within the limits of this state, belong to the Wyandots, Shawanoeese and Ottowas.—Several attempts have been made to extinguish their title by purchase, all of which have failed. The Wyandots are the most ancient inhabitants, and are considered the chief owners of the soil. It is probable, however, that in a few years, the extinguishment will be effected, as the lands are becoming useless to the natives, for the want of game. Civilized habits are making some progress among these Indians. The society of Friends, are the chief agents in this work; and, probably, from their correct habits, they are better qualified for the undertaking than any other. The government, with a commendable zeal for the preservation of the primitive inhabitants, afford every aid and encouragement on their part to prevent the unexampled destruction which has attended the natives of this continent, from the first arrival of the Europeans down to the present time. Many have advanced the idea, that the Indians could not be civilized.— Nothing can be more erroneous. All history of ancient times will contradict such a position. The government of the United States have never lost sight of this object; and have expended large sums of the public money, in attempts to introduce civilized life and such of the domestic arts as were suited to their condition among their savage neighbors. These laudable attempts have, in a great measure, failed, from causes over which the government had no control. I allude more especially to the agency of foreign powers—to the British above all others—who, from their contiguity to our Indians, their influence over them, and their known enmity to the government and people of the country, have, on all occasions, warned the Indians from receiving instruction from us; have misrepresented our views, by attributing them to selfish, corrupt, and improper motives, and by encouraging the Indians in their thirst of war and bloodshed ; by inculcating on their minds at all times that the Americans are their natural enemies, and to hold no confidence with them. These causes, with others of minor character, have chiefly contributed to prevent the civilizing the natives, and introducing the Gospel among them ; and it is very questionable whether any better success will attend our endeavors in this way, so long as the British authorities in Canada pursue their late and present system of policy towards the Indians and people of the United States. And I think it clearly follows, that if the Indians are to be civilized, it will be by the joint efforts of both nations ; and if a union in sincerity, in such a good cause, could be effected, the result could not be doubted. The measures of the British government, in relation to the Indians, is fast effecting their destruction; and with the knowledge of this fact, it is difficult to reconcile the conduct of a nation, who, with one hand are expending thousands in civilizing and christianizing the natives of one continent, while with the other they are pursuing measures here, that have for their object their destruction.

There are many ancient fortifications in and about Piqua. The present race of Indians are entirely ignorant of the cause or time of their erection. Some of these forts are of great extent, and some of them so small that they do not enclose more than half an acre. The excavations are all from the inside, and the entrance into them from the north. The ditches of some of them, are at this time six feet high above the surface of the surrounding grounds ; some of them are constructed in masses of gravel and stone, where it would have been extremely difficult if not altogether impracticable to erect them without the aid of iron tools.— There is one on my farm, which encloses about seventeen acres; it is of a circular form, the walls all round in part built of stone. The stone for the purpose, have been carried from the river, about

O o

600 yards distant. The trees on all these forts, are as large as those in the surrounding forests; and hence the conjecture, that the forts are not less than 400 years standing. I cannot find that any of them are to be found due north of this county; they can be traced south and south-west, to the Floridas.

Emigrants approaching this country from New-York, or the states east of that, would save much labor and expense, to land at Fort Meigs or Lower Sandusky; from the former to proceed by water up the Miami-of-the-Lakes to Fort Defiance or Fort Wayne, and ascend the Auglaize or St. Marys. If their destination was the new state of Indiana, from Fort Wayne they could pass a portage of eight miles, haul their craft over, and descend the Wabash to any given point below.

MONTGOMERY COUNTY,

Lies south of Miami, north of parts of Butler and Warren, east of Preble and west of Green. It is twenty-four miles long and twenty-two wide. The great Miami runs through it from north to south, near its western boundary. The Stillwater branch, waters the north-west corner, for about fourteen miles, on a direct line; Mad river winds five or six miles through the eastern side of the county, before entering the Miami, a little above Dayton. Besides these there are Franklin, Bear and Wolf creeks from the west, and Hole's creek from the east; all entering the Great Miami. The surface is uneven, consisting of rich hills and narrow vallies, except on the large streams, where there are wide and valuable bottoms, particularly on Mad river. The upland is heavily timbered, and equal to any in the state. There yet remain valuable tracts of public lands to be entered.

Dayton, is handsomely situated on the east bank of the Great Miami, a little below the confluence of the Mad river and Stillwater, and is at present the seat of justice. It was planned and surveyed under the direction of General Wilkinson, in 1796, whose title failed. The present proprietor is Daniel C. Cooper, who has given eight lots for county purposes, schools and churches. The public buildings are a court house, Methodist meeting house, Presbyterian church, academy and library; a bank called the

" *Dayton Manufacturing Company,*" with a capital of $100,000;
a post-office, and a printing-office, issuing a weekly newspaper, entitled the " *Ohio Republican.*" A bridge is about to be erected
over the mouth of Mad river. There are about 130 dwelling
houses, besides mechanics' shops—there are several grain and saw
mills near the town, at the mouth of Mad river, and on Wolf creek.
Dayton is the largest village between the Miamis, except Cincinnati.

Near the mouth of Hole's creek, on a plain, are remains of ancient works, of great extent. One of the embankments incloses
about 160 acres, and the walls are in some parts nearly twelve
feet high.

WARREN COUNTY,

Is situated south of Montgomery and a part of Green, north of
parts of Hamilton and Clermont, west of Clinton, and east of Butler. It is traversed by the Little Miami, from north-west to south-
east; together with the numerous tributary creeks and rivers; the
largest of which are Todd's and Cæsar's creeks, running into the
Little Miami from the east; Turtle creek from the west, and
Dick's and Clear creeks, flowing into the Great Miami. The
surface of this county is happily waving, being no where too hilly
to admit of convenient cultivation, or so level as to become wet
and marshy: its southern half has generally a thin soil, and oak
timber; its northern, is equal in fertility to any land in the state
—timbered with poplar, sugar maple, black walnut, bass wood,
blue ash, &c.

Lebanon, the seat of justice, is situated nearly in the centre of
the county, on the post road, between Cincinnati and Chillicothe,
between two branches of Turtle creek, near their junction. It is
four miles east of the Little Miami, and thirty north-east of Cincinnati. Its situation is healthy. Excellent water is obtained, at
the depth of twenty-five or thirty feet; building materials, clay,
lime, stone and wood, abundant. It has a court house, stone jail,
Baptist and Methodist meeting houses, school house, post-office,
printing-office, at which is printed a paper, called the " *Western
Spy,*" a public library; a banking association, called the " *Le-*

banon Miami Banking Company," with a capital limited to 250,000 dollars; besides several stores and mechanics' shops.

Franklin, another handsome village of this county, stands on the east bank of the Great Miami, ten miles south-west of Lebanon, and 34 from Cincinnati. Timber and other building materials, are plentiful, and grist and saw mills are numerous in its vicinity. It has a post-office, and about fifty-five families.

Waynesville, stands on the east bank of the Little Miami, ten miles north-east of Lebanon. It is inhabited and surrounded principally by Friends or Quakers. It has a post-office, a brick meeting house, 80 by 40; brick school house, grist and saw mills convenient—situation healthy.

Six miles from Lebanon, and above the mouth of Todd's Fork, are curious remains of aboriginal works. The form of one of the forts is trapezodial; the walls are of earth, and generally eight or ten feet high; but in one place where it crosses the brow of the elevated hill on which it stands, it is eighteen feet high; the Little Miami lies to the west, and deep ravines on the north, south-east and south; making it a position of great strength; it has numerous angles, retreating and salient, and generally acute. It has 80 gateways. The area of the whole enclosure is nearly 100 acres. Two mounds are situated a few rods to the east, which are about nine feet high. They are not far apart and walls extend from them in opposite directions to the adjoining ravines. Traces of several roads are yet visible: two of them are sixteen feet wide and elevated about three feet like our turnpikes.

CLERMONT COUNTY,

Is bounded south by the Ohio river, east by Adams and Highland counties, north by Clinton and Warren, and west by Hamilton. It is large and will probably be divided. It is watered on the west by the Little Miami, which separates it for twelve or fifteen miles from Hamilton; by the East Fork of the Little Miami, Stone Lick and O'Bannon's creeks; on the south, by the Ohio river, for the distance of forty miles, and by fifteen large creeks, emptying into the same river—the principal of which are Red Oak creek, which waters the north-east corner; Straight creek, White

Oak creek, very large, heads in Highland county, Bullskin, Bear, Big Indian, Little Indian, Cross and Muddy creeks. Its southern parts along the Ohio are hilly; the interior and northern parts level.—The bottoms of the Ohio, in this county, are wide, rich and heavily timbered. The prevailing timber on the uplands is oak.

Williamsburgh, the seat of justice, is situated on the north bank of the East Fork of the Little Miami, thirty miles east-north-east of Cincinnati, on the shortest road to Chillicothe. It is well supplied with water for mills and domestic use. It has a stone court house, post-office and two printing offices, which issue two weekly newspapers, called the " *Political Censor,*" and " *Western American.*"

Milford, stands on the east bank of the Little Miami, ten miles from its mouth. In the vicinity of this village are to be seen the remains of several ancient fortifications.*

Neviltown, is situated on the bank of the Ohio, at the mouth of Bear creek. *Stanton,* is situated at the mouth of Red Oak creek, near the north-eastern corner of the county. Emigrants would find many advantageous situations for settlements in this county, particularly on the Ohio bottoms.

Several *new* villages are commenced on the margin of the Ohio, between Muddy and Eagle creeks.

CLINTON COUNTY,

Is bounded south by Clermont and a part of Highland counties; east by parts of Highland and Fayette; north by Green,

---

* The largest of these forts is situated on the top of the first hill above the confluence of the East Fork with the Miami. It consists of a square enclosure, three sides of which have each a single opening, and the fourth two. From this side there is a semicircular projection, covering nearly as much ground as the square itself. It has three openings, at unequal distances. From the junction of these two figures on the west, there run two parallel banks, which terminate at a circular wall, from which two others are extended southwardly. These are divergent, and between them, near their termination, there are three banks connected at the inner end. From the north-east corner of the figure first described, there are discernible for two miles in the same direction, appearances which indicate a road in former times. The ground at present is raised from one to two feet high. The width of this causeway appears to have varied from 20 to 30 feet.— On the opposite side of the Miami river, above Round-bottom, there are similar works of considerable extent. *Picture of Cincinnati.*

and west by Warren. It is about twenty miles long and fifteen wide, and is watered, principally, by branches of Paint creek, running into the Scioto, and Todd's Fork of the Little Miami.— The surface of this county is generally level—in some parts marshy; it contains much good land, the greater part in a state of nature.

Wilmington, the only village deserving mention, is the seat of justice. It is nearly equidistant between Cincinnati and Chillicothe, or about fifty miles from each.

GREEN COUNTY,

Has Clinton south, Fayette and Madison east, Champaign and Montgomery west. It is about twenty-four miles square; and is watered by the Little Miami, which runs in a transverse direction through the county, from north-west to south-east; Mad river waters the south-west corner. Cæsar's and Massie's creeks, tributaries of the Little Miami, from the east, water large portions of the county. The western side of the county is watered by Sugar, and Big and Little Beaver creeks.

The Great Falls of the Little Miami, are in this county: in the course of a mile the river is precipitated from several successive tables, which produces a vast number of fine mill seats.

The vallies are wide, rich and productive; the uplands generally of a second quality, with a proportion of oak barrens.

Xenia, the seat of justice, is situated nearly in the centre of the county, on Shawanœse creek. It is three miles east of the Little Miami, and fifty-five north-east of Cincinnati. It has a brick court house, an academy and church; a post-office, and a printing-office which emits a weekly paper, entitled the " *Ohio Vehicle.*" The situation is healthy.

CHAMPAIGN COUNTY,

Lies north of Green, west of Delaware, south of the Indian lands, and east of Miami county. The great Miami meanders through its south-western corner; many of its numerous tributary streams water its southern side. Mad river waters the interior parts, or rather traverses it from its north-western to its south-eastern corner. The East Fork of Mad river irrigates an extensive portion of the county lying between Mad river and Delaware county. In addition to these are King's and Nettle creeks, and numerous rivulets and runs. No county in the state possesses a greater number of durable streams, or finer situations for mills. Its name is a correct index to its surface ; it has extensive alluvions or champaign tracts on the east side of Mad river : on the west side are rich heavy timbered lands : barren and swampy prairies are to be found towards the eastern side. It is, however, a large and fertile county, and holds out great advantages to emigrants.

Urbanna, the county seat, is situated on a large and fertile prairie, two miles east of Mad river. Two permanent brooks flow through it, and well water is easily obtained. The number of dwelling houses is upwards of 100, chiefly of wood. It has a post-office, a printing-office, in which is published a paper called the *" Spirit of Liberty,"* and a banking company. Fevers and agues are annual visitants. Timber, clay and quarries of sandy limestone are convenient.

Springfield is situated eleven miles south of Urbanna, on the south side of the East Fork of Mad river ; on the south it has a copious and durable creek, with falls of thirty feet descent. A woollen manufactory has been erected at these falls.

A few miles below Dayton, are mounds of great elevation. One, situated on a prairie, half a mile from the Franklin road, is said to be upwards of 100 feet in height, and 286 feet diameter at the base. The whole mound is covered with large forest trees.—— From its summit one has an extensive view of the circumjacent country. There is no appearance of the earth having been taken from the surrounding surface.

Note—The above described counties of Hamilton, Butler, Preble, Darke, Miami, Montgomery, Warren, Clermont, Clinton, Green and Champaign, are all watered by the Great and Little Miamis ; and wh ch embrace a district about ninety miles in length, and sixty broad. This is usually called the " Miami Country."

DELAWARE COUNTY,

Has Madison and Pickaway south, Licking and Knox counties east, Indian lands north, and Champaign west. It is finely
watered by the Scioto, the Whetstone Fork, Big-belly, Allum, and
Walnut creeks ; all large streams, which traverse the county from
north to south, parallel with each other, at the distance of from
four to ten miles apart. Soil and surface, well adapted to all the
purposes of cultivation. Improved lands are high, owing to the
facility with which produce is transported to market. The chief
towns are Delaware, and Norton, on Whetstone, and New-Balti-
more, on the Scioto—all new and thriving villages.

FRANKLIN COUNTY,

Situated nearly in the centre of the state, has Pickaway south,
parts of Fairfield and Licking east, Delaware north, and Madison
west. It is finely watered by the Scioto, and Whetstone rivers,
Big belly creek and its two forks, Allum and Walnut creeks.—
The surface of this county is gently waving, except along the
vallies of the streams; soil, similar to that of Delaware and
Champaign.

Columbus, the metropolis of the state, is situated on the east
bank of the Scioto, on an elevated prairie, of several hundred acres,
and of a soil equal in durability to any in the world. The length
of the town is one mile and forty rods, is parallel to the river having a straight line on the east; the course of the streets is north
12 deg. 30 min. west, their width 87 feet, alternately intersected
at every third lot, by an alley or a cross street, 37 and 33 feet
wide, and 24 in number ; Broad street, (120 feet wide) which commences at the river, where a bridge is about to be erected, and
communicates at the eastern extremity of the town with the main
road leading to Newark, Zanesville and Pittsburgh. This road is
several miles entirely straight and not far from mathematically level. Contiguous to Broad street on the north, High street on the
west, and State street on the south, is the Public square, including
ten acres, the most beautiful and central spot in the town; on

which is erected and nearly completed, the state house, built of brick, of sufficient magnitude and considerable elegance; and the state offices, all in one block, of one hundred feet in length.— The Penitentiary is situated in the south-west corner of the town. The whole number of buildings is upwards of 300. Some are rude and temporary, but the greater part are elegant and commodious; nearly 200 of which are dwelling houses. There are about a dozen stores, six taverns, a post-office, two printing-offices, and a number of mechanics' shops. There are two springs issuing east of the town and discharging into the river; one on the north and the other on the south, almost encircle the town. They are deemed capable of moving machinery sufficient for most manufactures or mills, a large part of the year. Situated, as this town is, on a high airy plain, in the centre of large and populous settlements, enjoying a safe and convenient navigation, and possessing great political and local advantages, it cannot fail in time, to rival the first cities in the western country. It was commenced in 1813. The rise of lots has been rapid, almost without a parallel. Lots nearest the public square, have sold for 2000 dollars, and no where in the town for less than 200. Boats of ten tons burthen can ascend to the town for six months in the year: and in freshets vessels of 200 tons, could descend into the Ohio. There is an abundance of timber, fit for ship building, in Franklin and Delaware counties.

Franklinton, is situated on the west bank of the Scioto, opposite Columbus, and just below the Whetstone branch.—It contains about seventy houses—and has been, in a manner, eclipsed by the metropolis.

Worthington, which is about equal in size to Franklinton, is a flourishing village, situated on the bank of Whetstone, 16 miles above Columbus.

PICKAWAY COUNTY,

Has Ross south, Fairfield east, Franklin north, and parts of Madison and Fayette west; the Scioto runs through this county.— The other streams are Deer, and Darby's creek from the west, and Lower Walnut from the east, all large and emptying into the

Scioto. The soil of this county is of the best quality. Pickaway plains which are about twelve miles long and three wide, is a prairie of inexhaustible fertility. Here are to be seen some of the first agricultural prospects in the state. The bottoms of the Scioto are wide and of the first quality. The towns are Circleville, Bloomfield, Jefferson, Livingston and Westfall.

Circleville, the seat of justice, is situated on the Pickaway bottom, about half a mile east of the Scioto. Its site is two mounds of earth, one circular, and the other square, containing about twenty acres. The first is enclosed by two circumvallations, whose perpendicular height is about fifteen feet above the adjoining ditch. In the centre of the town is a small vacant circle. From this focus the streets diverge in regular *radii*, intersecting the walls at equal distances. The greater part of the buildings are within the external circle. It contains about 250 buildings, a post-office, court house of an octagonal form, and thirteen stores, &c. The growth of this town has been rapid—it owes its existence to the wealth of the surrounding plantations rather than to political causes or commercial advantages.

MADISON COUNTY,

Has Fayette south, Franklin and Pickaway east, Delaware north, and Champaign and Green west. It is watered by the North Fork of Paint and Darby's creek. The eastern parts are broken, or moderately hilly; especially the dividing ridge between the waters of Paint and Little Miami. Towards the western parts, are prairies and barrens, but the greater part first rate land. It is pretty thickly settled, and has few unseated lands inviting to settlers.

New-London is the chief town—it contains about 100 buildings.

FAYETTE COUNTY,

Has Highland and Scioto south, Ross and Pickaway east, Madison north, and Green and Clinton west. It is watered by the North and West Forks of Paint creek, and head branches of Cæsar's creek. In soil, surface, and general aspects, it closely resembles Clinton, already described. Washington is the chief town.

HIGHLAND COUNTY,

Has Adams south, Pike east, Ross, Clinton and Fayette north, and Clermont west. It is copiously watered by forks of Brush and Paint creeks, and by small creeks and brooks running into the East Fork of the Little Miami; its surface is generally hilly; free from stagnant waters or marshes, which insures health to the inhabitants. It is thinly settled, and offers many eligible situations to industrious emigrants.

Mounds and old forts are to be seen in many parts of the county. On the head branches of the East Fork of the Little Miami, is an ancient work, different in figure to any hitherto discovered. It consists of a square enclosure, with " *nine* banks of long parapets united at one end, exhibiting very exactly the figure of a gridiron. In this fort most of the gateways are guarded by straight or crescent-formed batteries."

ADAMS COUNTY,

Has the Ohio river south, Scioto county east, Highland county north, and Clermont west. It is hilly and broken along the Ohio —is watered by Eagle, Brush and Isaac's creeks, and by waters of Paint and Little Miami. It has a hilly and broken surface, rich, deep soil, heavy forests of oak, hickory, sugar maple, black walnut, black elm and sycamore. Although a populous county, it has yet considerable bodies of unseated lands, belonging to individuals, mostly non-residents. There is an abundant supply of iron-ore on Brush creek, upon which Gen. M'Arthur and a Mr. James erected a furnace last autumn. It has several villages.

West-Union, the seat of justice, is situated on a branch of the East Fork of the Little Miami, on the road leading from Limestone, in Kentucky, to Chillicothe. It has about 100 houses—a court house, jail, printing-office and post-office, six stores, four inns, and a great number of mechanics. The surrounding country is rolling and perfectly healthy; no instance of billious fever and ague has occurred; springs and mill seats abundant. Wild lands worth from five to twenty dollars.

Manchester, stands on the bank of the Ohio, near the lower end of Massie's island, fifteen miles above Maysville ; it is pleasantly situated, commands a view of the Ohio; but appears stationary ; it has about forty *old* houses.

Adamsville, is situated just below the mouth of Brush creek, and eight miles above Manchester, which it resembles in appearance and size. Here are fine bottoms, which continue wide for twelve miles above and below the mouth of Brush creek.

SCIOTO COUNTY,

Situated on both sides of the river of the same name, has the Ohio river south, Gallia east, Ross and Pike north, and Adams west. It is watered by the Scioto and Ohio rivers, Little Scioto river, Turkey, Pine, Stout's, Twin's and Scioto creeks.

The bottoms of the Ohio and Scioto, in this county, are wide, and of the first quality. The hills near the Ohio are covered with white oak and hickory, and generally of a third quality, but suitable to pasturage and wheat. Many unseated bottom tracts could be purchased for six, eight, or ten dollars, at a bargain.— Turkey and Pine creeks abound with fine sites for mills, which are but partially improved.

Portsmouth, the seat of justice, stands on a peninsula formed by the confluence of the Scioto with the Ohio. Its site is pleasant, gently inclining to the south. It contains about 100 houses, mostly new.

Alexandria, is situated on the margin of the Ohio, two miles below Portsmouth, and immediately below the Scioto. It was formerly the county seat, but was abandoned in consequence of an inundation caused by an extraordinary rise of the Ohio. The water rose four feet above the level of the plain on which it is built. I measured the bank of the Ohio at this place last June, and found it to be 70 feet above the surface of the water, which was then at an ordinary height. There are fifteen old buildings, and a tavern well supported by the votaries of Bacchus. Indolence and dissipation characterize the inhabitants. They have a constant supply of excellent fish. I saw a catfish caught at the mouth of Scioto, weighing seventy four pounds. The bottoms for many miles above and below the mouth of Scioto, are from one to two miles in width, and as rich as can be desired. Mounds and walls are numerous; a wall from four to seven feet high extends from the Great to the Little Scioto—a distance of seven miles.

PIKE COUNTY,

Lies on both sides of the Scioto river—has Scioto county south, Ross east and north, and Highland west. It is watered by the Scioto and its tributary creeks and brooks; the surface is considerably broken; timber, oak, hickory and maple; soil generally poor, except on the bottoms.

Piketon, situated on the east bank of the Scioto, is the county seat. Mounds are numerous throughout the county.

ROSS COUNTY,

Is situated on both sides of the Scioto, which divides it about equally. It has parts of Scioto and Pike counties south, Athens and Gallia east, Fairfield and Pickaway north, and Fayette and Highland west; and is watered by Paint creek on the west side of the Scioto; Kenneconic and Salt creeks on the east. This is a rich healthy county. The inhabitants are mostly wealthy, and have elegant buildings, large and well improved farms; the traveller on approaching a farm-house is forcibly struck with the indications of *plenty*, which are presented at every step; such as immense fields of grain, large stacks of wheat, capacious corn cribs well filled even in summer; numerous herds of stock, cattle, horses, hogs, sheep, common and merino; yards swarming with poultry; and should he have occasion to enter the hospitable mansion, he will there find the same proofs of abundance and perfect independence; every thing is on the scale of external wealth; a plenteous board, elegant and costly furniture, well dressed children and servants. In short,

> " A clean fire-side and a jorum,"

and what is better, a friendly welcome, without any of those sour looks and sly watchings of the motion of your knife and fork, too often witnessed in the north. The above remarks apply to all the rich counties of this state, as well as to those of Kentucky, Tennessee and Louisiana.

Chillicothe, the seat of justice, and formerly of the state government, is situated on the west bank of the Scioto, (66 miles from its mouth) on a beautiful and extensive plain. It is laid out on a large scale, with a great number of out-lots attached to it.— The plan is regular; the streets cross each other at right angles, and every square is divided into four parts by lanes crossing each other also at right angles; the streets are 66 feet wide, the alleys 16; the lots contain four acres each. It contains about 500 buildings, and about 4000 inhabitants. It has several stately public buildings, four churches, several rope walks, about 40 dry good stores, cotton and woollen factory, besides breweries, distilleries, and tanneries. In short, it is a brisk and elegant town, in the centre of fertile and populous settlements, and surrounded by a great number of handsome and tasty country seats. It has three printing offices, two issuing weekly newspapers, the "*Freedonian,*" and "*Supporter,*" and one for books; a post-office and a land-office for the disposal of the public lands. Gentlemen of taste would find Chillicothe an agreeable residence.

Bainbridge, is situated on a small branch of Paint creek on the Maysville road, 38 miles north-east of West-Union, and 26 south-west of Chillicothe. It is surrounded by a well settled country—it has about fifty houses—land in its vicinity worth 25 dollars an acre. About a mile to the northward of this village, are some of the best mills in the state, belonging to Gen. Massie, who is besides the proprietor of Bainbridge. Wild lands around this town are too high to be advantageously purchased for farming. It belongs to the favorites of *Plutus,* who obtained it for a song, but now refuse to sell it, in parcels, unless at an exorbitant price. So much for the blindness of legislation.

It has several other villages—the principal of which are Amsterdam and Adelphi.

The vallies of Paint and Scioto, and indeed many of the adjacent hills abound with the vestiges of an immense ancient population; and perhaps, the curious antiquary, can no where in the western country find a richer field for his researches.

Ten miles west of Chillicothe, on one of the elevated and steep ridges of Paint creek, are walls of stone, now in ruins, extending along the brow of the hill, for nearly a mile and a half, and enclosing upwards of 100 acres. It was formed of undressed freestone, and appears, from the quantity of stones, to have been twelve or fifteen feet high, and four or five thick ; many of the stones bear the marks of fire. The wall bears the appearance of having been shaken down by an earthquake. Mr. James Foster, of Chillicothe, who particularly examined it, says, that within the area there were about thirty furnaces—from some of which he took cinders that resembled in every way those formed in blacksmith's forges. From some of them he got pieces of burnt unwrought clay, that resembled pumice stone, but are of a pale blue color. Those lying on the surface of the earth are covered with coats of *rusty mail*, which probably had lain there since the days of Lycurgus.   The first is nearly circular, with ten passes or gateways placed at regular distances, at one of which there is the appearance of a well or spring, enclosed with a stone wall. Trees from three to five feet in diameter, which were obviously preceded by a more gigantic growth, if we may judge from the long traces left by those that have mouldered into their native dust. No stones are to be found within one mile of the walls. " At the bottom of the hill, on the south-west side, are the ruins of the *town*, or rather *city*. The cellars and the stone foundations of the houses still remain. The streets are in regular squares. Near it there is a large mound perfectly level to the top. It was from all appearances the residence of a warlike race." The surrounding country abounds with iron ore, and with excavations, which the inhabitants suppose to have been formerly made in search of that mineral. I have myself seen the ruins of several ancient stone buildings, in Ross and Pickaway counties; one within a few miles of Chillicothe, near the Maysville road, appeared, as measured by the eye, sixty feet long by thirty wide; the stones were generally large and ragged without the least mark of the hammer, or any other iron tool. Six large beech and sugar maple trees were growing within the enclosure. A mound thirty feet high, and perfectly conical was standing on the site of Chillicothe for several years after the first white settlements. It has lately been levelled with the earth, to make room for a fine brick house ; this want of respect for *aboriginal antiquities*, is too often evinced by the people of the west. On a high hill, on the opposite side of the Scioto, is another mound of equal magnitude. There are probably seven hundred similar ones in the counties of Athens, Ross and Pickaway.

FAIRFIELD COUNTY.

A large and wealthy interior county, bounded on the North by Licking, east by Muskingum and Washington, south by Athens and Ross, and west by Pickaway and Franklin counties. It is 36 miles long by 30 broad; and contains 900 square miles. It is divided into the twenty following townships, namely, Amanda, Reading, Liberty, Madison, Jackson, Hopewell, Bern, Bloom, Thorn, Hocking, Falls, Violet, Greenfield, Clear creek, Pleasant, Walnut, Richland, Rush creek, Pike and Perry. The villages regularly laid out and called towns, are, in addition to Lancaster, the county seat, the seven following, namely; Somerset, Clinton, New-Lebanon, Jacksonville, Greencastle and Centreville. This county embraces perhaps the most elevated tract of country, of similar extent between the Muskingum and Scioto rivers. The land is therefore drier, and more peculiarly adapted to the production of wheat and other kinds of grain than that of several adjacent counties. The principal streams are the head waters of Hockhocking river. The face of the country about Lancaster in the central part of the county presents a peculiar aspect. The land seems generally level; but abrupt, precipitous and coni form piles of rocks, producing very little timber or herbage, are occasionally interspersed in a promiscuous manner, in every direction. They are of divers altitudes and magnitudes. Some people might perhaps conjecture them to have been works of art, did not their numbers and magnitude preclude the idea. One of these called Mount Pleasant, about one mile northerly from Lancaster, is very remarkable. It is situated near a large prairie, and encompassed by a large plain. The south-west front of this huge pile of rocks is about 500 feet in perpendicular height : the base is about a mile and a half in circumference; while the top is but about 30 by 100 yards across it. *Ohio Gazetteer, page 50.*

Lancaster, a flourishing post town and seat of justice in this county. It is handsomely situated in the centre of the county, in Hocking township, near the source of Hockhocking river, on the road leading from Zanesville to Chillicothe. It contains between 100 and 200 houses, and a population of 6 or 700 inhabitants. Here are likewise twelve mercantile stores, a handsome

brick court house and jail, a Methodist meeting house, a bank, an
English and German printing-office, from which are published
weekly newspapers in both languages, and a market house with a
market on Wednesdays and Saturdays. Various kir s of mechanical business are likewise here industriously prosecuted. Distance,
28 miles south-easterly from Columbus, 36 south-westerly from
Zanesville, and 34 north-easterly from Chillicothe. N. lat. 39 45,
W. lon. 5 35.   *Ibid, page 77.*

LICKING COUNTY,

Has Fairfield county south, Muskingum and Coshocton east,
Delaware and Franklin north, and Madison west; and is watered
by Licking river and its two forks; Wakatomika and Walnut
creeks, all large and boatable.

Wherever we find the traces of former population, as demon-
strated by the existence of mounds, fortifications, and ruins of
buildings, we are sure to find land of an excellent quality. This
county is full of antiquities.*

Newark is a thriving little town situated in the forks of Licking, on the road between Zanesville and Columbus. *Granville* is

---

* Those in the vicinity of Newark " cover, or rather pass over in different directions, more than 1500 acres of ground, and appear to have had
an intended connection with, or approached to each other. The one
most remarkable for size is circular, and is, by actual measurement,
three-fourths of a mile in circumference. It has but one gateway or entrance, which is ten rods wide; the wall from the bottom of the ditch is
from 18 to 35 feet. It is highest near the entrance, where each side terminates somewhat in the form of a basin. The one most remarkable of
form, and mathematical regularity of parts, lies about three-fourths of a
mile north of the one first mentioned. It is a regular octagon ; all the
sides being, by actual measurement, equal; the walls or lines being about
three feet high. At each angle, except one, is an opening or gateway, opposite to which, within, is a raised work of the same height of the wall :
a parallelogram whose length covers the entrance From the out angle
or opening, you pass between parallel walls, which are ten rods apart, into another circular work, the walls of which are about the same height of
the foregoing. The compass when set in the centre between the parallel
walls, and in direction with them, leads you directly to the only part
where there has been a place for passing in and out of the circle: and this
place affords evidence of having been a covered way, with towers, or
ground more elevated than the wall, on each side. The octagon and circle may contain each from twenty to thirty acres, and are near to where
a principal branch of Licking river appears to have flowed.

Q q

also a considerable village. The surface, soil, timber and water of this county, is inviting to settlers. It has had a rapid settlement; and presents strong inducements to emigrants.

ATHENS COUNTY,

Has Gallia south, Washington east, Washington and Fairfield north, and Ross west. It is watered by the Great Hockhocking, and its branches; by Racoon, Federal, Shade, and Salt creeks, and an immense number of brooks. Compared to such counties as Ross, Franklin, Pickaway, and Licking, it may be said to be poor, in soil and improvements. The southern parts, adjoining Gallia county, consist of oak hills and deep narrow vallies. It is thinly inhabited; in many places it is from four to twenty miles between houses; but this is only true, as it respects the eastern portion.— Game is abundant—such as bears, deer, foxes, racoons, &c. Wild turkies are more numerous in this than in any other part of the state. The range is rich, and will probably continue so for many years to come.

Mounds and embankments are to be seen in every part of the county. I opened several; but found nothing except stone axes, arrows, and bones : at the bottoms there was uniformly a stratum of ashes intermixed with coals, brands and fragments of calcined bones. Almost every farm contains several mounds.

Athens, is pleasantly situated on the east bank of the Great Hockhocking, on a peninsula formed by a considerable bend of that river. 37 miles above its confluence with the Ohio, and nearly in the centre of the *College* townships, reserved by congress in the grant to the Ohio company for the endowment of a University. The names of these townships are Athens and Alexander ; the last lies on the south side of the river ; they contain 46,080 acres. The lands are leased in small farms of from 100 to 160 acres, to applicants forever, upon terms never to be altered—the rent of each tract being the interest of the appraised value of the land in a state of nature.

The town is laid out in a regular form—is elevated about 100 feet above the bottoms. The soil is a dry rich loam, well adapted for gardens. There are numerous springs of never failing excel lent water. The total number of buildings is about 100. There is an academy in a very flourishing state under the instruction of an able teacher, in which are taught all the branches of a liberal education; and a spacious new college is now building. The present revenue of the university is about 2500 dollars, the education of youth is to be gratuitous.

The greater part of the college lands are very fertile; but some tracts are broken and of a thin soil. The settlements commenced in 1797, and the town and county of Athens have proved unusually healthy. Many of the settlers are from New-England, who affirm that sickness had rarely visited their families. The Hockhocking is navigable 6 miles above Athens for batteaux.— The bottom lands are better and more extensive than those of the Muskingum. In front of the town they are more than one mile wide. There are fine quarries of freestone in the vicinity of the town. About two-thirds of the village lots are leased, and the residue fast settling. The uplands are timbered with white and black oak, hickory and chesnut; occasionally interspersed with sugar-maple, ash and beech. The bottoms are covered with buckeye, pawpaw, elm, black walnut, spice-wood and honey-locust.— Fish in considerable quantities are taken from the rivers. Coal mines, chalybeate and sulphur springs, are so plentiful that no township is without several of each kind.

GALLIA COUNTY,

Is bounded south and east by the Ohio river, Athens county north, Lawrence and Jackson west. It is watered by the Little Scioto, Leading, Racoon, Indian Guyandot, and Big Stone creeks. Like Athens, it is large and hilly, and thinly settled. It has much poor land, consisting of oak ridges, of a thin gravelly soil. These hills skirt the Ohio through the whole extent of Scioto, Gallia, Washington, and Belmont counties; extending back 30 or 40 miles; they become more elevated as we ascend the river; nevertheless, the soil becomes better east of the Muskingum; and as high up as Steubenville, it may be said to be rich. The bottoms of the Ohio are wide. There are bodies of good land in the interior parts, on which the principal part of the timber is pitch pine, very lofty and straight. This kind of land is much esteemed by the inhabitants; the soil is sandy, mixed in places with loam and gravel; but it produces corn, wheat, oats and potatoes, as abundantly as deeper soils.

Galliopolis is delightfully situated on the bank of the Ohio, three miles below the Great Kenhaway. The bottom on which it is built, is elevated fourteen feet above the highest rise of the river. The soil is a rich, yellow clay, rendered mellow, like loam, by a proportion of fine sand. The streets are wide, and run in parallels with the river upwards of one mile and a quarter in length. The high lands in the rear of the town, approach within half a mile of the river. This town was settled by a colony of 500 French, in 1790; but the present number of inhabitants is considerably short of that number. There are about 76 houses, a court house, church, and printing-office. The inhabitans have beautiful gardens. They make good wine, from a species of native vines, which were found on the islands a short distance above the town, and which, since they have been domesticated, produce grapes almost equal in size and flavor to the muscadins of France. There is a vineyard in the vicinity of this place, of six acres, which is expected the present year to produce 1000 gallons of wine. A mound of 18 or 20 rods in circumference is situated near the academy. Other remains of ancient works are visible both on the bottoms and neighbouring hills.

LAWRENCE COUNTY.

Bounded south by the Ohio river, west by Scioto county, north by Jackson, and east by Gallia. It is watered by Symmes', and Indian Guyandot creeks—surface, broken; soil, chiefly of an inferior quality—timber, principally oak. This county was recently laid off, and is not yet organized.

JACKSON COUNTY.

Is bounded north by Ross and Athens, east by Athens and Gallia, south by Gallia and Scioto counties. It is 24 by 20 miles in extent, comprizing 414 square miles. It was established in the winter of 1816. Surface, hilly; soil, generally of a second quality. Timber—oak, and hickory on the uplands. The *Scioto Salt*

Works, which belong to the United States, and at which considerable quatities of salt are made, are situated nearly in the centre of this county, on the easternmost branch of Salt creek, 28 miles S. E. of Chillicothe. It is expected that the seat of justice will be near these works. The principal streams are the three forks of Salt creek and the head branches of Symmes' creek.

WASHINGTON COUNTY,

Is bounded north by Muskingum, Guernsey and Monroe counties, southeast by the Ohio river—south and west by Athens and Fairfield. It is 63 miles long from east to west, and from 12 to 31 in breadth, containing about 1100 square miles. It is watered by the Ohio and Muskingum rivers, Little Muskingum, Pawpaw, Duck, Wolf, Miegs and Little Hocknocking creeks. A large proportion of this county is hilly—soil poor, and timber chiefly oak. The bottoms, however, of the Ohio and Muskingum and the large creeks, are pretty extensive and of the first quality.

Marietta—Is situated on the first bank of the Ohio, immediately above the entrance of the Muskingum. Like most of the towns on that fine river, its site and appearance is "*pleasant*." Yet, hitherto, its growth has not kept pace with public expectation, nor realized the sanguine anticipations and early predictions of its proprietors. It contains about 100 houses, exclusive of 35 or 40 on the opposite bank of the Muskingum, where fort Harmer formerly stood —it has besides, a court house, jail, market house, academy, two churches, a bank, post-office, printing-office, two rope walks, steam gristmill, several mercantile stores, and four well furnished inns. In March 1816, a large Commercial and Exporting Company was formed, since which the shipbuilding business has revived. The St. Clair, a brig of 120 tons burden, was the first sea-rigged vessel, ever launched from the banks of the Ohio. She was built by Com. Preble in 1799. N. lat. 39 34.

Belpre, a beautiful village, or rather settlement, extending several miles along the Ohio river, commencing at the mouth of Congress creek and reaching to the Little Hockhocking, and up that river several miles; this is the most populous part of the county.

Waterford, a post township on the Muskingum river, 22 miles above Marietta. It is a handsome, rich settlement extending several miles along the fine bottoms of that river. Ancient fortifications are numerous in this county.*

MUSKINGUM COUNTY,

Bounded north by Coshocton, east by Guernsey, south by Washington and Fairfield, and west by Fairfield and Licking counties. It is watered by the Muskingum and Licking rivers, and by Coal, Jonathan, Wakatomika, Salt and Wills' creeks. It is large and populous, having an area of about 820 square miles, and a popu-

---

* The largest SQUARE FORT, by some called *the town*, contains forty acres, encompassed by a wall of earth from six to ten feet high, and from twenty-five to thirty-six feet in breadth at the base. On each side are three openings, at equal distances, resembling three gateways. The entrances at the middle are the largest, particularly that on the side next the Muskingum river. From this outlet are the remains of a *covertway*, formed of two parallel walls of earth, 231 feet distant from each other, measuring from centre to centre. The walls at the most elevated part on the inside are 24 feet in height, and 42 in breadth at the base, but on the outside average only five feet high. This forms a passage of about 360 feet in length, leading by a gradual descent to the low grounds, where it probably at the time of its construction reached the margin of the river. Its walls commence at 60 feet from the ramparts of the fort, and increase in elevation as the way descends towards the river; and the bottom is crowned in the centre, in the manner of a well formed turnpike road. — Within the walls of the fort, at the north-west corner, is an oblong, elevated square, 188 feet long, 132 broad, and nine feet high; level on the summit, and nearly perpendicular at the sides. At the centre of each of the sides the earth is projected, forming gradual ascents to the top, equally regular, and about six feet in width. Near the south wall is another elevated square, 150 feet by 120, and eight feet high; similar to the other, excepting that instead of an ascent to go up on the side next the wall, there is a hollow way ten feet wide leading twenty feet towards the centre, and then rising with a gradual slope to the top. At the the south-east corner is a third elevated square 108 by 54 feet with ascents at the ends; but not so high nor perfect as the two others. A little to the southwest of the centre of the fort is a circular mound, about 30 feet in diameter and five in height; near which are four small excavations at equal distances, and opposite each other. At the south-west corner of the fort is a semi-circular parapet, crowned with a mound, which guards the opening in the wall. Towards the south-east is a smaller fort, containing twenty acres, with a gateway in the centre of each side and at each corner. These openings are defended with circular mounds. On the outside of the smaller fort is a mound, in form of a sugar-loaf, of a magnitude and height which strike the beholder with astonishment. Its base is a regular circle 115 feet in diameter; and its perpendicular altitude is 30 feet. It is surrounded with a ditch four feet deep and fifteen wide, and defended by a parapet four feet high, through which is an opening or gateway towards the fort 20 feet wide.

There are other walls, mounds and excavations, less conspicuous and entire, but exhibiting equal proofs of art and design.   *Harris's Tour.*

lation of about 12,000 souls. Surface generally hilly ; the lovers
of romantic scenery will find ample gratification on the sharp, elevated ridges between Salt and Will's creeks, on the Wheeling road.
Extensive beds of stone coal are found in various parts of the county, especially in the hills bordering the Muskingum river.

Zanesville, is situated on the east bank of the Muskingum river,
opposite Putnam and the mouth of Licking, 50 miles by land above
Marietta. It contains about 240 houses, generally small but neat
and well built. It has a court house, jail, market house, methodist
meeting house, three glass factories, two banks, land office, nail factory, 22 mercantile stores, paper mill, several oil mills, numerous
saw and grain mills, post-office, book-bindery, two printing-offices,
in which are published the " *Muskingum Messenger*" and " *Zanesville Express.*"

Opposite the town, the Muskingum falls six feet in the space of
a few rods, and Licking river forms a cascade at its entrance. A
canal is now opening around the Muskingum rapids, through the
town, by an association called the " Zanesville Canal and Manufacturing Company," who intend to manufacture iron in all its various branches, cotton, wool, hemp, flax, paper, &c.

Putnam, is situated on the right bank of the Muskingum, directly opposite Zanesville. It has about seventy houses, seven
stores, and a cotton factory. These two towns are connected by
two bridges. The upper bridge is so constructed that one may
cross Licking or the Muskingum from or to either side of Licking. The country around these places, in every direction, is settled, and generally well cultivated. Coal abounds in the hills, and
is often found in sinking wells. Four miles up Licking, is a forge
and furnace, extensively carried on by Dillon & Son.

KNOX COUNTY.

Has Licking south, Coshocton east, Richland north and Delaware west. It is watered by the Whitewoman branch of the
Muskingum, Owl creek, and branches of Licking and Scioto. It
will rank among the most fertile counties of the state.

Mount Vernon, is the seat of justice; it is new but rapidly increasing in size and improvements. The largest streams are all
boatable.

COSHOCTON COUNTY,

Clinton, is situated on the north side of Owl creek, 2 miles N. W. of Mount Vernon; it contains 37 houses and a post-office. Knox county has a monied institution called the *"Owl Creek Bank."*

Bounded north by Wayne, east by Tuscorawas, south by Muskingum, and west by Knox counties. It is about 30 miles square. The Muskingum river runs through the southeastern part;—the other streams are Wills' creek and Whitewoman's river. Surface generally uneven. It deservedly ranks among the best counties of the state. The bottoms of Whitewoman's and Tuscarawas are wide and highly productive. The uplands are generally heavy timbered; oak in places, with rich poplar and black walnut lands interspersed. It abounds with freestone, coal and limestone.

Coshocton, the seat of justice, is situated near the forks of the Muskingum, 40 miles north of Zanesville, and contains about 80 houses and 4 stores.

RICHLAND COUNTY,

Has Knox south, Wayne east, Huron and Medina north, and Indian lands west. It is watered by the head branches of the Huron, East Fork of the Sandusky, Clear Fork, a branch of the Muskingum, Muddy creek, &c. Its name represents the quality of its soil. It will rank with any county in the state in point of fertility. It is new and contains large bodies of rich unsettled lands.

Mansfield and *Green* are the largest villages; they are new but thriving.

TUSCARAWAS COUNTY,

Has Guernsey south, Harrison east, Wayne and Stark north, and Coshocton west. It is watered by the Tuscarawas, Stillwater, Conoton, Sugar and Sandy Creek.

New-Philadelphia, the seat of justice for Tuscarawas county.— It is situated on the eastern branch of Muskingum river, on a large, level, and beautiful plain, opposite the mouth of Sugar creek.

It contains the county buildings, five stores, and 47 dwelling-houses. Distance, 50 miles north-east from Zanesville, and 100 north-eastwardly from Columbus. N. lat. 40 32, W. lon. 4 30.

Gnadenhutten, a post town, originally established by some Moravian missionaries, on the eastern branch of the Muskingum river, eleven miles southerly from New-Philadelphia.

Schoenbrun, a Moravian missionary settlement, three miles below New-Philadelphia.

WAYNE COUNTY,

Is bounded south by Coshocton, east by Stark, north by Medina and part of Portage, and west by Richland. It was organized in the year 1808, and is 30 miles long by 29 broad, containing 870 square miles. It is divided into the following townships: Wooster, Springfield, Mohiccan, Boughman, East Union, Paint, Perry, Salt Creek, Prairie, Lake, Sugar Creek and Chester. The principal streams are Killbuck, running nearly a south course, and navigable up to Wooster, for boats of from 10 to 14 tons; Apple creek, a tributary of Killbuck, a very good stream for mills; Sugar creek, near the south-east corner of the county, is likewise a good stream for mills; Chippeway, in the N. E. and Mohiccan John creek, in the west side of the county, which is a very considerable stream in its different ramifications in this county, and in Richland. The Lake Fork and Jerome's Fork, are navigable for boats of 10 or 12 tons, 18 miles above the south boundary of the county. The soil is generally excellent. The creek bottoms are extensive and very fertile, producing immense crops of corn, when properly cultivated. The upland is very productive in wheat, rye, oats, corn, flax, &c. The timber on the upland is very tall, and generally composed of white and black oak, walnut, cherry, hickory, and some few chesnuts: the prevailing timber on the bottoms and low lands is ash, elm, sycamore, sugar maple and soft maple, together with some beech, interspersed with a variety of wild plums, crab apples, grape vines, buckeye, hazle, &c. The prices of land vary according to situation and natural and artificial advantages, being from three to fifty dollars an acre.

The principal towns in this county are Wooster, Paintville and Jeromesville.

Wooster, the seat of justice for the county, commenced building in 1811, and now contains 60 dwelling houses, together with seven stores, four taverns, and a large and excellent brick banking-house, for the German Bank of Wooster, a public land office, for the sale of the United States' lands, a public school house and a meeting house for the Baptist society. Many of the buildings being built of brick, are large and elegant. In the town are five master carpenters, employing ten hands each, four blacksmith shops, two cabinet makers, two tan yards, one chair maker, one carriage maker, three taylors, three shoe makers, two hatter's shops and one brewery. There is likewise in this town, one ordained clergyman, of the Baptist persuasion, one lawyer and two physicians. The road from Pittsburgh to Mansfield and Upper Sandusky, and likewise that from Erie to Columbus passes through this place. The road from Zanesville to Granger and Cleveland passes through this town, as likewise might be added the road from the termination of the great Cumberland road north-westerly to Lower Sandusky, and thence to Perrysville, at the head of ship navigation, on the Miami-of-the-Lake, and onward to Detroit. The population consists chiefly of emigrants from Pennsylvania. There are, however, some from the state of New-York, and the eastern states.— The population amounts to about 6500.* Its surplus produce is consumed by the numerous emigrants, who are crowding into the county. Ultimately its commerce will find its way to the shores of Lake Erie, distant only 46 miles.

Jeromesville—A new village on Jerome's creek, near the Indian village, and fifteen miles west of Worcester.

Jeromestown, an Indian village and settlement, on the road from Wooster to Mansfield.

Paintville—A new town on the road from Wooster to New Philadelphia, fifteen miles S. E. of the first place.

Artificial mounds of considerable size is found in this county. A brick was found in 1816, in digging a cellar in Wooster, under the

---

* Letter from Wm. B. Raymond, Dec. 28, 1816.

stump of a large oak tree, and about four feet below the surface of the earth. It was of the size and appearance of a common brick. There were two others found in that cellar, that were less perfect in shape and consistence.

STARK COUNTY,

Has Harrison and Tuscarawas south, Columbiana east, Portage north, and Wayne west. The Tuscarawas branch of the Muskingum river runs from north to south entirely through the county, on the western side, and is navigable as high up as the county extends for keel-boats of any burthen. Big Sandy, a large creek, falls into the Tuscarawas near the southern boundary of the county. Nimishillen is a large creek which falls into Big Sandy on the north side, about four miles from its confluence with the Tuscarawas, and is one of the best mill streams in the state, with a sufficiency of water at all times of the year to drive water works of any description. Adjoining this creek, and about four miles from Canton are immense banks of iron ore of a superior quality. The building of a furnace is now in contemplation. There are in the neighborhood of Canton, a number of excellent bridges; the first of importance is a toll bridge over the Tuscarawas river, about eight miles west of Canton, and one mile from Kendal, on the road from Canton to Wooster. It is 612 feet in length, erected on stone piers about 20 feet in height. The next in importance is over Nimishillen creek, one mile east of Canton, 650 feet in length, built on wooden piles; besides a number of others of less importance over the several branches of the Nimishillen creek.

Canton, the seat of justice, is handsomely situated on an elevated plain, in the forks of Nimishillen creek. Its latitude has never been ascertained by actual observation, but being about eleven English miles south of the northern boundary of the county, may be correctly enough stated at 40 deg. 50 min. north latitude, and four deg. 30 min. west longitude from Washington City; and is distant from Steubenville 50 miles north-west; from Pittsburgh 95 miles west, from Columbus 120 miles north-east. The first settlement in this county commenced in the spring of 1806, since which time the emigration has equalled, if not surpassed any thing ever witnessed in any part of the state. Agreeably to a census taken in the spring of 1815, the white male inhabitants over 21 years of age amounted to 1325, which being multiplied by 6, the probable number for every white male over 21 years of age, which is a moderate calculation, being mostly settled with young growing families, would give 7950 ; to which, add a probable increase for one year and eight months, say 1500, would give the present population at 9450. In the town of Canton, there are about eighty dwelling houses and upwards of 500 inhabitants. Also, nine mercantile stores, (besides six in other parts of the county) one cut nail factory, one wool carding machine, an oil mill, a fulling mill, four tanneries, four taverns, three boot and shoemakers, four tailors, two saddlers ; besides a number of carpenters and cabinet makers. About seven miles west of Canton, and adjoining the beautiful village of Kendal, is a woollen manufactory established by Thomas Roach, now in successful operation, on an extensive scale, and manufacturing cloth of a superb quality.*

Kendal, a new and flourishing post town, seven miles west from Canton, on the eastern side of the Tuscarawas creek. It contains fifty houses and four stores. Many rich farmers reside in its vicinity.

Osnaburgh, a new village five miles east of Canton, on the road leading to New-Lisbon.

GUERNSEY COUNTY,

Has parts of Washington and Monroe south, Bellmont and part of Harrison east, Tuscarawas north, and Muskingum west ; watered almost exclusively by Wills' creek and its branches. Surface broken, soil generally second quality. It is divided into nine townships, viz : Cambridge, Wills, Westland, Oxford, Seneca, Madison, Buffalo, Wheeling and Richland. The bottoms of Wills' creek are fertile and well cultivated. The culture of foreign grapes has been introduced into this county.

Cambridge, the chief town and seat of justice, is situated on the right bank of Wills' creek, at the intersection of the road leading

---

* Letter of John F. Coulter, of Canton, January, 1817.

from Zanesville to Wheeling. It has about sixty houses, three taverns, four stores, and a post-office. Wills' creek has good mill seats, a little above this town. A toll bridge 175 yards long has been built across Wills' creek, at this place.

MONROE COUNTY,

Has Washington south, the Ohio river east, Belmont north, and Guernsey west. It is watered by branches of Duck, Pawpaw, Little Muskingum, Sunfish and Capteena creeks, all running into the Ohio. In surface, soil, timber and productions, it closely resembles Belmont and Guernsey. Coal mines and iron ore have been discovered on Sunfish creek.

Woodfield, a new town, is the county seat. It is situated on high ground, in Centre township, in a central part of the county, fourteen miles from the Ohio river, and 35 miles N. W. of Marietta.

BELMONT COUNTY,

Has Monroe south, the Ohio river east, Harrison north and Guernsey west. It is watered by Indian Wheeling, M'Mahon's and Capteena creeks. It is hilly and broken, excepting the bottoms of the Ohio. Timber—oak, hickory, sugar maple, &c.

St. Clairsville, the seat of justice for the above county, is situated on an elevated hill, 70 mills eastwardly from Zanesville, and 11 west of Wheeling. The surrounding country is broken, but remarkably healthy. This town contains upwards of 150 houses, court house, jail, three houses for public worship, for Friends, Methodists, and Presbyterians; a market, two printing-offices, fifteen stores, a bank, and about 750 inhabitants.

HARRISON COUNTY,

Has Belmont south, Jefferson east, parts of Columbia and Stark north and Tuscarawas west. It is watered by Stillwater and other branches of the Tuscarawas, and creeks and brooks running into the Ohio. Its surface waving, and in most parts hilly. Timber—oak, chesnut, hickory, with some sugar maple, cherry and black walnut. This county is settled chiefly by emigrants from Pennsylvania. It abounds with coal mines, freestone, limestone, and a fine white, soft, tenacious clay, fit for manufacturing purposes.

Cadiz, a small village of 20 houses, is situated on a hill, 26 miles west of Steubenville, on the Zanesville road. This county has four or five other villages, mostly new and small.

JEFFERSON COUNTY,

Has a part of Belmont south, Ohio river east, Columbiana north, and Harrison west. It is watered by Indian Short, Indian, Wills' and Yellow creeks, all running into the Ohio. The surface of this county is broken; but the soil is of an excellent quality, and capable of producing wheat, corn, rye, oats and flax. It is one of the oldest settled counties in the state. The principal towns are Steubenville and Mount-Pleasant.

Steubenville, is delightfully situated on the first and second banks of the Ohio, 72 miles by water below Pittsburgh, and 20 above Wheeling. It is nearly as large as Pittsburgh, and promises to rival the first cities of the west; it contains about 400 houses, many of them elegant and costly. Its growth, for the last four years has been uncommonly rapid. I passed it in 1805, and found it so small as scarcely to be preserved in recollection during an absence of eleven years. In approaching this town in April 1816, by water, I was surprised to hear the *music* of its ponderous steam engines, several miles before I had a view of the town. It has about 40 mercantile stores, 6 taverns, post office, bookstore and printing-office, at which is published the " *Western Herald.*"

It has a fine woollen manufactory, the machinery of which is propelled by steam; steam paper mill, producing paper of a superior quality; and in quantities more than sufficient to supply ten of the surrounding counties. A steam grist mill; stone cotton factory, brewery, distillery, soap and candle factory. It is not long since lots in this village, 60 by 180 feet, sold for one hundred dollars each; many of them now command from 10 to 15,000 dollars each.

Mount Pleasant, twelve miles north of Steubenville, has about 150 houses, 7 stores, 3 taverns, 3 saddler's, 3 hatter's, 4 blacksmith's, 4 weaver's, 6 boot and shoe maker's, 8 carpenter's, 3 taylor's, 3 cabinet maker's, 1 baker's, 1 apothecary's, and 2 waggon maker's shops ; 2 tanneries; 1 shop for making wool carding machines ; 1 with a machine for spinning thread from *flax ;* 1 nail factory ; 2 wool carding machines. The public buildings are a meeting house belonging to the society of Friends, built of brick, two stories high, 92 feet by 60 ; a brick school house, 46 by 22 feet, and a brick market house, 32 by 16. Within the distance of six miles from the town, are 9 merchant mills, 2 grist mills, 12 saw mills, a paper mill with 2 vats, a woollen factory with 4 looms, and 2 fulling mills.

COLUMBIANA COUNTY.

Has Jefferson and the Ohio river south, Pennsylvania east, Trumbull and a part of Portage north, and Stark west. It is watered by Little Beaver and branches of Big Beaver river. This county in surface, soil, extent and character of population, has a strong resemblance to Jefferson. It is rich in agricultural products, mills, coal mines, iron ore and valuable timber. It contains about forty grist and saw mills ; several extensive manufactories of cotton and woollen, a furnace and several forges.

Fairfield, is the seat of justice. There are eight or ten other villages, nearly new.

Note—The counties of Columbiana, Stark, Wayne and Richland are bounded north by New Connecticut, or the 41st degree of latitude. On the south these counties are bounded by Jefferson, Harrison, Tuscarawas, Coshocton and Knox ; south of these and north of the Muskingum, are Belmont, Monroe, Guernsey and parts of Muskingum and Washington—between the Muskingum and the eastern branches of the Miami, or more properly the Miami country, are Gallia, Athens, Fairfield, Licking, Franklin, Champaign, Pickaway, Ross, Pike, Scioto, Adams, Highland, Clinton, Fayette and Delaware. The counties situated north of lat. 41, are comprised within the tracts usually termed *New Connecticut,* and the *Fire Lands.*

NEW CONNECTICUT,

Is bounded by Lake Erie on the north, by Indian lands west, by the parallel of N. lat. 41. south, and by Pennsylvania east. Its length is 120 miles, and average width about 45, and its area about 5349 square miles or 4,000,000 acres. It is divided into seven counties, viz :—

ASHTABULA COUNTY,

Is bounded by Lake Erie north, Geauga west, Trumbull south, and Pennsylvania east. It is watered by the Ashtabula, and numerous creeks.

TRUMBULL COUNTY,

Lies south of Ashtabula, north of Columbiana, west of Pennsylvania, and east of Portage county. It is watered by branches of the Big Beaver, running into the Ohio, and Grand river of the Lake.

PORTAGE COUNTY,

Lies north of Stark and Wayne, west of Trumbull, south of Geauga, and east of Medina ; and is watered by branches of Ashtabula, Big Beaver, Tuscarawas, and Grand and Chagrin rivers.

GEAUGA COUNTY,

Has Lake Erie north, Cayahoga county west, Portage south, and Ashtabula east; and is watered by Grand and Chagrin rivers.

CAYAHOGA COUNTY,

Lies west of Geauga, south of Lake Erie, east of Huron, and north of Medina. It is watered by Cayahoga and Rocky rivers besides numerous large creeks.

MEDINA COUNTY.

Is bounded south by parts of Wayne and Richland, east by Portage, north by Cayahoga, and west by Huron. It is watered by head branches of Cayahoga, Rocky and Black rivers, and the extreme branches of the Muskingum.

HURON COUNTY,

Is bounded south by Richland, or the parallel of N. lat. 41, and Indian lands ; east by Medina and Cayahoga counties, north by Lake Erie, and west by Indian lands. It is large enough, when properly settled, to form three additional counties ; and is watered by Black, Vermillion, and Huron rivers, Pipe and Cold creeks, and Sandusky and Portage rivers.

SURFACE, SOIL, TIMBER.

The surface of this extensive tract, is neither hilly nor champaign; but sufficiently undulating to give a quick motion to the streams, and afford facilities in removing the timber from the earth. All the large streams have gullied for themselves, deep narrow vallies. The Ashtabula and Grand rivers, flow four or five hundred feet below the surface of the bordering hills. The banks of the Chagrin, Cayahoga, and Rocky rivers, are less elevated ; and those of the streams west of the last named river, gradually diminish as we proceed westwardly : For example, the banks of Pipe creek, Sandusky, and Portage, are comparatively low; and the country west of Huron river, also approaches to the champaign character. The whole tract has a northern inclination.

The timber of these tracts, consist of oak—white, black, red and yellow; chesnut, elm—red, white and slippery ; linden or basswood, hickory, black walnut and beech; maple, sugar and soft ; cucumber tree, ash—red, white, blue and black ; white pine, spruce, hemlock, larch, horse chesnut, sycamore, wild cherry, dogwood, honey locust, aspin, black poplar, birch—black and white ; alder, witch hazel, spice wood, sassafras, crab apple, plum, red mulberry, service tree, horn-beam and cotton tree.

The soil is loam, sandy in places. deep, black vegetable mould, clay and gravel.

From the western limits of Pennsylvania to the mouth of Rocky river, is a strip of country, bordering on Lake Erie, about three

S s.

miles wide, generally of a sandy and gravelly soil, covered with two or three inches of black mould, and a growth of hickory, chesnut and oak, with some black walnut and butternut. This soil proves peculiarly congenial to the growth of wheat, corn, rye, oats, barley and fruit—but not so natural to grass, as the country immediately south, which has a moister and deeper soil; and which is clothed with a heavy growth of sugar maple, beech, tulip, cucumber and black walnut. The beech and maple country is preferred by many, on account of its greater fertility, and the luxuriance of its pasturage and meadows. The plants and shrubs are such as are common to the western counties of New-York and Pennsylvania, besides, several unknown to these states.*

GEOLOGICAL.

The order of the earth's strata is, 1. A deep vegetable mould, except in places near the lake ; loam or clay of great thickness ; in oak and chesnut land, reddish and friable ; in the beech and maple region, grey. 2. Gravel or sand, of unequal depths, according to the elevation or depression of the surface ; wherever sand is found, it is stratafied with water marks. 3. Ash-colored freestone, compact slate, or blue clay. 4. Quicksand, where water is obtained, which is excellent under sand stone, and unpleasant under blue clay.

The fossil productions of these counties, are of great importance to the inhabitants. Coal is found on the south and south-east parts of the Western Reserve, and near Lake Erie on Rocky

---

* Mr. Granger enumerates the following species, viz : Leather wood, papaco, (*annona tribola*) many species of elder, hazel-nut, sumac, ninebark, red-bud, wild rose and eglantine, honeysuckle and woodbine, grapes, mealy tree, or guelder rose, buttonwood, raspberries, blackberries, dewberries, gooseberries, black currants, whortleberries, ivy, mountain ivy, mountain laurel, bitter-sweet, prickly ash, May apple, wintergreen, rattle weed, sweet flag, puccoon or blood root, centaury, cucumber root, ladies' bedstraw, poke, winter cherry, Indian turnip or wake robin, gentian, ginseng, Virginia snake root, Seneca snake root, black flower, white hellebore, Solomon's seal, mint, cat mint, balm, pennyroyal, thorn apple, wild hops, Indian berry, cresses, pleurisy root, wild ginger or coltsfoot, wild oats, (*zizania aquatica*) worm seed, cardinal flower, partridge berry, mullen, deadly night-shade, skunk cabbage, water hemlock, cicuta, cranberry, strawberry, hoarhound, elecampane, May weed, arrow head, henbane, ground ivy, gold thread, Columbo, Avens, and Indian hemp, (*Urtica Whitlowia,*)

river. Almost every town has salt licks : when bored to the depth of 200 feet, they are said to be rich. Salt has been made in Trumbull county, without boring. Sulphur, chalybeate, and aluminous springs are numerous.

Allum and copperas are found in the high slate banks of the large streams.* Iron-ore, bog and rock, is abundant, and proves to be good. Gypsum, chrystalized and grey, is found on the Caya-hoga and Sandusky rivers. Limestone is found in every county; but is most abundant in Huron, on the prairies between Huron and Sandusky rivers. Mill-stones, grind-stones and whetstones, are made in several parts of the Reserve.

The road from Erie to Cleveland continues, the greater part of the way, on an alluvial ridge, of about the height and width of a well raised turnpike road. When closely examined, one is ready to exclaim, " this was once the margin of Lake Erie; this mound has been raised by its waves." This natural turnpike consists of sand, pebbles, and shells, similar to those on the beach of the lake.

TOWNS AND SETTLEMENTS.

Warren, the seat of justice for Trumbull county, is the oldest village in the northern parts of Ohio. It is situated near the Mahoning branch of the Big Beaver. This country is the most populous of any in the Reserve, and has several forges, and a furnace. Wild lands are worth from 5 to 15 dollars an acre. Improved farms have been sold as high as 15 dollars, for an entire tract.

Harpersfield, the seat of justice for Ashtabula, is situated on the road leading from Erie to Cleveland, some miles east of Ashtabula river. Here is an old settlement, extending along the road for several miles—and is chiefly remarkable for the abundance of the peach orchards, the most extensive of any in the United

* Ralph Granger, Esq. of Warren, is the only writer, I believe, who has thrown much light on the geology of this country. " Allum," he says, " is very abundant. Almost all the schistus would afford it upon upon roasting and exposure."

States, and fine dairies. *Austinsburgh,* is situated a few miles south of Harpersfield. There are numerous mills on the Ashtabula. Pine timber is found, in limited quantities, on the Ashtabula, Grand and Chagrin rivers. Pine boards are exported to Canada from Grand river.

Paynsville, is situated on the left bank of Grand river, about one mile from the lake. It has about forty houses—several mills and three stores; it has a high, dry, sandy plain in its rear.

Ravenna, the seat of justice for Portage, is situated in the centre of populous settlements; in its neighborhood, is an abundance of iron ore, which is very rich—a ton and a half of ore yields *one ton of iron.*

Cleveland, is situated on the right bank of the Cayahoga, half a mile from Lake Erie. Its site is dry, sandy and elevated two hundred feet above the level of the river and lake; nevertheless, bilious fevers and agues, have frequently afflicted the inhabitants. The cause is to be ascribed to the surf of the lake's choaking up the river, and causing a stagnation of its waters, for three miles upwards. There are about forty or fifty houses. The view of the lake is charming. The soil for three or four miles east and south is sandy. Timber—oak and hickory.

Hudson, is situated on the road leading from Cleveland to Canton, near Tinker's creek, running into the Cayahoga.

Medina and *Huron* are now receiving a great number of emigrants. The first is beautifully watered, has large borders of unimproved lands; vast quantities of iron ore; a furnace is now building; as is also a great number of mills. The land between the Cayahoga and Rocky rivers, near the lake, is poor; to the west of Rocky river the aspect and quality of the soil improves very much, until we approach Black river; between which and Vermillion the soil is generally of a second quality, except on the lake shore, and generally too low to suit nice judges of farming land. Up Vermillion there is much poor white oak land, too wet to be healthy. I consider the mouth of Black and Vermillion rivers, to be unsuited to health. The banks of these streams are low, and in some places marshy for some distance upwards. From the Vermillion to Huron, the country continues of a rich soil, but too low, in many situations, to promise health. The bottoms of Huron have proved sickly for eight or ten miles up, after which the country is uncommonly healthy. Timber—sugar maple, beech, elm, oak, chesnut; honey locust and buckeye, on the bottoms. So salubrious is the air, and so excellent the water above the forks, that it has already become proverbial with the inhabitants, residing near the mouth of the river, to say, that " the people living above the forks have received leases of their lives." The prairies commence within one mile of Huron, six or seven miles from the lake, and extend to the Miami-of-the-Lakes, interspersed with large and small bodies of wood land. The country between Huron and Sandusky, a few miles from the lake, has proved favorable to health, especially on Pipe and Cold creeks. From Pipe creek to Croghansville is 34 miles, the first half of the way prairie, variegated with strips and islets of wood land, and small ponds ; the last, timbered land, oak, hickory, black walnut, basswood.

Croghansville, is situated on the left or west bank of the Sandusky, near Fort Stephenson, eighteen miles from lake Erie. It contains about 30 houses. Fort Stephenson is situated on the west bank of the Sandusky, at the distance of 200 yards from the river, where the second banks are about 50 feet high. Seven miles above the fort are the Seneca and Delaware Indian villages. The distance from this post to Fort Meigs, is forty miles ; the road passes through the Black Swamp, which is four miles wide. The country between this road and the great meadow is too flat for cultivation, though the soil is extremely rich.

Venice, a new town, on the margin of Sandusky, is just commenced building. Since July, 1816, thirty lots have been sold ; one saw and one grist mill, are in operation within three fourths of a mile of its site, on Cold creek, a never failing stream. A grist mill, with four run of stones, a paper mill, and other water machinery, are about to be erected.

POPULATION.

The population at this moment is believed to amount to about 450,000 souls.

Enumeration of the white male inhabitants over 21 years of age, within the State of Ohio, in the year 1816.

COUNTIES.		COUNTIES.	
Tuscarawa, - - -	776	Gallia, - - -	1326
Coshocton, - - -	589	Delaware, - - -	984
Montgomery, - . -	2047	Pike, - - -	453
Warren, - - -	2413	Scioto, - - -	774
Harrison, - - -	1458	Fairfield, - - -	2733
Preble, - - -	1067	Licking, - - -	1267
Butler, - - -	2377	Fayette, - - -	741
Knox, - - -	850	Belmont, - - -	2439
Pickaway - - -	1355	Miami, - - -	1116
Stark, - - -	1335	Highland, - - -	591
Franklin, - - -	1351	Richland, - - -	591
Trumbull, - - -	1361	Madison, - - -	1566
Geauga, - - -	523	Jefferson, - - -	2937
Clermont, - - -	2448	Washington, - -	1419
Wayne, - - -	759	Monroe, - - -	271
Portage, - - -	1153	Muskingum, - -	2238
Cayahoga, - - -	494	Ross, - - - -	3311
Ashtabula, - - -	639	Hamilton, - - -	3725
Clinton, - - -	920	Columbiana, - -	2725
Athens, - - -	792	Champaign, - -	2097
Guernsey, - - -	953	Huron, - - -	388
Green, - - -	1615		
Adams, - - -	2083	Total,	64,550

INDIANS.

The following statement shews the number of Indians, of all ages and sexes, within the limits of the state of Ohio, in 1816.*

Wyandots, on Sandusky river and its waters, - - - 695

Shawanœse, on the head of the Auglaize river, and on the upper waters of the Miami of Ohio ; principal village, Wapaghkonetta, 27 miles north of Piqua, - - - - - - - 840

Delawares in Ohio, on the head waters of the Sandusky & Muskingum, 161

Senecas, who reside between Upper and Lower Sandusky, at and near Seneca Town, - - - - - - 450

Senecas, Munseys, and Delawares, on the head waters of the Miami of Ohio, at and near Lewis' Town, 30 miles N. E. of Piqua, - 434

Ottowas, who inhabit the south shores of Lake Erie, about Miami Bay, near fort Meigs, and on the Auglaize river—numbers not stationary—about - - - - - - 450

TOTAL, 3036

*This statement was furnished by J. Johnston, Esq. of Piqua.

TENNESSEE,

IS situated between 35 and 36 30 N. lat. bounded north by Kentucky, west by the Mississippi river, south by the New State, [Mississippi] and Alabama Territory; East by North Carolina. The rivers have all a western direction, flowing into the Tennessee, Cumberland, and Mississippi.—The state is divided into East and West Tennessee, by the Cumberland mountains. East Tennessee is watered by the Holston, Notachucky, French Broad, Tellico, Richland, Clinch, Big Emery, and Hiwasee rivers, all head branches of the Tennessee. West Tennessee is watered by Cumberland, Tennessee, Elk, Buffaloe, Duck, Swan, Wolf of Cumberland, Oby, Forked Deer, Obian, Hatchy, and Wolf of the Mississippi.

The Tennessee is one of the largest rivers in the western country, being nearly as long and as broad as the Ohio, and navigable for large boats, 1100 miles. It enters the Ohio 13 miles, below the mouth of Cumberland, and 57 above that of the Ohio. Several of its tributaries are also large navigable rivers, particularly Holston, Notachucky, French Broad, Tellico, Hiwassee, Clinch and Duck; all of which are from the south, except the two last. The surface and soil of this state west of the Cumberland mountains, is nearly similar to the southern counties of Kentucky, and the northern parts of Mississippi, and the Alabama Territory.— The greater part of the country is broken, free from swamps, and remarkably healthy. The fertile cotton lands produce forest trees of an extraordinary growth. Cane abounds in the vallies and on the rich hills. Saltpetre, tobacco, cotton, hogs, and cattle, are the grand staples. There is a large body of rich land, belonging to the United States, between Duck river and the Muscle Shoals, and south of the Tennessee river, below the Shoals, extending to the Mississippi, and down that river to the mouth of the Wolf— containing about 6,000,000 of acres. This part of the state affords fine situations for enterprising emigrants. The water in many parts, is excellent; the bottoms of Duck and Buffalo rivers, are very valuable, free from stagnant waters, and bearing thick cane brakes. There is a deficiency of water on the limestone lands, in consequence of the fissures in the beds of the creeks, which causes the water to sink and form subterranean streams, which only show themselves in the bottoms of the *coves* and *sinks*. Yet the soil is of the best quality, and well adapted to the cotton culture. Iron ore, freestone, and caves abounding with saltpetre, is found in various parts of the new cession. By far the greater part of West Tennessee is admirably well watered. I have travelled extensively in this state, and never saw 50 acres of swampy ground, unless at the confluence of some of the large rivers, where the newly formed alluvion had not acquired the consistence of *terra firma*.— Fevers are almost unknown to the inhabitants, except on the bottoms of the Cumberland, Tennessee and Mississippi rivers. I know of no country where diseases are so rare, or where physicians have so little employ ; children, remarkably robust and healthy. The climate proves congenial to northern constitutions.— About half a dozen families removed to this state, from the state of New-York, nearly 30 years ago. Residing in the same county from which they migrated. I have twice had occasion to visit them, in Overton county, near the junction of Oby and Wolf rivers.— The unprecedented health and increase of *Simeon Barber's* family, since their residence in Tennessee, deserves to be put on record. He left New-York with a wife and eight children, five girls and three boys : his daughters are all married. The eldest has *ten* children, the second *ten*, the third *eleven*, the fourth *ten*, and the fifth *five ;* the eldest son *ten*, the second *seven*, the third *three ;* making a *total* of SIXTY-SIX, *all perfectly formed, and living in May*, 1816. They have enjoyed almost uninterrupted health.— Old Mr. Barber has six or seven great grand-children, which makes the increase from one family upwards of 70 souls. Not a single death occurred in the different branches of the family, until two of the sons removed to Indiana, in 1816, when two of the children died of the whooping cough. Mr. Barber is now 77 years of age, and his wife 74. I do not recollect having ever seen in the northern states, the heads of any single family, of so advanced an age, possessing so great a degree of activity, bodily and mental vigor, or of so young and healthful appearance. Mr. B. thinks nothing of walking fifteen or twenty miles ; and labors occasionally in his fields. None of the other families which accompanied him, have had the same rapid increase of numbers ; but they have enjoyed fine health, and all concur in representing the country as healthy beyond example. Indeed, from my own experience and observation, I do not hesitate to pronounce the country between Cumberland and Tennessee rivers, as incomparably the most healthy of any part of the western country, from the Great Lakes to the Gulf of Mexico. Perhaps the country south of Tennessee river—from the French Broad to the Mississippi, as far south as the junction of the Black Warrior and Tombigbee rivers—might with justice be included in the salubrious region. The southern half of the late Mississippi Territory, and Louisiana, are not *generally* unfavorable to health, but *locally* so. The same remark also applies to Ohio, Indiana, and the Michigan, Illinois, North-Western, and Missouri Territories.

The Cumberland Mountains run through the state from north to south, and spurs or lateral branches extend west to the vicinity of Nashville. Their summits between Wolf river (of Cumberland) and the Big Emery, are dreary and precipitous, in places; and bear frequent evidences of the action of water—even on the highest peaks. As we approach the head branches of Wolf and Oby, the soil becomes deep and fertile, even on the knobs and ridges where the ascents and declivities are so steep as to render it impracticable to travel on horseback. Upon these hills, or rather small mountains, are found tulip, beech, and sugar maple trees of the largest dimensions ; little or no underwood; abundance of ginseng and various other medicinal plants. Between the mountains, are " *coves*" of ten, fifteen or twenty arches, similar to those in Wayne county, (Ken.) already described, with the best freestone water, and covered with the largest trees and canebrakes. No situation can be more lonesome and secluded than these gloomy retreats, when found at the distance of fifty or sixty miles from the residence of a human being. I once had occasion to pass, alone, from Clinch river to Nashville, a distance of nearly two hundred miles, across the mountains : the nature of the country rendered it necessary to perform the route on foot. For the convenience of water, I was obliged to encamp several nights in these abodes of desolation and silence. In several instances, I was forcibly impressed with the power of solitude. The air—nay, all nature, appeared at rest—not a sound struck the ear ; the very leaves were

T t

330 **WESTERN GAZETTEER, &c.**

as motionless as icicles. In this awful stillness, the wolf's dire howl would have been music to my ear.

Caves, of great depth and extent, are found throughout the state; in the Cumberland Mountain, on the summit of an elevated peak, is one of unfathomable profundity—A stone thrown or dropt into its frightful orifice, returns no sound. I once drank at a subterranean brook, in Sullivan county, which was large enough to drive a mill, and as I judged, at least 400 feet beneath the surface of the earth.*

---

* This cave is on the summit of a high hill; within a few rods of its mouth there is a *crater*, gulf, or *sink*, 400 feet deep, and about 200 yards wide at the top, gradually narrowing towards the bottom like a funnel, but too steep to admit of *voluntary* descent. The descent into the cave is easy—after which several spacious rooms are passed—when we come to a narrow passage—through which one is obliged to creep, and use great caution to prevent the extinction of the torch, as there is a pretty strong current of air constantly setting towards the mouth of the cave : beyond this passage, at the distance of twenty paces, commences a difficult descent of several hundred feet, which brings one within hearing of the murmurs of the brook; still 70 paces distant—and to reach which, without a broken neck, the utmost care is necessary. The bottoms and stones of this brook are similar in every respect to common brooks in mountainous countries. The water was cold and perfectly agreeable to the taste. I was told by the person who acted as a guide, that we could see *day light* by ascending the stream a few rods, which I found to be the case. But the aperture which admitted the light, prevented our ingress to the crater, being barely sufficient to enable us to survey the huge and frightful masses which projected from the sides, or lay in chaotic piles at the bottom of the gulf.

APPENDIX.

SKETCHES OF SOME OF THE WESTERN COUNTIES OF PENNSYLVANIA.

BEAVER COUNTY,

IS situated on both sides of the Ohio river and Big Beaver creek, in the western part of Pennsylvania; it is bounded on the west by Brook county of Virginia, and Columbiana county of the state of Ohio, by Mercer county on the north, Butler on the east, and Alleghany county on the south-east; its length from north to south on the west side is about thirty-six miles, in breadth eighteen miles; divided into fifteen townships, containing in the year 1810, 12,168 inhabitants; the number must be considerably increased since. The climate and situation may be considered very favorable to health; the face of the country generally hilly, interspersed with tracts of excellent land, and others not so fertile, though suitable for the production of good crops of well filled wheat; the bottom land produces corn in abundance. Unimproved land sells at four dollars, improved farms from six to twelve dollars per acre; the price of wheat previous to the late war, was from sixty to sixty-seven cents per bushel; it is now from $1 to $1 25; rye, from 75 cts. to $1; barley, $1; corn, 75 cents; oats, 37 1-2 cents; beef, 5, and pork, from 6 to 7 dollars per cwt.; salt from $6 50 to $7 50 per barrel of 250 lbs. nett wt. The country is well situated for commerce, having the Ohio river passing through the southern part of the county, and the Big Beaver creek, which is navigable for Durham boats (except the falls) to several miles above Warren, in Trumbull county, state of Ohio, intersecting the county from north to south, till it empties into the Ohio river near Beaver-town.

Beaver-town contains between 50 and 60 dwelling houses, an excellent brick court-house, a stone prison, a banking house, a printing-office, and a new brick building for an academy. The road from Pittsburgh to Detroit, and to places situate in the north-eastern part of the state of Ohio passes this way. There are in this county two furnaces and one forge for making iron : one of the furnaces is at Bassingheim, or Conoquenessing, a creek putting into Big Beaver, on the east side; the other furnace, and the forge, are at Brighton, on the falls of Big Beaver. Those falls are a continuation of rapids for more than two miles; they are well calculated for giving motion to machinery, and susceptible of great improvement. In addition to the above, there are erected on them, 4 grist-mills, 4 saw-mills, 1 trip-hammer, 1 woollen manufactory, 1 oil-mill, and 1 cotton-spinning factory: and there yet remain unoccupied situations, and water sufficient for many more. The chief articles of export, are flour, porter, beer, cast and bar-iron, sent down the river; those carried up to Pittsburgh, consist of grain, beef-cattle, beer, porter, pig-iron, castings, pot-ash, linseed-oil, woollen cloth, cotton yarn, country linnen, &c. The county abounds with iron ore, stone coal, and limestone. There are several villages in the county; in one of which, Greensburgh, about ten miles north of Beaver-town, is an academy, where the languages are taught. It may be remarked, that all kinds of grain, common to the climate, are generally cultivated in the county.*

MERCER COUNTY,

Is bounded south by Beaver, east by Venango, north by Crawford and east by the state of Ohio. It is watered by the Big Beaver, Pymahoning, Shenango, Neshamoe and Sandy creeks.—There is much good land in this county—a considerable part of it is beech and maple land; well watered and healthy.

BUTLER COUNTY,

Is bounded east by Armstrong, north by Venango, west by Beaver and south by Alleghany. It is watered by Buffaloe creek running into the Alleghany, and by Connoquenessing and its various branches running into Big Beaver. The timber is principally oak—soil light, but producing small grain and grass—surface moderately hilly. This county is chiefly remarkable for being the residence of the Harmonists.

HARMONIE SOCIETY,

This Society originated in the dutchy of Wurtemburgh, about 30 years ago, and emigrated from that country to the United States in consequence of the rigor and intolerance of the Lutheran church, George Rapp, the principal leader of the Society, and several followers, arrived in Philadelphia in 1803. They were the next year followed by the whole Society, who embarked at Amsterdam, to the number of 160 families. Rapp purchased 5700 acres of land, in this county. In February, 1805, a constitution was organized, whose principles were the same as the first Apostolic church, (See Acts iv. 32.) " And the multitude of them that believed, were of one heart, and of one soul: neither said any

---

* Letter of A. Mendenhall, Esq. of Beaver-town, March, 1817.

of them, that aught, of the things which he possessed was his own; but they had all things common." There is no such thing as individual property—every thing belongs to the Society—all labor is in common. All the produce and provisions, are deposited in a large brick store, and served out according to the wants of the different members. During the winter of 1805, they erected 18 log houses, 18 by 24, and a large barn. Ground to the amount of 150 acres, was cleared for corn, 40 for potatoes and 15 for meadow. A grist and saw mill were erected, and a race way dug three-fourths of a mile long. Thirty additional houses were built in the autumn of the same year. In 1806, 300 acres of land were cleared for corn, 58 for meadow; a public inn, several dwelling houses, a framed barn, 100 feet long, and an oil mill were erected. The next year, among other improvements, 400 acres were cleared; a brick store house, saw mill and beer brewery were built. Every succeeding year has added to their wealth and buildings. They have now several capacious brick and framed barns—a brick meeting house, ware house, fulling, dying, grist and hemp mills—carding machines, spinning jennies, distilleries, &c. The annual quantity of produce, consisting of wheat, rye, oats, barley and potatoes, exceeds 40,000 bushels, besides 5000 lbs. of flax and hemp, 100 gallons of sweet oil, distilled from the white poppy, and the product of twelve acres of vineyard. This truly economical people appropriate every foot of earth within the limits of their little republic, to some object of utility. Hills which are too steep for the plow or the drag, are planted with the vine. Their vineyard is situated on the south side of a steep hill, and exhibits to the eye a succession of benches, rising one above the other, like the galleries of our churches—the front of each bench or flat being walled up with stones, to prevent the sliding or caving of the earth.— They have about 3000 acres of ground cleared; have a large stock of cattle, and about 1000 sheep; part of which are *merino*. Their *cloth* has obtained a high reputation. There are about 100 mechanics, who work for the country as well as the society. The number of common laborers amounts to about 700 men, who will readily dispose of a large job of work—a 100 acre field is scarcely the labor of a day. Nothing can exceed their industry. Idleness and intemperance are unknown among them. Food, clothing and physic, are all received from the public stores. Their costume is very plain; the women dress with no motive of conquest. All are in *uniform*—a linsey or woollen jacket and petticoat, a close black cap, with a patch of cotton or wool on the crown, and tied under the chin, are their constant attire. The whole Society attends divine worship on Sunday. The venerable Rapp fills the pulpit. Every thing, in short, proceeds with the regularity of clock work.

Their village is called *Harmonic*, after the society. It is situated on the right bank of the Connoquenessing creek, which heads near the Alleghany river, and runs into the Big Beaver, about 50 miles above its entrance into the Ohio. Over this creek they have a bridge 220 feet long.—The creek affords many facilities for water machinery. The surrounding country is excellent for pasturage—but not of the first quality for grain. This interesting little colony have principally removed to the banks of the Wabash, below Vincennes, where they have commenced the culture of the vine, and the manufacture of broad cloths from merino wool.

VENANGO COUNTY,

Lies north of Butler, east of Mercer, south of Crawford and west of Armstrong. It is watered by Alleghany river, French, Sugar, Sandy, Oil, Mahoning and Toby's creeks. Soil light and gravelly, except on the bottoms ; timber, oak, chesnut, beech, sugar maple and ash. It is thinly settled, abounding with desolate plantations, " where the fox looks out of the window, and the tall grass waves to the wind."

Franklin, the seat of justice, is situated partly on the right bank of French creek, and partly on the west side of the Alleghany river, at their confluence. It contains about 40 houses ; surrounding country poor and broken ; but healthy. Eleven miles northeast of Franklin, are the celebrated oil springs, which rise from the bed of Oil creek, about one mile from its entrance into the Alleghany river. The supply of oil is inexhaustible ; one can collect a gallon in an hour or two. The place must have been much frequented in former times, as both banks of the creek abound with excavations. covering several acres, made no doubt by persons in search of the oil.

CRAWFORD COUNTY,

Is about 50 miles square : bounded east by Warren, north by Erie, and west by Mercer, and the Ohio state line ; south by Venango. It is finely watered by French creek, Cussawago, Little Conneaut, Pymahoning, Mud and Sugar creeks, and branches of Oil and Broken Straw creeks. Much of this country, west of French creek, is rich beech and maple land.—The southern part oak timbered ; soil light and poor for grain, except rye ; grass grows well. The bottoms of French creek, between Meadville and Mud creek, are wide and rich ; timber, oak, black walnut, bass wood, some honey locust and sugar maple. East of French creek, towards Warren, the timber is pine, oak, hemlock, maple—soil poor, surface broken, and beautifully watered. Above Mud creek, the timber is beech, butternut, black walnut, sugar maple, elm, with very little underwood ; soil black and deep, readily yielding to the foot, covered in places with nettles, like the country near the dividing ridge, between Colt's Station and Le Bœuf. There are already a considerable number of people from the eastern states established in this county, who are much pleased with the country. Wild land sells at from $3 to 10, according to situation.

Meadville, is situated on the cast side of French creek, on an extensive plain or bottom, and contains about 120 houses. Its growth has been slow, and the rise of property discouraging.— Town lots in central situations, are remarkably low, not above four hundred dollars for the most eligible. They were sold at auction by the proprietor. Mr. Mead, at Pittsburgh, in Dec. 1797, at the average price of $40. It has several stores and taverns, an academy, a college in prospective, arsenal, jail, court-house, post office, printing-office, at which is published a newspaper and magazine.

ERIE COUNTY.

Is bounded east by New-York, north by lake Erie, west by Ohio and south by Crawford. It is beautifully watered by fifteen or twenty handsome creeks, issuing from innumerable springs, and flowing into lake Erie; the largest of which is Twenty Mile, Sixteen Mile, Four Mile, Elk, Walnut, and Conneaut; besides French creek flowing into the Alleghany; Le Bœuf, Sugar and Miles' creeks—all running into French creek. This county is about 55 miles long, and has an average width of 30 miles; it is partly formed from the triangular tract ceded by the United States to Pennsylvania, containing 202,187 acres, which extends from the western boundary of New-York, along lake Erie 45 miles, being 18 miles wide at its base, and terminating in a point 3 miles east of the eastern limits of New-Connecticut. No section of the United States of equal extent is better supplied with mill seats and facilities for the various kinds of hydraulic machinery; but which at present are little improved. However, the spirit of improvement has commenced; land has within the last four years nearly quadrupled in value; and the settlements are fast extending. From the New-York state line to that of the state of Ohio, near Conneaut, to the distance of three miles from the lake, the soil is a sandy loam, intermixed in places with gravel and covered with two or three inches of vegetable mould; timber, chesnut, (very large) hickory, black walnut, oak, basswood, and some hemlock. This kind of land is much esteemed by Pennsylvanians; being highly favorable to grain and fruit; and in a manner exempt from frost during the season of vegetation. This narrow strip is now selling at from eight to sixteen dollars an acre, by the farm. In 1813, few improved lots were valued at more than five dollars an acre; and in 1798, the " Population Company" of Philadelphia, were making gratuitous grants of 200 acres to every actual settler, throughout the Triangle: three miles from the lake the country rises about 100 feet, and it is at the point of this elevation that the beech and maple country commences, and continues so with little variety of soil, timber and aspect, to the southern limits of the county. The timber consists of sugar maple, beech, tulip, (white wood) elm, bass wood, cucumber, white ash, butternut, interspersed with some hemlock—all large and lofty. Springs of excellent water are numerous. The soil is a deep grey loam, easily ploughed—producing fine timothy and clover ; the inhabitants confine themselves to stock-raising and dairies ; the forests have very little underwood—one will frequently meet with bodies of land on which the chief timber is sugar maple. say six or eight trees to an acre. with scarcely a single bush or shrub, but covered with a luxuriant and troublesome growth of nettles, the genuine *Urtica Whitlowi,* five or six feet high, and almost impassable.

Erie, stands on the margin of a bay, formed by two peninsulas ; has an excellent harbor for light shipping, and contains about 100 houses. It has a court house, jail, post-office, and a printing-office, from which is issued the " *Genius of the Lakes.*" Its site is a plain, and the banks of the basin, or lake, i- about 70 feet high, very steep. The largest peninsula, (*Presqu' Isle*) is seven miles long, and from half a mile to a mile and a half broad. It is a perfect desert, or heap of sand, thrown up by the surf of the lake, covered with ponds, cranberry marshes, dwarf pines, and shrubby oaks. The little peninsula is not more than half a mile long : a considerable stream of never failing water, large enough to drive a mill, enters the lake at the east end of the town. Erie is 97 miles S. S. W. of Buffalo, 136 nearly N. of Pittsburgh, and about 100 E. of Cleveland. Its trade is already considerable. The The ship-yard is about two miles above the town. The *oak* timber for the United States' ships of war, was cut near the spot ; the masts were hauled several miles. A turnpike, across the portage 16 miles long, extends from Erie to Le Bœuf creek.

Waterford, stands on the bank of Le Bœuf creek, sixteen miles south of Erie ; it contains fifteen or twenty houses, and is the point of embarkation for descending French creek into the Alleghany and Ohio.

WARREN COUNTY,

Is bounded east and north by Cattaraugus and Chatauque counties, (N. Y.) west by Crawford, and south by Venango, is large enough when settled for three or four counties of the usual size ; and is watered by the Alleghany and Connewango rivers, Broken Straw, Great and Little Oil creeks, besides numerous other large streams, running into the Alleghany from the south. The northern half of this county, watered by the head branches of Oil and Broken Straw creeks and the Connewango, will admit of dense settlements, as the land is uniformly good ; similar to the beech and maple lands of Erie county and the Holland Purchase in New-York ; and abounding with excellent springs, and meadows of nettles ; some small tracts of pine and hemlock ; but two-thirds of the county is covered with ash, beech, sugar maple, and locust, with little underwood. The remainder, although susceptible of settlement and cultivation, is chiefly valuable for the almost exhaustless quantities of pine timber, and convenient mill-seats, which are to be found in great numbers on all the streams, except Connewango, which is a deep languid stream from the New-York state line to its junction with the Alleghany. Broken Straw creek is about forty yards wide, and joins the Alleghany seven miles below the mouth of Connewango; it is brisk for the space of nineteen miles from its mouth—where it forks and becomes gentle. There are about twenty saw-mills established on its banks, all actively employed in slitting the immense white-pine forests growing along its borders. Oil creek, nearly equal in size, also abounds in mills and pine timber. This creek enters the Alleghany about forty miles below Broken Straw; the intervening country, for the distance of twenty miles from the Alleghany, is broken, of a light gravelly or clayey soil, stoney, and covered with pine, hemlock, beech, birch, and some sugar maple. There are at present very few settlements, except along the banks of the above named streams; and these depend on the lumber business, rather than the cultivation of the soil. The pines of the hills are uncommonly large, tall, and straight, suitable for shingles and masts.

Warren, the seat of justice for the county, is situated on the right bank of the Alleghany river at the entrance of the Connewango. Its site is a large dry plain, washed on the south and east by those rivers, and margined in the rear by very high hills. It contains about twenty-five houses and a saw mill. The Alleghany is here 150 yards wide, and the Connewango 100. The bottoms are narrow, but rich; soil of the uplands loamy; timber, near Warren, oak, chesnut and hickory. There is a safe and easy harbor or eddy abreast the town, at which almost all the boats and rafts, descending the Alleghany from Olean, or the Connewango, from Chautauque lake, stop to procure refreshments and relaxation. Provisions are usually scarce and exorbitantly high in price. Nothing but enterprize is wanting to give this village a respectable appearance and extensive trade. Wild lands throughout the county, from $3 to 8 an acre; and improved farms at a very small advance, say from $8 to 12 an acre. Deserted cabins are frequently met with between Warren and Meadville. About two miles north-east of Warren, is a small insulated spur of the Alleghany mountains, whose summit affords a boundless view of the surrounding country. From this elevated point, one surveys a circle of territory of 80 miles diameter.

> " A scene so rude, so wild as this,
> Yet so sublime in barrenness,
> Ne'er did my wand'ring footsteps press,
> Where'er I hap'd to roam."

U u

ARMSTRONG COUNTY.

Lies east of Butler and north of Alleghany—is very large and thinly settled; and watered by the Alleghany river, Toby's and Kiskiminitas creeks. It contains great quantities of iron ore, and extensive forests; surface, almost mountainous; soil, generally poor.

Kittaning, the seat of justice, is a pleasant village of about 70 houses, situated on the left bank of the Alleghany, thirty miles above Pittsburgh.—The bottoms are wide, and finely cultivated; in the rear a coal hill rises to the height of 200 feet. It is here that the Alleghany has become broad, deep and majestic—the prospect changes; we lose sight of the high barren hills, which constantly present themselves from Cornplanter's village to Arm-strong.

ALLEGHANY COUNTY,

Is bounded north by Butler, west by Beaver, south by Washington, east by Westmoreland. It is finely watered by the Alleghany, Monongahela, and Ohio rivers. It is watered, west of the Alleghany and Ohio rivers, by Seweekly, Pine, and Bull creeks, all pure and wholesome streams. Plum and Sandy creeks, enter the Alleghany from the east; and Chartier's creek, falling into the Ohio, about one mile below Pittsburgh.

Pittsburgh.—This city is situated on the point of land formed by the junction of the Alleghany and Monongahela rivers, and at the head of the Ohio. It is a large and flourishing place, possessing a greater number and variety of manufacturing establishments, than any other inland town in America. It contains about 1000 houses; bridges are about to be erected over the Alleghany and Monongahela rivers.—It is in N. lat. 36 43—321 miles west of Philadelphia, and 136 south of Lake Erie. The scenery of the surrounding hills is enchanting. All the hills which border the town, are stored with a boundless supply of stone coal. The principal manufacturing establishments are, a steam grist-mill, steam engine factory, slitting-mill, to which is attached a nail factory, the first of the kind in America; a cannon foundery, air furnace, cotton and woollen factories, two potteries, three breweries, &c.— There are four printing-offices, and two bookstores. A complete description of this interesting town would fill a volume.

WASHINGTON COUNTY,

Lies south of Alleghany county, and east of Brooke county in Virginia. It is a rich, well cultivated, healthy, and undulating country, abounding in coal-mines, iron-ore, and producing fine crops of grass and grain.

Washington, is situated on a pleasant ridge, 26 miles south-west of Pittsburgh. It has about 300 houses, court house, jail, two churches, several valuable manufactories, a printing-office, and post-office. The United States' great turnpike road from Cumberland to the western country, passes through this place.

Cannonsburgh, lies 14 miles S. W. of Pittsburgh; situated on the declivity of a steep hill, having Chartier's creek at the bottom. This village was commenced in 1797, by a Mr. Cannon. It now contains upwards of 150 houses. It owes its prosperity, chiefly to its college, which is becoming respectable. The original building, designed for a college, has been suffered to go to decay. The *new* edifice, when completed, will be three stories—180 feet in front; the wings each, 70 in front and 40 in width—the centre 40 in front by 60 back. " A combination of local advantages—the state of religion and morals—the abundance and cheapness of provisions, in a fertile country—inexhaustible mines of coal at hand; and the quietness and salubrity of the village, combine in rendering this a most eligible seat for a literary institution. The benefits of such an institution to the western country, growing as it is in wealth, population and refinement, are incalculable."

SKETCHES OF SOME OF THE WESTERN COUNTIES OF VIRGINIA.

BROOKE COUNTY.

This county is long and narrow; bounded north and west by the Ohio river, south by Ohio county and east by Beaver county, Pa. It is watered by several streams, the largest of which is Harman's creek, which empties into the Ohio river one mile above Steubenville. It has extensive bottoms along the Ohio. The uplands are rich, well watered, and producing fine crops of grain, grass, flax, hemp and peas; and well adapted to fruit. There is an abundant supply of coal in the hills; and emigrants in search of a pleasant and healthy residence, will find fine situations along the Ohio river, between Charleston and Wheeling.

Charleston, is pleasantly situated on the left bank of the Ohio, six miles below Steubenville and 17 above Wheeling. It contains nearly 200 buildings—ten or twelve stores, court house, jail, church, extensive pottery, printing-office and book-store. Buffalo creek joins the Ohio at the south end of the town, on which are a number of valuable grist-mills. This town is 50 miles southwest of Pittsburgh, by land; by water, 82.

OHIO COUNTY,

Is bounded west by the Ohio river, north by Brooke, east by Green and Harrison, and south by Wood county—watered by Grave and Fish creeks. This county, like Brooke, is hilly; has rich and extensive bottoms, and large quantities of unsettled lands.

The bottoms of Grave creek contain interesting vestiges of ancient population. On coming close to this mound, says the author of the Pittsburgh Navigator, you are surprised at its mountain-like appearance, and the darkness occasioned by the height of the trees on its summit over those on the plain below. Its perpendicular elevation is about 75 feet, 180 yards in circumference around its base, and 40 on its flat on the top. It appears to be a very regular circle, and forms in its rising an angle of about 80 degrees. The centre of its top is sunk in perhaps four feet, forming a basin of that depth and about eight or ten feet over. Its summit bears an aged white oak of four feet in diameter, and its sides are richly clad with a luxuriant growth of all the different kinds of trees of the forest, and of the same size and appearance. It stands in an extensive plain, having neither ditch nor rising ground near it, nor can it be discovered where the earth of which it is formed has been taken from. East of the big mound, there are several small ones in the open fields, and a number of fortifications, whose particular dimensions I did not take.

Wheeling, stands on a high bank, peninsulated by the Ohio river and Wheeling creek. The buildings are chiefly on one street, running parallel along the banks of the river, for three-fourths of a mile. The town contains about 200 houses, fourteen stores, court house, jail, church, two potteries for stone ware, nail factory, market house, rope walk and boat yard. When the Great Cumberland road, which it is supposed will intersect the Ohio at this place, is completed, Wheeling must rapidly increase in size and commercial importance.

RANDOLPH COUNTY.

A distant correspondent has communicated a sketch of this county, and pointed out the most eligible route for emigrants from New England; which is, to " cross the North River at Newburgh, the Delaware at Easton, the Susquehannah at Harrisburgh; thence through Carlisle, Shippensburgh, Chambersburgh, Green-Castle, Hancock, Cumberland, Western-Port; thence over the Alleghany —cross Cheat river at Goff's; thence to William Wamsley's and Daniel Barret, Esq's. upon the Buchanan river, or from Wamsley's to Beverly, formerly called Tygert's valley—having a brick court house and jail, public offices, and several stores; it is laid out in half-acre lots, upon three parallel streets. Building lots sell from 30 to 100 dollars. Beverly is handsomely situated, between two branches of the Valley river, and bids fair to become a place of considerable business; an association, called the New-England Company, owning large tracts of land upon the waters of Valley and Buchanan rivers, are now rapidly settling by New-England people. A large appropriation of land is made by the Company for the permanent support of moral and religious instruction. Schools and libraries are now opened in different parts of the county, having a missionary furnished by the Hampshire Missionary Society in Massachusetts. The Buchanan river is one of the principal waters of the Monongahela, uniting with the Alleghany from the north at Pittsburgh, form the Ohio. The soil of Randolph is deep and rich, producing to great perfection all species of crops that can grow in New-England, and others which cannot grow north of Virginia. Fifty bushels of corn to the acre, is a moderate crop; other grain in proportion. The usual price of wheat, is from four shillings to one dollar; rye and corn, two shillings and sixpence to three shillings. Mechanics are much wanted for the erection of mills, dwellings, &c. The face of the land is undulating and hilly, furnishing excellent mill-seats.— The water is pure, and the climate healthy. The summers are moderately cool, and winters very mild; having in spring and autumn, together, at least three months the advantage of New-England. The timber consists of oak, walnut, elm, sugar, ash, maple, bass-wood—principally hard wood. The forests furnish rich pastures for cattle, stone coal, and salt licks. Taxes are light. Several planters fatten and sell from sixty to ninety head of cattle annually, which are driven across the Alleghany to Richmond, Alexandria, Washington and Baltimore, at the average distance of about two hundred miles, and always command cash. Roads are opening in various directions, and a state road is about to be laid out from Staunton to the Ohio river, and expected to pass through the Company's land. The Little Kenhaway takes its rise and has boatable water upon the land, affording an easy communication with the Ohio river near Marietta, thence to New-Orleans, or up the Muskingum, with a few miles land carriage, may enter the Cayahoga river, Lake Erie, and thence to the Canada markets—or by the projected canal of New-York, may enter the North River. These lands, when more generally known, will probably be considered equal to any other in the market."

SKETCHES OF SOME OF THE WESTERN COUN-
TIES OF NEW-YORK.

The six western counties of this state, viz : Genesee, Allegany, Niagara, Cattaraugus, and Chautauque, except the eastern parts of the two first, constitute the " Holland Purchase," which contains about 4,000,000 of acres. This extensive tract is bounded east by a transit line running north from the Pennsylvania state line to Lake Ontario, being 97 and a half miles and eleven chains long; north by lake Ontario, west by the river Niagara, lake Erie and the Triangle of Presqu' Isle; and south by Pennsylvania. It is about 100 miles in length, with an average breadth of about 70 miles. The southern parts of this Purchase are watered by the Alleghany and its tributaries, Oswyhec, Oil, Ishau and Olean; Great Valley, and Jokki creeks; Connewango river, and branches of Broken Straw and French creeks. The waters flowing into Lake Ontario, are the Genesee river and Allen's creek; into Niagara river, Tonawanda, Murderer's, Eleven-Mile, and Ellicott's creeks; into Lake Erie, Buffalo, Quaquagagahaun, (Sunfish) Cahnahatchie, Cattaraugus, Silver, Canadaway, and Chautauque creeks. This tract was purchased, in 1797, from the Seneca Indians and the state of Massachusetts, by the late Robert Morris, of Philadelphia, for less than six cents an acre. It was surveyed into townships of six miles square, in 1790, under the direction of Joseph Ellicott, Esq. The sale of lots commenced in 1799, at from $1,25 to $2,50 an acre; the price of wild lands, at present, is from $4 to 12 : improved lands from $12 to 20, or upwards. The dividing ridge between the waters of the Ohio and the lakes, forms a zig-zag course ; approaching to within 15 or 20 miles of the Alleghany, and to within a few miles of the lake alternately. For instance, the Genesee river, Buffalo, Cattaraugus, and Chautauque, creeks, head within a short distance of the Pennsylvania line ; and the east branch of the Connewango, rises within *five* miles of Lake Erie ; the western branch, and Chautauque Lake, to within *nine* miles of the same lake. The surface south of the dividing ridge, is broken—in some places, near the Alleghany, mountainous ; to the north it gradually subsides, and becomes nearly level at and north of the road leading from Canandaigua to Buffalo. The soil is principally a deep grey loam—timber, in most parts, beech, sugar-maple, basswood, elm, white ash, with some hemlock, butternut, and black cherry. White-oak, chesnut, and hickory, are found on the shore of Lake Ontario, on the banks of Tonawanda and Genesee ; on the Cattaraugus, Canadaway, and Chautauque ; west of Chautauque creek, the shores of lake Erie abound with beautiful chesnut groves. A strip of rich, springy, beech and sugar maple land, abounding with meadows of

he Urtica Whitlowi, runs through the whole extent of the Pur-
hase from east to west, lying near the dividing ridge to the north ;
and, on an average, about 20 miles wide.

The southeastern corner of the purchase, as well as that part of
Alleghany county lying east of the transit line, is covered with extensive groves of some of the finest white pine timber in America ; and so advantageously situated, that the inhabitants can convey it at their option to the Ohio market by the Alleghany, to
Baltimore by the Tioga, Canisteo, Conhocton, and Susquehanna
rivers ; by the Genesee river to Rochester, and Canada ; the white
pine region extends from the Conhocton to the Connewango, or
rather to Oil creek in Pennsylvania. The supply of this valuable
building material is immense ; perhaps 500,000 acres—of majestic, close set groves, of the first quality—free from crooks or knots.
Yet, when we consider the extent of the demand, and the over-
action and havoc which will follow casual good markets, a few
years, it is feared, will be sufficient to level those extensive forests
with the earth.

Chautauque Lake, within twenty miles of the western extremity
of the tract, is 22 miles long, and from two to six wide, extending
north and south; at the head of which is the pleasant village of
Fredonia, which has a good boat and raft navigation to Pittsburgh
and New-Orleans ; the portage from Fredonia to Lake Erie, is
nine miles, over a good road. Chautauque creek, which heads
ten or fifteen miles southwest of Fredonia, and enters Lake Erie
at Portland, is remarkable for the immense depth of its bed, being
four or five hundred feet below the surface of the country, and is
a good stream for mills. East of Chautauque Lake, six or eight
miles, are the three Casdaga Lakes, from one to five miles in circumference, and discharging their waters into the east branch of
the Connewango river. A few miles east of these lakes, is the
Great Buffalo Swamp, nine miles long and three wide, obviously
the ruins of an ancient lake. The Connewango meanders lazily
through its whole extent, from north to south. It is covered by
brambles, flags, and alders, with a few islands of woodland. It is
very miry—and in some places will tremble beneath one's feet for
several rods. The surounding country, on all sides, except at the
outlet, is high and fertile. The Seneca Indians call it *Cah-ih-ta-
wa-na.*

Cattaraugus, called by the Indians *Ca-ta-gus-ka-honh,* (stink-
ing banks) is an interesting stream, about 37 miles long, very
crooked, having a brisk current, numerous mill-seats, high perpendicular slate banks in places, and wide rich bottoms for the first
ten miles.

The Indian tribes resident on this Purchase, consist of about
3500 Senecas, 350 Tuscaroras, 200 Onondagas, and 75 Cayugas.
In the sale of the tract to Mr. Morris they reserved two reservations on the Genesee river, at Kennedea, and Ononda, about six
miles square each ; one 7 miles square on the Tonawanda, 7 miles

from Batavia; one 4 miles square, belonging to the Tuscaroras near Lewiston; one 10 miles square at the forks of Buffalo; one 10 miles long and 4 wide on the Cattaraugus, commencing 4 miles from lake Erie; one 20 miles long and 1 wide, lying on both sides of the Alleghany river, commencing 20 miles below Hamilton on Alleghany, and being almost one continued forest of lofty pines, of great value; and sufficient, if properly managed, to render the whole Seneca tribe rich.

Buffalo, is delightfully situated near the northeastern margin of Lake Erie, about two miles above its outlet, and on the great road leading from Albany to Ohio. It is built on an inclined plain, elevated about thirty feet above the surface of the lake. The situation affords a most beautiful prospect of the lake, Niagara river and the Canada shore. The surrounding country is of a rich soil; but the improvements are mostly new and not very extensive. Buffalo was laid out for a village about nine years ago, and was a place of considerable trade at the commencement of the late war. But in December, 1813, it was entirely destroyed by the British; since that time its growth has been rapidly increasing. It is now incorporated, and contains a bank, court house, jail; post-office, exchange office. custom-house, 17 stores for groceries and dry goods; three druggist stores, two printing offices and a book-store; a market house, brewery and bakery; three blacksmiths, three cabinet and chair shops; a hat factory and hat warehouse; one saddlery, one stone-cutter; three tailor's shops; one tinnery; two silversmiths; a Fire Company; a public library; a Presbyterian Society, with an ordained minister and Moral Society.— Application has been made for an Insurance Company, and measures have been taken for the improvement of the harbor. The whole number of buildings is nearly 200, and the number of inhabitants about 1000. They are chiefly emigrants from different parts of this state, and from most of the eastern states. Many of the buildings are of brick, from two to three stories high, and make a very handsome appearance. The court house is of brick, 50 feet square, with a piazza in front, and when completed will be the best building in this part of the country. The principal streets run from north to south, from 66 to 100 feet wide; these are intersected by others of equal width. Buffalo creek enters the lake a few rods west of the village. Five miles from the lake it divides into three branches, which water a fine body of land. Buffalo possesses natural advantages for trade, equal, if not superior, to any internal place in the United States; having at present a ship navigation for 1000 miles west, through lakes Erie, Huron and Michigan, and with little expense, in improving the navigation at the entrance into Lake Superior, may be extended to a distance as much farther to the west; and a boat navigation may be easily opened from the south part of Lake Michigan, to communicate with the Mississippi river. The navigation eastward,

after passing the falls of Niagara, is continued, with but little interruption, to Montreal.

The Holland Purchase also contains several other flourishing
villages, such as *Black Rock*, at the outlet of Lake Erie, of about
30 houses ; *Manchester*, at the Falls of Niagara ; Lewiston, opposite Queenston ; Batavia, the seat of justice for Genessee county ;
40 miles east of Buffaloe, on the Tonawanda creek ; Warsaw, on
Allen's creek, 18 miles south of Batavia ; Hamilton, on Alleghany ;
Pomfret on Canandaway, 10 miles west of Cattaraugus ; Fredonia, the seat of justice for Chautauque county.

BRIEF SKETCHES OF THE GREAT NORTHERN
LAKES.

LAKE ONTARIO,

Is about 200 miles long and 70 wide. Its water is deep, cold,
and transparent. It receives from the south, Black, Oswego, and
Genesee rivers; besides several large creeks. Pumice stones
have been found on its western shore : Volney thinks that its basin is the crater of an extinguished volcano. The river Niagara,
connecting the Lakes Ontario and Erie, is 36 miles long, about
one mile wide, very deep, and of a swift current.

LAKE ERIE,

Is about 300 miles long and 40 wide. Its tributaries from the
south enter in this order, Buffalo, Quaquagagahaun, Cattaraugus, Conneaut, Ashtabula, Grand river, Cayahoga, Rocky, Black,
Vermillion, Huron, Sandusky, Portage, Toussaints, Miami, Raisin, Little Huron, Strait of Detroit. From the northern shore it
receives Barbue, Chenette, Grand, Loutre and Aux Cedres. The
anchorage of this lake is bad, as the bottom in most parts, consists
of smooth slate and limestone rocks. The best and only harbors
for shipping on the southern shore, are Erie basin, Sandusky and
Miami bays. The British have a safe harbor at Malden.—A chain
of islands extend from Sandusky bay to near Malden ; the most
important of which is Put-in-Bay, where there is an excellent harbor for boats and shipping.

LAKE ST. CLAIR,

Is situated about equidistant between lakes Erie and Huron.
Its form is nearly circular—its banks low and level. Its depth,

except near the shore, is *invariably twenty-one feet.* This I ascertained when on board the Lady Prevost, Capt. Turner, in Oct. 1813. The severe gales of ten or twelve days continuance, prevented this vessel from getting out of the lake. She was obliged frequently to change her moorings, and traversed the lake in every direction; and the ignorance of Capt. T. and the pilot, rendered it necessary to take constant soundings, by which means it was discovered that the bottom of the lake was a perfect plain, composed of a deep stratum of white clay, remarkably tenacious, and from which it required great force to disengage the anchor. Nevertheless the water of the lake is transparent, when not disturbed by storms. The rivers which disembogue into this lake are Ruskin, Thames, Bell, and Bear, which enter from the British and Huron from the American side. Its islands are Isle *Aux Pesches*, Thompson's Island, Hay Island, *Chenal Ecarte*, and Horsen's Island. The British shore presents some beautiful settlements. The American coast is partially settled. The surrounding country is fertile and perfectly *champaign* to the distance of 30 miles in every direction. From the centre of the lake in a clear day, one sees in the direction of Lake Michigan, the elevated ridges of distant hills, which afford some relief to the eye, from the immensity of the horizon.

LAKE HURON,

Is about 1100 miles in circumference, of a triangular form—receiving from the north-west the tributaries of Lake Superior, and from the south-east that of Lake Michigan. It has two deep bays on its southern coast, Saganaum and Thunder bays; to the east, Thunder and Matchadash. A chain of islands called the Manitoualin, making a safe navigation for boats and canoes; between this, the rivers from the east are Natasawaga, Sandy and Des Francois, from Lake Nippising; from the north, Otassalon, Mississaki, and Chaho; its waters are deep, transparent, and abound with fish.

LAKE MICHIGAN,

Is about 300 miles long and 70 wide; a considerable part of its eastern coast consists of light sand hills. It receives about 40 rivers most of which have already been described. Its southern extremity is supposed to be in 41 50 N. latitude. Its bays and rivers afford valuable sturgeon fisheries. It lies entirely within the United States territory. The islands of this lake are mostly situated towards its northern end.

LAKE SUPERIOR,

Is about 500 miles long and 1500 in circumference. Its southern extremity is in 46, 46, north latitude.

"Lake Superior is the largest and most magnificent body of fresh water in the world; it is clear and pellucid, of great depth, and abounding in a great variety of fish, which are the most excellent of their kind. There are trouts of three kinds, weighing from five to fifty pounds, sturgeon, pickerel, pike, red and white carp, black bass, herrings, &c. &c. and the last and best of all, the Ticamang, or white fish, which weighs from four to sixteen pounds, and is of a superior quality in these waters. This lake may be denominated the grand reservoir of the river St. Lawrence, as no considerable rivers discharge themselves into it.— The principal ones are, the St. Louis, the Nipigon. the Pic, and the Michipicoten. Indeed, the extent of country from which any of them flow, or take their course, in any direction, cannot admit of it, in consequence of the ridge of land that separates them from the rivers that empty themselves into Hudson's bay, the gulf of Mexico, and the waters that fall into Lake Michigan. which afterwards become a part of the St. Lawrence. [Mackenzie.]

PUBLIC LANDS.

Copy of an estimate, furnished to the Senate in 1812, of the Public Lands unsold, on the 30th Sept. 1811, in the state of Ohio, and in the Michigan, Indiana, Illinois, and Mississippi Territories. To ascertain the quantity since acquired from the Indians, the quantities sold in the respective territories, and the balance remaining unsold, will require much time and labor.

STATE OR TERRITORY,	To which the Indian title has been extinguished.	To which the Indian title has'nt been extinguished.	TOTAL.
State of Ohio, - - - (a)	6,725,000	5,575,000	12,300,000
Michigan Territory, - - (b)	5,100,000	11,400,000	16,500,000
Indiana and Illinois south of parallel of latitude passing by the southern extremity of lake Michigan(c)	33,000,000	23,200,000	56,200,000
Territory west of lake Michigan & north of said parallel, (d)	5,500,000	34,500,000	60,000,000
Mississippi Territory, - (e)	5,900,000	49,100,000	55,000,000
Total,	56,225,000	143,775,000	200,000,000

(a) Remaining unsold at the Land Offices of Marietta, Canton, Steubenville, Zanesville, Chillicothe and Cincinnati,   6,974,000

Deduct part of Cincinnati in Indiana, - - -   673,735

  6,300,449

Estimated part of cession of Ottowas, &c. - - -   425,000

  6,725,449

INDIAN CESSIONS AND ANNUITIES.

TREATY OF GREENVILLE.

AT the treaty of Greenville, held August 3, 1795, the United States obtained all the lands to which the Indian title had not been previously extinguished, lying eastwardly and southwardly of a line commencing at the mouth of the Cayahoga river, running up the same to the portage between it and the Tuscarawas branch of the Muskingum, down this river to old Fort Lawrence; thence westwardly to the commencement of the portage between Loramie's creek and the St. Mary's; thence a westwardly course to Fort Recovery, on the Massissinway; thence south-westerly so as to intersect the Ohio river at the confluence of Kentucky river. The following sessions were also obtained from the Indians at the same treaty :—

1. One piece of land six miles square, at the mouth of Loramie's creek. 2. Two miles square, at the head of St. Marys, near

---

(*b*) After deducting 200,000 acres for private claims.

(*c*) Remaining unsold at the Land Offices of Jeffersonville, Vincennes, and part of Cincinnati, S. W. of fort Recovery, 4,730,771
Add part of Cincinnati district in Indiana, - - 675,786
Cessions of Kaskaskias in August 1803, and Piankashaws December 1805. - - - - - - - 11,800,000
Cessions of Pottawattamies, Miamis, Weaws, &c. of 1809, 3,200,000
do. of Sacs and Foxes, of Nov. 1804. - - - 13,600,000

33,504,557
Deduct for private claims, 500,000

(*d*) Part of the cession of the Sacs and Foxes. 33,004,557
(*e*) Very uncertain, deducting 83,000 acres for private claims not ascertained.

NOTE.—The public lands remaining unsold and unceded, east of the Mississippi, amount to about 200,800,000 of acres.

	ACRES
In Ohio about	12,800,000
Indiana,	20,000,000
Michigan,	26,000,000
Illinois,	30,000,000
North-Western.	68,000,000
Mississippi and Alabama,	34,000,000
Tennessee,	10,000,000
Total,	200,800,000

The public lands in Louisiana and the Missouri Territory, are supposed to amount to 400,000,000 of acres; one half of which may be considered uninhabitable.

Girtytown. 3. Six miles square, at the head of the navigable waters of the Auglaize river. 4. Six miles square, at the confluence of the Auglaize and Miami rivers. 5. Six miles square, at the junction of the St. Marys and St. Josephs. 6. Two miles square, at the head of the little river branch of the Wabash, eight miles southwest of Fort Wayne. 7. Six miles square, at the Weaw town, (Ouitanon) on the Wabash. 8. Twelve miles square, on the Miami near Fort Meigs. 9. Six miles square, at the mouth of the Miami-of-the-Lakes. 10. Six miles square, on Sandusky bay. 11. Two miles square, at Croghansville near Sandusky river. 12. A tract six miles wide, extending from the river Rouge to Lake St. Clair. 13. The island of Michilimackinac and the Isle De Bois Blanc. 14. Six miles square, on the main to the north of the island of Michilimackinac. 15. Six miles square, at the mouth of Chicago river. 16. Twelve miles square, at the mouth of the Illinois. 17. Six miles square, at Peoria at the south end of Illinois lake.

Annuities. In consideration by these cessions, the United States agreed to deliver goods to the following amount, viz: To the Wyandots, $1000; to the Delawares, $1000; to the Shawanoese, $1000; to the Miamis, $1000; to the Ottowas, $1000; to the Chippewas, $1000; to the Pottawattamies, $1000; and to the Kickapoos, Weaws, Elk river, Piankashaws and Kickapoo tribes, $500 each.

In 1805, at a treaty held at Fort Industry, the United States obtained an extinction of Indian claims as far west as a meridian line intersecting the southern shore of Lake Erie, at a point 120 miles west of the western boundary line of Pennsylvania, or six miles west of Pipe creek, including the *Fire Lands*, (now Huron county.—Annuity, $1000, to the Wyandot, Munsee, Delaware, and Seneca tribes.

In 1807, Gen. Hull obtained a relinquishment of the Indian title to the lands lying east of a line running due north, from the mouth of the Auglaize to the parallel of the outlet of Lake Huron, thence north-east to the White Rock, in that lake, except eight or ten small reservations. For this cession the United States paid $10,000, shortly after the ratification of the treaty; *i. e.* $3,333 to the Ottowas; $3,333 to the Chippewas; $1,666 to the Wyandots; $1,666 to the Pottawattomies, together with an *annuity* forever of $1000, to be apportioned on the above ratio among the aforesaid tribes.

By the treaty of Brownstown, (Nov. 1808) with the Wyandots Chippewas, Ottowas and Pottawatamics, Gen. Hull obtained the cession of a strip of land, extending from Fort Meigs to the *Fire Lands*, about 70 miles long and 1 wide, for the purpose of a road and a line of settlements.

The extinction of Indian claims of the southern part of Indiana, has been effected at various treaties. The annuities were 150 bushels of salt to the Delawares and Shawanœse, &c. $300 to the Delawares, (for five years;) $200 to the Piaukashaws, for 10 years; $600 (permanently) to the Miamis ; $250 to the Eel rivers; $250 to the Weaws; $500 to the Pottawattames, for five years.

Additional.—(Sept. 30, 1809)—$500 to the Miamis, 500 to the Delawares, $250 to the Eel rivers, and $500 to the Pottawattamies; besides $200 paid down.

In August, 1803, Gen. Harrison obtained from the Kaskaskia and Illinois Indians, a cession of all their lands in the Illinois Territory, excepting one reservation of 350 acres, near Kaskaskia, and another of 1280 acres to be located at the option of the Indians. Annuity for the same, $1000 ; besides a donation of $300 for the erection of a church; $500 for miscellaneous purposes, and $100 annually for seven years, towards the support of a priest. This was a tract about 200 miles long and 100 wide, extending along the east bank of the Mississippi from the mouth of the Illinois to that of the Ohio.

In December, 1805, the Piankashaws ceded all the lands lying between the Wabash and the Kaskaskia purchase above described, for which they receive a yearly annuity of $300.

In November, 1804, the Sacs and Foxes ceded to the United States, all the lands within these boundaries : Beginning at a point on the Missouri, opposite the mouth of Gasconade river ; thence northwardly to the Jaustioni; down that river (thirty miles) to the Mississippi ; thence up the Mississippi to the mouth of the Ouisconsin ; up that river 36 miles in a direct line ; thence to Sakagan Lake; thence down Fox river of the Illinois ; thence down the Illinois to the Mississippi and the point of beginning—: supposed to contain about 14,000,000 acres : for which they receive a permanent annuity of $1000.

In November, 1808, the Great and Little Osages ceded all the lands lying east of a line, beginning at Fort Clark, on the Missouri, five miles above Fire Prairie, and running thence a due south course to the river Arkansas, and down the same to the Mississippi; for which they received 1000 dollars down, and a permanent annuity of 500 dollars.

In September, 1805, Gen. Z. M. Pike obtained from the Sioux, nine miles square at the mouth of the St. Croix ; and two strips extending on both sides of the Mississippi, from the mouth of the St. Peters to the Falls of St. Anthony—containing altogether, 100,000 acres ; for which we paid 2000 dollars.

In August, 1816, the Pottawattamies and Ottowas relinquished about 6,000,000 acres of land at the south end of Lake Michigan, lying on the Kenkakee, (Theskaki) Chicago, and Milwakee rivers ; for which the United States are to pay them a permanent annuity of 1000 dollars in goods, at first cost, without charge for transportation.

In 1786, the Chickasaws ceded an extensive district on the south side of Tennessee, below the Muscle Shoals—for which they received 20,000 dollars. By a late treaty, they have ceded lands north of Tennessee, for which government paid them 4500 dollars, and an annuity of 12,000 for ten successive years.

In 1805, the Cherokees ceded large tracts of lands, lying between Duck, Tennessee and Clinch rivers, for which they received 14,000 dollars, and an annuity of 3000. In 1806 they ceded additional tracts, on Duck and Elk rivers, for which the United States gave them 10,000 dollars. In 1816 they relinquished large tracts; for which the United States paid them 500 dollars, and an annuity of 600 dollars for ten years.

The Choctaws have relinquished lands, at different times, for which they have been paid 60,500 dollars—with an annuity of 3,000 dollars in perpetuity, and 6,000 dollars for twenty successive years.

DIRECTIONS TO EMIGRANTS.

—⊙⊙—

GREATFIELD, (Scipio, Cayuga County, N. Y.)
6 month 2, 1817.

Thy question, *"Whether a residence in Indiana will be favorable to the health of Emigrants from higher latitudes?"* should be considered in two points of view, though in strictness, it might be confined to the effects of a warmer climate on the constitution.

I am aware of the difficulty of finding two places which differ in nothing but in temperature; where the atmosphere is equally dry, pure, elastic, heavy, electrical, and equal at all times in its currents. Without such agreement, comparisons must be imperfect; but from a general review of the warmer parts of the temperate zone, I know of no series of facts which should determine that question in the negative. The most remarkable instances of longevity on record, take their date from countries further south than the object of this enquiry ; and though the limits of human life have been abridged since that day, I cannot discover why we may not assign a full average of health to those parallels of latitude.

Clark mentions in his travels in Greece, that an English sea captain had been long in search of a spot the most exempt from disease, where he might pass the remnant of life; and that after having visited various parts of the world with this object in view, he fixed on the Isle of Scio. That author adds, he was not disappointed; the south point of this island is in lat. 38 14, and making allowance for the difference of climate, we must pass far to the south of Indiana to find winters equally mild.

I notice these instances because many of our citizens appear to have drawn their ideas of warm climates from the maritime parts of the southern states. But the formation and climate of that district is essentially different from those of the same parallels west of the mountains. There the distressing heats of the day are often protracted till towards midnight, and the degree is so extraordinary as to prevent the refreshment of sleep, even to the native exhausted by fatigue. During this time on the opposite side of the Alleghany, evening is attended by a refreshing coolness, and while I was in Indiana, though near midsummer, I passed no night in which a blanket was not comfortable.

This coolness at evening appears to be peculiar to the country north and west of the Alleghany mountains. Cramer informs us that it extends southwardly to Mobile. Why should the climate of New-York be more healthy than that of Indiana ? It is a fact well known to many, that in summer we have weather as hot as in the West-Indies. This heat has been sufficient to produce from our marshes every form of fever that has prevailed on our western waters. The mortality attending dysentery in different parts of this state, appears to have been as great as in any cases of that malady to the south. Typhus has ravaged our most airy situations, and in the northern parts of our county, epidemics have been uncommonly fatal. Emigrants suffering from rheumatism or consumption have much to hope from that climate, and I know of no disease in that country to balance this advantage.

There are now living in Vincennes, four Frenchmen who were at the defeat of General Braddock, who have lived in that place between fifty and sixty years. There are also two French women between eighty or ninety years old, and one person of the name of Mills, lately died aged 115 years. These instances may show, that there is nothing peculiarly destructive to human life in that country, and it should be remembered that these have not been selected from a large city, but a frontier town of small population.

I shall now pass to a more important view of the subject.— The ease and safety with which families can descend the Ohio, has made that river the great thoroughfare of emigration to the south-western states ; and the loss of health, and often of life, experienced by new comers, ought to be more frequently imputed to the injudicious manner of performing that navigation, than to the unhealthiness of those countries.

As the messenger is waiting, my remarks must be brief, but I hope their importance will attract the notice of some of the thousands of our citizens who heedlessly press on to destruction.

Descend the river in Autumn after the frosts have commenced, for by that time the offensive smell from the shores will have abated. Use no river water without filtering. This operation is expeditiously performed in a vessel like an upright churn with two bottoms. These are three or four inches apart, and the upper, in which a number of small holes are bored, receives in the centre, a tube, one inch in diameter, extending above the vessel and communicating with the cavity between the bottoms. After spreading a cloth fill the upper part with well washed sand, and let the water (from a vessel above) down through the tube. In a short time it will rise through the sand divested of its impurities or sediment in sufficient quantities for every culinary purpose. In a few days the apparatus may need cleansing; as the filth will be chiefly below, a hole opened in the lower bottom will allow it to pass off. (See Melish's Travels, vol. I page 158.) If the water has not an agreeable coolness, cider or strong beer should be mixed with it for drink, as the warmth, without such stimulus will relax the tone of the stomach, and predispose to disease.

Lay in plenty of good wholesome provisions. Travellers should never change their diet for the worse. The fatigues of mind and body, in most cases, require that it should be for the better. To live economically is to live comfortably. Any additional expense in provisions would not go far in paying a Doctor's bill, without taking into view loss of time, and of comfort, or the expenses of nursing.

Go not in a vessel with a bad roof. A crowded boat is an inconvenient place to dry wet clothes; and the damage sustained in furniture would more than pay the expense of being comfortably sheltered, without considering the probable loss of health. Bending their boards over head, is not sufficient; I have seen none of these roofs that would not admit a driving shower of rain.

If spirituous liquors are taken, let the quantity be cautiously regulated. Every excess debilitates the system, and to think of escaping disease by keeping always " full," is desperate folly.— When fever attacks such subjects it is commonly fatal. Some men who have travelled much, and who have no moral or religious scruples to dissuade them, totally abstain from spirits in unhealthy situations. Eating rich wholesome food guards the stomach much better from infection, nor would I omit in the list of such articles, well cured ham and strong coffee.

If the weather become warm, guard well against the smell of bilge water. But if you must descend in the spring, go early.— Avoid all delay, and remember you are fleeing for your lives. I have seen the havoc, and I believed not till then. Nail boards over head to keep off the heat of the roof, for sometimes it will remind you of an oven.

On landing, you ought first to secure yourselves from the inclemency of the weather. Water from brooks should be filtered—but depend not on these during summer. If springs are not convenient, dig wells; it is much cheaper to do this than to be sick. Much of the sickness of new countries proceeds from bad water.

Let nothing tempt to fish in warm weather immediately on changing your climate. The effluvia of the shores is poison. To get wet and lie out all night is little short of madness. But fresh fish are unwholesome, unless it be for a slight change of diet. We know of no country that has been healthy where the inhabitants live on fresh fish. But if you must have them, buy them; any price is cheaper than health. If you must fish, do it in the day time, and be comfortably sheltered at night. Be also cautious of using much fresh meat from the woods.

If you feel indisposed, wait not till you are *down sick*, but take medicine without delay. If the stomach be foul, which is the case at the commencement of all fevers, take an emetic and then brace up with bark. If this is too bad, take pearl-ash dissolved in water, half a gill, not too strong, three times a day, fasting. Whatever may be the offending cause, (except the case be *mechanical*,) it will in some measure neutralize it, though there may be cases in which it will be insufficient. I have seen no medicine quicker in its operation, and on myself the most distressing symptoms were relieved in half an hour. Since that it has been tried with equal success by others. In dysentery it has been considered a *specific*, and probably no medicine will better merit that character; for we know of no case of this disease where relief was not obtained by the use of it. It may be procured at Vincennes, and probably at Cincinnati, but it is scarce and dear in the western country.

Keep away from the flats on the rivers, and let not the fertility of the soil induce you to cultivate it, until you are naturalized to the climate; or more properly recovered from all the fatigues attending emigration, for it is necessary that the mind should be composed as well as the body. Land of an inferior quality in a high, airy situation will yield greater *real profits*.

Let me caution the emigrant on one point more and I have done. The water in the Ohio country, as in this (which is only a continuation of it) is in many places strongly impregnated by lime.—The effects of this on children just weaned, have often proved fatal by inducing dirrahœ, which soon exhausts the patient, and no medicine can give relief while the *occasional cause* is not removed. This is easily done by refusing water, and giving cows' milk. If the disease is far advanced, paragoric may be necessary to abate the irritability. I first discovered the benefit of this treatment on one of my children, who seemed wasting to a skeleton, and have witnessed much of its good effects since.

I have sketched these in great haste. Many of these ideas will probably soon appear in my Journal,* which I am now preparing for the press.

Very respectfully, thy friend,

DAVID THOMAS.

S. R. Brown, *Auburn.*

Emigrants who prefer the southern parts of Ohio, Indiana, Tennessee and Mississippi, and who remove from the northern parts of New-York, Vermont, New-Hampshire, Province of Maine, &c. would do well to embark at Hamilton, on the Alleghany river, where they ought to arrive about the 20th of March, in order to descend the river the first freshets. Boats are easily procured on the spot, of various sizes: the navigation of the Alleghany is easy and safe; only two or three accidents have happened since the settlement of the country. Those who intend settling near the banks of the Ohio, or Mississippi, would do well to descend on rafts of white pine boards, which, if properly constructed, are as safe and more convenient for a family, than a common boat.— Boards of an excellent quality can be purchased at Hamilton for 75 cents per 100 foot—if not wanted for building, by the emigrant, they will command a ready sale at all the villages and towns between Pittsburgh and Louisville. Provisions are scarce and extravagantly high at Olean Point; consequently travellers and families ought to lay in a stock in the rich and populous counties of Cayuga and Ontario. It would be ruinous for families to embark as late as the first of May.

The road from Geneva to Hamilton is good in winter, horrible in April, tolerable in summer. The distance from Hamilton to Pittsburgh, by water is 300 miles.

	Distances.
Kilbuck's Eddy,	20
Jamison's Indian town,	10
Cold Spring (Indian village,)	6
Sky Prairies (Indian Tavern,)	4
Cornplanters,	10
Hoop's mills,	16
Women,	4
Broken Straw,	7
Oil Creek,	40

* Mr. Thomas has recently visited many parts of the western country, and surveyed it with the eye of a philosopher. His *Journal*, which is nearly prepared for the press, will, no doubt, afford a rich geographical treat.

		Distances.
Franklin,	- - - - - -	10
Sandy Creek,	- - - - - -	10
Scrub Grass,	- - - - -	8
Montgomery Falls,	- - - - -	7
Patterson's Falls,	- - - - -	7
Toby's creek from the east,	- - - -	10
Catfish Falls,	- - - - - -	11
Redbank creek from the east,	- - -	7
Mahoning creek,	- - - - -	7
Sloan's Ferry,	- - - - -	14
Nicholson's Falls,	- - - - -	7
Kittanning,	- - - - - -	7
Freeport, west side,	- - - - -	4
Plumb creek,	- - - - - -	18
Pittsburgh,	- - - - -	12

256

The distance from Pittsburgh to the mouth of the Ohio, by water, is 1188 miles.

Hamilton's island, (below Pittsburgh,)	- -	3
Big Beaver creek,	- - - - -	29
Beavertown,	- - - - - -	30
Georgetown,	- - - - - -	42
Willis's Creek,	- - - - - -	71
Steubenville,	- - - - - -	73
Charlestown,	- - - - - -	79
Warren,	- - - - - -	87
Little Grave creek,	- - - - -	107
Little Muskingum river,	- - - -	168
Marietta,	- - - - - -	172
Vienna,	- - - - - -	179
Blannerhasset's island	- - - - -	191
Letart's rapids,	- - - - -	245
Point Pleasant,	- - - - -	283
Great Sandy,	- - - - -	341
Little Sandy,	- - - - -	364
Alexandria,	- - - - -	393
Salt Lick creek	- - - - -	418
Maysville,	- - - - - -	458
Augusta,	- - - - - -	479
Cincinnati,	- - - - - -	424
Vevay,	- - - - - -	466
Great Miami,	- - - - -	551
Kentucky river,	- - - - -	627
Louisville,	- - - - - -	705
Bule river,	- - - - - -	762
Green river,	- - - - -	925

ADDITIONS AND CORRECTIONS.

PAGE 10—From Flint river to the Georgia line, I do not recollect seeing any land whatever, fit for cultivation. It is low, flat, excessively poor, and badly watered, abounding in cypress ponds, bay galls and saw palmetto flatts, fit only for the present occupants, gouffres, salamanders and bull snakes.—*Barnett, U. S. Com.*

PAGE 16—From more recent information from Madison county, it appears that the present population exceeds 15,000 souls. Great numbers of intruders have established themselves on the public lands, on both sides of the Tennessee river. Mr. Barnett, who was lately employed by government to survey a part of the new cessions, states that " where water was scarce, it was not uncommon to see from four to eight families encamped at one spring."— He supposes that 300 families of this description cultivated patches of corn last season, in a single valley south of Tennessee river, other parts were quite populous. Strife already prevails in some parts, as to the right of occupancy. The greater part are in destitute circumstances, having expended their all in reaching the *promised land.*

PAGE 18—The *Theakaki* is latterly written *Kenkakee*; " it rises in a flat marshy country in the neighborhood of the St. Josephs of the Lake, and runs a meandering course westwardly, passing the southern extremity of Lake Michigan, at the distance of 20 or 30 miles from it. Near the head of this river is a small creek, putting into the St. Josephs, through which boats have sometimes passed, in time of high water, from the St. Josephs to the Kenkakee."

PAGE 23—The paragraph describing the valley of the Illinois was extracted from the " Description of the Western Country," by an officer of the U. S. army. This writer appears to have drawn a too highly colored picture of the bottoms of the Illinois. Major Long, topographical engineer, speaks less favorably of the country.

" The valley of the Illinois varies in its width from three to ten miles—is generally flat and marshy, and for the most part subject to inundations when the river has no more than a medial height. In some parts of it, however, prairies and bottoms of considerable extent are to be met with, elevated much above high water mark. In ascending the river the bluffs gradually decrease in height;

being about 150 feet high at the mouth, and about 100 at the head of the river. Included in the bluffs are strata of lime-stone, slate and coal, which occasionally make their appearance along the surface of the declivities."

PAGE 43—*Indiana*—According to Gen. Harrison, " the finest country in all the western world, is that which is bounded eastwardly by the counties of Wayne, Franklin, and part of Dearborn, Switzerland and Jefferson ; westward by the tract called the New Purchase; and extending northwardly some small distance beyond the Wabash ; this tract containing perhaps 10 millions of acres, is principally the property of the Miamis : part of it of the Miamis and Delawares. It includes all the head waters of the White river; the branches of the Wabash which fall in from the south or south-east ; that part of it which the Delawares occupy is the finest indeed from their towns to the Wabash, and on the Wabash is also good ; having the finest mill streams, and land of the first quality ; well timbered, and intermixed with small rich prairies. The streams are very small until you get pretty high up the Wabash; as one branch of the White river runs parallel with, and so near to the Wabash, that the streams must necessarily be short. The Kentucky militia say, that in approaching Ouitanan, near White river, they passed through the finest country they had ever seen; north of the Wabash, the land is not so good *off the rivers.*

PAGE 40—In describing *White river*, no notice was taken of the Eel river branch, which joins the North Fork from the west, about 20 miles above the entrance of the Teakettle Fork, and waters the eastern part of Harrison's Purchase. There is another river of this name, entering the Wabash above Tippecanoe. There is no such river as " *Pomme*," tributary to the Wabash. On some maps it is written, " *Dela Panse*"—on others " *Calemut*." There are *three* streams running into the Wabash, called " *Pettite*," or Little Rivers.

CARVER's PURCHASE.

The following additional information was received from Mr. BENJAMIN GORTON, just as the printing of this volume was closing, and, as it may be of some service, to those who may have an interest in the tract of territory to which it relates, the Publisher, with that view, gives it a place here.

In the second Edinburgh edition of Carver's Travels is particularly described the reasons why and wherefore the *Naudowessies* of the plains, freely and voluntarily gave the said grant, which was for effecting a treaty of peace between the said *Naudowessies* and the Chippeway nation, who were then coming in great numbers to destroy them. by which means they were pacified, with difficulty, and turned back and left them. As he by this means

rescued them from certain destruction—they, having a grateful
sense thereof, freely and voluntarily made him a present of the following tract of land—as described in his Deed, which stands recorded in the said second Edinburgh Edition, as follows:—

"To Jonathan Carver, a chief under the most mighty and po-
tent George the third, king of the English and other nations, the
fame of whose courageous warriors have reached our ears, and has
been more fully told us by our good Brother Jonathan aforesaid,
whom we rejoice to see come among us and bring us good news
from his country—WE, CHIEFS OF THE NAUDOWESSIES
who have hereto set our Seals, do by these presents, for ourselves
and heirs forever, in return for the many presents and other good
services done by the said Jonathan to ourselves and allies, give,
grant and convey to him, the said Jonathan, and to his heirs and
assigns, forever, the whole of a certain tract or territory of land,
bounded as follows, viz: From the Falls of St. Anthony, running
on the east bank of the Mississippi, nearly south-east, as far as the
south end of Lake Pepin, where the Chippeway river joins the
Mississippi; and from thence eastward five days travel, accounting twenty English miles per day; and from thence north, six
days travel, accounting twenty English miles per day; and from
thence again to the Falls of St. Anthony, on a direct strait line.—
WE DO for ourselves, heirs and assigns forever, give unto the said
Jonathan, his heirs and assigns forever, all the said lands, with all
the trees, rocks and rivers therein, reserving for ourselves and
heirs the sole liberty of hunting and fishing on land not planted or
improved by the said Jonathan, his heirs and assigns, to which we
have affixed our respective seals, at the Great Cave, May the 1st,
one thousand seven hundred and sixty-seven.

"HAWNOPAWJATIN, his X mark.
"OTOHTONGOOMLISHEW, his X mark."

The above particulars were carefully taken from the aforesaid
second Edinburgh edition of Carver's Travels, by Benjamin Gorton, of Troy, state of New-York, in the year 1795, when he made
a purchase of some of the lands from the heirs, and had the perusal
of the aforesaid book, belonging to Mary Carver, widow of the
said Jonathan, deceased.

It was about that time asserted, that Captain Carver went to
England, and that he had a daughter in that country whom he called his only heir; and that when he died, in England, he left this
girl all his title to this land, and that the papers were left in the
care of one Dr. Letsom, who is since dead, as we are told: That
there has been a plea made that this girl is the only heir, and of
course that the title of those heirs must fail; but this is impossible,
as his widow was living in Deerfield, Massachusetts, not long
since, certainly in the year 1795; therefore, all those pleas are
vain: That there was such a deed made to the said Carver, as be-

fore described, no one will pretend to doubt, and that he went to England to obtain a grant from the crown is also certain. Whether he ever did obtain such grant from the king of Great-Britain, we have never been able to learn. If it is the case, the title is unquestionably as good as any patent lands under the crown, before our revolutionary war. If it is not the case, the Indian title is undoubtedly good, and the deed will be found recorded in Wakontebe Cave, or the Great Cave before mentioned, below the Falls of St. Anthony, which the Naudouwessies of the Plains will confirm, if any person appears to take possession as the true and lawful heirs of Jonathan Carver, to which the government of the United States will probably have no objection, as the Indian title must, at all events, be extinguished, and the heirs of Carver can have no greater plea of title, until they prove a title from the crown, which may be known by searching the English records, between the year 1767, and the American revolutionary war, which may easily be done.

The First American Frontier
AN ARNO PRESS/NEW YORK TIMES COLLECTION

Agnew, Daniel.
A History of the Region of Pennsylvania North of the Allegheny River. 1887.

Alden, George H.
New Government West of the Alleghenies Before 1780. 1897.

Barrett, Jay Amos.
Evolution of the Ordinance of 1787. 1891.

Billon, Frederick.
Annals of St. Louis in its Early Days Under the French and Spanish Dominations. 1886.

Billon, Frederick.
Annals of St. Louis in its Territorial Days, 1804-1821. 1888.

Littel, William.
Political Transactions in and Concerning Kentucky. 1926.

Bowles, William Augustus.
Authentic Memoirs of William Augustus Bowles. 1916.

Bradley, A. G.
The Fight with France for North America. 1900.

Brannan, John, ed.
Official Letters of the Military and Naval Officers of the War, 1812-1815. 1823.

Brown, John P.
Old Frontiers. 1938.

Brown, Samuel R.
The Western Gazetteer. 1817.

Cist, Charles.
Cincinnati Miscellany of Antiquities of the West and Pioneer History. (2 volumes in one). 1845-6.

Claiborne, Nathaniel Herbert.
Notes on the War in the South with Biographical Sketches of the Lives of Montgomery, Jackson, Sevier, and Others. 1819.

Clark, Daniel.
Proofs of the Corruption of Gen. James Wilkinson. 1809.

Clark, George Rogers.
Colonel George Rogers Clark's Sketch of His Campaign in the Illinois in 1778-9. 1869.

Collins, Lewis.
Historical Sketches of Kentucky. 1847.

Cruikshank, Ernest, ed,
Documents Relating to Invasion of Canada and the Surrender of Detroit. 1912.

Cruikshank, Ernest, ed,
The Documentary History of the Campaign on the Niagara Frontier, 1812-1814. (4 volumes). 1896-1909.

Cutler, Jervis.
A Topographical Description of the State of Ohio, Indian Territory, and Louisiana. 1812.

Cutler, Julia P.
The Life and Times of Ephraim Cutler. 1890.

Darlington, Mary C.
History of Col. Henry Bouquet and the Western Frontiers of Pennsylvania. 1920.

Darlington, Mary C.
Fort Pitt and Letters From the Frontier. 1892.

De Schweinitz, Edmund.
The Life and Times of David Zeisberger. 1870.

Dillon, John B.
History of Indiana. 1859.

Eaton, John Henry.
Life of Andrew Jackson. 1824.

English, William Hayden.
Conquest of the Country Northwest of the Ohio. (2 volumes in one). 1896.

Flint, Timothy.
Indian Wars of the West. 1833.

Forbes, John.
Writings of General John Forbes Relating to His Service in North America. 1938.

Forman, Samuel S.
Narrative of a Journey Down the Ohio and Mississippi in 1789-90. 1888.

Haywood, John.
Civil and Political History of the State of Tennessee to 1796. 1823.

Heckewelder, John.
History, Manners and Customs of the Indian Nations. 1876.

Heckewelder, John.
Narrative of the Mission of the United Brethren. 1820.

Hildreth, Samuel P.
Pioneer History. 1848.

Houck, Louis.
The Boundaries of the Louisiana Purchase: A Historical Study. 1901.

Houck, Louis.
History of Missouri. (3 volumes in one). 1908.

Houck, Louis.
The Spanish Regime in Missouri. (2 volumes in one). 1909.

Jacob, John J.
A Biographical Sketch of the Life of the Late Capt. Michael Cresap. 1826.

Jones, David.
A Journal of Two Visits Made to Some Nations of Indians on the West Side of the River Ohio, in the Years 1772 and 1773. 1774.

Kenton, Edna.
Simon Kenton. 1930.

Loudon, Archibald.
Selection of Some of the Most Interesting Narratives of Outrages. (2 volumes in one). 1808-1811.

Monette, J. W.
History, Discovery and Settlement of the Mississippi Valley. (2 volumes in one). 1846.

Morse, Jedediah.
American Gazetteer. 1797.

Pickett, Albert James.
History of Alabama. (2 volumes in one). 1851.

Pope, John.
A Tour Through the Southern and Western Territories. 1792.

Putnam, Albigence Waldo.
History of Middle Tennessee. 1859.

Ramsey, James G. M.
Annals of Tennessee. 1853.

Ranck, George W.
Boonesborough. 1901.

Robertson, James Rood, ed.
Petitions of the Early Inhabitants of Kentucky to the Gen. Assembly of Virginia. 1914.

Royce, Charles.
Indian Land Cessions. 1899.

Rupp, I. Daniel.
History of Northampton, Lehigh, Monroe, Carbon and Schuykill Counties. 1845.

Safford, William H.
The Blennerhasset Papers. 1864.

St. Clair, Arthur.
A Narrative of the Manner in which the Campaign Against the Indians, in the Year 1791 was Conducted. 1812.

Sargent, Winthrop, ed.
A History of an Expedition Against Fort DuQuesne in 1755. 1855.

Severance, Frank H.
An Old Frontier of France. (2 volumes in one). 1917.

Sipe, C. Hale.
Fort Ligonier and Its Times. 1932.

Stevens, Henry N.
Lewis Evans: His Map of the Middle British Colonies in America. 1920.

Timberlake, Henry.
The Memoirs of Lieut. Henry Timberlake. 1927.

Tome, Philip.
Pioneer Life: Or Thirty Years a Hunter. 1854.

Trent, William.
Journal of Captain William Trent From Logstown to Pickawillany. 1871.

Walton, Joseph S.
Conrad Weiser and the Indian Policy of Colonial Pennsylvania. 1900.

Withers, Alexander Scott.
Chronicles of Border Warfare. 1895.